Multidisciplinary Applications of Deep Learning–Based Artificial Emotional Intelligence

Chiranji Lal Chowdhary
Vellore Institute of Technology, India

A volume in the Advances in Computational
Intelligence and Robotics (ACIR) Book Series

Published in the United States of America by
    IGI Global
    Engineering Science Reference (an imprint of IGI Global)
    701 E. Chocolate Avenue
    Hershey PA, USA 17033
    Tel: 717-533-8845
    Fax: 717-533-8661
    E-mail: cust@igi-global.com
    Web site: http://www.igi-global.com

Library of Congress Cataloging-in-Publication Data

Names: Chowdhary, Chiranji Lal, 1975- editor.
Title: Multidisciplinary applications of deep learning-based artificial
  emotional intelligence / Chiranji Lal Chowdhary, editor.
Description: Hershey PA : Engineering Science Reference, 2022. | Includes
  bibliographical references and index. | Summary: "This book explores
  artificial intelligence applications in emotional intelligence including
  machine learning and deep learning and presents up-to-date technologies
  and solutions to the main aspects regarding the applications of
  artificial intelligence in emotional intelligence applications"--
  Provided by publisher.
Identifiers: LCCN 2022018656 (print) | LCCN 2022018657 (ebook) | ISBN
  9781668456736 (h/c) | ISBN 9781668456743 (s/c) | ISBN 9781668456750
  (ebook)
Subjects: LCSH: Affect (Psychology)--Computer simulation. | Artificial
  intelligence--Industrial applications. | Emotional intelligence. | Deep
  learning (Machine learning)
Classification: LCC Q343 .M85 2022 (print) | LCC Q343 (ebook) | DDC
  006.3--dc23/eng20220722
LC record available at https://lccn.loc.gov/2022018656
LC ebook record available at https://lccn.loc.gov/2022018657

This book is published in the IGI Global book series Advances in Computational Intelligence and Robotics (ACIR) (ISSN: 2327-0411; eISSN: 2327-042X)

British Cataloguing in Publication Data
A Cataloguing in Publication record for this book is available from the British Library.

All work contributed to this book is new, previously-unpublished material. The views expressed in this book are those of the authors, but not necessarily of the publisher.

For electronic access to this publication, please contact: eresources@igi-global.com.

Advances in Computational Intelligence and Robotics (ACIR) Book Series

Ivan Giannoccaro
University of Salento, Italy

ISSN:2327-0411
EISSN:2327-042X

MISSION

While intelligence is traditionally a term applied to humans and human cognition, technology has progressed in such a way to allow for the development of intelligent systems able to simulate many human traits. With this new era of simulated and artificial intelligence, much research is needed in order to continue to advance the field and also to evaluate the ethical and societal concerns of the existence of artificial life and machine learning.

The **Advances in Computational Intelligence and Robotics (ACIR) Book Series** encourages scholarly discourse on all topics pertaining to evolutionary computing, artificial life, computational intelligence, machine learning, and robotics. ACIR presents the latest research being conducted on diverse topics in intelligence technologies with the goal of advancing knowledge and applications in this rapidly evolving field.

COVERAGE

- Adaptive and Complex Systems
- Artificial Intelligence
- Cognitive Informatics
- Automated Reasoning
- Computational Intelligence
- Brain Simulation
- Neural Networks
- Evolutionary Computing
- Robotics
- Algorithmic Learning

IGI Global is currently accepting manuscripts for publication within this series. To submit a proposal for a volume in this series, please contact our Acquisition Editors at Acquisitions@igi-global.com or visit: http://www.igi-global.com/publish/.

Titles in this Series

For a list of additional titles in this series, please visit: www.igi-global.com/book-series/advances-computational-intelligence-robotics/73674

Principles and Applications of Socio-Cognitive and Affective Computing
S. Geetha (VIT University, Chennai, India) Karthika Renuka (PSG College of Technology, India) Asnath Victy Phamila (VIT University, Chennai, India) and Karthikeyan N. (Syed Ammal Engineering College, India)
Engineering Science Reference • © 2023 • 330pp • H/C (ISBN: 9781668438435) • US $270.00

Revolutionizing Industrial Automation Through the Convergence of Artificial Intelligence and the Internet of Things
Divya Upadhyay Mishra (ABES Engineering College, India) and Shanu Sharma (ABES Engineering College, India)
Engineering Science Reference • © 2023 • 300pp • H/C (ISBN: 9781668449912) • US $270.00

Convergence of Big Data Technologies and Computational Intelligent Techniques
Govind P. Gupta (National Institute of Technology, Raipur, India)
Engineering Science Reference • © 2023 • 335pp • H/C (ISBN: 9781668452646) • US $270.00

Design and Control Advances in Robotics
Mohamed Arezk Mellal (M'Hamed Bougara University, Algeria)
Engineering Science Reference • © 2023 • 320pp • H/C (ISBN: 9781668453810) • US $305.00

Handbook of Research on Applied Artificial Intelligence and Robotics for Government Processes
David Valle-Cruz (Universidad Autónoma del Estado de México, Mexico) Nely Plata-Cesar (Universidad Autónoma del Estado de México, Mexico) and Jacobo Leonardo González-Ruíz (Universidad Autónoma del Estado de México, Mexico)
Information Science Reference • © 2023 • 434pp • H/C (ISBN: 9781668456248) • US $315.00

Applying AI-Based IoT Systems to Simulation-Based Information Retrieval
Bhatia Madhulika (Amity University, India) Bhatia Surabhi (King Faisal University, Saudi Arabia) Poonam Tanwar (Manav Rachna International Institute of Research and Studies, India) and Kuljeet Kaur (Université du Québec, Canada)
Engineering Science Reference • © 2023 • 300pp • H/C (ISBN: 9781668452554) • US $270.00

Artificial Intelligence for Societal Development and Global Well-Being
Abhay Saxena (Dev Sanskriti Vishwavidyalaya, India) Ashutosh Kumar Bhatt (Uttarakhand Open University, India) and Rajeev Kumar (Teerthanker Mahaveer University, India)
Engineering Science Reference • © 2022 • 292pp • H/C (ISBN: 9781668424438) • US $270.00

701 East Chocolate Avenue, Hershey, PA 17033, USA
Tel: 717-533-8845 x100 • Fax: 717-533-8661
E-Mail: cust@igi-global.com • www.igi-global.com

Chiranjilal Lal Chowdhary would like to dedicate this book to his beloved wife Amru Choudhary for all her support in life; without that support, he would not have reached the present position.

Editorial Advisory Board

Table of Contents

Detailed Table of Contents

Chapter 1

*Subramaniam Meenakshi Sundaram, GSSS Institute of Engineering and Technology for
Women, India*
Tejaswini R. Murgod, GSSS Institute of Engineering and Technology for Women, India
Sowmya M., GSSS Institute of Engineering and Technology for Women, India

With the advent of technology, we have seen drastic changes in the way of life. Right from automation to improved security systems, technology got us covered. Machines deployed with intelligence stand the potential to drive cars, perform medical procedures, control traffic, and possibly everything that we can think of. Several large and small-scale organizations are adopting AI technologies to amplify their growth and surpass prior business results. Emotional AI can also help businesses to solve sensitive issues at the workplace. The global outlook is that AI imbibed into automation or robotics is going to revolutionize the markets and workforces. As per market estimates, over the next five years, the affective computing market will witness new heights surging to a growth rate of 43.0% CAGR in terms of revenue, with the global market reaching to US$ 1710 million by 2024 up from US$ 200 million in 2019. In the forecast period from 2019-2024, development around touchless AI models are expected to grow in the affective computing market between 2017 and 2025.

Chapter 2

Amita Umesh Dessai, Goa College of Engineering, India
Hassanali G. Virani, Goa College of Engineering, India

This chapter analyzes 57 articles published from 2012 on emotion classification using bio signals such as ECG and GSR. This study would be valuable for future researchers to gain an insight into the emotion model, emotion elicitation and self-assessment techniques, physiological signals, pre-processing methods, feature extraction, and machine learning techniques utilized by the different researchers. Most investigators have used openly available databases, and some have created their datasets. The studies have considered the participants from the healthy age group and of similar cultural backgrounds. Fusion of the ECG and GSR parameters can help to improve classification accuracy. Additionally, handcrafted features fused with automatically extracted deep machine learning features can increase classification accuracy. Deep learning techniques and feature fusion techniques have improved classification accuracy.

    Jagan Mohan Nagula, National Institute of Technology, Silchar, India
    Murugan R., National Institute of Technology, Silchar, India
    Tripti Goel, National Institute of Technology, Silchar, India

Machine learning (ML) and deep learning (DL) techniques play a significant role in diabetic retinopathy (DR) detection via grading the severity levels or segmenting the retinal lesions. High sugar levels in the blood due to diabetes causes DR, a leading cause of blindness. Manual detection or grading of the DR requires ophthalmologists' expertise and consumes time prone to human errors. Therefore, using fundus images, the ML and DL algorithms help automatic DR detection. The fundus imaging analysis helps the early DR detection, controlling, and treatment evaluation of DR conditions. Knowing the fundus image analysis requires a strong knowledge of the system and ML and DL functionalities in computer vision. DL in fundus imaging is a rapidly expanding research area. This chapter presents the fundus images, DR, and its severity levels. Also, this chapter explains the performance analysis of the various ML DL-based DR detection techniques. Finally, the role of ML and DL techniques in DR detection or severity grading is discussed.

    Bandaru Sri Chandra Nikitha, RV College of Engineering, India
    Basavaneni Silpa, RV College of Engineering, India
    Sindhu R. Rajendran, RV College of Engineering, India
    Ramavenkateswaran N., RV College of Engineering, India

The present world is overwhelmed with digital technologies: ubiquitous platforms of cloud computing and the internet of everything. Artificial intelligence (AI) is a technology that enables a machine to simulate human behaviour. The detailed facial expressions are captured by AI-enabled effective imaging and recognition processes of human vision. In artificial emotional intelligence (AEI), a new paradigm of human-computer interaction with AI-enabled cloud and internet connectivity could transpire healthy emotional intelligence (EI). As per the WHO world health report in 2018, globally, an estimated 264 million people are affected by depression and increased in recent years pertinent to COVID-19 lockdown-induced socio-economic factors. Hence, its paramount importance for the government and researchers to give serious consideration to developing EI. EI including human behaviours, digital well-being, and decision-making can be mentored using predictive data analytics. In this chapter, recent trends, preferrable ML algorithms, and research approach to EI components are discussed.

    Akshat Mishra, Vellore Institute of Technology, India
    Swetank Kaushik, Vellore Institute of Technology, India
    Srinivasa Perumal R., Vellore Institute of Technology, Chennai, India
    Chiranji Lal Chowdhary, Vellore Institute of Technology, India

The notion of agile supply chains is gaining traction in academia and has been enthusiastically adopted by private corporations. A variety of factors differentiate agile supply networks. They should not only be network-based but also market-sensitive, with tightly linked virtual and crucial operations. If agile supply chains are to adapt for ever-faster turnaround time towards both volume and variety changes, they must integrate supply and demand. The agile supply chain must be able to swiftly modify the output to satisfy customer needs and move from one version to the next. Of course, information technology is essential to the smooth running of agile teams. However, this chapter will focus on two additional essential facilitators of supply chains. Agility, which has gotten less emphasis yet is vital to the success of these kinds of procedures, has gotten less attention.

    Santhakumari Sadhasivam, School of Information Technology and Engineering, Vellore Institute of Technology, Vellore, India
    Kamalakannan J., School of Information Technology and Engineering, Vellore Institute of Technology, Vellore, India

Emotions have a vital role in human beings, and it is tough to define because of their intangible nature. Emotions vary over time and from person to person. Sometimes, emotions that sound good to people also may harm human beings. It depends upon one's health conditions and circumstances. Emotions are related to neurological, physiological, or cognitive processes. Though emotions are intangible, many invasive and non-invasive techniques are available to read the electrical activity in the brain to sense the different kinds of emotions. EEG is a non-invasive technique used in brain wave analyses. The main goal of this chapter is to give a brief introduction to EEG, characteristics of the brain waves, which part of the brain is responsible for emotions, the neurological structure of emotions, and lists of deep learning algorithms used to classify the various emotions. This chapter also contains data sets of emotions and a few key challenges in this field. For researchers with engineering backgrounds who are naive to this field, this chapter could be helpful.

    Niranjan Rajpurohit, Jaipuria Institute of Management, Jaipur, India
    Jevin Jain, NMIMS, India
    Yash Agrawal, Intellibuzz TEM Pvt. Ltd., India

Artificial neural networks (ANNs) and their applications have revolutionized several industries and functions, including HR, in a short span of time. These state-of-the-art AI solutions build together or independently a more efficient way for the human resource managers to predict the potential success of an employee in his or her work team. Extant research has established the positive effect of emotional intelligence on team effectiveness. Emotional intelligence is playing an increasingly bigger role in determining one's success as an effective team member. People with higher EQ are better able to work in teams, adjust to the change, and are flexible in workplace. This chapter attempts to design a model, deploying neural networks, to aid in increasing project team effectiveness.

    Avani K. V. H., BMS College of Engineering, India
    Deeksha Manjunath, BMS College of Engineering, India
    C. Gururaj, BMS College of Engineering, India

Thyroid nodule is a common disease on a global scale. It is characterized by an abnormal growth of the thyroid tissue. Thyroid nodules are divided into two types: benign and malignant. To ensure effective clinical care, an accurate identification of thyroid nodules is required. One of the most used imaging techniques for assessing and evaluating thyroid nodules is ultrasound. It performs well when it comes to distinguishing between benign and malignant thyroid nodules. But ultrasound diagnosis is not simple and is highly dependent on radiologist experience. Radiologists sometimes may not notice minor elements of an ultrasound image leading to an incorrect diagnosis. After performing a comparative study of several deep learning-based models implemented with different classification algorithms on an open-source data set, it has been found that ResNet101v2 gave the best accuracy (~96%), F1 score (0.957), sensitivity (0.917), etc. A simple and easy-to-use graphical user interface (GUI) has also been implemented.

Chapter 9

Sujigarasharma K., School of Information Technology and Engineering, Vellore Institute of Technology, Vellore, India

Rathi R., School of Information Technology and Engineering, Vellore Institute of Technology, Vellore, India

Visvanathan P., School of Information Technology and Engineering, Vellore Institute of Technology, Vellore, India

Kanchana R., Computer Science and Engineering, Vel Tech Ranganathan Dr.Sagunthala R&D Institute of Science and Technology, Chennai, India

One of the important aspects of human-computer interaction is the detection of emotions using facial expressions. Emotion recognition has problems such as facial expressions, variations of posture, non-uniform illuminations, and so on. Deep learning techniques becomes important to solve these classification problems. In this chapter, VGG19, Inception V3, and Resnet50 pre-trained networks are used for the transfer learning approach to predict human emotions. Finally, the study achieved 98.32% of accuracy for emotion recognition and classification using the CK+ dataset.

Chapter 10

Vanmathi C., Vellore Institute of Technology, India

Mangayarkarasi R., Vellore Institute of Technology, India

Prabhavathy P., Vellore Institute of Technology, India

Hemalatha S., Vellore Institute of Technology, India

Sagar M., Vellore Institute of Technology, India

A human's words, facial expressions, gestures, tone of voice, and even keyboard force can all be used in conjunction with artificial intelligence technologies to perform emotion intelligence (EI) identification. The development of artificial emotional intelligence has made it possible for people and robots to interact in a manner that is more natural, similar to the way that humans engage with one another. The expansion of the internet of things and wearable technology has a positive impact on the development of emotion detection software in the healthcare sector. This system contributes to society by making use of many forms of technology. There is always going to be a trade-off between price and functionality. The development of software with emotional intelligence relies on the collection of extensive datasets and the development of reliable modelling techniques. This chapter uses case studies, computing, and AI-based research methods to analyze emotional intelligence systems and their effects on human-computer interaction in the healthcare sector.

Nomvula J. Ndhlovu, University of South Africa, South Africa
Leila Goosen, University of South Africa, South Africa

In order to provide readers with an overview of, and summarize, the content of this chapter, the purpose is stated as answering the primary research question: To what extent can multidisciplinary artificial intelligence in education (AIED) applications enhance higher education teaching and learning at an open and distance e-learning (ODeL) institution in South Africa? It is important to note that this is done against the background of multidisciplinary applications of deep learning-based artificial emotional intelligence.

Parvathi R., Vellore Institute of Technology, Chennai, India
Pattabiraman V., Vellore Institute of Technology, Chennai, India

The Google Play Store is one of the most well-known and widely used Android app stores. On the Play Store, there is a lot of new information not only by the developers of the programme but also by the users who provide reviews and ratings. All of this information may be used to provide valuable insight into app popularity, which can be quite beneficial to app creators. The authors used a Google Play Store raw data collection from the Kaggle website. The data set includes a variety of features that can be used to forecast app success. Many classifier models are used to predict the popularity of apps in this study and determined which one give the best results. In the classification model, user reviews are added as a numerical feature. This feature has been found to considerably improve classification accuracy. Surprisingly the social aspects have a significant impact on the popularity of an app are also considered in this study.

Iuliia Pinkovetskaia, Ulyanovsk State University, Russia

The purpose of study was to evaluate the indicators characterizing the development of the healthcare system in the regions of Russia. The study used official statistical information on the activities of medical organizations located in all 82 regions of Russia for 2020. The density functions of the normal distribution were used as models. The research showed that on ten thousand people living in the region are an average of 48 doctors, 85 hospital beds, 289 patients who were served daily in organizations engaged in outpatient treatment. These indicators are higher than in many other countries, which creates prerequisites for the development of emotional intelligence in the Russian healthcare sector. In most regions the salary in the healthcare sector did not differ significantly from the average salary in the corresponding region. The proposed methodological approach and the results obtained have a scientific novelty, since the assessment of regional features of medical care in the regions of Russia has not been carried out before.

    Zahra Alidousti Shahraki, University of Isfahan, Iran
    Mohsen Aghabozorgi Nafchi, Shiraz University, Iran

Today, many changes have been seen in the life of people in society with the development of new technologies. For example, developing various new communication platforms and applications such as social networks has been able to affect the lifestyle and communication of people in different age groups. The elderly are one of the most important sections of society, and other age groups have been affected by new applications and social networks in recent years. One of the important issues that should be considered for the elderly people is to provide a suitable environment to improve their quality of life because they are one of the most vulnerable groups in society who, due to old age and various diseases, don't have this power to do their daily routine, and this affects their moods. So, designing new intelligence applications for improving their emotional intelligence can play an important role to facilitate their work and communications. In this chapter, the authors discuss new artificial intelligence applications that can control the emotional intelligence of the elderly.

    Neelu Khare, Vellore Institute of Technology, India
    Brijendra Singh, Vellore Institute of Technology, India
    Munis Ahmed Rizvi, Vellore Institute of Technology, India

Machine learning and deep learning play a vital role in making smart decisions, especially with huge amounts of data. Identifying the emotional intelligence levels of individuals helps them to avoid superfluous problems in the workplace or in society. Emotions reflect the psychological state of a person or represent a quick (a few minutes or seconds) reactions to a stimulus. Emotions can be categorized on the basis of a person's feelings in a situation: positive, negative, and neutral. Emotional intelligence seeks attention from computer engineers and psychologists to work together to address EI. However, identifying human emotions through deep learning methods is still a challenging task in computer vision. This chapter investigates deep learning models for the recognition and assessment of emotional states with diverse emotional data such as speech and video streaming. Finally, the conclusion summarises the usefulness of DL methods in assessing human emotions. It helps future researchers carry out their work in the field of deep learning-based emotional artificial intelligence.

Preface

Emotional intelligence has emerged as an important area of research in the artificial intelligence field as it covers a wide range of real-life domains. Though machines may never need all the emotional skills that people need, there is evidence to suggest that machines require at least some of these skills to appear intelligent when interacting with people. To understand how deep learning-based emotional intelligence can be applied and utilized across industries, further study on its opportunities and future directions is required.

Multidisciplinary Applications of Deep Learning-Based Artificial Emotional Intelligence explores artificial intelligence applications, such as machine and deep learning, in emotional intelligence and examines their use towards attaining emotional intelligence acceleration and augmentation. It provides research on tools used to simplify and streamline the formation of deep learning for system architects and designers. Covering topics such as data analytics, deep learning, knowledge management, and virtual emotional intelligence, this reference work is ideal for computer scientists, engineers, industry professionals, researchers, scholars, practitioners, academicians, instructors, and students. In the chapter "Artificial Intelligence and Data Analytics Based Emotional," the study is about the systematic literature review that uses new generation techniques for developing different techniques to make life easier from different emotional AI methods. Right from automation to improved security systems, technology got us covered. Machines deployed with intelligence stand the potential to drive cars, perform medical procedures, control traffic, and possibly everything that we can think of. Several large and small-scale organizations are adopting AI technologies to amplify their growth and surpass prior business results.

The next chapter "Emotion Detection and Classification Using Machine Learning Techniques," analyzes 57 articles published from 2012 on emotion classification using bio signals such as ECG & GSR. This study would be valuable for future researchers to gain an insight into the emotion model, emotion elicitation and self-assessment techniques, physiological signals, pre-processing methods, feature extraction, and machine learning techniques utilized by the different researchers. A maximum of the investigators have used openly available databases, and some have created their datasets. The studies have considered the participants from the healthy age group and of similar cultural backgrounds. Fusion of the ECG and GSR parameters can help to improve classification accuracy. Additionally, Handcrafted features fused with automatically extracted deep machine learning features can increase classification accuracy. Deep learning techniques and feature fusion techniques have improved classification accuracy.

Chapter 3

Machine learning (ML) and deep learning (DL) techniques play a significant role in diabetic retinopathy (DR) detection via grading the severity levels or segmenting the retinal lesions. High sugar levels in the blood due to diabetes causes DR, a leading cause of blindness. Manual detection or grading of the DR requires ophthalmologists' expertise and consumes time prone to human errors. Therefore, in the chapter "Role of Machine and Deep Learning Techniques in Diabetic Retinopathy Detection," the ML and DL algorithms help automatic DR detection using fundus images. The fundus imaging analysis helps the early DR detection, controlling, and treatment evaluation of DR conditions. Knowing the fundus image analysis requires a strong knowledge of the system and ML and DL functionalities in computer vision. DL in fundus imaging is a rapidly expanding research area. This chapter presents the fundus images, DR, and its severity levels. Also, this chapter explains the performance analysis of the various ML DL-based DR detection techniques. Finally, the role of ML and DL techniques in DR detection or severity grading is discussed.

Chapter 4

The present world is overwhelmed with digital technologies: ubiquitous platforms of cloud computing and the internet of everything. Artificial intelligence (AI) is a technology that enables a machine to simulate human behavior. The detailed facial expressions are captured by AI-enabled effective imaging and recognition processes of human vision. In artificial emotional intelligence (AEI), a new paradigm of human-computer interaction with AI enabled cloud and internet connectivity could transpire healthy emotional intelligence (EI). As per the WHO world health report in 2018, globally, an estimated 264 million people are affected by depression and increased in recent years pertinent to COVID lockdown-induced socio-economic factors. EI including human behaviors, digital well-being and decision-making can be mentored using predictive data analytics. In the chapter "Role of Machine Learning in Artificial Emotional Intelligence," recent trends, preferable ML algorithms and research approach to EI components are highlighted.

The notion of agile supply chains is gaining traction in academia and has been enthusiastically adopted by private corporations. A variety of factors differentiate agile supply networks. They should not only be network-based but also market-sensitive, with tightly linked virtual and crucial operations. If agile supply chains are to adapt for ever-faster turnaround time towards both volume and variety changes, they must integrate supply and demand. The agile supply chain must be able to swiftly modify the output to satisfy customer needs and move from one version to the next. Of course, information technology is essential to the smooth running of agile teams. The chapter "Role of Emotional Intelligence in Agile Supply Chains" will focus on two additional essential facilitators of supply chains. Agility, which has gotten less emphasis yet is vital to the success of these kinds of procedures, has gotten less attention.

Chapter 6

Emotions have a vital role in human beings, and it is tough to define because of their intangible nature. Emotions vary over time and from person to person. Sometimes, emotions that sound good to people also may harm human beings. It depends upon one's health conditions and the circumstances. Emotions are related to neurological, physiological, or cognitive processes. Though emotions are intangible, many invasive and non-invasive techniques are available to read the electrical activity in the brain to sense the different kinds of emotions. EEG is a non-invasive technique used in brain wave analyses. The main goal of chapter on "Neural Patterns of Emotions in EEG and fMRI" is to give a brief introduction to EEG, Characteristics of the brain waves, which part of the brain is responsible for emotions, the neurological structure of emotions, and lists of deep learning algorithms used to classify the various emotions. The chapter "Neural Patterns of Emotions in EEG and fMRI" also contains data sets of emotions and a few key challenges in this field. The researchers with engineering backgrounds who are naive to this field, this chapter could be helpful.

Chapter 7

Artificial neural networks (ANNs) and their applications have revolutionized several industries and functions, including HR, in a short span of time. These state-of-the-art AI solutions, build together or independently, a more efficient way for the human resource managers to predict the potential success of an employee in his or her work team. Extant research has established the positive effect of Emotional

Intelligence on Team Effectiveness. Emotional Intelligence is playing an increasingly bigger role in determining one's success as an effective team member. People with higher EQ are better able to work in teams, adjust to the change and are flexible in workplace. In the chapter "A Neural Network Approach to Increase Project Team Effectiveness Through Emotional Intelligence," it is attempted to design a model, deploying neural networks, to aid in increasing project team effectiveness.

The chapter "Deep Learning-Based Detection of Thyroid Nodules" deals with thyroid nodules which are common disease on a global scale. Thyroid nodules are divided into two types: benign and malignant thyroid nodules. To ensure effective clinical care, an accurate identification of thyroid nodules is required. One of the most used imaging techniques for assessing and evaluating thyroid nodules is ultrasound. It performs well when it comes to distinguishing between benign and malignant thyroid nodules. But ultrasound diagnosis is not simple and is highly dependent on the radiologists' experience. Radiologists sometimes may not notice minor elements of an ultrasound image leading to an incorrect diagnosis. After performing a comparative study of several deep learning-based models implemented with different classification algorithms on an open-source data set. It has been found that ResNet101v2 gave the best accuracy (~96%), F1 Score (0.957), sensitivity (0.917), etc. A simple and easy-to-use Graphical User Interface (GUI) has also been implemented.

The next chapter on "Emotion-Based Human-Computer Interaction" is highlighting the important aspects of human-computer interaction is the detection of emotions using facial expressions. Emotion recognition has problems such as facial expressions, variations of posture, non-uniform illuminations and so on. Nowadays Deep Learning techniques become important to solve these classification problems. In this chapter VGG19, Inception V3 and Resnet50 pre-trained networks are used for the transfer learning approach to predict human emotions. Finally, the study achieved 98.32% of accuracy for emotion recognition and classification using the CK+ dataset. Another chapter titled "A Study of Human Interaction Emotional Intelligence in Healthcare Applications" is focused on some case studies, computing, and AI-based research methods to analyze emotional intelligence systems and their effects on human-computer interaction in the health care sector. A human's words, facial expressions, gestures, tone of voice, and even keyboard force can all be used in conjunction with artificial intelligence technologies to perform Emotion Intelligence (EI) identification. Recent advancements in artificial intelligence detectors are in high demand by health care practitioners for decision making and early therapy prediction. The expansion of the internet of things and wearable technology has a positive impact on the development of emotion detection software in the healthcare sector. This system contributes to society by making use of many forms of technology. There is always going to be a trade-off between price and functionality. The development of software with emotional intelligence relies on the collection of extensive datasets and the development of reliable modelling techniques.

In this chapter "To What Extent Can Multidisciplinary Artificial Intelligence Applications Enhance Higher Education?" the purpose is stated as answering the primary research question: To what extent can multidisciplinary Artificial Intelligence in Education (AIED) applications enhance higher education teaching and learning at an Open and Distance e-Learning (ODeL) institution in South Africa? It is important to note that this is done against the background of multidisciplinary applications of deep learning-based artificial emotional intelligence.

The Google Play Store is one of the most well-known and widely used Android app stores. On the Play Store, there is a lot of new information. Not only by the developers of the programme, but also by the users who provide reviews and ratings. All of this information may be used to provide valuable insight into app popularity, which can be quite beneficial to app creators. We used a Google Play Store raw data collection from the Kaggle website. The data set includes a variety of features that can be used to forecast app success. Many classifier models is used to predict the popularity of apps in this study and determined which one give the best results. In the classification model, user reviews is added as a numerical feature. This feature has been found to considerably improve classification accuracy. Surprisingly the social aspects have a significant impact on the popularity of an app are also considered in Chapter "Google Play Store Apps Data Analysis and Popularity Predictions using Artificial Emotional Intelligence".

The purpose of chapter "Providing the Population With Medical Services in the Context of Emotional Intelligence" was to evaluate the indicators characterizing the development of the healthcare system in the regions of Russia. The study used official statistical information on the activities of medical organizations located in all 82 regions of Russia for 2020. The density functions of the normal distribution were used as models. The research showed that on ten thousand people living in the region are an average of 48 doctors, 85 hospital beds, 289 patients were served daily in organizations engaged in outpatient treatment. These indicators are higher than in many other countries, which creates prerequisites for the development of emotional intelligence in the Russian healthcare sector. In most regions the salary in the healthcare sector did not differ significantly from the average salary in the corresponding region. The proposed methodological approach and the results obtained have a scientific novelty, since the assessment of regional features of medical care in the regions of Russia has not been carried out before.

Machine learning and deep learning play a vital role in making smart decisions, especially with huge amounts of data. Identifying the emotional intelligence levels of individuals helps them to avoid superfluous problems in the workplace or in society. Emotions reflect the psychological state of a person or represent a quick (a few minutes or seconds) reaction to a stimulus. Emotions can be categorized on the basis of a person's feelings in a situation: positive, negative, and neutral. Emotional intelligence seeks attention from computer engineers and psychologists to work together to address EI. However, identifying human emotions through deep learning methods is still a challenging task in computer vision. The chapter "Deep Learning Methods for Modelling Emotional Intelligence" investigates deep learning models for the recognition and assessment of emotional states with diverse emotional data such as speech and video streaming. Finally, the conclusion summarizes the usefulness of DL methods in assessing human emotions. It helps future researchers carry out their work in the field of deep learning-based emotional artificial intelligence.

This edited volume is targeted for undergraduate and graduate students, practitioners, researchers, clinicians and data scientists who are interested in getting information on latest developments in the field of Artificial Emotional Intelligence. This will guide the researchers to the leading edge of the literature on multidisciplinary applications of deep learning-based artificial emotional intelligence.

Chiranji Lal Chowdhary
Vellore Institute of Technology, India

Chapter 1
Artificial Intelligence and Data Analytics–Based Emotional Intelligence

Subramaniam Meenakshi Sundaram
https://orcid.org/0000-0003-2352-0714
GSSS Institute of Engineering and Technology for Women, India

Tejaswini R. Murgod
GSSS Institute of Engineering and Technology for Women, India

Sowmya M.
GSSS Institute of Engineering and Technology for Women, India

ABSTRACT

With the advent of technology, we have seen drastic changes in the way of life. Right from automation to improved security systems, technology got us covered. Machines deployed with intelligence stand the potential to drive cars, perform medical procedures, control traffic, and possibly everything that we can think of. Several large and small-scale organizations are adopting AI technologies to amplify their growth and surpass prior business results. Emotional AI can also help businesses to solve sensitive issues at the workplace. The global outlook is that AI imbibed into automation or robotics is going to revolutionize the markets and workforces. As per market estimates, over the next five years, the affective computing market will witness new heights surging to a growth rate of 43.0% CAGR in terms of revenue, with the global market reaching to US$ 1710 million by 2024 up from US$ 200 million in 2019. In the forecast period from 2019-2024, development around touchless AI models are expected to grow in the affective computing market between 2017 and 2025.

INTRODUCTION

The booming growth of Machine Learning (ML) and Artificial Intelligence, like most transformational technologies, is both exciting and scary (Dwivedi et al., 2021). It is exciting to consider all the ways

DOI: 10.4018/978-1-6684-5673-6.ch001

our lives may improve, from managing our calendars to making medical diagnoses, but it is scary to consider the social and personal implications as well. As machine learning continues to grow, we all need to develop new skills in order to differentiate ourselves. With advances in Artificial Intelligence, machines can do better than human beings in gathering data, analyzing data, interpreting the results, determining a recommended course of action and implementing the course of action (Chowdhary & Acharjya, 2018). A smart machine might help the doctor to diagnose an illness at a faster rate and even provide necessary recommendation treatment for the same.

It takes a person, however, to sit with a patient, understand their life situation (finances, family, quality of life, etc.), and help determine what treatment plan is optimal. Similarly, a smart machine may be able to diagnose complex business problems and recommend actions to improve an organization. Organizations are using data and insights to enhance customer experience, optimize profit & growth and operational efficiency (Chowdhary, 2021). Using data analytics we get the right information at the right time. Industries today offer data landscape modernization, analytics; provide master data management and data quality as a service. With these the data processing needs in real-time, batch and big data, they deploy analytics models at scale and get consistency and quality of data.

Emotional Intelligence (EI) has always been important, but cultivating the competencies that underpin emotional intelligence will be increasingly significant as automation and Artificial Intelligence replaces all, or part of many jobs. Emotional intelligence closely relates to attention and the executive functions of our brain. Essentially, emotional intelligence is a set of competencies and skills that we use to shift our attention between self-focus, other focus and beyond. We can use these skills to accurately judge our own and other people's emotional expressions, to regulate our own emotions and discern their impact on others. If success and happiness is the goal, these skills are fundamental.

Mayer & Salovey (1997) defined EI as a mental ability, suggesting that emotionally intelligent people perceive emotions more accurately. This enables them to use emotions to facilitate thinking, to understand them and their meanings, and to manage their own emotions as well as someone else's in a more optimal way. In a nutshell, EI can be defined as the meta-ability to perceive and understand emotions, as well as to manage them appropriately and adaptively.

When data is universally accessible, AI teams are focused on development and deployment, and IT infrastructure is flexible and unbounded. AI that is data-driven, production-oriented and cloud-enabled should available anytime, anywhere and at any scale. The enterprise-ready AI is fast becoming a reality. With organizations producing data at unprecedented rates, technology can turn this data into insights and efficiencies that cannot come fast enough. New digital technologies are quickly reshaping the financial services industry and financial institutions are turning AI and machine learning to meet both increased regulatory requirements and customer demand for web-based and mobile access to banking products. Research institutions and medical facilities are using the ability to analyze massive data sets to sequence the human genome, develop new forms of treatment, speed and improve patient care, and better manage electronic health records. The future of manufacturing is connected, automated and digitally driven. As plant floor operations technologies converge with IT, numerous use cases across the manufacturing cycle become possible to ignite innovation, create more efficient operations, reduce downtime and improve worker productivity.

In the following sections we highlight AI and EI, Artificial Emotional Intelligence, technologies adopted for EI, applications of Emotional Intelligence, challenges of AI, Data Analytics and Emotional Intelligence and the future of Artificial Emotional Intelligence

ARTIFICIAL EMOTIONAL INTELLIGENCE

Emotions and Intelligence are allied spectacles and hence veritable intelligent agents are modeled taking into account the emotional quotient. Research and development in artificial intelligence have imbibed emotional intelligence as an important focus theme to scan across real-life disciplines. Noteworthy key-ins have been incorporated to evolve fresh imminent across the sphere of emotional intelligence and algorithms which deploy intelligent software decisions. Agents who delve into teaching-learning process are very alluring for merging emotional facets in artificial intelligence. It is an incredible fact that emotions play an imperative component in intelligent behavior and persuade the human judgment-making process. Recent EI research focuses on strategic features such as emotion detection, emotional agents, text emotion detection and modeling the setting of artificial and autonomous task agents.

Design and Development of technology tools endowed with emotional intelligence are the trending research focus booming up in artificial intelligence domain. The global outlook is that AI imbided into automation or robotics is going to revolutionize the markets and workforces. Improvisation in AI which is escalating to leaps and bounds will give rise to smarter "thinking" jobs than monotonous "doing" jobs (Balakrishnan et al., 2019).

Artificial emotional intelligence is vital for integration of future robots into the human society. This work introduces one possible approach to representation and processing of emotional mental states and attitudes (appraisals) in a cognitive architecture (Samsonovich, 2012). Artificial emotional intelligence could be the key to a human-level artificial intelligence in general. From this perspective, adding advanced emotional capabilities to cognitive architectures (Gray, 2007) is a critical milestone on the roadmap to human-level artificial intelligence.

Today's large volumes of surveillance data pose a challenge of extracting vital information from the data automatically. The task may remain unsolved even after relevant objects; features and apparent relations have been identified and represented in a symbolic format. In many important cases, the remaining task involves higher cognitive analysis of human mental states (elements in human Theory of Mind), which today requires a human analyst. Biologically-inspired affective cognitive architectures increasingly attract attention in this context as an efficient, robust and flexible solution to the challenge of real-world sensory data analysis. At the same time, modeling of higher cognition in cognitive architectures is often limited to simplistic algorithms and separated from biologically inspired information processing.

Examples of potential applications of future intelligent agents that will be based on this approach include: (i) detection, anticipation and control of ad hoc social interactions related to spontaneous violence, accidents or a natural disaster, (ii) detection of individual and group activities that are likely to be related to terrorism, (iii) prediction of a potentially harmful individual condition: e.g., psychological breakdown of a human operator, driver, or air traffic controller. Meta cognitive theory-of-mind skills that a human analyst must have in order to be efficient in the above tasks include the abilities to infer, attribute, simulate and predict mental states of actors involved in the ongoing action. The approach developed in this work supports the view that an artifact can and should have similar meta-cognitive abilities in order to be human-level intelligent and successful in solving tasks of the mental state analysis.

Emotional intelligence represents an ability to validly reason with emotions and to use emotions to enhance thought. Physiological research was revealing the existence of neural pathways for unconscious emotional processing. Neurologists have made progress in demonstrating that emotion is as, or more, important than reason in the process of making decisions and deciding actions. The significance of these findings should not be overlooked in a world that is increasingly reliant on computers to accommodate to user needs. Emotional Intelligence involves the concepts like managing emotions, understanding emotions, facilitating thought and perceiving emotions (Zhang et al., 2022).

TECHNOLOGY AND EMOTIONAL INTELLIGENCE

Fuzzy Logic Systems (FLS) produce acceptable but definite output in response to incomplete, ambiguous, distorted, or inaccurate (fuzzy) input. Fuzzy Logic (FL) is a method of reasoning that resembles human reasoning. The approach of FL imitates the way of decision making in humans that involves all intermediate possibilities between digital values YES and NO. The conventional logic block that a computer can understand takes precise input and produces a definite output as TRUE or FALSE, which is equivalent to human's YES or NO. The fuzzy logic works on the levels of possibilities of input to achieve the definite output. Fuzzy logic can control machines and consumer products (Wang et al., 2022). This may not give accurate reasoning, but acceptable reasoning. Fuzzy logic helps to deal with the uncertainty in engineering.

The Artificial Neural Network (ANN) is a system of hardware and/or software patterned after the operation of neurons in the human brain. These ANNs are a variety of deep learning technology, which also falls under the umbrella of AI. Commercial applications of these technologies generally focus on solving complex signal processing or pattern recognition problems. Examples of significant commercial applications include handwriting recognition, speech-to-text transcription, oil-exploration data analysis, weather prediction and facial recognition. A neural network is even capable of beating human performance in the area of image recognition. The artificial neural networks have soared and the technology continues to improve (Cavus et al., 2022).

Emotions form a fundamental aspect of the human existence, an aspect which has been widely ignored by technology for the simple reasons that the emotions cannot be quantifiable and because the technology did not really exist to read them (Hornung et al.,, 2022). It may sound futuristic, but the times are near when computers can read our emotions and the concept of emotional intelligence is not far off. We can call this as a blend of psychology and computer science. Affective computing, as it is being called is the latest trend and being developed for use in many applications. Affective computing also coined as artificial emotional intelligence, or emotion AI is the study and development of systems which are programmed to simulate, interpret and process human affects. Affective computing is an interdisciplinary field which spans computer science, psychology, and cognitive science blended all together. This is based on the concept that something as ephemeral as emotion can be quantified and captured as its own data point. With multiple pattern recognition tasks, AI can be vastly superior when compared to humans when it comes to reading subtle emotions on a user's face.

APPLICATIONS OF EMOTIONAL INTELLIGENCE

Emotional Intelligence is the ability to identify, evaluate, control, and express emotions in an effective and positive way. An individual with high EQ is able to communicate better, lessen their anxiety and stress, resolve conflicts, improve relationships, empathize with others, and overcome life's challenges. Emotional intelligence affects the quality of lives because it influences human behavior and relationships (Singh et al., 2022). Developing a high EI can help determine success, it can affect the choices by creating options we might not have thought otherwise or considered to be possible. The way a child manages emotions can have an impact on everything from his or her relationships with other students. Higher levels of emotional intelligence are able to keep a check on emotions better and be empathetic to others around them. This can help them develop improved self-motivation and more effective communication skills-essential skills to helping students become more confident learners. On the other hand, students who lack emotional intelligence can become less connected to school, negatively affecting performance in a classroom. EI involves emotional literacy (recognizing own feelings and the feelings of others), managing emotions (being able to control emotions effectively) and developing empathy (understanding and sharing the feeling of others).

The potential application for affective computing is limitless, especially when the market for affective computing systems has just started to evolve. With affective technology being adopted globally across multiple domains, the applications extend to healthcare, media & advertisement, market research, automotive, retail, communication and education. In education, e-learning programs could automatically detect when the learner is having difficulty to read and understand to further offer additional explanations or information. Additionally, e-therapy could help deliver psychological health services online as effectively as live in-person counseling.

The medical domain seems to gain the most, where affective computing applications are being created to assist people on the autism spectrum interact. Technology can enable medical devices to alert the wearer the changes happening to their biometric data like the heart rate, temperature, and etc. moments before and after a dangerous epileptic seizure.

Research labs are working on devices programmed to sense every emotion that ranges from pain to depression, something which is difficult to accurately diagnose at present and even programs which can monitor movements which are associated with acute chronic pain to offer vital suggestions for physiotherapy for the cure. Summing up, the time is near; where our refrigerator might suggest us to skip the ice cream tonight because the stress is high and suggest us to take a soothing soup instead, and our car may warn us to drive attentively because we are talking on the phone while driving, and our phone might encourage us to take breaks because we are getting frustrated after that bad office day.

Affective computing systems automatically identify emotions. Affective computing is also called emotion detection, emotion AI, artificial emotional intelligence or affective AI. Affective computing is an emerging technology that enables computers and systems to identify, process, and simulate human feelings and emotions. It is an interdisciplinary field that leverages computer science, psychology, and cognitive science. While it may seem unusual that computers can do something that is so inherently human, research shows that they achieve acceptable accuracy levels of emotion recognition from visual, textual, and auditory sources. With the insights gained from emotion AI, businesses can offer better services for their customers and make better decisions in customer-facing processes like sales, marketing, or customer services.

ADVANCEMENTS OF EMOTIONAL INTELLIGENCE

There is a lot of development in the field of AI has been a groundbreaking revolution in the always changing field of technology. Chatbots are more like friends to us nowadays as they try to understand what we are inquiring (Senthilkumar & Chowdhary, 2019). The important development in the field of chatbots is the introduction of emotional AI. Emotional AI can also help businesses to solve sensitive issues at the workplace. Spot is one such chatbot that enables employees to namelessly report improper behavior at the workplace without conversing with a human. The chatbot asks open-ended questions which would give them plenty of information to apply their algorithms and analyze the situation. Julia Shaw, Co-founder of Spot, who also happens to be a memory scientist and criminal psychologist believes that in such situations, no human involvement will cause more victims to tell the truth.

Additionally, Loris is messaging software which will train people to develop their skills without a human trainer. It trains employees on building listening and empathy skills to deal with different kinds of customers as well as varied nature of colleagues. As consumers are spending most of their time looking at their mobile screens, businesses can manage conversations with their consumers at a large scale and chatbots will play a major role in it. A bot agency named Sciensio deploys an AI technique that comprehends client purpose and gives applicable answers that may not jump out to humans who take everything literally. While new apps are being developed, there are services building Emotional AI tools which can be deployed into systems. The travel industry is constantly approaching emotional AI to interact with customers personally to offer them the best holiday. Marketing professionals, as well as governments, want to know how everyone feels when we fill out any form or reply to queries. Where personalization has been a turnaround factor for companies to interact, gain and retain customers, companies want to be approached as more reliable and trustworthy. For this, they need to know more about their customers wherein they can genuinely solve their problems, offer products and services which are suitable for every customer according to their needs and requirements.

Well, nowadays where technology is constantly bringing up something new, chatbot seems to be the only rescue option which can provide flexible responses to how users feel and reaching out to the user during a crisis. Also, medical appointments and other such sensitive tasks can be elevated and be solely handled by chatbots as they can detect someone in urgency or need, and accordingly respond to such situations where we humans can fail sometimes. This is very crucial as it enables to give the best service pouring in maximum customer satisfaction, and to some extent, customer loyalty too. After seeing such use cases where emotional AI can altogether help in having a deeper conversation with users, every business should assure to deploy emotional AI as it can provide the most useful response.

RECENT CHALLENGES OF AI, ANALYTICS AND EI

Big Data Analytics and Data Fusion due to the enormous increase in data through digitalization, big data has become a business-critical resource. A large amount of computing power and various tools for analyzing data are required to utilize the data. Businesses can use data to improve their core business, but also to create completely new business models. Mass data analytics is already a well-established technology for processing and retrieving such information. Necessary functions include: editing and refining raw data for analysis, visualizing data for the user, and various statistical methods for extracting relevant data and making predictions based on the data collected. Artificial intelligence tools aim to automate this process and enable the analysis of massive amounts of data.

Data analysis methodologies can be divided into three types namely: (1) Data analytics refers to evaluating data based on past events, (2) Predictive analytics makes assumptions and tests based on historical data to predict future events, and (3) Artificial intelligence / machine learning analyzes data, makes assumptions and produces predictions on a scale that human analysis alone cannot achieve. One advantage of computers over humans is the ability to retrieve and recall vast amounts of information that can be accessed quickly, for example, via the Internet. If the data is of sufficient quality, the machine can outperform human performance in limited machine learning tasks. Often too little attention is paid to the collection, naming, or the notation and modification of good quality data for data analysis or machine learning methods, although the performance of the methods is largely dependent on it.

We must be able to choose the right tools for each application. Most of the time that goes into data analysis takes time to edit and clean up the data for automatic analysis. Typically, this takes at least 80% of the time of the entire analysis process. Business applications are an important application area for data analysis and artificial intelligence. The problem with applying machine learning to business databases is that most of them are too dirty or sparse in terms of machine learning. So, for the time being, there are few real machine learning applications compared to normal business analytics. Prediction is not required in many applications, as statistical reasoning and analysis of variances are sufficient in 80-90% of cases according.

In addition, data interpretability is usually more important in business applications than absolute accuracy. For this reason, traditional statistical methods are still dominant compared to black-box methods of neural networks. However, due to the hype of artificial intelligence, many methods implemented by conventional methods are referred in media as artificial intelligence, although they actually are not. The greatest benefit of artificial intelligence in business applications may therefore come from intelligent assistants who only help the user to make a decision. Due to its speed and other capacity, the machine is also able to combine data from different sources in an unprecedented way. A good example is a recent article on a study published by Nature Human Behavior, which found that human happiness is diminished by air pollution

Daily human emotional expressions or likes are unreliable, but over a longer period of time they provide reliable information about the user's average emotional state. Jaron Javier, a pioneer of the Internet, regards Facebook and Google's business models as shaping people's behavior, which goes much further than ordinary advertising. Computational models using advanced statistical mathematics and machine learning provide users with both "carrot" and sometimes "stick" - thus gradually changing their behavior to the benefit of businesses.

FUTURE OF ARTIFICIAL EMOTIONAL INTELLIGENCE

Human emotional intelligence refers to the ability to recognize our own emotions and those of others and to use this knowledge to guide our own behavior and achieve our goals. The importance of emotional intelligence for different applications is clear. For example, when making shopping decisions, feeling of a particular product is often more important than the details of the product. Studies have shown that when it comes to deciding between several options, it is very difficult for a person to do so by mere logical reasoning. Salespeople who can read the customer's feelings are better salespeople. When a customer views a product in a store or shop window, their feelings tell us what they like and what they don't.

In understanding emotions and social skills, man is superior to machines, and this competitive advantage should be exploited. Nowadays, when interconnected intelligent devices control our communication and our daily lives, attention to emotions plays a central role in artificial intelligence - we can talk about Emotion AI or Affective Computing. Communication with technology is becoming more interactive, resembling the interaction between people. Intelligent devices in our environment are able to capture people's emotions and moods and create more personalized user experiences.

According to cognitive explanations, humans use emotions to process information from both their bodies and their environment. The human mind is thought to function in that it constantly processes and directs its emotions. Feelings arise as a result of judgments and interpretations. Feeling creates motivation for action as well as repeating our behavior. Although cognitive explanations focus on exploring information processing, they also accept that physiological state can alter emotion. Studies have shown the effect of the physiological states of the body on the experience of feeling.

Applications of Emotion AI Emotions play a central role in human-to-human interaction. When talking to a robot or chatbot, one finds "machine-like", insensitive speech disgusting. In particular, empathy that is the ability to understand the feelings of the interlocutor is seen to play a significant role in good interpersonal communication. The same flaw more generally applies to interaction in digital media, where we often do not see our interlocutor. Emotional intelligence can be used in many ways in computer assisted teaching. For example, if the subject to be taught has not been understood or the student is not attentive enough, it is readily apparent from the student's expressions and changes in emotional state.

Challenges and future perspectives of emotional artificial intelligence research are still largely in its infancy. Much of the research, as well as the basic theories of emotion recognition, has been made for a small number people with acted, non-natural expressions. The spontaneous natural expressions in our daily lives are very varied and different. The state-of-the-art technology is therefore most suitable for applications where emotion recognition accuracy is not critical. The context greatly influences to expressions.

The best success in recognizing emotions can be achieved by learning, if possible, personal emotion models for each person. This is similar to what was the case with the much easier problem of speech recognition. Speaker-dependent, that is, speech recognition system trained individually by each person's speech samples is much easier than speaker-independent - and only after significant improvements through deep learning and massive training data can speaker-independent recognition be successful nowadays. The ways in which people express their emotions vary enormously, so it is not possible to achieve sufficiently good results for many applications using a common model. Focusing on only one application can improve recognition. In fact, this has been typical for most machine vision applications. Generally, in a given application, variations in the imaging conditions can be minimized and application-specific test data collected to the widest possible range of people, and these techniques facilitate analysis to obtain sufficiently high reliability

CONCLUSION

By integrating emotional intelligence with the existing artificial intelligence, AI is taking a crucial turn on its journey to becoming a transformational technology. Today, approximately 52% consumers around the world use AI powered technology. However, even the most sophisticated AI technologies lack essential factors like emotional intelligence and the ability to contextualize information like human beings. This is the sole reason why AI has not succeeded in taking over a major aspect of our careers and lives. Therefore, infusing emotions, empathy, and morality into AI is the next milestone technologists wish to accomplish, and a considerable amount of effort is being put in the process. Since 2020, artificial emotional intelligence is deemed to be a technological reality. While we humans keep on struggling to see one another, emotionally intelligent AI has advanced rapidly. Cameras in smart phones are omnipresent and ubiquitous, and face-tracking programming has already advanced enough to analyze the tiniest details of our facial expressions. The most progressive ones can even differentiate faked feelings from genuine ones.

Also, voice recognition and natural language processing algorithms are showing signs of improvement at discovering our opinion and emotional state from the audio. The technologies that analyze emotional responses from faces and voice are as of now way beyond the aptitudes of a normal human, and in numerous areas surpass the capacities of even the most skilled people. As the world digitally changes, each business is being judged based on ease of use and customer service. To succeed, there is a requirement for companies to offer an astounding experience that encourages them to meet and surpass their ideal business results, as well as remaining ahead of contenders. In making AI emotionally intelligent, it can make a deeper, intimate connection with customers. In spite of the fact that emotional AI is not widespread, tech giants and startups in different segments, including automotive and retail, have put resources into making their technology more human through computer vision and voice recognition. Hardly in another two years, will 10% of individual gadgets have emotional AI capacities. However, with new technology, comes new risks and reading feelings are one of them. Emotional AI is an integral asset that can give new metrics to comprehend individuals and redefine products and services in the future. In any case, it is imperative to consider and evaluate any risk. Unlike humans, AI can use your entire online history, which by and large is more data than anyone can recollect about any of their companions. Probably the most progressive machine learning algorithms created at Facebook and Google have just been applied on a secret stash of data from billions of individuals. These algorithms definitely realize what are our wants, inclinations and emotional triggers are, based on our communication, friends and cultural context. In numerous areas, they comprehend us better than we know ourselves.

While organizations need to make further connections with their shoppers by building and deploying emotional AI technologies, responsibility measures should be included. Thus, they will be able to keep up client trust and guarantee that appropriate actions are taken to solve issues, i.e bias or data breaches. This is the place software testing comes into picture.

As we move into a touch less, automated time, the competition to consummate these advancements follows; nonetheless, programming testing should be top of mind so as to give a frictionless, high-quality digital experience that results in effective results for all included. Faultless and right software is viewed as the norm by clients, so it is important to guarantee that each interaction an application or system has with a customer fulfills their physical, mental and emotional needs. To accomplish this impeccable experience, business leaders must research each conceivable user journey through continuous, automated testing.

Ensuring this tech is powerful and blunder free is crucial for its adoption and longevity. Testing the customer experience should be executed for online organizations, as this will find weak areas of an application or gadget, and permit groups to fix any issues with the product. Applications and services that perform well and give clients what they need will build up client trust and loyalty. As per market estimates, over the next five years, Affective Computing market will witness new heights surging to a growth rate of 43.0% CAGR in terms of revenue, with the global market reaching to US$ 1710 million by 2024 up from US$ 200 million in 2019. In the forecast period from 2019-2024, development around Touch less AI models are expected to grow at new heights taking the maximum pie of the affective computing market between 2017 and 2025. There are a few challenges as well into the adoption, these include slow digitization rate prevalent across emerging economies couples with exuberant cost of making affective computing systems with other operational challenges are the major speed breakers to the dominance of the global affective computing market.

REFERENCES

Balakrishnan, S., Janet, J., & Rani, S. S. (2019). Symbiotic transformational technology on the rise: artificial intelligence in emotional intelligence. *CSI Communications Magazine, 43*, 14-17.

Cavus, N., Mohammed, Y. B., Gital, A. Y. U., Bulama, M., Tukur, A. M., Mohammed, D., Isah, M. L., & Hassan, A. (2022). Emotional Artificial Neural Networks and Gaussian Process-Regression-Based Hybrid Machine-Learning Model for Prediction of Security and Privacy Effects on M-Banking Attractiveness. *Sustainability, 14*(10), 5826. doi:10.3390u14105826

Chowdhary, C. L. (2021). Simple Linear Iterative Clustering (SLIC) and Graph Theory-Based Image Segmentation. In Handbook of Research on Machine Learning Techniques for Pattern Recognition and Information Security (pp. 157-170). IGI Global.

Chowdhary, C. L., & Acharjya, D. P. (2018). Singular Value Decomposition–Principal Component Analysis-Based Object Recognition Approach. In Bio-Inspired Computing for Image and Video Processing (pp. 323-341). Chapman and Hall/CRC. doi:10.1201/9781315153797-12

Dwivedi, Y. K., Hughes, L., Ismagilova, E., Aarts, G., Coombs, C., Crick, T., Duan, Y., Dwivedi, R., Edwards, J., Eirug, A., Galanos, V., Ilavarasan, P. V., Janssen, M., Jones, P., Kar, A. K., Kizgin, H., Kronemann, B., Lal, B., Lucini, B., ... Williams, M. D. (2021). Artificial Intelligence (AI): Multidisciplinary perspectives on emerging challenges, opportunities, and agenda for research, practice and policy. *International Journal of Information Management, 57*, 101994. doi:10.1016/j.ijinfomgt.2019.08.002

Gray, W. D. (Ed.). (2007). *Integrated models of cognitive systems* (Vol. 1). Oxford University Press. doi:10.1093/acprof:oso/9780195189193.001.0001

Hornung, O., & Smolnik, S. (2022). AI invading the workplace: Negative emotions towards the organizational use of personal virtual assistants. *Electronic Markets, 32*(1), 123–138. doi:10.100712525-021-00493-0

Mayer, J. D., & Salovey, P. (1997). *Emotional development and emotional intelligence*. Basics Books.

Samsonovich, A. V. (2012, July). An approach to building emotional intelligence in artifacts. *Workshops at the Twenty-Sixth AAAI Conference on Artificial Intelligence*.

Senthilkumar, M., & Chowdhary, C. L. (2019). An AI-Based Chatbot Using Deep Learning. In *Intelligent Systems* (pp. 231–242). Apple Academic Press. doi:10.1201/9780429265020-12

Singh, D., Kaur, M., Jabarulla, M. Y., Kumar, V., & Lee, H. N. (2022). Evolving fusion-based visibility restoration model for hazy remote sensing images using dynamic differential evolution. *IEEE Transactions on Geoscience and Remote Sensing, 60*, 1–14. doi:10.1109/TGRS.2022.3155765

Wang, X., Xu, B., & Guo, Y. (2022). Fuzzy Logic System-Based Robust Adaptive Control of AUV with Target Tracking. *International Journal of Fuzzy Systems*, 1–9. doi:10.100740815-022-01356-2

Zhang, K., Ren, W., Luo, W., Lai, W. S., Stenger, B., Yang, M. H., & Li, H. (2022). Deep image deblurring: A survey. *International Journal of Computer Vision, 130*(9), 2103–2130. doi:10.100711263-022-01633-5

Chapter 2
Emotion Detection and Classification Using Machine Learning Techniques

Amita Umesh Dessai

Goa College of Engineering, India

Hassanali G. Virani

Goa College of Engineering, India

ABSTRACT

This chapter analyzes 57 articles published from 2012 on emotion classification using bio signals such as ECG and GSR. This study would be valuable for future researchers to gain an insight into the emotion model, emotion elicitation and self-assessment techniques, physiological signals, pre-processing methods, feature extraction, and machine learning techniques utilized by the different researchers. Most investigators have used openly available databases, and some have created their datasets. The studies have considered the participants from the healthy age group and of similar cultural backgrounds. Fusion of the ECG and GSR parameters can help to improve classification accuracy. Additionally, handcrafted features fused with automatically extracted deep machine learning features can increase classification accuracy. Deep learning techniques and feature fusion techniques have improved classification accuracy.

INTRODUCTION

Emotions indicate the way people prompt their feelings and communicate with the external world. Paul Ekman's theory recognizes the seven basic discrete emotions Fear, anger, disgust, sadness, happiness, surprise, and contempt experienced by human beings. The emotions can be distinguished from their biological processes and characteristics and usually do not persist for long. James Russell's Circumplex model of emotion separates the emotions in a two-dimensional circular space (Emotion classification, 2022). The valence indicates the pleasantness of the emotions and arousal intensity of emotions. Happiness has high valence and high arousal. Electroencephalogram (EEG), Electromyogram (EMG), respira-

DOI: 10.4018/978-1-6684-5673-6.ch002

tion rate (RT), Galvanic skin response(GSR) or Electrodermal activity (EDA), skin temperature(ST), heart-related methods like Electrocardiogram (ECG), Blood volume pulse (BVP), enable the detection of emotions. In a virtual classroom environment reliant on students' emotions suitable teaching plans can be formulated. The passengers can get alert if the driver is found angry or in stressful conditions. Companies can assess the emotions of their customers and then decide the strategy for marketing their products. In the healthcare field, robots can judge patient's emotional states and alter their actions appropriately. Human-computer interaction systems monitor the discomfort experienced by patients who aren't able to express their emotions verbally. Emotions are detected in geriatric patients to provide them assistance. Remote monitoring of the health of the elderly is done depending on the emotions experienced by them. The patients are provided assistance based on their emotions. Emotions can be detected using smart devices for real-time applications like healthcare, online classroom environment, advertising products. In this survey, the Inclusion criteria are ECG, BVP, GSR, and the exclusion criteria are Facial, Voice signals, EEG, EMG, ST, Respiration rate for emotion detection. The research papers built on the openly available databases using ECG and GSR signals are published in the year 2012. This survey focuses on the recently published papers from the year 2012 to 2020. A total of 47 research papers are from the years 2016 to 2020. This chapter reviews ten papers published in the year 2016 and nine papers during the years 2017 and 2018 respectively. Twelve papers in this review are from the year 2019, seven papers during the year 2020. Mainly total number of 9 papers is from Elsevier, 8 numbers of papers are from IEEE transaction and 8 papers from MDPI sensors databases. Factors like the number and age of participants, gender proportionality, cultural & social background, and intellectual, physical, mental well-being of the subjects were considered. Emotions experienced by the participants mapped on the Valence Arousal scale. Pictures, Audio, Audiovisuals, virtual reality, the real-time environment used for emotion elicitation. Self-assessment manikins (SAM), Questionnaire, Participant's ratings, Participant's feedback, Android-based application assess the emotions experienced by the participants. The fusion of the ECG and GSR parameters leads to an enhancement in classification accuracy.

The paper structured as follows. The Section Background reviews the emotion models, emotion elicitation methods, methods of self-assessment by the participants. Next Section on "Emotional Intelligence" reviews the publicly available databases for research, devices used for acquiring these signals, and the participant's details. "Emotion Detection" and "ECG, GSR Signal Preprocessing" Sections mention the pre-processing methods, feature extraction, and feature selection techniques. The feature selection techniques assist in selecting the optimum features needed for classification. Next Section "Classifications and Fusion" explains the classification techniques and the fusion techniques for classifying the emotions. Last Sections are Future directions and Conclusion. Figure number 1 lists an overview of the various attributes for emotion recognition and classification using the ECG & GSR signals.

BACKGROUND

Egger Maria, Ley Matthias, Hanke Sten in their paper give a review of emotion detection. The outward physical expressions in Facial recognition lead to falsified emotion classification. EEG gives emotion classification with high accuracy, but it is suitable for clinical applications. Speech recognition extracts semantics from speech while voice recognition analyses the acoustic of spoken words. The accuracy of voice recognition is lesser than Facial recognition and EEG since the talking style and rates differ in individuals. Photoplethysmography (PPG) is used in smartwatches to calculate heart rate variability (HRV).

Figure 1. Overview of Emotion classification

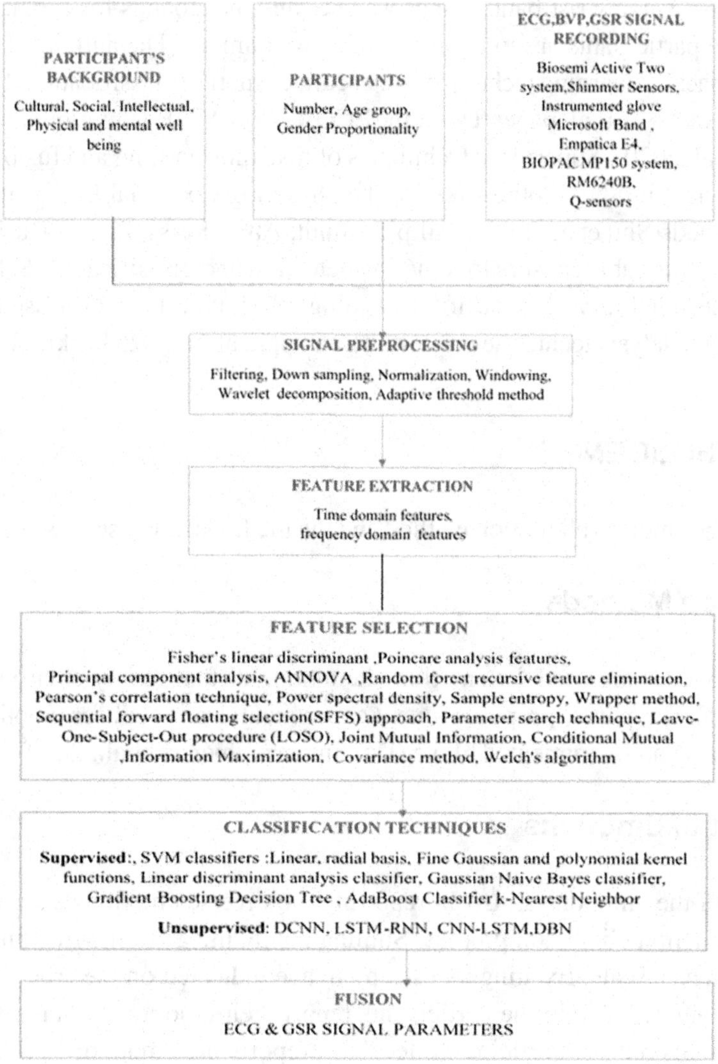

HRV calculated from ECG correlates up to 88% with calculations from PPG data. Electrodermal activity (EDA) or Galvanic skin response (GSR) measures skin conductivity. The skin conductivity decreases during the relaxed state and increases when subjected to efforts. A decreased respiration frequency indicates a relaxed state and deep and fast breathing indicates happiness or anger. Slow respiration patterns indicate depressive emotions. EMG uses Facial muscles for emotion detection. The paper concluded that bio signals can be used for the two-dimensional measurements using the valence and Arousal model. The paper mentions the future scope that emotion recognition with the sole use of smartwatches would be possible during everyday activities (Egger et al., 2019).

Aaron Frederick Bulagang & others reviewed the various ECG and GSR signal acquisition methods, signal processing, feature extraction, classification methods. However, this paper does not mention the deep machine learning techniques. The authors also propose the usage of virtual reality for emotion elicitation (Bulagang et al., 2020; Chowdhary et al., 2018). Stanisław Saganowski & others review the usage of wearable sensors like wrist bands, smartwatches and, headbands for capturing the HR, GSR, EEG signals when the participants are in their real-life environment. The authors also mention, signal processing and deep machine learning techniques for accurate emotion classification (Saganowoski et al., 2020). Patrícia Bota & others in their paper review the ECG, GSR, BVP, Respiration signals for classifying the emotions (Bota et al.,2020). Supervised techniques of machine learning and fusion techniques, used for classifying emotions .Lin Shu & others review the physiological signal-based emotion recognition and classification methods(Shu et al.,2028).Philip Schmidt, Attila Reiss, Robert Durichen, Kristof Van Laerhoven mention the Wearable sensors for emotion detection and classification(Schmidt et al.,2019). The authors,review the suitability of a specific physiological signal, the sensor used for capturing the data, signal processing, analysis technique concerning an application (Dzedzickis et al., 2020).

EMOTIONAL INTELLIGENCE

This section reviews the emotion elicitation method and the methods of the self-assessment of emotions.

Emotion Elicitation Methods

Sounds, images, and videos are used for emotion elicitation. Virtual reality environment can be used for emotion elicitation. The paper, proposes a new experimental protocol for emotion elicitation and biosignal recording using an instrumented glove (Domínguez-Jiménez et al., 2020)

Self-Assessment of Emotions

The self-assessment of the emotions assists in reporting the diverse emotions experienced by the participants during the emotion elicitation process. Smiling happy image to the frowning unhappy image is indicated on the Valence scale. Exciting to a sleepy image indicated on the arousal scale (Bradley et al., 1994) . Questionnaire's, wherein the participants report their emotions as a reply to questions, are used in four papers in this review. Participant's feedback reports the emotions in five papers .Emotion assessment through a survey is also used (Domínguez-Jiménez et al., 2020) . EnvBodySens Android-based app where the participants can report their emotions in real-time environments is used (Kanjo et al. 2018). The emotion elicitation & emotion self-assessment methods, explored in the various studies, are listed in table number 1 given below.

EMOTION DETECTION

This section reviews the factors like the participant's background, physiological signals used for recognizing the emotions and the instruments used to capture these signals.

Table 1. Emotion Elicitation & Self-Assessment

REFERENCE NO.	EMOTION ELICITATION METHOD	EMOTION SELF ASSESSMENT METHOD
DEAP DATABASE (Koelstra et al.,2012)	40 music videos of one minute duration	Emotions were rated on a 9 point scale by the participants. Visualization done using Self-assessment manikins (SAM) .
MAHNOB DATABASE (Soleymani et al.,2012)	20 videos	Dominance, arousal, valence predictability on a scale of 1 to 9, self-assessment manikins (SAM)
ASCERTAIN DATABASE (Subramanian et al.,2018)	Videos(movie clips)	Valence and Arousal ratings based on engagement of the video, Familiarity
AMIGOS DATABASE (Miranda-Correa, et,al.,2021)	16 short videos,4 Long videos(movie clips)	Self-assessment of affective levels (valence, arousal, control, familiarity, liking and basic emotions) on a scale of 1 to10
DREAMER DATABASE (Katsigiannis et, al.,2018)	Audio-visual stimuli(Videos)	Participants ratings , SAM
(Lee et, al.,2019)	DEAP database, Music videos in a silent room	DEAP Database
(Al Machot, et,al.,2019)	a)DEAP Database b)MAHNOB Database	a)DEAP Database b)MAHNOB Database
(Ferdinando,et,al.,2014)	MAHNOB Database	MAHNOB Database
(Nakisa, et,al.,2018)	Video clips	A keyword was used to represent each emotion such as neutral, anxiety, amusement, sadness, joy or happiness, disgust, anger, surprise, and fear.
(Domínguez-Jiménez,et,al.,2020)	70 Video clips	Post stimuli survey to report the emotions
(Romeo,et,al.,2022)	a)DEAP database b)6 movie clips	a)DEAP dataset b)SAM(9 point scale)
(Kanjo, et,al.,2019)	Walking around the city centre in Nottingham, UK on specific routes.	SAM(5 step)
(Zhang,et,al.,2018)	Video clips, Video induction is a multimodal (audio,visual and cognitive)	–
(Agrafioti,et,al.,2012)	International Affective Picture System (IAPS),data	–
(Dar,et,al.,2020)	a.Dreamer Database b.AMIGOS Database	a.Dreamer dataset b.AMIGOS dataset
(Lee, et,al.,2020)	DEAP Database	DEAP Database

Participant's Details

Psychologically the emotions are expressed differently by the, unlike genders. In the various tests, females score higher than males in response to emotions, except for anger. Women experience emotions like happiness more intensely (The Conversation, 2021).

Participant's Background

The cultural differences impact the emotional arousal levels based on the study conducted on the East and Western people (Lim et al., 2016). The emotional content might be lower in the naturalistic database owing to the disturbances in the surroundings and the quality of the signal recording instrument. AS-CERTAIN database includes the personality traits of the members in addition to emotions. The authors propose to investigate correlates between affective physiological responses and soft-biometrics and how apriori knowledge of personality can impact the design of user-centered studies (Subramanian et al.,2018). AMIGOS database considers the mood and personality traits of the members along with the affect. The authors showed that social context has a significant effect on the valence and arousal ratings of the members (Miranda-Correa et al., 2021). The paper mentions that the on-body modality is the more robust data source for emotion detection. When on body data is fused with the environmental and location data, accuracy improves by 7% (Kanjo, et al.,2019). Other attributes like pollution levels, population density is also considered. Participants are with prior experience in acting in two papers. Participants in the two papers have no hearing impairments hence suitable for audio-based emotion induction.

ECG, BVP, GSR signals

The electro-cardiac signals in the heart are measured using the ECG signal. The P wave represents atrial depolarization, the QRS complex indicates ventricular depolarization, and the T wave represents ventricular repolarization. Pan Tompkins adaptive thresholding algorithm extracts R peaks from the ECG signal. The changes in arousal and valence levels result in variations in the R -R interval (Shimmer Solicits Clinical Research, 2022). The PPG sensor detects variations in the heart rate and blood flow in arteries. Infrared light is focused with the help of the light-emitting diode on the body's surface. Hemoglobin in the blood cells absorbs the red light and is reflected by the other tissues. The volume of blood present in the tissues decides the concentration of light returned to the PPG photodetector (Shimmer Solicits, 2022; Chandresekhar, U. & Chowdhary, 2013) .The inter-beat interval detected from the BVP gives the heart rate. The normal range of the heart rate is between 50 to 70 beats/minute and increases during sympathetic arousal. GSR increases due to the rise in arousal levels. Later, the skin conductance reduces due to the reabsorption since the duct of the sweat gland fills. Extra sweat pours out of the duct, leading to a decrease in skin conductance. GSR signals, however, are unable to detect the valence levels of emotions efficiently (Emotion Recognition, 2022).

Signal Recording Instrument

Biosemi Active Two system, Smart wristband (Empatica E4), Microsoft Band 2 devices are used for capturing the ECG & GSR data wirelessly from the participants. Microsoft Band 2 tracks fitness and is compatible with Windows, Android smartphones through a Bluetooth connection. The Shimmer 3 ECG (Electrocardiogram) sensor detects the electrical signals in the heart. Seven number of papers have used Shimmer sensors. GSR Shimmer sensor kit measures the skin conductance using the electrodes attached to two fingers. Figure number 2 shows the ECG Shimmer sensor kit, capturing the ECG signal (shimmer solicits, 2022).

And the figure number 3 shows the GSR shimmer sensor (shimmer solicits, 2022) capturing the GSR signal.

The increase in sweat on the skin results in a larger current flowing (shimmer solicits, 2022). biopac MP 150 data acquisition system used in total six number of papers. power lab data acquisition system developed by ad instruments are used by some researchers.rm6240b signal recording system and omron hem-7051 electronic sphygmomanometer device is also used. Wearable off-the-shelf sensors monitor

Figure 2. ECG Shimmer Sensor

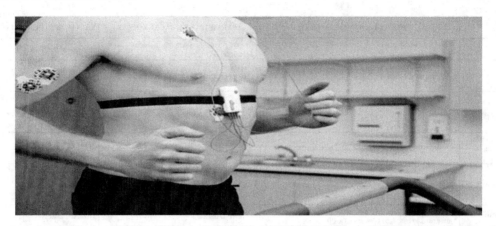

sports activities and have become popular among young people. HR, GSR signals can be gathered using these devices (de arriba pérez et al., 2018). This paper reviews the sensors like an instrumented glove, tea sensor, nonin sensor, e-health sensor platform v2.0, zephyr bioharness and pulse oximeter as listed in table number 2.

ECG, GSR SIGNAL PREPROCESSING

This section reviews the preprocessing methods, feature extraction, and feature selection techniques for ECG, GSR, and BVP signals.

Figure 3. GSR Shimmer Sensor

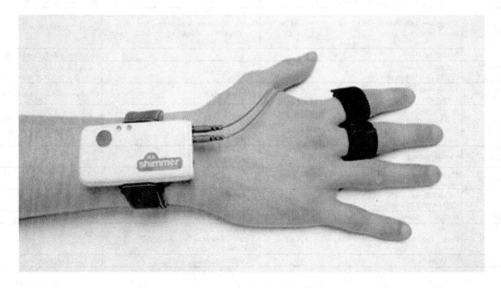

Table 2. Signal Recording

REFERENCE NO.	PARTICIPANT'S DETAILS	PARTICIPANT'S BACKGROUND	SIGNAL RECORDING INSTRUMENT
DEAP DATABASE (Koelstra et al.,2012)	32 healthy participants, 16 Males, mean age 26.9	Diverse cultural backgrounds (European, North American)	Biosemi Active Two system
MAHNOB DATABASE (Soleymani,2012)	27 participants, 11 Males	Different cultural and educational backgrounds	Biosemi Active Two system
ASCERTAIN DATABASE (Subramanian et al.,2018)	58 users,21 female, mean age 30	Frequent movie watchers and fluent in English. Big five personality traits.	Wearable off the shelf sensors
AMIGOS DATABASE (Miranda-Correa, et,al.,2021)	40 healthy participants 13 females aged between 21 and 40.	Personality traits and mood of individual and groups.	Shimmer sensor kit
DREAMER DATABASE (Katsigiannis et, al.,2018)	25 healthy volunteers, aged between 22 and 33 years old	–	Shimmer sensor
(Lee et., al.,2019)	a)DEAP dataset b)four participants, aged between 20 to 30	a)DEAP Database	a)DEAP dataset
(Al Machot et., al.,2019)	a)DEAP Database b)MAHNOB Database	a)DEAP Database b)MAHNOB Database	a)DEAP Database b)MAHNOB Database
(Ferdinando et., al.,2014)	MAHNOB Database	MAHNOB Database	MAHNOB Database
(Nakisa et., al.,2018)	20 participants, aged between 20 and 38 years	–	Smart Wristband (Empatica E4)
(Domínguez-Jiménez et., al.,2020)	42 healthy subjects, between 18–25 years	–	Instrumented glove to acquire PPG and GSR signals
(Romeo et., al.,2022)	a)DEAP dataset b) Twenty-nine volunteers, 14 females, age ranging from 20-30 years	DEAP Database	a) DEAP dataset b) Smartwatch sensors (Microsoft Band 2)
(Kanjo et., al.,2019)	40 females, average age of 28 years	–	Microsoft wrist Band
(Zhang et., al.,2018)	aged from 18 to 30 years, 29 students, 15 males and 14 females	Tianjin University, China.	BIOPAC MP150 system
(Agrafioti,et,al.,2012)	44 volunteers	–	BIOPAC MP 150 system
(Dar et., al.,2020)	a.Dreamer database b.AMIGOS database	a.Dreamer Database b.AMIGOS Database	a.Dreamer Database b.AMIGOS Database
(Lee et., al.,2020)	DEAP Database	DEAP Database	DEAP Database
(Sarkar et., al.,2021)	a.AMIGOS database b.Dreamer database	a.AMIGOS Database b.Dreamer Database	a.AMIGOS Database b.Dreamer Database
(Shi et., al.,2017)	Forty-eight healthy volunteers, 25 females and 23 males, aged between 20 and 26 years	Students from Shandong University and had no history of cardiovascular disease, mental illness, or alcohol records	RM6240B signal recording system and OMRON HEM-7051 electronic sphygmomanometer device
(Kanjo et., al.,2019)	Sixty healthy students, 30 males and 30 females aging from 20 to 26 years.	Physically and mentally healthy, without any Angio cardiopathy, mental sickness, and denied use of alcohol or any medicine	RM6240B signal recording system and OMRON HEM-7051 electronic sphygmomanometer device
(Mickael et., al.,2015)	Data of 100 children younger than 30 months old	–	Q-sensors used for GSR measurement
(Agrafioti,et,al.,2012)	Twenty-five healthy volunteers, 10 males, 15 female,in the age-group of 19–28 years	None had hearing impairment or a history of mental disorder, Iranian subjects,non musician,all were right-handed subjects	BIOPAC MP100 system
(Pollreisz et., al.,2017)	20 to 25 years old	–	Smart Wristband (Empatica E4)
(Goshvarpour et, al.,2017)	11 females, mean age: 22.73 ± 1.68 years	College students	Power Lab data Acquisition System developed by AD Instruments
(Minhad et., al.,2017)	Twenty three volunteers, 8 males and 15 females, aged between 23 to 36 years.	Malaysian origin	Cloth snap wet electrode and dry electrode
(Selvaraj et., al.,2013)	Sixty healthy volunteers, Inclusive of thirty under graduate students from the university (18 to 25 years old), fifteen school children (9 to 16 years old) and fifteen adults (39 to 68 years old)	–	Power Lab data Acquisition System developed by AD Instruments
(Bong et., al.,2012)	5 healthy subjects	–	Power Lab data Acquisition System developed by AD Instruments
(Mickael et., al.,2015)	35 participants, mostly between 18 and 30 years old,46% women	French origin	EDA:TEA sensor HR: Nonin sensor
(Harper et., al.,2020)	a)AMIGOS database b)DREAMER database	a)AMIGOS database b)DREAMER database	a)AMIGOS database b)DREAMER database
(Wei et., al.,2018)	MAHNOB database	MAHNOB database	MAHNOB database
(Greco et., al.,2017)	Twenty-five healthy subjects, aged between 25–35 years	No history of injury of the auditory canal or partial or full incapability of hearing	GSR:BIOPAC MP150
(Ayata et., al.,2018)	DEAP database	DEAP DATABASE	DEAP DATABASE

continued on following page

Table 2. Continued

REFERENCE NO.	PARTICIPANT'S DETAILS	PARTICIPANT'S BACKGROUND	SIGNAL RECORDING INSTRUMENT
(Shukla et, al.,2021)	AMIGOS database	AMIGOS database	AMIGOS database
(Keren et, al.,2017)	Remote Collaborative and Affective Interactions (RECOLA) Database,27 subjects	French-speaking adults during the resolution of a collaborative task	–
(Kanjo et, al.,2018)	40 participants, females, average age of 28.	Low stress conditions, Participants walking in similar weather conditions	on-body sensors
(Ragot et, al.,2017)	19 volunteers, 12 women and 7 men, average age was 33.89 years ± 8.62	All subjects were from French, francophone, normal vision, participants had not taken any somatic drug	BIOPAC MP150 and Smart Wristband (Empatica E4)
(Rakshit et, al.,2016)	33 healthy subjects, 13 Females, 20 Males, with average age 27	–	Pulse oximeter
(Matsubara et, al.,2016)	5 participants, aged between 20 to 25	Japanese, engineering department of university	Smart Wristband (Empatica E4)
(Ferdinando et, al.,2016)	MAHNOB Database	MAHNOB Database	MAHNOB Database
(Ranganathan et, al.,2016)	emoFBVP Database, Ten participants	Professional actors, Participants have completed basic coursework in acting/non-verbal communication	Zephyr BioHarness
(Ferdinando et, al.,2017)	MAHNOB Database	MAHNOB Database	MAHNOB Database
(Gjoreski et, al.,2017)	DEAP DATABASE	DEAP DATABASE	DEAP DATABASE
(Yoo et, al.,2017)	6 males (average age 25.6 years) and 5 females (average 22.1 year)	Graduate students, no physical and mental illness, no psychotropic medication, smoking, coffee, drugs, and alcohol not allowed prior to the experiment.	Sensors
(Liu et, al.,2016)	–	Participants were Junior in Jilin University of Changchun, China.	e-Health Sensor Platform V2.0
(Santamaria-Granados 2019)	AMIGOS database	AMIGOS database	AMIGOS database
(Hassan, 2019)	DEAP database	DEAP database	DEAP database
(Li, C., Xu, C. et, al.,2016)	30 healthy subjects, 15 male and 15 female, age ranges from 23 to 32 years	Tianjin University, China.	BIOPAC MP150 system

Preprocessing Of ECG, BVP, GSR Signals

The raw ECG, BVP, GSR signal acquired from the body contains various noise signals, baseline drift. Hence the processing makes it compatible with the feature extraction stage. ECG, GSR signals contain noise signals such as muscle artifact, motion artifact, and external electrical noise caused due to the interference from mains. Frequencies in the noise signals are Muscle artifact: 5 to 50Hz, Respiratory: 0.12 to 0.5Hz, Line frequency 50Hz or 60Hz. The ECG signal acquired during motion leads to the baseline drift. Baseline Subtraction used in four papers. Down sampling, Averaging technique, used in four papers and Normalization technique used in seven number of papers. The baseline wandering path finding algorithm is used for preprocessing of the ECG signal from the AMIGOS database (A.Dessai et al., 2021),

Windowing strategy used in (Kanjo et al., 2019; Keren,2017), Fourier Transform method used in (Mickael Menard et al.,2015), and Adaptive thresholding technique to detect the R peaks from the ECG signal is used in four papers.

Feature Extraction techniques

Feature extraction techniques help to extract the relevant features from the pre-processed ECG, BVP & GSR signals. Empirical mode decomposition is used for finding the emotion patterns in ECG (Agrafioti et al., 2012). The parameters such as Root mean square and standard deviation of the Successive Differences between adjacent R-R intervals, the number of pairs of adjacent NN intervals differing by more than 20ms, Frequency-domain features such as power spectral density for very low frequency, low frequency, high frequency and the ratio of high frequency to low frequency are calculated for the ECG

Figure 4. Preprocessing, Feature Extraction, Feature Selection Stages

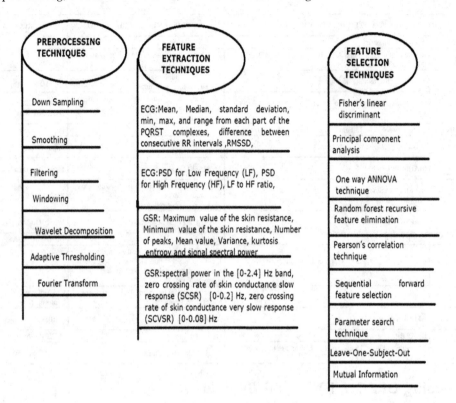

and BVP signals. The features calculated for GSR signals are the Maximum value of the skin resistance, Minimum value of the skin resistance, Number of peaks, Mean value, Variance, kurtosis, Average rising time of the GSR signal, decay time, latency, Entropy, Signal power.

Feature Selection Techniques

Linear discriminant analysis and Fisher's linear discriminant calculate the linear combination of features, used for the dimensionality reduction before the classification. The principal component analysis (PCA) technique computes the Principal components of the data, to obtain lower-dimensional data. PCA is used for dimensionality reduction. KPCA, based on the technique of kernel methods, was used in a total five number of papers (Goshvarpour, 2017; Guo,2016; Perez-Rosero, 2017; Subramanian, 2018; Zhang, 2018). One-way ANNOVA compares the means of two or more samples (Emotion Recognition, 2022). Random forest recursive feature elimination algorithm constructs several decision trees during training time (Domínguez-Jiménez, 2020). The parameter search technique chooses a set of optimum hyperparameters (Harper, 2020). Pearson's correlation technique measures the linear correlation between two sets of data, used in (Lee, 2020; Shi, 2017). Wrapper's method explores all possible combinations of features to improve the accuracy (De Arriba Pérez et al., 2018). The sequential forward floating selection (SFFS) approach starts with the best single feature initially, then the process continues pairing with one of the remaining features (Naji, M. et al., 2013). Figure number 4 lists the preprocessing, feature extraction, and feature selection techniques used in the various studies in this review.

Classification and Fusion Techniques

This section reviews the practices used for classifying the emotions and the classification accuracies reported in different studies. The machines identify the trends in the information through the training phase and utilize these patterns during the testing phase for data classification without being programmed explicitly.

Machine Learning Classifiers

KNN algorithm (supervised technique) classifies the data using the length between the data points. KNN does not get trained to find the relevant features in the data during the training period. KNN uses the value of k and the distance function. KNN is unsuitable for large datasets (The professionals point, 2019). The paper concluded that the Gradient boost decision tree outperforms other classifiers (SVM, KNN, and Gaussian NB) in all situations, demonstrating its predictive power on the multichannel physiological dataset (Zhang et al., 2018). The ECG has rich emotion-relevant features that could signify changes in human emotions. Support vector machine (SVM): The data is separated into different planes using the support vectors. The testing phase classifies the unknown data. Non-linear kernels are used for transformation

Like polynomial radial basis functions when the data is not linearly separable (Lee et al., 2020). Romeo mentions that multiple instance learning (MIL) approach detects the utmost emotional events rather than the continuous affective changes (Romeo et al., 2022). The proposed MIL approaches act at the bag level to classify the overall emotional response in consideration of the local response. The standard supervised learning approaches do not consider the local information but only provide a global response averaged over the entire video sequence. The arousal recognition task discloses a relatively lower accuracy compared to valence classification. The EMDD-SVM attained the greatest accuracy for solving the arousal task. The choice of the number of instances for each physiological signal (synchronously recorded over each video) can change for each subject and depends on several factors, such as the type and duration of stimuli. The paper proposes the maximization of entropy and mutual information by selecting the correct number of instances via the information theory. Future works mentioned in the paper may be devoted to extending the MIL-based approach in a different scenario which would involve modeling, discriminating, and localizing self-reported emotion. Identifying when the emotional response occurs within the labeled time window could further inform the personalization that technology can provide to the person. During physical rehabilitation, knowing when a person becomes anxious during an exercise could help the rehabilitation system to understand in what part of the exercise routine the person may psychologically struggle. This could lead to the proposal of a simplified version of the exercise part to expose the patient gradually to the movement as a physiotherapist would do. Also can provide other types of support, such as breathing reminders to reduce anxiety and tension. Table number 3 lists the various supervised classification techniques.

Deep Machine Learning

The feature extraction in deep techniques is done automatically, unlike traditional machine learning with manual feature extraction. Deep machine learning needs powerful hardware due to the complex mathematical structures used in the algorithm. Deep Machine learning takes more time to get trained

Table 3. Supervised Classification Techniques

REFEREN. NO.	PHYSIOLOGICAL SIGNAL	CLASSIFICATION TECHNIQUES	CLASSIFICATION ACCURACY
DEAP DATABASE (Koelstra et al.,2012)	ECG,GSR	Gaussian Naive Bayes classifier	46.2% and 45.5% for arousal and valence respectively
MAHNOB DATABASE (Soleymani et al.,2012)	ECG,GSR	SVM-RBF classifier	46.2% and 45.5% for arousal and valence respectively
ASCERTAIN DATABASE (Subramanian et al.,2018)	ECG,GSR	Naive Bayes, Linear SVM classifier	SVM:0.56 and 0.57 for ECG signals for valence and arousal levels respectively GSR:0.64 for valence,0.61 for arousal
AMIGOS DATABASE (Miranda-Correa, et,al.,2021)	ECG,GSR	SVM classifier	ECG:0.576 and 0.592 for Valence and Arousal respectively GSR:0.531 and 0.548 for Valence and Arousal respectively
DREAMER DATABASE (Katsigiannis et, al.,2018)	ECG	SVM with RBF classifier	0.6237 for valence and arousal
(Ferdinando et,al.,2014)	ECG	SVM classifier	47.69% and 42.55% for arousal and valence
(Domínguez-Jiménez et,al.2020)	ECG,GSR	SVM,,LDA,DT,NB classifier	100% for amusement and sadness
(Romeo et, al.,2022)	ECG,GSR	SVM classifier	a)Accuracy of 68% and 69% for valence and arousal respectively b) Consumer dataset (i.e. 32% low arousal vs 68% high arousal)
(Zhang et, al.,2018)	ECG,BVP,GSR	Gradient Boosting Decision Tree (GBDT) classifier	Accuracy:93.42%
(Perez-Rosero et, al.,2017)	BVP,GSR	a)Linear discriminant analysis (LDA) classifier b) SVM classifiers with linear, radial basis and polynomial kernel functions	SVM with radial basis Kernel function 72.5%
(Taylor, et al.,2015)	GSR	Neural networks, random forests, Naive Bayes, nearest neighbour, logistic regression, and support vector machines (SVM) classifier	SVM:78.93%
(Guo et, al.,2016)	ECG	SVM classifier	Two and Five emotion states and obtain 70.4% and 52% accuracy, respectively.
(Shu et, al.,2020)	ECG	KNN,,RF, DT , GBDT, and AdaBoost classifier	Except KNN, the accuracies of RF, DT, GBDT, and the AdaBoost are over 0.80
(Feng et, al.,2018)	GSR	SVM and KNN classifier	a)SVM:48%, 86% and 75% for "Acceptance", "Joy" and "Boredom" b) 64% classification accuracy
(Naji et, al.,2013)	ECG	SVM classifier	Average valence classification accuracy of 94.91% and average arousal classification accuracy of 93.63%
(Pollreisz et, al.,2017)	ECG,GSR	Decision Tree classifier	64.66%
(Goshvarpour et, al.,2017)	ECG,GSR	Probabilistic Neural Network classifier	Using PCA, the highest recognition rate of 100% was achieved for sigma =0.01
(Minhad et, al.,2017)	ECG,GSR	SVM classifier	ECG: Audio visual:65.6% GSR: Audio visual:62.18%
(Selvaraj et, al.,2013)	ECG	a)Bayesian Classifier, b)Regression Tree, c)K- nearest neighbor d)Fuzzy K-nearest neighbor	a)40.22% b)64.12% c) 65.45% d) 64.11%
(Bong et, al.,2012)	ECG	a)K-nearest neighbor (KNN) b)Support Vector Machine (SVM) classifier	a) 77.69% (HR) b) 66.09%
(Mickael Menard et, al.,2015)	HR,GSR	SVM classifier	a)HR: 89.58% b)GSR: 85.57%
(Wei et, al.,2018)	ECG,GSR	SVM classifier	ECG: 68.75% GSR: 57.69%
(Greco et, al.,2017)	GSR	KNN classifier	Arousal:77.3% Valence:84%
(Ayata et, al.,2018)	PPG,GSR	Random forest(RF), kNN and decision tree classifier	PPG: 70.92% and 70.76% accuracy rate for arousal and valence prediction respectively GSR:71.53% and 71.04% accuracy rate for arousal and valence prediction respectively
(Shukla et, al.,2021)	GSR	Support vector machine (SVM) classifier and radial basis function (RBF) kernel classifier	85.75%(F1-score: 0.63) for arousal ,83.9% (F1-score: 0.61) for valence .
(Kanjo et, al.,2018)	ECG,GSR	KNN, SVM,Random Forest (RF) classifier	KNN:86% SVM:84% RF:84%
(Ragot et, al.,2017)	HR,GSR	SVM classifier	HR: 70% for arousal and 66% for valence
(Rakshit et, al.,2016)	HR	SVM classifier	Average model accuracy is 83.8%.
(Matsubara et, al.,2016)	ECG,GSR	SVM with Grid search technique classifier	Accuracy:90.9%
(Ferdinando et, al.,2016)	ECG	KNN classifier	55.8% for valence, 59.7% for arousal
(Ferdinando et, al.,2017)	ECG	KNN classifier	Arousal: 66.1%% Valence:64.1%
(Yoo et, al.,2016)	ECG,GSR,PPG	Back Propagation neural network classifier	85.9%
(Liu et, al.,2016)	GSR	SVM classifier with RBF kernel function	66.67%
(Hassan et, al.,2019)	GSR,PPG	Fine Gaussian SVM (FGSVM) classifier	89.53% accuracy

Table 4. Deep Machine Learning Techniques

REFERENCE NO.	PHYSIOLOGICAL SIGNAL	CLASSIFICATION TECHNIQUES	CLASSIFICATION ACCURACY
(Lee et, al.,2019)	PPG	DCNN classifier	DEAP:75.3%,76.2% for valence and arousal respectively
(Al Machot et, al.,2019)	GSR	DCNN classifier	The accuracy for subject-independent classification is 78% and 82% for MAHNOB and DEAP respectively and to 81% and 85% subject-dependent classification for MAHNOB and DEAP respectively.
(Nakisa et, al.,2018)	BVP	LSTM-RNN classifier	LSTM RNN: 46.8%
(Kanjo et, al.,2019)	HR,GSR	CNN-LSTM classifier	Accuracy:94.7%
(Dar et, al.,2020)	ECG,GSR	1D-CNN,LSTM classifier	AMIGOS ECG: 98.73%, GSR: 63.67%. DREAMER:ECG:89.25%
(Lee et, al.,2020)	PPG	CNN classifier	Accuracy for valence:82.1%,, accuracy for arousal: 80.9%.
(Sarkar et, al.,2021)	ECG	Self-supervised deep multi-task CNN And Fully-Supervised CNN classifier	a)AMIGOS: Self-Supervised CNN, arousal 88.9% valence 87.5% Fully-Supervised CNN, arousal 84.4%, valence 81.1% a)DREAMER: Self-Supervised CNN, arousal 85.9%, valence 85% Fully-Supervised CNN:Arousal 70.7%, valence 66.6%
(Harper et, al.,2020)	ECG	a)CNN-LSTM(Non Bayseian) classifier b) CNN-LSTM(Bayseian) classifier	AMIGOS a)CNN-LSTM(Non Bayseian) 79%,78% b) CNN-LSTM(Bayseian) 90%,88% DREAMER a)CNN-LSTM(Non Bayseian) 70%,66% b)CNN-LSTM(Bayseian) 86%,83%
(Keren et, al.,2017)	ECG,GSR	CNN-RNN classifier	Concordance correlation coefficient (CCC) Arousal: ECG: .309,GSR: .101 Valence: ECG .210,GSR .336
(Gjoreski et, al.,2017)	BVP	DNN classifier Random Forest, Support Vector Machine, Gradient Boosting Classifier, and AdaBoost Classifier	–
(Santamaria-Granados et, al.,2019)	ECG,GSR	DCNN classifier	ECG:82% arousal,72% valence GSR:71% arousal,75% valence

(Empowering AI Leadership, 2022) .A convolutional neural network (CNN), contains many layers with some layers for feature extraction and some for classification. In CNN, filters perform the convolution operation on the data. Supervised or unsupervised methods, used for training CNN networks. A recurrent neural network (RNN) is suitable for the sequence of data as input. RNN is good for predicting time series data and for processing sequential information. The constraint of RNN is that it cannot use evidence from the distant past due to the unattainability of long-term memory. Hence to report these issues, Long-short-term memory (LSTM) provided that can learn long patterns. The paper considers the AMIGOS dataset and applies deep CNN to ECG and GSR signals (Santamaria-Granados et al. 2019). Table number 4 lists the various deep classification techniques.

Feature Fusion

The feature extraction of the ECG and GSR parameters is done separately. However, Fused feature vector input to the classifier results in improved classification accuracy (Ayata et al., 2018).

Table number 5 lists the fusion of ECG and GSR parameters and their classification accuracies. Figure number 5 lists the various classifiers used.

Table 5. Fusion

REFERENCE NO.	FUSION OF PARAMETERS	ACCURACY
AMIGOS DATABASE (Miranda-Correa, et,al.,2021)	ECG,GSR	0.570 and 0.585 for Valence and Arousal respectively
(Dar et, al.,2020)	ECG,GSR	81.5%
(Ayata et, al.,2018)	PPG,GSR	Arousal: Classifier – RF 72.06% Valence: Classifier – RF with 71.05%
(Keren et, al.,2017)	ECG,GSR	concordance correlation coefficient (CCC) Arousal:0.43 Valence:0.407
(Hassan et, al.,2019)	PPG,GSR	-

FUTURE RESEARCH DIRECTIONS

This chapter surveys the articles based on the ECG, BVP, and GSR signals for classifying emotions using machine learning techniques. Valence Arousal Scale is used in the overall 37 number of papers. Sound signals for emotion elicitation, in only three papers (Goshvarpour, 2017; Greco,2017; Naji,2013) and pictures have been used in another three papers (Agrafioti, 2012; Yoo,2016; Ragot,2017). Videos for inducing emotions in the total number of 33 papers. Five papers (Kanjo,2018; Kanjo, 2019; Keren,2017; Matsubara,2016; Ranganathan,2016) have detected the emotions in the real-time environment .Two papers propose virtual reality environments for emotion elicitation(Bulagang,2020; Shu,2018) .Self-assessment manikins (SAM) are used in the total 21 number of papers where the participants report their emotions using a set of images. Majority of the studies for self-assessment of emotion use SAM. Android-based application has been the new approach where the participants can use their mobile to report their emotions in a field-based environment. The physical and mental well-being of the subjects

Figure 5. Classification techniques

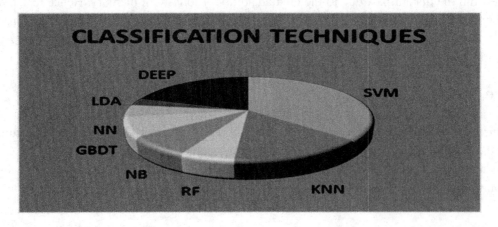

plays a significant role, so this review primarily focuses on healthy participants free from any medication with a mean age of around 30. In this review, the total number of participants is less than or equal to sixty and Bong & others have explored the data of five participants (Bong, 2012). Biosemi Active two system detects the ECG signal in total no. of thirteen papers. Smart wristband (Empatica E4) wearable device used for real-time physiological data acquisition (Matsubara, 2016; Nakisa, 2018; Pollreisz,2017; Ragot,2017). High pass, low pass, notch filters, filter the noises in the ECG signals, used in 15 number of studies (Electrocardiogram-Based Emotion Recognition Systems,2022).Total number of 27 papers have computed various time and frequency domain features. GSR time & frequency domain features are extracted in 18 number of reviewed papers. KNN is used for classification in the total 10 number of papers in this study. In this review, classification is done using SVM in a total 24 number of papers.

Deep machine learning techniques are used for classification in total 13 number of papers in this study. There is an improvement in the classification accuracy using Deep machine learning techniques. Deep learning offers a better performance as compared to the other machine learning techniques even with the limited amount of raw data and post-processed time-series data (Khan, 2021). In this survey, feature level fusion used in five research papers. The Valence Arousal scale two-dimensional Russell's model is explored in most of the studies. Most of the studies have used videos for emotion elicitation. Virtual reality, in the future, could be used for inducing emotions. Many of the studies have used SAM for the self-assessment of emotions. This chapter has explored the participants from France, Malaysia, China, Europe, America, Japan with diverse cultural backgrounds. The number of participants is not exceeding sixty. More participants, help in averaging out the assessment of a particular emotion experienced by the participants, hence reducing the biasing effect. In this study, equal gender proportion was considered except for (Goshvarpour, 2017) and (Kanjo,2018), where all-female participants and one healthy female graduate student in (Perez-Rosero, 2017) experience the emotions. The study explores the adult age group with no physical or mental illness. Subject-independent emotion recognition is an inspiring field due to the variations in the emotions based on age, gender, culture, other social factors, and surrounding environment used in most studies. The majority of the studies have explored the DEAP database. ASCERTAIN & AMIGOS databases aren't explored much by the researchers. SVM classifier is most popularly used. Deep machine learning techniques and feature fusion techniques have been used in a limited number of studies. The benchmark datasets with emotion elicitation using the virtual reality environment that would mimic a real-time environment, more participants of diverse cultural backgrounds, diverse age groups, and health conditions can be built in the future. The classification accuracy can be enhanced using suitable Signal preprocessing, feature extraction techniques. Deep machine learning and fusion techniques could improve classification accuracy.

CONCLUSION

Emotions indicate the state of the mental and physical well-being of the individuals. Human-computer interaction systems, using suitable machine learning techniques enable the diagnosis of these emotions resulting in the appropriate actions. Emotion classification using the ECG, BVP, GSR signals is a focal point for research. This chapter has reviewed the utilization of the supervised and unsupervised techniques for emotion classification using the bio-signals. Around 57 articles published from 2012 on emotion classification using RR intervals and skin conductance are analyzed. The various emotion elicitation & self-assessment techniques, pre-processing methods, feature extraction, and machine learning techniques have been explored. Videos are used for emotion elicitation by most researchers. SAM is used for assessing emotions. Preprocessing & feature extraction techniques help in improving the signal quality before classification. Supervised machine learning techniques are explored in most of the studies. However, deep machine learning & fusion techniques used in the limited number of studies

REFERENCES

Agrafioti, F., Hatzinakos, D., & Anderson, A. K. (2012). ECG Pattern Analysis for Emotion Detection. *IEEE Transactions on Affective Computing*, *3*(1), 102–115. doi:10.1109/T-AFFC.2011.28

Al Machot, F., Elmachot, A., Ali, M., Al Machot, E., & Kyamakya, K. (2019). A Deep-Learning Model for Subject-Independent Human Emotion Recognition Using Electrodermal Activity Sensors. *Sensors (Basel)*, *19*(7), 1659. doi:10.339019071659 PMID:30959956

Ayata, D., Yaslan, Y., & Kamasak, M. E. (2018). Emotion Based Music Recommendation System Using Wearable Physiological Sensors. *IEEE Transactions on Consumer Electronics*, *64*(2), 196–203. doi:10.1109/TCE.2018.2844736

Bong, S. Z., Murugappan, M., & Yaacob, S. (2012). Analysis of electrocardiogram (ECG) signals for human emotional stress classification. *Communications in Computer and Information Science*, *330*, 198–205. doi:10.1007/978-3-642-35197-6_22

Bota, P., Wang, C., Fred, A., & Silva, H. (2020). Emotion Assessment Using Feature Fusion and Decision Fusion Classification Based on Physiological Data: Are We There Yet? *Sensors (Basel)*, *20*(17), 4723. doi:10.339020174723 PMID:32825624

Bradley, M. M., & Lang, P. J. (1994). Measuring emotion: The self-assessment manikin and the semantic differential. *Journal of Behavior Therapy and Experimental Psychiatry*, *25*(1), 49–59. doi:10.1016/0005-7916(94)90063-9 PMID:7962581

Bulagang, A. F., Weng, N. G., Mountstephens, J., & Teo, J. (2020). A review of recent approaches for emotion classification using electrocardiography and electrodermography signals. *Informatics in Medicine Unlocked*, *20*, 100363. doi:10.1016/j.imu.2020.100363

Chandrasekhar, U., & Chowdhary, C. L. (2013). Classification of ECG beats using features from two-stage two-band wavelet decomposition. *Journal of Theoretical and Applied Information Technology*, *49*(3), 922–928.

Chowdhary, C. L., Das, T. K., Gurani, V., & Ranjan, A. (2018). An improved tumour identification with gabor wavelet segmentation. *Research Journal of Pharmacy and Technology*, *11*(8), 3451–3456. doi:10.5958/0974-360X.2018.00637.6

Dar, M. N., Akram, M. U., Khawaja, S. G., & Pujari, A. N. (2020). CNN and LSTM-Based Emotion Charting Using Physiological Signals. *Sensors (Basel)*, *20*(16), 4551. doi:10.339020164551 PMID:32823807

De Arriba Pérez, F., Santos-Gago, J. M., Caeiro-Rodríguez, M., & Fernández Iglesias, M. J. (2018). Evaluation of commercial-off-The-Shelf wrist wearables to estimate stress on students. *Journal of Visualized Experiments*, (136). Advance online publication. doi:10.3791/57590 PMID:29985338

Dessai, A., & Virani, H. (2021). Emotion Detection Using Physiological Signals. *2021 International Conference on Electrical, Computer and Energy Technologies (ICECET)*, 1-4. 10.1109/ICECET52533.2021.9698729

Domínguez-Jiménez, J., Campo-Landines, K., Martínez-Santos, J., Delahoz, E., & Contreras-Ortiz, S. (2020). A machine learning model for emotion recognition from physiological signals. *Biomedical Signal Processing and Control, 55*, 101646. doi:10.1016/j.bspc.2019.101646

Dzedzickis, A., Kaklauskas, A., & Bucinskas, V. (2020). Human Emotion Recognition: Review of Sensors and Methods. *Sensors (Basel), 20*(3), 592. doi:10.339020030592 PMID:31973140

Egger, M., Ley, M., & Hanke, S. (2019). Emotion Recognition from Physiological Signal Analysis: A Review. *Electronic Notes in Theoretical Computer Science, 343*, 35–55. doi:10.1016/j.entcs.2019.04.009

Electrodermal activity. (n.d.). In *Wikipedia*. Retrieved March 21, 2022, from https://en.wikipedia.org/wiki/Electrodermal_activity

Emotion classification. (n.d.). In *Wikipedia*. Retrieved March 21, 2022, from https://en.wikipedia.org/wiki/Emotion_classification

Emotion Recognition from Physiological Signal Analysis. (n.d.). Retrieved March 21, 2022, from https://www.researchgate.net/publication/333061423_Emotion_Recognition_from_Physiological_Signal_Analysis_A_Review

Empowering A. I. Leadership: AI C-Suite Toolkit. (n.d.). Retrieved March 21, 2022, from https://www3.weforum.org/docs/WEF_Empowering_AI_Leadership_2022.pdf

Feng, H., Golshan, H. M., & Mahoor, M. H. (2018). A wavelet-based approach to emotion classification using EDA signals. *Expert Systems with Applications, 112*, 77–86. doi:10.1016/j.eswa.2018.06.014

Ferdinando, H., Seppanen, T., & Alasaarela, E. (2016). Comparing features from ECG pattern and HRV analysis for emotion recognition system. *2016 IEEE Conference on Computational Intelligence in Bioinformatics and Computational Biology (CIBCB)*. 10.1109/CIBCB.2016.7758108

Ferdinando, H., Seppänen, T., & Alasaarela, E. (2017). Enhancing emotion recognition from ECG signals using supervised dimensionality reduction. *Proceedings of the 6th International Conference on Pattern Recognition Applications and Methods*. 10.5220/0006147801120118

Gjoreski, M., Gjoreski, H., Luštrek, M., & Gams, M. (2017). Deep affect recognition from R-R intervals. *Proceedings of the 2017 ACM International Joint Conference on Pervasive and Ubiquitous Computing and Proceedings of the 2017 ACM International Symposium on Wearable Computers*. 10.1145/3123024.3125608

Goshvarpour, A., Abbasi, A., & Goshvarpour, A. (2017). An accurate emotion recognition system using ECG and GSR signals and matching pursuit method. *Biomedical Journal, 40*(6), 355–368. doi:10.1016/j.bj.2017.11.001 PMID:29433839

Greco, A., Valenza, G., Citi, L., & Scilingo, E. P. (2017). Arousal and valence recognition of affective sounds based on Electrodermal activity. *IEEE Sensors Journal, 17*(3), 716–725. doi:10.1109/JSEN.2016.2623677

Guo, H., Huang, Y., Lin, C., Chien, J., Haraikawa, K., & Shieh, J. (2016). Heart rate variability signal features for emotion recognition by using principal component analysis and support vectors machine. *2016 IEEE 16th International Conference on Bioinformatics and Bioengineering (BIBE)*. 10.1109/BIBE.2016.40

Hany, F., Ye, L., Seppänen, T., & Alasaarela, E. (2014). Emotion Recognition by Heart Rate Variability. *Australian Journal of Basic and Applied Sciences, 8*(14), 50-55.

Harper, R., & Southern, J. (2020). A Bayesian Deep Learning Framework for End-To-End Prediction of Emotion from Heartbeat. *IEEE Transactions on Affective Computing*, 1–1. doi:10.1109/TAFFC.2020.2981610

Hassan, M. M., Alam, M. G., Uddin, M. Z., Huda, S., Almogren, A., & Fortino, G. (2019). Human emotion recognition using deep belief network architecture. *Information Fusion, 51*, 10–18. doi:10.1016/j.inffus.2018.10.009

Kanjo, E., Younis, E. M., & Ang, C. S. (2019). Deep learning analysis of mobile physiological, environmental and location sensor data for emotion detection. *Information Fusion, 49*, 46–56. doi:10.1016/j.inffus.2018.09.001

Kanjo, E., Younis, E. M., & Sherkat, N. (2018). Towards unravelling the relationship between on-body, environmental and emotion data using sensor information fusion approach. *Information Fusion, 40*, 18–31. doi:10.1016/j.inffus.2017.05.005

Katsigiannis, S., & Ramzan, N. (2018). DREAMER: A Database for Emotion Recognition Through EEG and ECG Signals From Wireless Low-cost Off-the-Shelf Devices. *IEEE Journal of Biomedical and Health Informatics, 22*(1), 98–107. doi:10.1109/JBHI.2017.2688239 PMID:28368836

Keren, G., Kirschstein, T., Marchi, E., Ringeval, F., & Schuller, B. (2017). End-to-end learning for dimensional emotion recognition from physiological signals. *2017 IEEE International Conference on Multimedia and Expo (ICME)*. 10.1109/ICME.2017.8019533

Khan, A. N., Ihalage, A. A., Ma, Y., Liu, B., Liu, Y., & Hao, Y. (2021). Deep learning framework for subject-independent emotion detection using wireless signals. *PLoS One, 16*(2), e0242946. doi:10.1371/journal.pone.0242946 PMID:33534826

Koelstra, S., Muhl, C., Soleymani, M., Jong-Seok Lee, Yazdani, A., Ebrahimi, T., Pun, T., Nijholt, A., & Patras, I. (2012). DEAP: A Database for Emotion Analysis;Using Physiological Signals. *IEEE Transactions on Affective Computing, 3*(1), 18–31. doi:10.1109/T-AFFC.2011.15

Lee, M., Lee, Y. K., Lim, M.-T., & Kang, T.-K. (2020). Emotion Recognition Using Convolutional Neural Network with Selected Statistical Photoplethysmogram Features. *Applied Sciences (Basel, Switzerland), 10*(10), 3501. doi:10.3390/app10103501

Lee, M. S., Lee, Y. K., Pae, D. S., Lim, M. T., Kim, D. W., & Kang, T. K. (2019). Fast Emotion Recognition Based on Single Pulse PPG Signal with Convolutional Neural Network. *Applied Sciences (Basel, Switzerland), 9*(16), 3355. doi:10.3390/app9163355

Li, C., Xu, C., & Feng, Z. (2016). Analysis of physiological for emotion recognition with the IRS model. *Neurocomputing, 178*, 103–111. doi:10.1016/j.neucom.2015.07.112

Lim, N. (2016). Cultural differences in emotion: Differences in emotional arousal level between the East and the West. *Integrative Medicine Research, 5*(2), 105–109. doi:10.1016/j.imr.2016.03.004 PMID:28462104

Liu, M., Fan, D., Zhang, X., & Gong, X. (2016). Human emotion recognition based on galvanic skin response signal feature selection and SVM. *2016 International Conference on Smart City and Systems Engineering (ICSCSE).* 10.1109/ICSCSE.2016.0051

Machine learning. (n.d.). In *Wikipedia*. Retrieved March 21, 2022, from https://en.wikipedia.org/wiki/Machine_learning

Matsubara, M., Augereau, O., Sanches, C. L., & Kise, K. (2016). Emotional arousal estimation while reading comics based on physiological signal analysis. *Proceedings of the 1st International Workshop on comics ANalysis, Processing and Understanding.* 10.1145/3011549.3011556

Menard, M., Richard, P., Hamdi, H., Dauce, B., & Yamaguchi, T. (2015). Emotion Recognition based on Heart Rate and Skin Conductance. *2nd International Conference on Physiological Computing Systems*, 26-32.

Minhad, K.N., Ali, S.H., & Reaz, M.B. (2017). A design framework for human emotion recognition using electrocardiogram and skin conductance response signals. *Journal of Engineering Science and Technology, 12*, 3102-3119.

Miranda-Correa, J. A., Abadi, M. K., Sebe, N., & Patras, I. (2021). AMIGOS: A Dataset for Affect, Personality and Mood Research on Individuals and Groups. *IEEE Transactions on Affective Computing, 12*(2), 479–493. doi:10.1109/TAFFC.2018.2884461

Naji, M., Firoozabadi, M., & Azadfallah, P. (2013). Classification of music-induced emotions based on information fusion of forehead Biosignals and electrocardiogram. *Cognitive Computation, 6*(2), 241–252. doi:10.100712559-013-9239-7

Nakisa, B., Rastgoo, M. N., Rakotonirainy, A., Maire, F., & Chandran, V. (2018). Long Short Term Memory Hyperparameter Optimization for a Neural Network Based Emotion Recognition Framework. *IEEE Access: Practical Innovations, Open Solutions, 6*, 49325–49338. doi:10.1109/ACCESS.2018.2868361

Perez-Rosero, M. S., Rezaei, B., Akcakaya, M., & Ostadabbas, S. (2017). Decoding emotional experiences through physiological signal processing. *2017 IEEE International Conference on Acoustics, Speech and Signal Processing (ICASSP).* 10.1109/ICASSP.2017.7952282

Pollreisz, D., & TaheriNejad, N. (2017). A simple algorithm for emotion recognition, using physiological signals of a smart watch. *2017 39th Annual International Conference of the IEEE Engineering in Medicine and Biology Society (EMBC).* doi:10.1109/EMBC.2017.8037328

Ragot, M., Martin, N., Em, S., Pallamin, N., & Diverrez, J. (2017). Emotion recognition using physiological signals: Laboratory vs. wearable sensors. *Advances in Human Factors in Wearable Technologies and Game Design*, 15-22. doi:10.1007/978-3-319-60639-2_2

Rakshit, R., Reddy, V. R., & Deshpande, P. (2016). Emotion detection and recognition using HRV features derived from photoplethysmogram signals. *Proceedings of the 2nd workshop on Emotion Representations and Modelling for Companion Systems.* 10.1145/3009960.3009962

Ranganathan, H., Chakraborty, S., & Panchanathan, S. (2016). Multimodal emotion recognition using deep learning architectures. *2016 IEEE Winter Conference on Applications of Computer Vision (WACV)*. 10.1109/WACV.2016.7477679

Romeo, L., Cavallo, A., Pepa, L., Bianchi-Berthouze, N., & Pontil, M. (2022). Multiple instance learning for emotion recognition using physiological signals. *IEEE Transactions on Affective Computing*, *13*(1), 389–407. doi:10.1109/TAFFC.2019.2954118

Saganowski, S., Dutkowiak, A., Dziadek, A., Dziezyc, M., Komoszynska, J., Michalska, W., Polak, A., Ujma, M., & Kazienko, P. (2020). Emotion Recognition Using Wearables: A Systematic Literature Review - Work-in-progress. *2020 IEEE International Conference on Pervasive Computing and Communications Workshops (PerCom Workshops)*. 10.1109/PerComWorkshops48775.2020.9156096

Santamaria-Granados, L., Munoz-Organero, M., Ramirez-Gonzalez, G., Abdulhay, E., & Arunkumar, N. (2019). Using deep Convolutional neural network for emotion detection on a physiological signals dataset (AMIGOS). *IEEE Access: Practical Innovations, Open Solutions*, *7*, 57–67. doi:10.1109/ACCESS.2018.2883213

Sarkar, P., & Etemad, A. (2021). Self-supervised ECG Representation Learning for Emotion Recognition. *IEEE Transactions on Affective Computing*, 1–1. doi:10.1109/TAFFC.2020.3014842

Schmidt, P., Reiss, A., Dürichen, R., & Laerhoven, K. V. (2019). Wearable-Based Affect Recognition—A Review. *Sensors (Basel)*, *19*(19), 4079. doi:10.339019194079 PMID:31547220

Selvaraj, J., Murugappan, M., Wan, K., & Yaacob, S. (2013). Classification of emotional states from electrocardiogram signals: A non-linear approach based on hurst. *Biomedical Engineering Online*, *12*(1), 44. doi:10.1186/1475-925X-12-44 PMID:23680041

Shi, H., Yang, L., Zhao, L., Su, Z., Mao, X., Zhang, L., & Liu, C. (2017). Differences of heart rate variability between happiness and sadness emotion states: A pilot study. *Journal of Medical and Biological Shimmer Solicits Clinical Research Community Input on Expanded*. Retrieved March 21, 2022, from https://shimmersensing.com/news/shimmer-solicits-clinical-research-community-input-on-expanded-open-wearables-initiative-owear/

Shu, L., Xie, J., Yang, M., Li, Z., Li, Z., Liao, D., Xu, X., & Yang, X. (2018). A Review of Emotion Recognition Using Physiological Signals. *Sensors (Basel)*, *18*(7), 2074. doi:10.339018072074 PMID:29958457

Shu, L., Yu, Y., Chen, W., Hua, H., Li, Q., Jin, J., & Xu, X. (2020). Wearable emotion recognition using heart rate data from a smart bracelet. *Sensors (Basel)*, *20*(3), 718. doi:10.339020030718 PMID:32012920

Shukla, J., Barreda-Angeles, M., Oliver, J., Nandi, G. C., & Puig, D. (2021). Feature extraction and selection for emotion recognition from Electrodermal activity. *IEEE Transactions on Affective Computing*, *12*(4), 857–869. doi:10.1109/TAFFC.2019.2901673

Soleymani, M., Lichtenauer, J., Pun, T., & Pantic, M. (2012). A Multimodal Database for Affect Recognition and Implicit Tagging. *IEEE Transactions on Affective Computing*, *3*(1), 42–55. doi:10.1109/T-AFFC.2011.25

Subramanian, R., Wache, J., Abadi, M. K., Vieriu, R. L., Winkler, S., & Sebe, N. (2018). ASCERTAIN: Emotion and Personality Recognition Using Commercial Sensors. *IEEE Transactions on Affective Computing*, *9*(2), 147–160. doi:10.1109/TAFFC.2016.2625250

Taylor, S., Jaques, N., Chen, W., Fedor, S., Sano, A., & Picard, R. (2015). Automatic identification of artifacts in electrodermal activity data. *2015 37th Annual International Conference of the IEEE Engineering in Medicine and Biology Society (EMBC)*. 10.1109/EMBC.2015.7318762

The Conversation. (n.d.). *In-depth analysis, research, news and ideas from*. Retrieved March 21, 2022, from https://theconversation.com/The

The professionals point. (n.d.). https://theprofessionalspoint.blogspot.com/2019/02/knn

Wei, W., Jia, Q., Feng, Y., & Chen, G. (2018). Emotion recognition based on weighted fusion strategy of multichannel physiological signals. *Computational Intelligence and Neuroscience*, *2018*, 1–9. doi:10.1155/2018/5296523 PMID:30073024

Yoo, G., Seo, S., Hong, S., & Kim, H. (2016). Emotion extraction based on multi bio-signal using back-propagation neural network. *Multimedia Tools and Applications*, *77*(4), 4925–4937. doi:10.100711042-016-4213-5

Zhang, X., Xu, C., Xue, W., Hu, J., He, Y., & Gao, M. (2018). Emotion Recognition Based on Multi-channel Physiological Signals with Comprehensive Nonlinear Processing. *Sensors (Basel)*, *18*(11), 3886. doi:10.339018113886 PMID:30423894

Zhao, L., Yang, L., Shi, H., Xia, Y., Li, F., & Liu, C. (2017). Evaluation of consistency of HRV indices change among different emotions. *2017 Chinese Automation Congress (CAC)*. 10.1109/CAC.2017.8243625

KEY TERMS AND DEFINITIONS

AMIGOS: Publicly available database for emotion classification.

Deep Learning: Machine learning technique.

Electrocardiography: Measurement of electrical activity of the heart.

Electrodermography: Measurement of electrical conductance of the skin.

Emotion Elicitation: Provoking emotions in the participants.

Emotion Self-Assessment: Emotions experienced by the participants.

Feature Extraction: Extraction of the relevant features from the data.

Fusion of Signals: Combination of signals.

Russel's Model: Two-dimensional model for emotion recognition.

Signal Processing: Removing unwanted signals from the data.

Chapter 3
Role of Machine and Deep Learning Techniques in Diabetic Retinopathy Detection

Jagan Mohan Nagula

ⓘ https://orcid.org/0000-0003-0978-4633

National Institute of Technology, Silchar, India

Murugan R.

National Institute of Technology, Silchar, India

Tripti Goel

National Institute of Technology, Silchar, India

ABSTRACT

Machine learning (ML) and deep learning (DL) techniques play a significant role in diabetic retinopathy (DR) detection via grading the severity levels or segmenting the retinal lesions. High sugar levels in the blood due to diabetes causes DR, a leading cause of blindness. Manual detection or grading of the DR requires ophthalmologists' expertise and consumes time prone to human errors. Therefore, using fundus images, the ML and DL algorithms help automatic DR detection. The fundus imaging analysis helps the early DR detection, controlling, and treatment evaluation of DR conditions. Knowing the fundus image analysis requires a strong knowledge of the system and ML and DL functionalities in computer vision. DL in fundus imaging is a rapidly expanding research area. This chapter presents the fundus images, DR, and its severity levels. Also, this chapter explains the performance analysis of the various ML DL-based DR detection techniques. Finally, the role of ML and DL techniques in DR detection or severity grading is discussed.

INTRODUCTION

The human eye is a perplexing system that allows individuals to identify one of their most essential detections. Our ability to comprehend and investigate our surroundings is based on our vision. Our eyes

DOI: 10.4018/978-1-6684-5673-6.ch003

always take in light when we look around us, which is crucial for the visual process.

The retina is a thin layer of the receptive layer that surrounds 66 percent of the eyeball, and it is the light stimulus that gives the sensation of visibility (Jagan Mohan et al., 2020b). The retina expands the brain, which is formed by zygotes from neural cells and is appropriately linked to the cerebrum by the optic nerve. The retina captures light and converts it into the object's liveliness. The liveliness of concussions activates neurons that carry electrical information from the eye to the brain's higher centers.

Diabetic retinopathy (DR) is a severe diabetic complication that causes retinal damage and blindness. It damages the retina vessels, resulting in fluid leaks and sensory abnormalities. According to (Steinmetz et al., 2021), DR is one of the most frequent ailments in the United States, the United Kingdom, and Singapore, alongside blinding conditions including cataracts and glaucoma.

This book chapter discusses the fundus image and publicly available databases associated with DR. In addition, this chapter covers the DR with clinically evident retinal feature symptoms, grading or categorization, and risk factors. This chapter describes various Machine Learning (ML) and deep learning (DL) techniques utilized in DR grading. It also explains how to increase ML and DL performance by preprocessing the fundus images. The chapter compares DR detection strategies utilizing ML and DL to other techniques in a quick comparison. It describes the role of ML and DL techniques and their potential for detecting or segmenting the DR stages. Finally, the conclusion concludes the chapter.

The Fundus Image

The fundus image is a 2-D image captured with the reflected light of 3-D retinal tissue. In 1850, H V H Savant invented the ophthalmoscope to capture fundus images. Fundus imaging aids in diagnosing and treating visual and chronic infections such as DR, hypertension, glaucoma, leukemia, and systemically malignancies with visual metastases, to name a few (Senior, 2010). The fundus imaging methods include digital fundus photography, autofluorescence, infrared reflectance, and contemporary fundus imaging technology developments (Chowdhary et al., 2016, Das et al., 2020).

Fundus image capturing uses the same principles as traditional imaging techniques (Mohan et al., 2020). Each image pixel is stored by turning the light into an electrical signal using a sensor. The image resolution can be improved by increasing the number of sensors on the camera.

As shown in Figure 1, the fundus image analysis aids in identifying DR retinal characteristics. Microaneurysms (MA) (Jagan Mohan et al., 2020a), exudates (EX) (Mohan et al., 2021b), hemorrhages (HEM), and Cotton-wool-spots (CWS) (Mohan et al., 2021a) are all DR retinal characteristics.

Table 1 lists the publicly accessible fundus databases and the # of images with a field of view (FOV), resolution, and purpose.

Diabetic Retinopathy

Diabetes patients are increasing at an astonishing rate worldwide due to various causes, including age, lack of physical activity, population growth, overweight, and urbanization. The number of diabetes patients is expected to rise to 366 million by 2030, up from 300 million in 2025 (Zhao & Jiang, 2020). Diabetes is the most common cause of visual impairment in laborer (working age) persons, according to (Pearce & Sivaprasad, 2020). The coronary arteries in the retina are disrupted in DR, leading them to spill liquids or fluids and distorting vision.

Figure 1. Fundus image with retinal lesions (Source: IDRiD database available publicly)

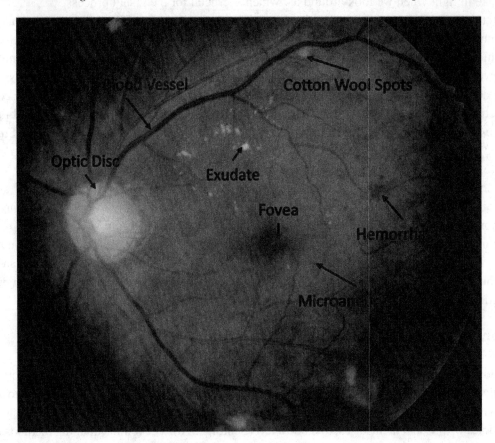

Table 1. DR database available publicly

Database	# of images	FOV (degrees)	Resolution	Task
APTOS (*APTOS: Diabetic Retinopathy Detection Kaggle [Internet]*, 2019)	5590	-	-	DR Classification
Kaggle (Decenciere et al., 2013; *Kaggle, Inc. Diabetic Retinopathy Detection Vol. (2016).*, n.d.)	88702	-	Variable	DR Classification
e-Ophtha (Decenciere et al., 2013)	463	50	1440 x 960 2048 x 1360	Detecting MA, EX DR vs Healthy
MESSIDOR-2 (Decencière et al., 2014)	1748	45	Variable	DR Classification
ROC (Jagan Mohan et al., 2020a)	100	45	1058 x 1061 1389 x 1383	Segmenting MA, HEM
DIARETDB0 (Kauppi et al., 2006)	89	50	1500 x 1152	Segmenting MA, HEM

DR is mainly divided into non-proliferative DR (NPDR) and Proliferative DR (PDR). Mild, moderate, and severe are the categories of non-proliferative DR.; the MA presence in NPDR is the first clinical sign of DR. Because of the blood vessel (BV) injury, oxygen supply to the retinal capillaries is reduced. Bulges on capillaries occur as small sac-like structures termed MA (Jagan Mohan et al., 2020a), which look like tiny red dots. The BVs in mild non-proliferative DR lose their ability to transport blood and begin to expand. The moderate, severe NPDR is defined by the presence of any of the MA, HEM, EX, or CWS.

The oxygen flow to retinal regions is cut off when retinal capillaries are blocked, resulting in puffy white patches known as CWS. The obstruction of the retinal arteries may provide enough pressure in the blood artery to cause it to rupture, leading to HEM. EX (Mohan et al., 2021a) is a condition in which proteins and lipids seep into the retina due to retinal vascular injury. The retina is starved of blood circulation due to growing obstruction of the more vascular system in severe non-proliferative DR, indicating the retina to generate new BVs. In advanced DR severity such as PDR, new BVs grow and causes permanent vision loss. Table 2 illustrates the phases of DR.

Table 2. DR stages

DR Stage	Observations	Severity
0	No lesions	Healthy eye
1	Presence of MA only	Mild
2	MA or Hem or EX or CWS	Moderate
3	More than 20 HEM in one of the four quadrants Venous bleeding No PDR	Severe
4	Neo Vascularization	PDR

DR is associated with several risk factors. Anyone with diabetes is susceptible to the DR. As a consequence, long-term progression of chronic high blood pressure and poor sugar management may raise the risk of developing an eye disease.

The global growth in DR-related vision disorders and blindness highlights the need to control diabetes individuals' visual loss effectively. To reduce DR-related blindness, various methods are available, ranging from prevention to early detection to active therapy. According to the researchers (Duh et al., 2017), the impact of medicine and its link with DR grade at index in predicting the course of blindness is another critical topic that has to be studied in future studies.

The study by Eszes et al. (Eszes et al., 2021) focused on the factors that cause DR, diabetic surveillance plans, regularity, and the influence of economic level. The study uses a portable fundus camera to acquire fundus photos of persons above 18 years old. There were also self-administered evaluations on self-health history and health-related behaviors, eyesight, HbA1c level, stage of disease, and participation at medical facilities. They also stated that while portable cams seem easy, they require extensive expertise to combat the reduced visual acuity for image evaluation, particularly in DL methods.

The risk of visual loss is reduced if DR is detected early and regularly screened. The number of ophthalmologists necessary is decreasing while the number of diabetes patients increases. The manual treatment of DR patients takes time and involves ophthalmologists with specialized training. As a result, an automated DR identification technology is needed to serve more people with diabetes while also reducing ophthalmologists' workload. The ML, DL, and their variations for detecting the DR are discussed in the following sections.

OVERVIEW OF THE ML AND DL TECHNIQUES

ML is a subset of artificial intelligence, a discipline that studies how machines learn different abilities and gain new information and how they recognize current understanding. ML is defined as a computer program that learns from experience concerning some assignment, programmed explicitly. Applications of ML include Data mining, computer vision, biometrics, medical diagnostics, speech and handwriting recognition, and robots. The categories of ML algorithms include

i. **Supervised learning**: A model is created through a training procedure that requires it to generate predictions and corrects them when other expectations are incorrect. The classifier is constructed until it reaches the appropriate accuracy of the training data. The learning works with the labeled data.
ii. **Unsupervised learning**: Deriving patterns from the incoming data is used to create a model. This might be to extract broad rules. It might be done using a statistical procedure to minimize redundancies consistently, or it could be done manually by sorting data by similarities. The learning works with the unlabeled data.
iii. **Semi-supervised learning**: The input data consists of both labeled and unlabeled instances. There is a targeted prediction problem, but the model must learn the structures to categorize and forecast the input.

As depicted in Figure 2, the ML in DR severity grading uses several preprocessing techniques to improve the retinal features in the fundus images. The preprocessing steps include image resizing, cropping, normalization for selecting the region of interest, and reducing the computational costs. In medical image analysis, collecting real-time images is a challenging task. Therefore, data augmentation techniques help in increasing the medical image database. The noise and other artifacts in the fundus image may lead to poor classification results. Therefore, noise removal and contrast adjustment techniques help remove the noise and improve the quality of the fundus images.

In ML, the features must be extracted manually. The manual feature extraction techniques include Gray-Level Co-Occurance matrix (K. Cao et al., 2019), Color, texture, and shape features (Padmanabha et al., 2017), Principle Component Analysis (PCA) (Bhatkar & Kharat, 2016), Discrete Wavelet Transform (Ur Rehman et al., 2018), Speeded-Up Robust Features (Mohan et al., 2021b), KAZE (Mohan, Murugan, Goel, et al., 2022) The extracted features help classify or segment the retinal lesions according to the ML algorithm used. As shown in Figure 2, it is recommended to consider the expert annotations in predicting the model's performance. Upon successful trials in clinical use cases, the model can be used in real-time application in DR grading. The following are the ML algorithms that are widely used in DR severity grading and other medical imaging applications.

i. Support vector machines (Abdelsalam & Zahran, 2021)
ii. K- Nearest Nieboors (Jagan Mohan et al., 2021)(Anupam et al., 2021)

Figure 2. Generalized ML model for DR severity grading

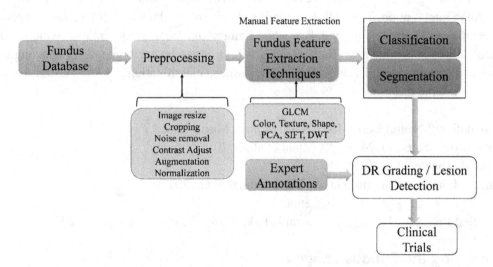

iii.   Naïve Bayes (Jagan Mohan et al., 2021)
iv.   Decision Trees (Aziza et al., 2019)
v.   Logistic regression (Tsao et al., 2018)

Artificial neural networks are used in DL techniques modeled by the neuronal structure. The phrase "deep learning" refers to methods for independently understanding the mathematical description of the hidden and essential relationships of fundus data. Unlike traditional machine learning methods, DL techniques require significantly less human direction since they do not rely on hand-crafted features, which may be time-consuming and difficult to build; instead, they acquire valuable characteristics from the fundus images. Furthermore, DL approaches extend substantially better than typical ML techniques when the amount of data expands. Figure 3 depicts a generalized paradigm for DR grading and lesion segmentation. The use of DL to detect and categorize DR has rapidly gained popularity.

Figure 3. Generalized DL model for DR severity grading

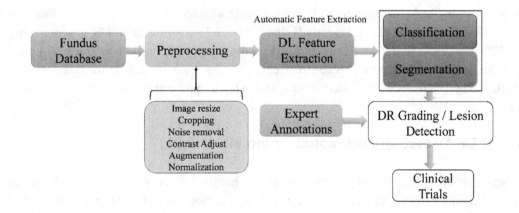

As depicted in Figure 3, the generalized DL-based DR grading model extracts features automatically without human intervention. The feature extraction step is the fundamental difference between the ML and DL techniques. However, DL models are data-hungry and require more images, which is challenging in medical image applications (Rautela et al., 2022). It can be overcome using data augmentation techniques to a certain extent. DL models in medical image classification or retinal lesion segmentation include the following techniques

i.   Convolutional Neural Networks (CNN) (Mohan, Murugan, & Goel, 2022)
ii.   Generative Adversarial Networks (Zhou et al., 2020)
iii.   U-Net (Mohan et al., 2021a)
iv.   Transfer Learning (Bhardwaj et al., 2021)(Kumar et al., 2022)
v.   Ensemble Learning (Jagan Mohan et al., 2021)
vi.   Modified Pre-trained Networks (Kassani et al., 2019; Shanthi & Sabeenian, 2019)

Preprocessing the Fundus Images

Preprocessing the fundus image data before feeding it into a DL model aids in obtaining more valuable features. Because fundus images are acquired with multiple camera lenses, noise in the fundus images may emerge from hardware components under varied environmental situations. Furthermore, all fundus images of exactly equal arrays are required for the FC layers in CNN. As a result, fundus image preprocessing is usually an essential stage in many of the data analyses assessed to reduce such variance, which ultimately impacts the success of the DR classifier and illustrates some minor details of the fundus. The following are some of the preprocessing steps used in DR classification techniques.

i.   Denoising (Jagan Mohan et al., 2020a)
ii.   Normalization (Goel et al., 2021)
iii.   Cropping (Zhang et al., 2017)
iv.   Color channel extraction (Jagan Mohan et al., 2020a)
v.   Contrast enhancement (Soomro et al., 2016)
vi.   Resizing (Chakrabarty, 2018)
vii.   Data augmentation (Araújo et al., 2020)

As reported in (Jagan Mohan et al., 2020a), the fundus images' noise removal and contrast improvement resulted in better MA detection with superior performance. The entropy of the fundus images reported in (Jagan Mohan et al., 2021) reveals that the model performance in DR grading is improved from 83.72% to 90.28%. As discussed earlier, image scaling, cropping, and normalization for picking the region of interest improve the model performance. Collecting real-time data in medical image analysis is a complicated process. As a result, data augmentation techniques contribute to expanding the medical database.

Review of DR Detection Techniques using ML and DL

Researchers worldwide are working on new ways to identify DR early via ML and DL approaches. The traditional data collecting methods like Fluorescein Angiography (FA) are now shifted to Digital

Fundus Camera for improved fundus images or to mass diagnose rapidly and efficiently by employing a high resolution and massive fundus image dataset. Let us discuss a few recent works suggested by the researchers.

Cao et al. (W. Cao et al., 2018) proposed an ML-based technique for the early detection of DR by finding the MA. In this work, the dimensionality of the feature space is reduced using PCA, and resultant features are used in classifying the MA and Non-MA candidates. They have reported an area under the curve (AUC) of 98.5% and an F measure of 0.926 on DIARETDB0, ROC databases. A multifractal geometry-based early DR detection technique is proposed in (Abdelsalam & Zahran, 2021) using an SVM classifier. This technique is evaluated on the private database collected from Mansoura University and reported an accuracy (Acc) of 98.5%.

A severe PDR is detected in (Yu et al., 2018) by finding the abnormal BV growth in the optic disc. This technique is evaluated on the Kaggle database. This technique uses a Gabor filter for BV segmentation, and morphological, and texture features are extracted, which are reduced to 18 using the recursive feature elimination (RFE) technique and classified using SVM. This method reported an Acc of 95.23%, Specificity (Sp) of 96.30%, Sensitivity (Se) of 92.90%, and AUC of 98.51%. Early detection of DR finding the MA is proposed in (Tavakoli et al., 2021). BV and optic disc are detected and masked using radon transform (RT) for detecting the MA using SVM. This technique is evaluated on a local database of 749 fundus images and reported a high Se of 100% and Sp of 93%.

Rodrigues et al. (Rodrigues et al., 2020) proposed a multi-model technique for finding the DR severity based on BV segmentation called ELEMENT. This approach functions on the threshold value and BV connectivity properties. This technique has reported an overall Acc of 97.40% and was evaluated on STARE, RC_SLO, VAMPIRE-FA, and CHASE DB. A genetic program (GP) based MA detection technique is proposed in (Usman & Almejalli, 2020). In this work, they considered 28 features obtained from preprocessed fundus images. Then, using fitness score binarization, they have calculated the expression that can be used in real-time applications. This technique was evaluated on MESSIDOR, DIARETDB1, and e-Optha and reported an Acc of 97%.

The DR classification can be done in two ways; one is a binary classification that detects healthy and DR fundus. The other is multi-class classification in which the severity of the DR is detected. The researchers (Xu et al., 2017)(Quellec et al., 2017) have proposed supervised CNN-based DR detection techniques based on a binary classification approach. These works are tested on the EyePACS database, reporting an Acc of 94.5% and AUC of 95.4%. Jiang et al. (Jiang et al., 2019) proposed a transfer learning-based DR binary classification method. This method was tested on a private database. The trained networks used in this approach are InceptionV3 and ResNet152 and reported an Acc of 88.21% and AUC of 94.6%.

The DR grading with lesion detection using CNN is proposed in (Wang et al., 2020). This technique helps to grade the DR by detecting the lesion present in the fundus image. This technique is evaluated on a private database and reported an Acc of 92.95%, Se of 99.39%, and Sp of 99.93%. A novel DR detection technique is proposed in (Jagan Mohan et al., 2021). This technique extracts the ensemble network features that combine ResNet101, VGG19, and InceptionV3. The dimensionality of the feature space is reduced using feature ranking techniques such as F Test, ReliefF, and Chi-score. The best features are used in the DR grading. This technique is evaluated on IDRiD, Kaggle, and MESSIDOR databases reporting an Acc of 97.78%, Se of 97.6%, and Sp of 99.3%. Qummar et al. (Qummar et al., 2019) proposed an ensemble network using the Kaggle database in DR classification. They have reported an Acc of 80.8%

Table 3. DR detection/grading techniques

Author	Method	Database	Se	Sp	Acc	AUC	F1 score	Purpose
(W. Cao et al., 2018)	PCA, ML	DIARETDB0 ROC	-	-	-	98.5	0.926	Early DR detection
(Abdelsalam & Zahran, 2021)	ML	Private data	-	-	98.5	-	-	Early DR detection
(Yu et al., 2018)	Gabor filter RFE SVM	Kaggle	92.90	96.30	95.23	98.51	-	Sever PDR detection
(Tavakoli et al., 2021)	RT SVM	Private data	100	93	-	-	-	Early DR detection
(Rodrigues et al., 2020)	ML	STARE, RC-SLO, VAMPIRE-FA, CHASE-DB	-		97.4	99.36	0.8579	Severe DR detection
(Usman & Almejalli, 2020)	GP	MESSIDOR, DIARETDB1, and e-Ophtha	98	96	97	-	-	-
(Xu et al., 2017)	CNN	EyePACS			94.5			DR binary classification
(Quellec et al., 2017)	CNN	EyePACS, DIARETDB1				95.4		DR binary classification
(Jiang et al., 2019)	Transfer Learning	Private data	-	-	88.21	94.6	-	DR binary classification
(Wang et al., 2020)	CNN	Private data	99.39	99.93	92.95	-	-	DR Grading with lesion detection
(Jagan Mohan et al., 2021)	Ensemble Features, SVM	MESSIDOR-2, Kaggle, IDRiD	97.6	99.3	97.78	-	0.974	DR Grading
(Qummar et al., 2019)	Ensemble network	Kaggle	-	86.7	80.8	-	-	DR Grading

and Sp of 86.7%. The EX segmentation using an improved U-Net model is proposed in (Mohan et al., 2021a). This technique helps in the early DR detection.

Most of the works were tested on specific fundus databases. Therefore it is necessary to check the state-of-the-art techniques on various databases to make the models generalize. Few researchers have suggested binary classification techniques, few others have proposed multi-class DR grading, and few authors have proposed DR classification through lesion detection. Table 3 shows the state-of-the-art results and the purpose of the technique.

Role of ML and DL in DR Classification

The ML and DL techniques play a vital role in medical imaging. AI is an emerging area that automates disease detection in the medical domain. In general, especially in India, only one ophthalmologist is there to treat one lakh, diabetic patients. However, as per the regulations, one ophthalmologist must be there for every twenty thousand people. Currently, there are only 12000 ophthalmologists in India for its

1,404,532,227 population as of April 2022. Manually treating diabetic patients is time-consuming and requires trained ophthalmologists. Therefore, an automated AI-based model is required to treat diabetic patients, reducing ophthalmologists' burden. Also, there is necessary to conduct eye camps on-site to serve people with diabetes in remote regions who cannot travel to the hospital. The AI models deployed in telephones or other embedded devices help treat diabetic patients in the initial screening. Based on the recommendation of the medical expert, necessary medications can be suggested.

The applications of AI in medical imaging are increasing in day-to-day life. The number of works reported in the medical imaging field during 2007-08 is around 100-150. However, the number increased to 1000-1100 during 2017-18, showing the role of AI in medical imaging.

Researchers have proposed several techniques in DR classification. These techniques recognize the complex structures in the fundus image, assessing retinal lesion features. In DR grading, the AI can use various imaging modalities at different stages of DR detection. However, most techniques are trained and tested with a limited database only. In general, the model's performance must be evaluated in the presence of a medical expert. To our knowledge, most of the procedures outlined thus far require verification in the presence of a medical professional. The performance of the models proposed by the researchers is limited to the database used. Therefore, a common platform must be developed to collect real-time images, thus helping the models train and improve the DR classification results, making the models generalize.

In general, the primary role of ML and DL in the healthcare domain is to analyze the correlations between clinical procedures and patient health improvements. ML and DL techniques are used to diagnose the disease, develop a set of rules for treating the patient, drug composition, adapted medicine, and patient nursing and attention. Some of the critical roles in clinical applications of ML and DL in the healthcare domain include Cardiovascular, Radiology, Oncology, Gastroenterology, and Psychiatry. ML and DL's system applications in medical imaging include disease diagnosis, telemedicine, electronic healthcare records, drug interactions, and the creation of new drugs.

CONCLUSION

Diabetes Mellitus is a chronic condition in which blood glucose levels rise due to the pancreas' failure to make or secrete enough insulin. Diabetes cases have increased dramatically in recent decades. Therefore, automated techniques in the medical domain are required to detect and diagnose diabetic retinopathy using fundus image analysis. This chapter has briefly introduced the fundus image, diabetic retinopathy, and stages. Also, it explains the overview of the machine and deep learning techniques, including the fundamental differences and types. It covers the basic preprocessing techniques used in diabetic retinopathy grading. Various techniques proposed by the researchers for diabetic retinopathy detection or grading are overviewed. Finally, machine and deep learning techniques in diabetic retinopathy detection and medical imaging are presented.

REFERENCES

Abdelsalam, M. M., & Zahran, M. A. (2021). A Novel Approach of Diabetic Retinopathy Early Detection Based on Multifractal Geometry Analysis for OCTA Macular Images Using Support Vector Machine. *IEEE Access: Practical Innovations, Open Solutions*, 9, 22844–22858. doi:10.1109/ACCESS.2021.3054743

Anupam, A., Mohan, N. J., Sahoo, S., & Chakraborty, S. (2021). Preliminary Diagnosis of COVID-19 Based on Cough Sounds Using Machine Learning Algorithms. *2021 5th International Conference on Intelligent Computing and Control Systems (ICICCS)*, 1391–1397. 10.1109/ICICCS51141.2021.9432324

APTOS: Diabetic retinopathy detection kaggle. (2019). Https://Www.Kaggle.Com/c/Aptos2019-Blindness-Detection/Data

Araújo, T., Aresta, G., Mendonça, L., Penas, S., Maia, C., Carneiro, Â., Mendonça, A. M., & Campilho, A. (2020). Data augmentation for improving proliferative diabetic retinopathy detection in eye fundus images. *IEEE Access: Practical Innovations, Open Solutions*, 8, 182462–182474. doi:10.1109/ACCESS.2020.3028960

Aziza, E. Z., el Amine, L. M., Mohamed, M., & Abdelhafid, B. (2019). Decision tree CART algorithm for diabetic retinopathy classification. *2019 6th International Conference on Image and Signal Processing and Their Applications (ISPA)*, 1–5.

Bhardwaj, C., Jain, S., & Sood, M. (2021). Transfer learning based robust automatic detection system for diabetic retinopathy grading. *Neural Computing & Applications*, 33(20), 13999–14019. Advance online publication. doi:10.100700521-021-06042-2

Bhatkar, A. P., & Kharat, G. (2016). Diagnosis of Diabetic Retinopathy Using Principal Component Analysis (PCA). *International Conference on Smart Trends for Information Technology and Computer Communications*, 768–778. 10.1007/978-981-10-3433-6_92

Cao, K., Xu, J., & Zhao, W.-Q. (2019). Artificial intelligence on diabetic retinopathy diagnosis: An automatic classification method based on grey level co-occurrence matrix and naive Bayesian model. *International Journal of Ophthalmology*, 12(7), 1158–1162. doi:10.18240/ijo.2019.07.17 PMID:31341808

Cao, W., Czarnek, N., Shan, J., & Li, L. (2018). Microaneurysm detection using principal component analysis and machine learning methods. *IEEE Transactions on Nanobioscience*, 17(3), 191–198. doi:10.1109/TNB.2018.2840084 PMID:29994317

Chakrabarty, N. (2018). A deep learning method for the detection of diabetic retinopathy. *2018 5th IEEE Uttar Pradesh Section International Conference on Electrical, Electronics and Computer Engineering (UPCON)*, 1–5.

Chowdhary, C. L., Sai, G. V. K., & Acharjya, D. P. (2016). Decreasing false assumption for improved breast cancer detection. *J. Sci. Arts*, 35(2), 157–176.

Das, T. K., Chowdhary, C. L., & Gao, X. Z. (2020). Chest X-ray investigation: a convolutional neural network approach. In Journal of Biomimetics, Biomaterials and Biomedical Engineering (Vol. 45, pp. 57-70). Trans Tech Publications Ltd.

Decenciere, E., Cazuguel, G., Zhang, X., Thibault, G., Klein, J.-C., Meyer, F., Marcotegui, B., Quellec, G., Lamard, M., Danno, R., Elie, D., Massin, P., Viktor, Z., Erginay, A., Laÿ, B., & Chabouis, A. (2013). TeleOphta: Machine learning and image processing methods for teleophthalmology. *IRBM*, *34*(2), 196–203. doi:10.1016/j.irbm.2013.01.010

Decencière, E., Zhang, X., Cazuguel, G., Lay, B., Cochener, B., Trone, C., Gain, P., Ordonez, R., Massin, P., Erginay, A., Charton, B., & Klein, J.-C. (2014). Feedback on a publicly distributed image database: the messidor database. *Image Analysis & Stereology*, *33*(3), 231. doi:10.5566/ias.1155

Duh, E. J., Sun, J. K., & Stitt, A. W. (2017). Diabetic retinopathy: Current understanding, mechanisms, and treatment strategies. *JCI Insight*, *2*(14), e93751. doi:10.1172/jci.insight.93751 PMID:28724805

Eszes, D. J., Szabó, D. J., Russell, G., Lengyel, C., Várkonyi, T., Paulik, E., Nagymajtényi, L., Facskó, A., Petrovski, G., & Petrovski, B. É. (2021). Diabetic Retinopathy Screening in Patients with Diabetes Using a Handheld Fundus Camera: The Experience from the South-Eastern Region in Hungary. *Journal of Diabetes Research*, *2021*, 2021. doi:10.1155/2021/6646645 PMID:33628836

Goel, T., Murugan, R., Mirjalili, S., & Chakrabartty, D. K. (2021). OptCoNet: An optimized convolutional neural network for an automatic diagnosis of COVID-19. *Applied Intelligence*, *51*(3), 1351–1366. doi:10.100710489-020-01904-z PMID:34764551

Jagan Mohan, N., Murugan, R., Goel, T., Mirjalili, S., & Roy, P. (2021). A novel four-step feature selection technique for diabetic retinopathy grading. *Physical and Engineering Sciences in Medicine*, *44*(4), 1351–1366. doi:10.100713246-021-01073-4 PMID:34748191

Jagan Mohan, N., Murugan, R., Goel, T., & Roy, P. (2020a). An improved accuracy rate in microaneurysms detection in retinal fundus images using non-local mean filter. *International Conference on Machine Learning, Image Processing, Network Security and Data Sciences*, 183–193. 10.1007/978-981-15-6315-7_15

Jagan Mohan, N., Murugan, R., Goel, T., & Roy, P. (2020b). Optic Disc Segmentation in Fundus Images using Operator Splitting Approach. *2020 Advanced Communication Technologies and Signal Processing (ACTS)*, 1–5. doi:10.1109/ACTS49415.2020.9350504

Jiang, H., Yang, K., Gao, M., Zhang, D., Ma, H., & Qian, W. (2019). An interpretable ensemble deep learning model for diabetic retinopathy disease classification. *2019 41st Annual International Conference of the IEEE Engineering in Medicine and Biology Society (EMBC)*, 2045–2048.

Kaggle, Inc. Diabetic retinopathy detection. (2016). Available at Https://Www.Kaggle.Com/c/Diabetic-Retinopathy-Detection

Kassani, S. H., Kassani, P. H., Khazaeinezhad, R., Wesolowski, M. J., Schneider, K. A., & Deters, R. (2019). Diabetic Retinopathy Classification Using a Modified Xception Architecture. *2019 IEEE International Symposium on Signal Processing and Information Technology (ISSPIT)*, 1–6. 10.1109/ISSPIT47144.2019.9001846

Kauppi, T., Kalesnykiene, V., Kamarainen, J.-K., Lensu, L., Sorri, I., Uusitalo, H., Kälviäinen, H., & Pietilä, J. (2006). DIARETDB0: Evaluation database and methodology for diabetic retinopathy algorithms. Machine Vision and Pattern Recognition Research Group, Lappeenranta University of Technology, 73, 1–17.

Kumar, V., Zarrad, A., Gupta, R., & Cheikhrouhou, O. (2022). COV-DLS: Prediction of COVID-19 from X-Rays Using Enhanced Deep Transfer Learning Techniques. *Journal of Healthcare Engineering, 2022*. doi:10.1155/2022/6216273 PMID:35422979

Mohan, N. J., Murugan, R., & Goel, T. (2020). Investigations of Diabetic Retinopathy Algorithms in Retinal Fundus Images. *International Journal of Image Processing and Pattern Recognition, 6*(1), 14–26.

Mohan, N. J., Murugan, R., & Goel, T. (2022). Machine Learning Algorithms for Hypertensive Retinopathy Detection through Retinal Fundus Images. *Computer Vision and Recognition Systems: Research Innovations and Trends, 39*.

Mohan, N. J., Murugan, R., Goel, T., & Roy, P. (2021a). Exudate Detection with Improved U-Net Using Fundus Images. *2021 International Conference on Computational Performance Evaluation (ComPE)*, 560–564. 10.1109/ComPE53109.2021.9752239

Mohan, N. J., Murugan, R., Goel, T., & Roy, P. (2021b). Exudate Localization in Retinal Fundus Images Using Modified Speeded Up Robust Features Algorithm. *2020 IEEE-EMBS Conference on Biomedical Engineering and Sciences (IECBES)*, 367–371. 10.1109/IECBES48179.2021.9398771

Mohan, N. J., Murugan, R., Goel, T., & Roy, P. (2022). Fast and Robust Exudate Detection in Retinal Fundus Images Using Extreme Learning Machine Autoencoders and Modified KAZE Features. *Journal of Digital Imaging, 35*(3), 496–513. Advance online publication. doi:10.100710278-022-00587-x PMID:35141807

Padmanabha, A. G. A., Appaji, M. A., Prasad, M., Lu, H., & Joshi, S. (2017). Classification of diabetic retinopathy using textural features in retinal color fundus image. *2017 12th International Conference on Intelligent Systems and Knowledge Engineering (ISKE)*, 1–5.

Pearce, E., & Sivaprasad, S. (2020). A review of advancements and evidence gaps in diabetic retinopathy screening models. *Clinical Ophthalmology (Auckland, N.Z.), 14*, 3285–3296. doi:10.2147/OPTH.S267521 PMID:33116380

Quellec, G., Charrière, K., Boudi, Y., Cochener, B., & Lamard, M. (2017). Deep image mining for diabetic retinopathy screening. *Medical Image Analysis, 39*, 178–193. doi:10.1016/j.media.2017.04.012 PMID:28511066

Qummar, S., Khan, F. G., Shah, S., Khan, A., Shamshirband, S., Rehman, Z. U., Khan, I. A., & Jadoon, W. (2019). A deep learning ensemble approach for diabetic retinopathy detection. *IEEE Access: Practical Innovations, Open Solutions, 7*, 150530–150539. doi:10.1109/ACCESS.2019.2947484

Rautela, K., Kumar, D., & Kumar, V. (2022). A Systematic Review on Breast Cancer Detection Using Deep Learning Techniques. *Archives of Computational Methods in Engineering*, 1–31. doi:10.100711831-022-09744-5

Rodrigues, E. O., Conci, A., & Liatsis, P. (2020). ELEMENT: Multi-Modal Retinal Vessel Segmentation Based on a Coupled Region Growing and Machine Learning Approach. *IEEE Journal of Biomedical and Health Informatics*, 24(12), 3507–3519. doi:10.1109/JBHI.2020.2999257 PMID:32750920

Senior, K. R. (2010). *The eye: the physiology of human perception*. The Rosen Publishing Group, Inc.

Shanthi, T., & Sabeenian, R. S. (2019). Modified Alexnet architecture for classification of diabetic retinopathy images. *Computers & Electrical Engineering*, 76, 56–64. doi:10.1016/j.compeleceng.2019.03.004

Soomro, T. A., Gao, J., Khan, M. A. U., Khan, T. M., & Paul, M. (2016). Role of image contrast enhancement technique for ophthalmologist as diagnostic tool for diabetic retinopathy. *2016 International Conference on Digital Image Computing: Techniques and Applications (DICTA)*, 1–8. 10.1109/DICTA.2016.7797078

Steinmetz, J. D., Bourne, R. R. A., Briant, P. S., Flaxman, S. R., Taylor, H. R. B., Jonas, J. B., Abdoli, A. A., Abrha, W. A., Abualhasan, A., Abu-Gharbieh, E. G., Adal, T. G., Afshin, A., Ahmadieh, H., Alemayehu, W., Alemzadeh, S. A. S., Alfaar, A. S., Alipour, V., Androudi, S., Arabloo, J., ... Vos, T. (2021). Causes of blindness and vision impairment in 2020 and trends over 30 years, and prevalence of avoidable blindness in relation to VISION 2020: the Right to Sight: an analysis for the Global Burden of Disease Study. *The Lancet. Global Health*, 9(2), e144–e160. doi:10.1016/S2214-109X(20)30489-7 PMID:33275949

Tavakoli, M., Mehdizadeh, A., Aghayan, A., Shahri, R. P., Ellis, T., & Dehmeshki, J. (2021). Automated Microaneurysms Detection in Retinal Images Using Radon Transform and Supervised Learning: Application to Mass Screening of Diabetic Retinopathy. *IEEE Access: Practical Innovations, Open Solutions*, 9, 67302–67314. doi:10.1109/ACCESS.2021.3074458

Tsao, H.-Y., Chan, P.-Y., & Su, E. C.-Y. (2018). Predicting diabetic retinopathy and identifying interpretable biomedical features using machine learning algorithms. *BMC Bioinformatics*, 19(9), 111–121. doi:10.118612859-018-2277-0 PMID:30367589

Ur Rehman, M., Abbas, Z., Khan, S. H., & Ghani, S. H. (2018). Diabetic retinopathy fundus image classification using discrete wavelet transform. *2018 2nd International Conference on Engineering Innovation (ICEI)*, 75–80.

Usman, I., & Almejalli, K. A. (2020). Intelligent Automated Detection of Microaneurysms in Fundus Images Using Feature-Set Tuning. *IEEE Access: Practical Innovations, Open Solutions*, 8, 65187–65196. doi:10.1109/ACCESS.2020.2985543

Wang, J., Luo, J., Liu, B., Feng, R., Lu, L., & Zou, H. (2020). Automated diabetic retinopathy grading and lesion detection based on the modified R-FCN object-detection algorithm. *IET Computer Vision*, 14(1), 1–8. doi:10.1049/iet-cvi.2018.5508

Xu, K., Feng, D., & Mi, H. (2017). Deep convolutional neural network-based early automated detection of diabetic retinopathy using fundus image. *Molecules (Basel, Switzerland)*, 22(12), 2054. doi:10.3390/molecules22122054 PMID:29168750

Yu, S., Xiao, D., & Kanagasingam, Y. (2018). Machine learning based automatic neovascularization detection on optic disc Region. *IEEE Journal of Biomedical and Health Informatics*, 22(3), 886–894. doi:10.1109/JBHI.2017.2710201 PMID:29727291

Zhang, D., Bu, W., & Wu, X. (2017). Diabetic retinopathy classification using deeply supervised ResNet. *2017 IEEE SmartWorld, Ubiquitous Intelligence & Computing, Advanced & Trusted Computed, Scalable Computing & Communications, Cloud & Big Data Computing, Internet of People and Smart City Innovation (SmartWorld/SCALCOM/UIC/ATC/CBDCom/IOP/SCI)*, 1–6.

Zhao, M., & Jiang, Y. (2020). Great expectations and challenges of artificial intelligence in the screening of diabetic retinopathy. *Eye (London, England)*, 34(3), 418–419. doi:10.103841433-019-0629-2 PMID:31827269

Zhou, Y., Wang, B., He, X., Cui, S., & Shao, L. (2020). DR-GAN: Conditional generative adversarial network for fine-grained lesion synthesis on diabetic retinopathy images. *IEEE Journal of Biomedical and Health Informatics*. PMID:33332280

Chapter 4
Role of Machine Learning in Artificial Emotional Intelligence

Bandaru Sri Chandra Nikitha
RV College of Engineering, India

Basavaneni Silpa
RV College of Engineering, India

Sindhu R. Rajendran
RV College of Engineering, India

Ramavenkateswaran N.
RV College of Engineering, India

ABSTRACT

The present world is overwhelmed with digital technologies: ubiquitous platforms of cloud computing and the internet of everything. Artificial intelligence (AI) is a technology that enables a machine to simulate human behaviour. The detailed facial expressions are captured by AI-enabled effective imaging and recognition processes of human vision. In artificial emotional intelligence (AEI), a new paradigm of human-computer interaction with AI-enabled cloud and internet connectivity could transpire healthy emotional intelligence (EI). As per the WHO world health report in 2018, globally, an estimated 264 million people are affected by depression and increased in recent years pertinent to COVID-19 lockdown-induced socio-economic factors. Hence, its paramount importance for the government and researchers to give serious consideration to developing EI. EI including human behaviours, digital well-being, and decision-making can be mentored using predictive data analytics. In this chapter, recent trends, preferrable ML algorithms, and research approach to EI components are discussed.

INTRODUCTION

Artificial intelligence can be referred to as a technology that enables a machine to resemble human behaviour and actions. Machine Learning is a branch of Artificial Intelligence. It helps the system grasp and

DOI: 10.4018/978-1-6684-5673-6.ch004

enhances itself from the experiences without having to be specifically programmed. The term "Machine Learning" has been given by Arthur Samuel. With the help of the statistical methods, the algorithms present are trained in such a way that they can categorize as well as make predictions that help in revealing the key insights. They influence the decision-making process in further cases. Since the 1940s digital computers have been designed in such a way that they can perform different kinds of complicated tasks like deriving a mathematical formula or playing a game. Artificial intelligence is an important branch of computer science which is associated with making some highly intelligent machines that are capable of performing functions that require human intelligence. The field of artificial intelligence is a combination of computer science and of strong datasets that help us to enable problem-solving. Artificial intelligence has some very important applications in the real world. The following are some of its examples: speech recognition, customer service, computer vision, Robo-advisors, self-driving cars, etc.

The idea of the "Machine that thinks" emerged around the late 1950s. In 1956, the term "Artificial Intelligence" was introduced by John McCarthy (Rajaraman, 2014). The first successful Artificial Intelligence software program was created in the year 1956 by Allen Newell, J.C. Shaw, and Herbert Simon (Newell et al., 1956). In 1967, Frank Rosenblatt built the first computer; it depends on the neural network, which learned everything through the terror method. As the years passed, different innovations were made in the world of artificial intelligence. Baidu's Minwa supercomputer used a convolutional neural network that can recognize and classify pictures with greater precision than the average human. Mattingly & Kraiger (2019) conducted around 58 tests based on emotional intelligence and its effect. Derek Leben had a strong belief that machines' judgement will be more valuable in the future since they make a reasonable judgement. In 2021, New York gave out 2,360 robotics pets that were capable of doing some physical movements and sounds. However, these pets could not meet the necessary emotional intelligent acceptance. Even today, artificial emotional intelligence has yet to obtain universal acceptance and adaptability in human and machine interaction pertinent to its complexity and challenges.

Artificial intelligence is its main goal and provides a base to solve problems independently. Machine learning is a key facilitator to solving problems at a greater speed than the human mind alone does. Data is the key to Machine Learning. The algorithms in Machine learning are the major reason for its success. The algorithms prepare mathematical models based on the data available to them. They help them in making decisions without being programmed explicitly. The ability to understand, utilize, handle, control and perceive emotions and detect emotions using artificial intelligence can be termed artificial emotional intelligence.

Machine Learning is widely useful in the following cases: Data security, Finance, Health care, Fraud detection, etc.

The following processes are used in Machine Learning processes: A selection technique, a blunders function followed by a model development technique. The systems learn and develop from experience through communicating with the people. Instead of coding each response, here in this case the system gets the opportunity to solve the situation and get practice making precise decisions.

The Neuro-inspired computing chips combine several talents stimulated by way of using neurobiological systems and could offer a power-green method to AI computing workloads.

- Many extraordinary varieties of neuro-inspired computing chips were developed over the previous few years, and diverse neuro-stimulated functions had been implemented in those chips, from the tool degree to the circuit and structure diploma (Cekic et al., 2022). Neuro-stimulated computing chips are still only in the early stages of development and for this reason, it's critical to find out the challenges and opportunities for the sphere.

- Providing a structure similar to the human brain to the systems might help in getting better results.
- A group of neuro-inspired computing chips have been developed especially for artificial intelligence applications that have similar neural structures to humans and some other animals.
- The Neuro-inspired computing chips seem to provide a great contribution to emotional artificial intelligence as they have various talents that are activated depending upon the way they use the neurobiological system.

The Internet of Things, or IoT, backs up billions of physical objects worldwide that can be connected to the Internet. It is possible that they collect and exchange information at some point in the field. Anything can be converted into an IoT tool because we only need a small controller and a few connection methods (Bluetooth or wifi).

- Everything around us becomes part of the IoT where we connect all the many objects and provide them with sensors that give them digital-level intelligence that enables them to pass real-time statistics without human involvement (Gillis, 2022).
- IoT provides instant better understanding by measuring and reporting specific real-world situations. Modern-day tool: The real-world situation can be tested and answered in real-time. If a heart rate reveals warnings of an unbalanced heartbeat, the patient may be able to slow down and relax to lower his or her heart rate by taking the appropriate dose, taking appropriate medication, consulting his or her doctor for similar guidance or even seeking medical help. If the site visitor monitoring system detects a cached copy on the dual trailer route, it can replace existing travel applications and allow passengers to select trade routes and avoid congestion. There are various IoT industrial applications on smart cars, robots, smart power, smart grid, etc. With the help of artificial emotional intelligence, we can see that we were able to avoid and predict some emergencies.

Smart devices that work based on Artificial Intelligence are great. The growing desire to improve home security has prompted the implementation of AI-enabled gadgets (Davy, 2003; Samantaray et al. 2021). These devices include a wide range of capabilities; including risk assessments, face thunder, and smart home integration, which also protect homeowners from security threats. Work that has to be done by humans is being supplemented by machines as with the help of artificial emotional intelligence they can predict the situation.

ARTIFICIAL EMOTIONAL INTELLIGENCE

The ability of computers to read a person's emotions by analyzing the data available to them including facial expressions, volume, touch, eye tracking, realistic and other features needed to understand a person's emotional state is called Artificial Emotional Intelligence. This makes machines capable of understanding not only the cognitive but additionally the emotive channels of human verbal exchange. And enables them to understand both nonverbal and verbal signals.

For visually understanding more information, human facial expressions are very useful. In the field of human-machine interaction, facial expression recognition is very important. As shown in figure 1,

Figure 1. Fundamental facial expressions considered for early emotion intelligent recognition (Singh et al., 2019)

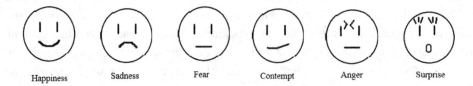

different emotions like anger, contempt, disgust, and fear. Happiness, sadness, and surprise can be recognized using facial expressions.

In 1995, "Affective Computing" entered into an act where MIT Media Lab could see that cameras, microphones and sensors could detect emotions.

With a combination of virtual computer vision, sensors, cameras, a lot of real-world information, background science and in-depth learning algorithms, these clever performance programs collect data and attempt to analyze and identify emotions. As data and detail increase algorithms become better at identifying emotions.

Necessity of Emotional Artificial Intelligence

Emotional Artificial Intelligence is an important marketing tool. It has the potential to develop a better relationship with customers. It also plays an important role in the industry. In the case of the advertising industry user, adaptability is very important to target a large number of viewers. The ability of the system to capture the user's mood is highly important, as this helps them to get feedback on the product. Moreover, it makes it easier for them to create some targeted ads. In the case of customer care, it is important to identify the customer's emotions on the phone and acting accordingly helps to provide a better customer experience. Changing the tone of voice, talking convincingly, etc. are some ways the system uses to please the customer. Moreover, it plays the biggest role in the case of health care as it helps to determine the mental health of real-world or her voice statistics, facial code removal, and eye size. We can anticipate and help alleviate depression in any stressful attack. The biometric sensors that are present in our devices help us to identify some emergencies beforehand and give us a chance to solve them in the best way possible.

How is Human Machine Interaction helping us in the development of the analysis of Artificial Emotional Intelligence?

Human-machine interaction plays a vital role in the development of artificial emotional intelligence systems. The machines are not coded to act accordingly. The machines learn to interact with humans through experience. The more the interactions take place between humans and machines, the more experienced they will become. It helps the machines to respond with better accuracy and take precise decisions according to the situation. Some of the modern gadgets and software like Alexa, Google assistant, etc. play an important role in the present-day world. By catching our voice they complete the assigned tasks. Though quite a large range of changes need to be performed on them, to adapt and act according to human emotions. Soon, even the machines around us will get mingled with us. It would be difficult to differentiate. They have developed a robot with emotions and artificial intelligence. It is named Sophia. It is the first robot to express over 60 human emotions.

Types of Emotional Intelligence:

There are 5 main parts of Artificial Emotional Intelligence. They are

1. Self-Awareness
2. Self-Regulation
3. Motivation
4. Empathy
5. Social skills

Self-Awareness

Self-Awareness is the functionality to judge personality socially and recognize how your conduct is being viewed with recognition by another. Its synonyms include "self-commentary," "introspection," and "self-targeted attention." Self-factors comprise private additives together with thoughts, emotions, and motives, as well as public (visible) additives which consist of looks, mannerisms, and others' opinions of self. If you're self-observant, you can understand the manner you're feeling, the manner you're performing, and how you seem. You in all likelihood have a sturdy draw close to your strengths and weaknesses, because of this which you understand in which and the manner you'll be maximum useful. These statistics may additionally want to make you a high-quality leader because you've been given a concept of what capabilities you may be lacking and therefore wherein and how you need another to use their capabilities (Mayer et al. 2016).

Self-recognition also can assist you to prepare yourself to reflect on consideration of your feelings effectively. It calls for self-mirrored image and intervention, so in case you're self-aware, while you get disappointed you could begin to reflect on why you feel as you do and discover that the feeling is a short-time period, out of location or encouragement for excessive brilliant movement. Doing this permits you to bear in mind your feelings as a part of a bigger photo so that you won't get affected by others. Being aware of the reason for your emotions can also provide you with a more feeling of management over the emotions, enhancing self-worth.

Self-Regulation

Self-regulation is the potential to remain balmy in emotional conditions. Although factors influence how you experience and could be your past trauma manipulation. If you're extraordinarily self-regulated, you're correct at managing the way you respond, you have a higher probability of making the correct decisions although the world is breaking down around you (Melissa, February 1, 2018). Also, in case you're rather self-controlled, you could easily adjust, due to the truth the ache that frequently comes from exchange received won't make you stagger.

Self-Regulation is an important skill for people who decide to take up jobs which might be expeditious and menacing. For instance, you have to be self-regulated as a firefighter. If he gets tensed, he could gasp and bypass out, jeopardizing himself and those he was looking to rescue.

Motivation

Motivation is the potential to make you with little to no strain from others. Some resources of intrinsic motivation consist of interest, a preference to satisfy your capacity, and a choice to peer you're imaginative and prescient come lifestyles. If you're surprisingly self-persuaded, you might need rewards like money or praise, however, they aren't the driving pressure at the back of your conduct. This way you have greater control over your productivity, due to the fact your motivation is self-generated.

Empathy

Empathy is the capability to recognize how people around you experience it and place yourself "in a personal situation." If you're exceedingly empathetic, you're additionally in all likelihood to sense ache when you observe other people in pain and pride while you understand another's satisfaction, permitting you to create an emotional bond with others (Singer, & Klimecki, (2014)

Cognitive Empathy

Cognitive empathy is being capable of putting yourself in some other vicinity and spotting their angle. It is also called 'perspective-taking'.

It allows us to place ourselves in someone else's situation, although it won't be compulsory for us to be enticed by their emotions. It is not truly healthy with the definition of empathy.

Effectively, cognitive empathy is 'empathy with the aid of notion', rather than through feeling.

Emotional Empathy

Emotional empathy is when you sense the alternative man or woman's emotions together with them, as in case you had caught the feelings. Emotional empathy is likewise referred to as 'private misery' or 'emotional contagion. This is towards the usual information of the phrase 'empathy', but extra emotional. Emotional empathy is probably the primary form of empathy that many people sense as kids. It may be seen whilst a mom smiles at her baby, and the toddler catches her emotion and smiles returned. Emotional empathy can be both good and bad:

Emotional empathy is ideal because we will without problems recognize and experience other humans' emotions. This is important for the ones in worrying professions, consisting of doctors and nurses, to respond to their sufferers accurately. It also means that we can reply to buddies and others while they're distressed (Cherry, 2015). Emotional empathy is horrific, due to the fact it is possible to turn out to be beaten utilizing one's feelings, and therefore not able to reply. This is referred to as empathy overload. Those with a tendency to end up crushed want to work on their self-regulation and particularly their willpower so that they become more capable of controlling their personal feelings.

Table 1. Elements of Emotional intelligence that uses Machine Learning according to year

	2010	2011	2012	2013	2014	2015	2016	2017
Self-regulation							2	3
Empathy					1			1
Motivation	1					1		2
Social skills		2		2		1	1	3
Emotions, and sentiment	2	2		2	5	13	10	11
Self-awareness								1

Compassionate Empathy

The call, for compassionate empathy, is constant with what we commonly understand through compassion. Like sympathy, compassion is a ready feeling situation for a person, but with an additional pass in the direction of motion to reduce the trouble. Compassionate empathy is the type of empathy that is typically maximally suitable.

Generally, folks who need or require your empathy don't simply want you to understand (cognitive empathy), and they don't require you to feel their pain or, something worse or, to cry along with them (emotional empathy). Instead, they need you to recognize and sympathize with what they may be going through and help them to do so to remedy the hassle, which is compassionate empathy.

Social Skills

Social Awareness is the potential to choose up on social groups and speak properly with everyone present there. Socially aware humans tend to be excellent listeners, who can effortlessly discern what's essential to the human beings they are talking with. Social focus is an effective device that could lead you to health, thrive, and probably end up a powerful chief.

Ultimately, social focus and relationship capabilities are carefully connected. For example, while college students try to remedy a struggle between them (courting competencies), the procedure is made less complicated while both can empathize with each other (social recognition).

Social consciousness allows children to enhance their social abilities with the aid of interconnecting with people from various backgrounds. Socially conscious students can identify the assets present and take advantage of them to cope with the requirements of society (Dollmat & Abdullah, 2021).

The elements of emotional intelligence that use ML according to year can be seen in table 1. It can be seen that every year more studies are made on emotions and sentiment.

Role of Machine Learning Algorithms in Artificial Emotional Intelligence

Machine learning helps to learn from experience rather than planned. Machine learning algorithms are the finest method for us to learn and develop the tools for real-world applications. Machine learning algorithms include Supervised, supervised, slow supervised mastering and reinforcement. Supervised mastering is a type of Device gaining knowledge of where machines are skilled using "well-labelled" data and based on those records, machines predict the output. In unsupervised learning, models are not trained using data sets. (Dollmat & Abdullah, 2021) Slightly supervised mastering is a combination of supervised and supervised mastering. In this case, the label or output you want is known as a small set of training data. Strengthening learning to learn by trial and error, by working with the environment (Chowdhary et al. 2015; Chowdhary et al., 2019).

The machine's ability to predict the situation by experience by recording various facial expressions, touching and analyzing the voice of different people. In-depth gaining knowledge of algorithms is primarily based on neural networks in which linked layers of neurons are used to manner information in the same way as the human brain. Many hidden layers are the idea for deep neural networks to research information activities in the situation of work sequence.

Different types of Algorithms concerning Artificial Emotional Intelligence

Machines have been developed to complete tasks in a much quicker and simpler way compared to humans. They are capable of completing all the tasks that a human can do mentally but they are incapable of making some decisions. As they lack an important element called emotions. With the help of artificial emotional intelligence, we can make machines capable of talking about emotional decisions also. Here are some algorithms that help us in achieving this goal:

Bayesian Network

This correctly nullifies the particular unfairness of previous records and the sound impact of instance statistics. It establishes an association constraint courting among stochastic variables and in the end, accomplishes the thrust of easing the computing of conditional opportunity

This productively eliminates the influence of previous knowledge and the sound of data sample data. It creates a link between the boundaries of random variables and, as a result, makes the calculation of conditional possibilities easier. The four sample elements are represented by element nodes A, B, D, and E, while the sample category is represented by class C. node. The following formula relationships are present in all feature nodes where conditions are independently satisfied.

$$C(n) = \sum_{i=0}^{N-1} S(i) \frac{\pi n}{i} \text{---} \tag{1}$$

The integrated distribution of the flexible set of feature factor nodes above can be calculated using the Bayes theorem as follows:

$$P = P(C) \prod_{i=1}^{\pi} P(Xi \mid C) \text{---} \tag{2}$$

For the background opportunities of class node C, the Bayesian network looks for flexibility through the flexible node sets of features. The background opportunities of the node C class could be calculated using the Bayes theorem and its conditional autonomy.

Figure 2. Architecture of an HMM-based Recognizer.

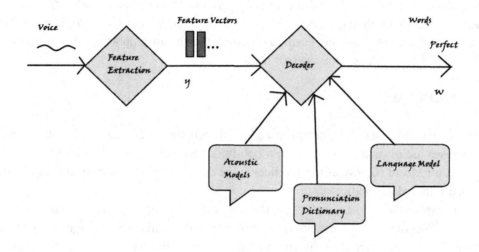

$$P(C) = \frac{P(C)}{x} \sum_{i=1}^{n} p(Xi \mid C) - \qquad (3)$$

The Bayesian Network is a simple program to build a highly efficient segmentation system to address weakly related variables. However, when input factors are linked, the self-reliant requirement of the Naive Bayesian network is violated, and the impact of segregation is poor (Weng & Lin, 2022).

It can be used for image processing by using mathematical operations. And using image processing, we can recognize the emotions of humans. As now this helps us to recognize human emotions, it makes it a little easier for the machines to make more precise decisions. (Vojković et al., 2021).

Hidden Markov Model

The HMM model is a statistical model, which is used to explain a Markov method with hidden unknown parameters. Since it is a directed graph model, it is applied in fields which include language processing and Emotion reputation. A quintuple may be used to describe a Hidden Markov Model. It comprises 2 nation units and 3 prob-capability matrices. Hidden Markov Models offer a smooth and effective framework for modelling time various spectral vector sequences. As a result of this, almost all large vocabulary continuous speech recognition (LVCSR) systems are primarily based more on Hidden Markov Model.

Whereas the vital minds underlying HMM-primarily based LVCSR are instead sincere, the simplifying assumptions and approximations concerned in direct implementation of those ideas ought to bring about a machine which has horrible accuracy and unacceptable sensitivity to modifications within the running surroundings. Hence, the practical software of HMMs in contemporary-day systems includes massive sophistication.

HMM-based speech recognition systems rely upon several assumptions: that speech signals may be properly represented through a set of spectrally derived feature vectors; that this collection can be modelled using an HMM; that the characteristic distributions can be modelled exactly; that there may be sufficient schooling information; and that the training and take a look at conditions are matched. In practice, all of these assumptions should be cosy to a degree and it's the volume to which the ensuing approximations can be minimized which determines the eventual performance (Gales & Young, 2008).

HMM-based speech recognition is a developing technology, and it has rapidly advanced commercial deployment. Its performance has already reached an extent which can support viable applications. The progress is continuous and there is a fall in error rates.

Gaussian Mixture Model

Gaussian mixture fashions are a considerably utilized set of regulations. To describe the statistics pattern distribution, it makes use of multiple Gaussian probability density distribution functions.

Gaussian Mixture Model (GMM) is used to decide the discriminatory power of the capabilities extracted from speech and glottal indicators.

In any pattern reputation package, increasing the intra class variance and decreasing the intra class variance of the attributes or talents are crucial issues to decorate the kind or recognition accuracy. Several research works can be made to bolster the discriminating potential of the extracted capabilities. The GMM has the potential in several pattern recognition applications mostly in Speech and image processing, but its feature of escalating the discriminative potential of the abilities isn't always substantially explored. Various applications of the Gaussian mixture model encourage us to signify GMM based totally on overall function enhancement. Low inter-class variance and high intra class variance of the competencies might also reduce the overall performance of classifiers, which leads to bad emotional reputation fees. GMM-based absolute clustering has been advised to lower the intra class variance and develop the Intra Class variance and complement the discriminative ability of the relative wavelet packet entropy and electricity capabilities. GMM application to labelling is initially based on the thought that each one of the data factors is generated from a finite mixture of Gaussian combination distributions and it is a probabilistic model (Muthusamy et al., 2015; Somayaji et al., 2020). The structure of GSM-based feature enhancement can be seen in figure 3.

In a model-primarily based method, positive models are utilized for clustering and seeking to optimize the fit of most of the facts and variations. Each cluster may be mathematically represented via a Gaussian (parametric) distribution.

The average emotion recognition rates are 92.79% and 84.58% using GSM based feature enhancement method, under speaker-dependent and speaker-independent experiments respectively. The findings display that the GMM-based function enhancement technique significantly complements the discriminatory power of the relative wavelet packet strength and entropy capabilities and therefore the overall performance of the speech emotion popularity machine may be more advantageous, especially within the reputation of multiclass emotions (Muthusamy et al., 2015).

Model Evaluation Criteria

In emotional popularity, a suitable estimation of the standards can be normally used to assess the efficiency of the version. In the case of Model Evaluation criteria, evolution criteria of random and uninterrupted emotion models have been introduced. When there is an uninterrupted version of emotions it makes the system even more efficient. The diagnostic precision level here gives the accuracy with which the emotions can be recognized.

Figure 3. GMM-based feature enhancement

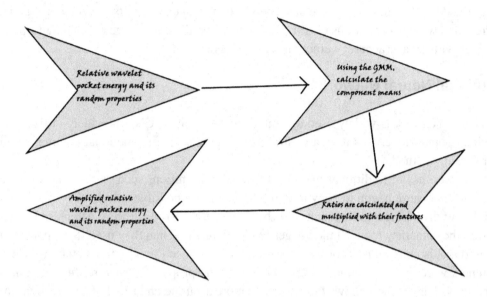

First, in a different sensory model, the test algorithm criteria are moderate to moderate memory loss and a moderate memory level, which can be determined using the techniques available:

N^i=total number of precisely recognized samples

N^t=total number of samples

$$UAR = \frac{1}{K} \sum_{i=1}^{k} \left(\frac{Nr^i}{K} \right)$$

$$WAR = \frac{1}{N} \sum_{i=1}^{k} Nr^t - \qquad (4)$$

K=total number of sample groups to be recognized

The correct recognition level, also called the average memory level, shows the perfect identification level for a particular group. However, occasionally, the precise diagnostic level is not sufficient to assess the efficiency of the algorithm. For instance, if only a sample of a particular type is recognized and the diagnosis is right, the diagnostic precision level is 100%. However, the classification method currently cannot detect other samples. As a result, researchers often use a moderate amount of weightless memory to test the performance of an algorithm (Weng & Lin, 2022).

The Pearson product-time coefficient, which can be determined using the following formula, is used as a test algorithm for the continuous sensory model.

$$C = \frac{1}{\sqrt{\sum_{i=1}^{N} Yi}} \sum_{i=1}^{N} \left(Yi - \underline{y} \right) - \qquad (5)$$

Y shows the average of the sample labels and N shows the total number of labels. The correlation coefficient is used to determine the correlation between the y and N, and its perfect and negative values indicate right and wrong correlations GMM-passively. When the percentage of the diagnostic precision level is higher with greater accuracy emotions can be recognized.

Convolutional Neural Network

As Deep Neural Network is widely used to analyze visual images, CNN is widely utilized in the picture and video popularity era, as it greatly diminishes the number of functional parameters due to the parameter sharing method.

Despite the success of traditional methods of facial recognition, such as the removal of complex features, researchers have begun to view in-depth learning as a possible solution.

CNN is in-depth facial recognition that could be trained in a few repositories. After removing the facial features from the data, they reduced the images to 48x48 pixels. Then they used the expansion method. The proposed architecture consists of two convolutional layers and two implementation-style modules.

Researchers were able to upgrade the production of the proposed structure through a network-in-network process. This method allows them to make more accurate and timely facial recognition.

Focused on the effect of pre-operated information on organizational adjustment to create a higher sense of order, Increased information, pivot adjustment, editing, 32x32 pixel dynamics and power suspension are the pre-CNN methods, which include two two-way convolution integration layers as shown in figure 4, that are fully integrated with 256 and 7 neurons. The ideal weight obtained in the preparation phase is used in the test phase. This experience was tested on three open-source platforms: CK +, JAFFE, and BU-3DFE. Scientists have shown that combining these previous management measures is far more powerful than implementing them independently. These previous management procedures were also developed. They proposed a clever CNN to identify AU facials. The organization uses two conversion layers, each followed by a high-end combination and finished with two fully integrated layers that reflect the established AU values.

The average maximum emotion recognition rate is 85% with convolutional neural networks. In the future, the efficiency rate can be improved by adding more face expression categories (Badrulhisham & Mangshor, 2021).

K- Nearest Neighbor Classifier

KNN is the simplest algorithm and it's completely constructed on the Supervised Learning technique. It checks the similarity between the already existing data and new data. Then it categories it and puts in a similar block concerning the previous cases. It stores the previous data, as a result of which it becomes easier to classify the newly imputed data. This algorithm does not make any assumptions; it makes reasonable decisions based on the data available. It is strong with noise training data.

KNN classifier is a form of initial-primarily grounded classifiers and spectaculars an appropriate magnificence tag for the brand's latest test vector employing the unrevealed test vector to acknowledge teaching vectors in agreement to a long way/alikeness function. Euclidean distance function turned into used and suitable fee was observed with the aid of looking for a value between 1 and 20 (Muthusamy et al., 2015). Under speaker-dependent and speaker-independent experiments, the maximum average recognition rates of K-NN classifiers are 59.14% and 49.12% respectively (Weng & Lin, 2022).

Figure 4. Structure of CNN Model

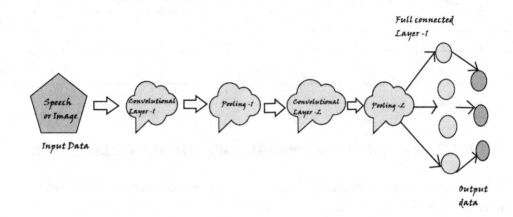

Support Vector Machines

Support vector machines (SVMs) are being used by an expanding number in perceptual science as a records-pushed type technique and function depletion approach. Whereas conventional statistical techniques usually compare group averages on selected variables, SVMs use a predictive algorithm to research multivariate patterns that optimally discriminate between businesses. Speech Emotion identification is the system of studying human feelings. People can identify their emotions with each other precisely. A support vector device (SVM) is one of the excellent algorithms for identifying and managing voice statistics.

Along with voice identification SVM also can identify facial expressions. It works along with the KNN. They identify the emotions and classify them accordingly. The KNN has previously stored data and they classify the new set of data into a similar category based on the previously stored data. With the help of this, SVM has a great capability to identify human emotions and make precise decisions.

COMPARISON OF ALGORITHMS CONCERNING EFFICIENCY

The 4 emotion capabilities of happiness, sadness, shock, and anger extracted from the artificial intelligence statistics gadget have been compared, and simulated experiments of single-mode and multimode emotion recognition algorithms have been finished. The research conclusions drawn show that the multimodal emotion recognition set of guidelines has a higher popularity impact than the single-modal emotion reputation for the emotional abilities in the artificial intelligence statistics system (Dollmat & Abdullah, 2021).

Table 2 shows the number of studies of each EI component that utilize machine learning according to year. It can be seen that the development of support vector machines is increasing from year to year.

Table 2. Machine learning implementation in different algorithms according to year

	2011	**2012**	**2013**	**2014**	**2015**	**2016**	**2017**	**2018**
K-NN				2	3	3	3	1
ELM					2			
Deep learning							1	2
SVM	1		1	3	8	7	6	8

RECENT DEVELOPMENTS IN ARTIFICIAL EMOTIONAL INTELLIGENCE

Recent advances in Emotional Artificial Intelligence seem to be very useful and helpful in predicting certain adverse events in advance. These uses include:

Human Machine Interaction

To have proper interaction between people and machines there is a need for an interface. We can consider the cases where a user interacts with the machine, turning the steering wheel, when we turn on/off the switch, etc. The same activities can be carried out without the requirement of manual function by using our gestures, mouse, using our mobile, touch screens or voice. The traffic lights automatically change their color when the car passes by using sensors. All the systems have been developed. For example, the chat boxes reply automatically to the questions asked by the customers and that way they keep learning. Voice assistants like Alexa and Google Assistant also have a great impact. (Erol et al., 2021) There is no requirement for touch also; all we need is to give the required commands through our voice. Although they are not perfect, they seem to be efficient in comparison with the current situation. Robots can understand the situation by reading, writing and observing speech and responding appropriately.

Automatic Driving

A fully automated driving system was introduced when we were empowered by a safe ride to our destination without human involvement. Artificial emotional intelligence provides a significant contribution to the sector of automatic driving. Though it has to face some challenges like interacting with multiple sensors and also keeping a correct track of the real-time data it still seems to be working great. The main places where AI plays an important role are in sensor data processing, planning the path, execution of path, frequently checking the vehicle's condition along with collecting information regarding the insurance. A deep neural network is shown in figure 5, in real-time; the number of layers and nodes are used in higher numbers.

Quantum AI

Quantum computing is a widely developing field of computer science (Kitchen & Drexel, 2021). It includes the amazing dynamics of quantum physics and the properties of the universe's smallest particles, to make computers have more new capabilities. The physics within the return of quantum computing

Figure 5. Deep Neural Networks

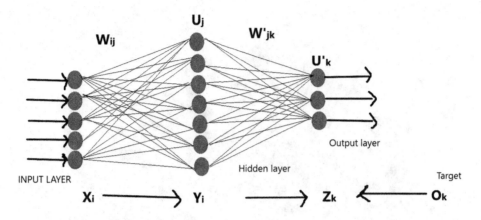

is complex, allowing quantum laptop systems to save and interpret statistics in dynamic "qubits" in the area of the "bits" of traditional computer systems. Bits can be considered as simple binary ones or zeros, which perform computer processing when millions of them are strung together. Whereas qubits are more versatile which even include negative values and can represent a broad range of varying levels (Kitchen & Drexel, 2021). Quantum computers operate faster than the human brain, computers in the first place. It can resolve impossible cases as well.

AI Conversations

Environmental AI seems to provide better and more satisfying customer service when the system tries to adapt to the human environment and perform appropriately. AI conservation can be referred to as the implementation of AI for the conservation of natural resources and wildlife, which can be seen in figure 6.

FUTURE DEVELOPMENTS IN ARTIFICIAL EMOTIONAL INTELLIGENCE:

As shown in figure 7, Future developments in artificial emotional intelligence include staff safety, medical diagnosis, fraud detection, connected home, driving safety, community services, smart Call center, video Games, Education and autonomous vehicles (Prentice et al., 2020),

Emotional Artificial Intelligence have the potential to detect employees' anxiety and stress. The emotions of a single person can have a great impact on that of the whole group, with the help of artificial emotional intelligence we will be able to read the gestures of the employee beforehand and provide a solution for it before the situation gets worse. Learning software prototypes had been evolved to match children's feelings. When a child gets frustrated because the project is just too difficult or too clean, the device adapts to the undertaking, so it'll be tougher. This helps in maintaining a balance among the children's emotions. According to an independent survey, about 30% of users admitted to lying to their vehicle insurance enterprise, so that it will get assistance. With the help of AI's ability to implement some rules and find out the suspicious activities going on, we can identify if the insurance claim is fair or not.

Figure 6. AI conservation (Raslin Saluja, June 21, 2021)

In this case with voice statistics, we can find out what the client's status is and respond appropriately. If a customer is angry, the transformation and height of the system are adjusted in such a way that it silences the customer. This develops a system where it's like a causal interaction between two humans. With experience, the machines learn more about emotions and act accordingly. With the help of computer vision, the system looks at the player's emotions and adapts them accordingly. The future of AI in video games could factor to automation and generated textual content; the AI-generated video games now checking out the fringes of modern-day gaming technology additionally spotlight their limits. It helps physicians to identify levels of anxiety and stress in patients. Doctor-patient relationships can be improved because of improved communication (Wilson & Djamasbi, 2015). It helps doctors in understanding the patient's emotions about treatment and can result in higher levels of patient satisfaction.

It can analyze the nature of the speaker and respond appropriately. When smart homes have an emotional artificial intelligence detector, they can understand the mood of the speaker and react accordingly.

This was introduced by the Department of Recreation to monitor the overall human condition with surveillance cameras. This will help in understanding the state of people. Car manufacturers can use a computerized monitoring system to track the emotional state of drivers. Excessive emotional state or drowsiness may result in warning the driver. The emotionality feature of AI was regarded as the strongest predictor of dangerous driving behaviours. It was concluded that the people with high EI scores were having less dangerous driving behaviour, leading to fewer accidents and fatalities. Shortly, the interior of autonomous vehicles will be equipped with various sensors, such as microphones and cameras that will

Figure 7. Future developments in AEI

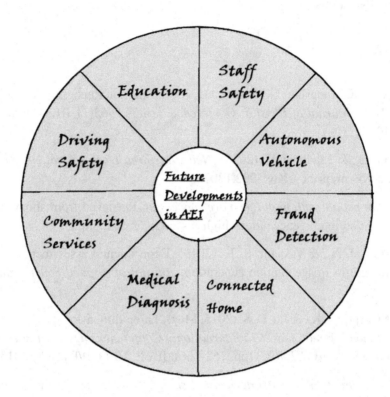

monitor the situation and determine how drivers perceive the driving experience. The cameras installed help AI in detecting the emotion of the driver and passenger and help in making the roads much safer.

CONCLUSION

Emotions play a position in organizational existence. Understanding those feelings facilitates people to control them. Emotional labor is difficult for people, whilst emotional intelligence may help people address the emotional demands in their jobs. Emotion recognition is significant for machine learning and artificial intelligence. Further developments in emotion recognition will make machines able to understand how people feel, which the first step to fulfill our needs is.

The use of Emotional Artificial Intelligence gives a far greater profound view of how machines can assist people in comparison to the traditional ways of AI these days. Traditional AI uses good judgment and performance to resolve and master answers in small quantities of time on a particular subject of interest, including dealing with mathematical calculations in medical fields. If we implement Emotional Intelligence in AI, the generation can grow into new regions of research. Many regions may be exposed like: Healthcare, Education, Consultation, and even Construction. All of the fields use emotional bias to construct stability for folks that are handling emotional troubles. We have discussed multimodal emotion recognition algorithms in this paper because they give higher efficiency than single modal emotion recognition algorithms. So, we hope to make further contributions to the development of multimodal emotion recognition algorithms.

REFERENCES

Badrulhisham, N. A. S., & Mangshor, N. N. A. (2021, July). Emotion Recognition Using Convolutional Neural Network (CNN). *Journal of Physics: Conference Series, 1962*(1), 012040. doi:10.1088/1742-6596/1962/1/012040

Cekic, M., Bakiskan, C., & Madhow, U. (2022). *Neuro-Inspired Deep Neural Networks with Sparse, Strong Activations.* arXiv preprint arXiv:2202.13074.

Cherry, K. (2015). *Are people with high IQs more successful.* Retrieved from about education: http://psychology. about. com/od/intelligence/a/does-high-iq-equal-success. htm

Chowdhary, C. L., Goyal, A., & Vasnani, B. K. (2019). Experimental assessment of beam search algorithm for improvement in image caption generation. *Journal of Applied Science and Engineering, 22*(4), 691–698.

Chowdhary, C. L., Muatjitjeja, K., & Jat, D. S. (2015, May). Three-dimensional object recognition based intelligence system for identification. In *2015 International Conference on Emerging Trends in Networks and Computer Communications (ETNCC)* (pp. 162-166). IEEE. 10.1109/ETNCC.2015.7184827

Davy, A. (2003). *Components of a smart device and smart device interactions.* Telecommunications Software and Systems Group.

Dollmat, K. S., & Abdullah, N. A. (2022). Machine learning in emotional intelligence studies: A survey. *Behaviour & Information Technology, 41*(7), 1485–1502. doi:10.1080/0144929X.2021.1877356

Erol, B. A., Majumdar, A., Benavidez, P., Rad, P., Choo, K. K. R., & Jamshidi, M. (2019). Toward artificial emotional intelligence for cooperative social human–machine interaction. *IEEE Transactions on Computational Social Systems, 7*(1), 234–246. doi:10.1109/TCSS.2019.2922593

Gales, M., & Young, S. (2008). The application of hidden Markov models in speech recognition. *Foundations and Trends® in Signal Processing, 1*(3), 195-304.

Gillis, A. S. (2020). What is iot (internet of things) and how does it work? *IoT Agenda, TechTarget, 11*.

Kitchen, K., & Drexel, B. (2021). *Quantum computing: A national security primer.* Academic Press.

Mattingly, V., & Kraiger, K. (2019). Can emotional intelligence be trained? A meta-analytical investigation. *Human Resource Management Review, 29*(2), 140–155. doi:10.1016/j.hrmr.2018.03.002

Mayer, J. D., Caruso, D. R., & Salovey, P. (2016). The ability model of emotional intelligence: Principles and updates. *Emotion Review, 8*(4), 290–300. doi:10.1177/1754073916639667

Muthusamy, H., Polat, K., & Yaacob, S. (2015). Improved emotion recognition using gaussian mixture model and extreme learning machine in speech and glottal signals. *Mathematical Problems in Engineering, 2015*, 2015. doi:10.1155/2015/394083

Newell, A., Shaw, J. C., & Simon, H. A. (1956). *Problem solving in humans and computers*. Rand Corp.

Prentice, C., Dominique Lopes, S., & Wang, X. (2020). Emotional intelligence or artificial intelligence–an employee perspective. *Journal of Hospitality Marketing & Management, 29*(4), 377–403. doi:10.10 80/19368623.2019.1647124

Rajaraman, V. (2014). John McCarthy—Father of artificial intelligence. *Resonance, 19*(3), 198–207. doi:10.100712045-014-0027-9

Saluja, R. (2021). *Steps taken by developed nations to protect the wildlife*. KIIT School of Law.

Samantaray, S., Deotale, R., & Chowdhary, C. L. (2021). Lane detection using sliding window for intelligent ground vehicle challenge. In *Innovative Data Communication Technologies and Application* (pp. 871–881). Springer. doi:10.1007/978-981-15-9651-3_70

Singer, T., & Klimecki, O. M. (2014). Empathy and compassion. *Current Biology, 24*(18), R875–R878. doi:10.1016/j.cub.2014.06.054 PMID:25247366

Singh, C., Kumar, A., Nagar, A., Tripathi, S., & Yenigalla, P. (2019, December). Emoception: An inception inspired efficient speech emotion recognition network. In *2019 IEEE Automatic Speech Recognition and Understanding Workshop (ASRU)* (pp. 787-791). IEEE. 10.1109/ASRU46091.2019.9004020

Somayaji, S. R. K., Alazab, M., Manoj, M. K., Bucchiarone, A., Chowdhary, C. L., & Gadekallu, T. R. (2020, December). A framework for prediction and storage of battery life in iot devices using dnn and blockchain. In *2020 IEEE Globecom Workshops (GC Wkshps)* (pp. 1-6). IEEE.

Vojković, L., Kuzmanić Skelin, A., Mohovic, D., & Zec, D. (2021). The Development of a Bayesian Network Framework with Model Validation for Maritime Accident Risk Factor Assessment. *Applied Sciences (Basel, Switzerland), 11*(22), 10866. doi:10.3390/app112210866

Weng, Y., & Lin, F. (2022). Multimodal Emotion Recognition Algorithm for Artificial Intelligence Information System. *Wireless Communications and Mobile Computing, 2022*, 2022. doi:10.1155/2022/9236238

Wilson, V., & Djamasbi, S. (2015). Human-computer interaction in health and wellness: Research and publication opportunities. *AIS Transactions on Human-Computer Interaction, 7*(3), 97–108. doi:10.17705/1thci.00067

Chapter 5
Role of Emotional Intelligence in Agile Supply Chains

Akshat Mishra
Vellore Institute of Technology, India

Swetank Kaushik
Vellore Institute of Technology, India

Srinivasa Perumal R.
Vellore Institute of Technology, Chennai, India

Chiranji Lal Chowdhary
https://orcid.org/0000-0002-5476-1468
Vellore Institute of Technology, India

ABSTRACT

The notion of agile supply chains is gaining traction in academia and has been enthusiastically adopted by private corporations. A variety of factors differentiate agile supply networks. They should not only be network-based but also market-sensitive, with tightly linked virtual and crucial operations. If agile supply chains are to adapt for ever-faster turnaround time towards both volume and variety changes, they must integrate supply and demand. The agile supply chain must be able to swiftly modify the output to satisfy customer needs and move from one version to the next. Of course, information technology is essential to the smooth running of agile teams. However, this chapter will focus on two additional essential facilitators of supply chains. Agility, which has gotten less emphasis yet is vital to the success of these kinds of procedures, has gotten less attention.

INTRODUCTION

The agile supply chain (Oliveira-Dias et al., 2022) necessitates that all businesses place a high value on so-called "personal qualities." Technical competence and intellect (IQ) alone may not ensure success, and in the battle to be quick, they may just be one qualifying element rather than the winning factor (Razmak

DOI: 10.4018/978-1-6684-5673-6.ch005

et al., 2022). The organization's emotional intelligence (EQ) is crucial in facilitating agility (Ma et al., 2022). The needs for these high-level talents are highlighted in our preliminary study.

An individual's emotional intelligence (EQ) is divided into five categories:

- Self-awareness is the ability to recognise one's own internal states, preferences, resources, and intuitions (Klussman et al., 2022). This includes the capacity to recognise one's emotions and the repercussions of those emotions, as well as understanding one's talents and limits and having a strong feeling of self-worth and potential.
- Self-control is the ability to control one's internal states, urges, and resources (Tang et al., 2022). This necessitates controlling disruptive impulses and emotions, upholding a high level of honesty and integrity, accepting responsibility for one's own performance, being adaptable to change, and being at ease with creative, inventive ideas, methods, and new information.
- Motivation of emotional inclinations that lead or assist in the achievement of objectives (Hur et al., 2022) This necessitates the abilities of always seeking to improve or meet a level of excellence, aligning with the group or organization's goals, being ready to act on opportunities, and persevering in pursuing goals despite hurdles and disappointments.
- Empathy is the ability to understand and empathise with the feelings, needs, and problems of another (Alzayed et al., 2022). This necessitates the ability to sense others' feelings and perspectives, as well as taking an active interest in their concerns; the ability to sense others' development needs and coach their abilities; the ability to anticipate, recognise, and meet customer needs; the ability to cultivate opportunities through various types of people; and the political awareness of reading a group's emotional currents and power relationships.
- The social skills are the ability to elicit desired reactions from others (Teglasi et al., 2022). This necessitates persuasion skills, such as the ability to listen openly and send persuasion messages; conflict management skills, such as the ability to negotiate and resolve disagreements; the ability to inspire and guide individuals and groups; the ability to initiate and manage change; and team capabilities, such as the ability to create group synergy in pursuing collective goals.

The preliminary outcomes of agility study (Sharma et al., 2022) support the requirement for the aforementioned abilities. Social skills, empathy, and drive are all important when developing a network. The requirement to be 'virtual' necessitates employees developing all five areas in order to sustain relationships that are critical to their existence. Market awareness necessitates a high level of client empathy. Process integration necessitates the development of all five areas.

A new poll conducted by the Society of Human Resource Management emphasises the importance of emotional intelligence in attaining a competitive edge. The survey looked at a group of top organisations that were chosen based on their profitability, cycle times, volume, and other important performance indicators (Schlaegel et al., 2022).

They discovered that the best organisations have the following skills in managing their "people assets":

- Organizational conviction in and adherence to core strategy.
- Establishing open lines of communication and creating trust with all internal and external stakeholders.
- A desire to create ties both inside and outside the company where they might provide a competitive advantage.

- Resource sharing, collaboration, and assistance.
- An environment that encourages risk-taking and collaborative learning.
- A desire to compete and develop on a regular basis.

These difficulties are easy to map into the five emotional intelligence abilities listed above, and they're essential for the creation of an agile supply chain (Najar, 2022).

We organize the rest of the chapter as follows. In next Section, we present the fundamentals and motivation of emotional intelligence in agile supply chain. We discuss background of emotional intelligence and agile supply chain in the Literature Survey Section. Now, we followed the method and materials in next Section. In next Section, we cover core applications with figures and their explanations. Some use cases discussed in a Section. Next Section considers the Challenges and future scopes of research. Finally in the last Section, we draw conclusions of this Chapter.

FUNDAMENTALS AND MOTIVATIONS

Leading firms have realised that the only way to acquire a competitive advantage is to use time compression in supply chain process design and operation. Companies must deliver more value for less money in less time in order to thrive, i.e. raise the proportion of time spent "adding value" in the whole supply chain process.

A supply chain's goal is to provide value to customers at a cheaper cost than the competition. A combination of concrete and intangible benefits, specific product features, as well as image, reputation, and responsiveness, make up value. Customers don't buy products; they buy benefits, as the old marketing saying goes. Customers' perceptions of value are getting increasingly influenced by the passage of time. It is also possible to highlight the role of time in cost reduction. As a result, time compression improves both sides of the equation's competitive advantage. Specifically, by lowering costs and gaining a competitive advantage.

Within organisations, focusing on time enhances responsiveness and agility. One of the key advantages is greater visibility into supply chain processes, which allows for improvements. However, using common tools and procedures to complete a successful time compression project in the supply chain does not guarantee success. Soft skills are essential to obtain access to knowledge and, as a result, to manage change, which necessitates the use of emotional intelligence.

Literature Survey

Several research works on emotional intelligence, agility, lean, and supply chain management are discussed in this section.

This research investigates the relationship of ambidextrous, agile, and lean supply chains to supply chain performance while examining the moderating effect of inter-island logistics. A theoretical design was developed to study the above relationship. As an initial analysis, hypotheses were tested with data from 34 manufacturing firms in Indonesia, using SmartPLS with 500 bootstrap samples. This research contributes to the supply chain management literature in three ways. First, it found that an agile supply chain mediates ambidextrous and lean supply chains to improve supply chain performance. Second, inter-island logistics, however, negatively moderates the relationship between an agile supply chain and supply chain performance. Finally, it strengthens the conceptual definition of the relationship between ambidextrous, lean, agile supply chains and supply chain performance (Alamsjah and Asrol, 2021).

Jianhua et al. (2009) studied the static scheduling problems of definite market demands with time constraints in agile supply chains, which consist of multi-stage members with limited capacities. They have also established a framework model to picture the supply chain's structure and an integer nonlinear programming (INLP) model to describe the scheduling problem. Then they have designed a two-step algorithm with lower complexity to resolve the INLP model. 1) the shortest response time scheduling algorithm to judge whether the supply chain can meet the demands' time constraints, 2) the lean scheduling algorithm to abstain the minimum inventory cost of the supply chain. Finally, they have also verified the practicality and effectiveness of the model and algorithms by a numeric experiment.

One of the features of agile supply chains is their organic combination of batch production mode and customization production mode. Aimed at this feature, components and parts of products can be divided into general parts which are made according to batch production and diversity parts according to customization production. And different inventory control strategies can be adopted corresponding to these two kinds of production modes. Moreover, the production activities of general parts present comparatively stronger continuity, and the production activities of diversity parts and the distributing and transporting of both kinds of parts present some discreteness. Therefore, agile supply chain systems can be considered as dynamic systems mixed with continuous variables and discrete ones. Based on above consideration, Hybrid Petri Net is used to model and simulate an agile supply chain hybrid dynamic system. The results of the simulation indicate that Hybrid Petri Net can effectively describe the dynamic characteristics of agile supply chain systems (Wang and Fu, 2007).

Emotional intelligence (EI) is a collection of quasi skills, attitudes, and talents that influence one's ability to respond quickly to environmental changes and stresses. Nevertheless, it is not always possible to monitor the effect of a multitude of variables involved in behavioural phenomena. In several different industries, Emotion Perception or Artificial Emotional Intelligence is now a $20 billion research area with applications. In a variety of ways, artificial emotional intelligence can operate through industries. Emotional readings may also be used by AI as relating to decision, such as in advertising campaigns. In terms of temporal dynamics, a powerful learning method is required to extract high-level representations of emotional responses. In terms of spatial dispersion, a learning process strategy is required to extract high-level assessment of emotional states. The recurrent neural network outperforms linear models in terms of prediction accuracy. A recurrent model is proposed in this paper to forecast the pattern between the variables of age, gender, occupation, marital status, and education in order to predict the EI. The appropriate recurrent model is capable of predicting EI with important correlations in most of its dimensions and could demonstrate the advantage over regression models in predicting EI using sociological parameters. This model will estimate the level of EI in the various occupational, professional, gender and age groups and provide a planning basis for addressing possible deficiencies in each group (Prabha et al., 2022).

Singh et al. (2021) attempt to rediscover the effect of emotional intelligence on stress through different algorithms designed through machine learning. The paper gives us food for thought on how Machine Learning can be used by HR professionals to predict the emotional quotient and thereby stress of all employees at the time of their induction into the organization, promotions, etc. This will tremendously save time, money, and effort. This significantly helps in building competitive human capital.

Sadri et al. (2021) uses a Blockchain Ethereum platform as a solution to leverage traceability in the blood donation supply chain (BDSC). Blockchain is a highly efficient, decentralized, and peer-to-peer distributed technology deploys to provide end-to-end traceability, safety, immutability, and security in the BDSC ecosystem. As a part of this study, a role-based smart contract solution is used to define the access per each role, which therefore assists to ensure traceability and security of information in the BDSC ecosystem.

The supply chain is a new business model for supply chain planning and transportation management with the goal of increasing supply chain flexibility. In his chapter, Chowdhary (2022) explains the framework of digitalization in agile supply chain management.

Methods and Materials

The need for improvement in time-based resource management is becoming more widely recognised inside enterprises. According to research, the time spent really 'adding value' within a manufacturing setting can be as little as 5% of the total process time, and in the context of the entire supply chain, things can be even worse - 'adding value' time has been found to be as little as one tenth of 1%. It's crucial to know what time compression isn't before you can appreciate what it can do for your competitive position:

- Time compression is not based on historical observation, work-study, or human performance measurement, and the associated old ways of working to the old business process.
- Time compression does not imply that individuals should work quicker at the expense of quality, safety, or their livelihood.

Instead, time compression is the process of eliminating waste time in the workplace, which leads to higher customer satisfaction, lower inventory levels, and better quality (see Bearings case study). People are working smarter rather than harder. Change management, business process reengineering, and comprehensive quality management programmes can all benefit from time compression. These are programmes that must address difficulties that are unique to a company's situation. The concept of 'time compression' complements and necessitates the existence and operation of these programmes in a way that fully uses the time-based approach.

It has been discovered that by concentrating on time in the supply chain, cost difficulties tend to disappear. Time is a unit of measurement shared by all supply chain partners, whereas cost and transfer price data can be interpreted in a variety of ways. In contrast to activity-based costing methodologies, which are commonly employed in supply chain analysis, focusing on time allows one to see "the forest rather than the branches." The study is also faster and more successful than a standard cost-based analysis, taking only around 20% of the time and resources. Analysis is pushed to a physical level by focusing on time. The time focus has proven to be easy to execute and provides quick effects.

Three criteria are used to define value-adding time:

- Whether the procedure (or aspects of the process) alters the nature of the consumable item (i.e., the customer's product).
- Whether the change to the consumable item results in something that the customer appreciates or cares about enough to pay for.
- Whether the process is correct the first time and will not need to be repeated to achieve the desired result that the client values.

Figure 1. Example for an Emotion Perceiving network

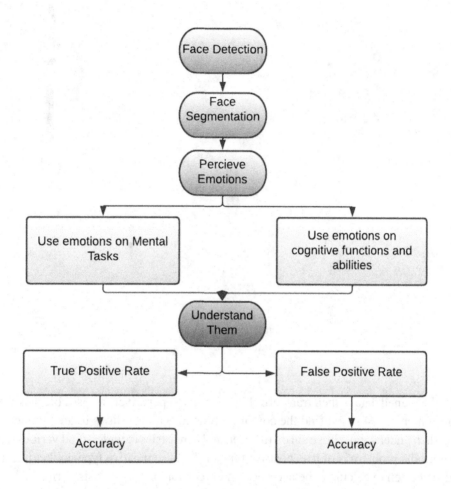

Queuing time, rework time, and time spent due to managerial indecision are the three types of non-value adding activities. One does not need to be concerned about the correct application of the definitions because, in most cases, 95 percentage of the time is lost, and thus there is plenty of room for improvement! The value-adding and non-value-adding operations can be visualised using a time-based process map.

Core Applications

The proposed procedure is for an emotion/mental task detection and analyser using deep neural networks along with facial description of the employees.

Here in the diagram, we can see that the model functions by firstly performing the Face Detection, hence perceiving only facial features and discarding various environmental factors.

Then the proposed diagram performs the task of Face Segmentation to segment various parts of the face for further analysis by forming contours and detecting facial reactions.

Figure 2. Face and Environment analysis through image data by passing it to a RPN network and ROI pool.

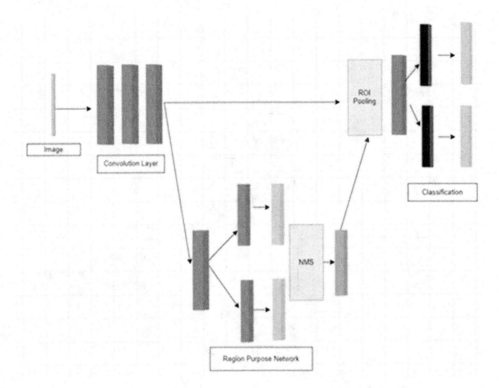

After that, the gained data is then transferred to an emotion perceiver, whose sole task is to use emotions to identify mental tasks, and find the cognition functions and abilities related to them.

The model then understands the strain on the user, and hence tries to understand various reaction types to detect weather the problem is of true positive type or the false positive type, and at last it produces a probability distribution to calculate the accuracy and precision of the analysis performed.

Figure shows the face detection (object detection) using Region Proposal Networks has shown to be more promising than face segmentation.

Face segmentation works by determining if each pixel in an image is part of a face. Face segmentation is accomplished by hand-crafted post processing (i.e., we determine how to do it rather than learning how to do it) to distinguish regions (rather than pixels) of faces. Trained the network to find the exact region of the face using Region Proposal Networks. Query the model to locate the face using several overlapping regions in the picture, and then combine the answers to locate faces in a more defined way.

The data from the region purpose network is then again passed to ROI along with the augmented data generated from the Convolution Layer. After that a pooling layer could be proposed which will then help in identification of the useful features from the feature map generated by RPN and CNN, then using this pooled data we can perform classification into relevant emotions by passing it into a DenseNet.

The proposed High-Level Design specifies how an emotional intelligence model could be developed for management of time-sensitive supply chain tasks.

The main components revolve around data extraction and generation of a learning model based around Emotional Competency of human factors. And therefore, reduce the time-consuming load from the manual analysis.

Figure 3. Suggestion for Emotional Intelligence system to optimize supply chains

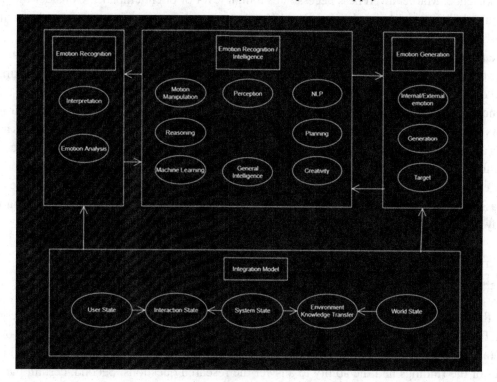

The proposed procedure constitutes of 4 modules:

1. Integration Model: This module basically perceives the user state, his actions and the way how they affect the environment, then it extracts relevant information and then passes it to the emotion generation and recognition modules.
2. Emotion Recognition: Main task of this module is to find out which actions, what kind of data and which results qualify as Emotions vectors to perform analysis upon, this module consults with the emotion recognition and intelligence module to verify the activity recognized.
3. Emotion Recognition/Intelligence: This module basically performs all heavy-lifting for the proposed methodology, it constitutes of Perception, motion manipulation, natural language processing, reasoning and planning engine, Then the Machine learning and intelligence modules to understand and develop learning models for the perceived tasks.
4. Emotion Generation: This module analyses the external factors then generate test cases for the recognized emotions, which are then further used to factor between internal and external emotions.

USE CASES

The preliminary outcomes of agility research support the need for the aforementioned abilities. Social skills, empathy, and motivation are all important when developing a network. The requirement to be 'virtual' necessitates workers developing all five areas in order to sustain relationships that are critical to their existence. Market awareness necessitates a high level of client empathy. Consider the political skills required for a supplier in-plant' at Bose! Process integration necessitates the development of all five areas.

An example of the value of EQ in comparison to IQ: A woman working at Cranfield was summoned to a software consulting firm that was losing a significant amount of business to another firm. There was little doubt that their products were technically superior, and that their staff have great technical competence and IQ. These technically brilliant persons, however, were discovered to have a low EQ ability. As a result, they were unable to effectively network and create connections with clients and suppliers. As a result, the company was underperforming. The good news is that EQ abilities can be learned.

A number of presenters at a recent Cranfield conference on agility emphasised the importance of EQ as a vital enabler for agility. "To remain competitive (agile and responsive), KJS will continue to focus on the basics...getting the best people, integrating planning, enabling technology, and avoiding waste," said Andy Richardson, UK Supply Chain Director of Kraft Jacobs Suchard.

CHALLENGES AND FUTURE DIRECTIONS

Through this study we have identified certain limitations that can be transformed into the future scope of research. First, the constrained time frame of the project restrained the researcher in collection of a large set of data both from the literature surveys and model comparisons. This constrained a certain degree of quality of the findings and the ability to answer the research questions. Second, certain parameters that influenced the interaction such as focality of the organization, time frame of relation, power, and monetary benefits between an interaction weren't considered. Future scope of the research can include a large sample size, and the influential parameters to provide interesting results. This would provide empirical evidence if one parameter superseded the other one and would signify the relation between them. Another interesting recommendation for future research would be to study the emotional intelligence of a set of supply chain professionals over a period of time and monitor their interaction levels with their buyers/suppliers to gauge their management performance levels.

CONCLUSION

Time compression and emotional intelligence are being viewed as crucial facilitators when the agile supply chain idea is developed and implemented in organisations. Of course, information systems are a critical component of any agile supply chain, but visibility of essential operations must first be gained before they can be properly applied. This necessitates the use of time compression techniques and a high level of emotional intelligence on the part of individuals involved in the project.

Increased agility will undoubtedly be crucial for all organisations in the future. Cranfield School of Management is building an Agile Supply Chain Research Centre in response to this. The goal of this centre is to identify the supply chain enablers and inhibitors, establish the important components of agile strategies, create a workable template for agility, and promote agile best practise across all industry sectors. Additional industrial partners are now being sought for this study.

REFERENCES

Alamsjah, F., & Asrol, M. (2021, December). Inter-island Logistics and the Role of an Agile Supply Chain to Achieve Supply Chain Performance: Initial Findings. In *2021 IEEE International Conference on Industrial Engineering and Engineering Management (IEEM)* (pp. 270-274). IEEE. 10.1109/IEEM50564.2021.9672866

Alzayed, M. A., Miller, S. R., & McComb, C. (2022). Does Empathy Beget Creativity? Investigating the Role of Trait Empathy in Idea Generation and Selection. In *Design Computing and Cognition'20* (pp. 437–454). Springer. doi:10.1007/978-3-030-90625-2_26

Chowdhary, C. L. (2022). Agile Supply Chain: Framework for Digitization. In *Innovative Supply Chain Management via Digitalization and Artificial Intelligence* (pp. 73–85). Springer. doi:10.1007/978-981-19-0240-6_5

Hur, W. M., Shin, Y., & Moon, T. W. (2022). Linking motivation, emotional labor, and service performance from a self-determination perspective. *Journal of Service Research*, 25(2), 227–241. doi:10.1177/1094670520975204

Jianhua, W., Nan, L., & Hui, G. (2009, October). Static Scheduling Model and Algorithms of Agile Supply Chain Under Definite Demands. In *2009 Second International Conference on Intelligent Computation Technology and Automation* (Vol. 3, pp. 984-987). IEEE. 10.1109/ICICTA.2009.703

Klussman, K., Curtin, N., Langer, J., & Nichols, A. L. (2022). The importance of awareness, acceptance, and alignment with the self: A framework for understanding self-connection. *Europe's Journal of Psychology*, 18(1), 120–131. doi:10.5964/ejop.3707 PMID:35330854

Ma, J., Zeng, Z., & Fang, K. (2022). Emotionally savvy employees fail to enact emotional intelligence when ostracized. *Personality and Individual Differences*, 185, 111250. doi:10.1016/j.paid.2021.111250

Najar, T. (2022, January). Lean-Agile supply chain innovation performance; the mediating role of dynamic capability, innovation capacity, and relational embeddednes. In *Supply Chain Forum: An International Journal* (pp. 1-22). Taylor & Francis.

Oliveira-Dias, D., Maqueira, J. M., & Moyano-Fuentes, J. (2022). The link between information and digital technologies of industry 4.0 and agile supply chain: Mapping current research and establishing new research avenues. *Computers & Industrial Engineering*, 167, 108000. doi:10.1016/j.cie.2022.108000

Prabha, R., Anandan, P., Sivarajeswari, S., Saravanakumar, C., & Babu, D. V. (2022, January). Design of an Automated Recurrent Neural Network for Emotional Intelligence Using Deep Neural Networks. In *2022 4th International Conference on Smart Systems and Inventive Technology (ICSSIT)* (pp. 1061-1067). IEEE. 10.1109/ICSSIT53264.2022.9716420

Razmak, J., Pitzel, J. W., Belanger, C., & Farhan, W. (2022). Brushing up on time-honored sales skills to excel in tomorrow's environment. *Journal of Business & Industrial Marketing*, ahead-of-print.

Sadri, S., Shahzad, A., & Zhang, K. (2021, February). Blockchain traceability in healthcare: Blood donation supply chain. In *2021 23rd International Conference on Advanced Communication Technology (ICACT)* (pp. 119-126). IEEE.

Schlaegel, C., Engle, R. L., & Lang, G. (2022). The unique and common effects of emotional intelligence dimensions on job satisfaction and facets of job performance: An exploratory study in three countries. *International Journal of Human Resource Management*, *33*(8), 1562–1605. doi:10.1080/09585192.2020.1811368

Sharma, S., Oberoi, J. S., Gupta, R. D., Saini, S., Gupta, A. K., & Sharma, N. (2022). Effect of agility in different dimensions of manufacturing systems: A review. *Materials Today: Proceedings*, *63*, 264–267. doi:10.1016/j.matpr.2022.03.054

Singh, S., Sharma, C., Sharma, S., & Verma, N. K. (2021, September). Re-Learning Emotional Intelligence through Artificial Intelligence. In *2021 9th International Conference on Reliability, Infocom Technologies and Optimization (Trends and Future Directions) (ICRITO)* (pp. 1-5). IEEE. 10.1109/ICRITO51393.2021.9596091

Tang, Y. Y., Tang, R., Posner, M. I., & Gross, J. J. (2022). Effortless training of attention and self-control: Mechanisms and applications. *Trends in Cognitive Sciences*, *26*(7), 567–577. doi:10.1016/j.tics.2022.04.006 PMID:35537920

Teglasi, H., Caputo, M. H., & Scott, A. L. (2022). Explicit and implicit theory of mind and social competence: A social information processing framework. *New Ideas in Psychology*, *64*, 100915. doi:10.1016/j.newideapsych.2021.100915

Wang, W., & Fu, W. (2007, August). Hybrid Petri Net Based Modelling and Simulation of Agile Supply Chain Dynamic Systems. In *2007 IEEE International Conference on Automation and Logistics* (pp. 2560-2565). IEEE. 10.1109/ICAL.2007.4339011

Chapter 6
Neural Patterns of Emotions in EEG and fMRI:
Emotions' Patterns in EEG Signals

Santhakumari Sadhasivam

School of Information Technology and Engineering, Vellore Institute of Technology, Vellore, India

Kamalakannan J.

School of Information Technology and Engineering, Vellore Institute of Technology, Vellore, India

ABSTRACT

Emotions have a vital role in human beings, and it is tough to define because of their intangible nature. Emotions vary over time and from person to person. Sometimes, emotions that sound good to people also may harm human beings. It depends upon one's health conditions and circumstances. Emotions are related to neurological, physiological, or cognitive processes. Though emotions are intangible, many invasive and non-invasive techniques are available to read the electrical activity in the brain to sense the different kinds of emotions. EEG is a non-invasive technique used in brain wave analyses. The main goal of this chapter is to give a brief introduction to EEG, characteristics of the brain waves, which part of the brain is responsible for emotions, the neurological structure of emotions, and lists of deep learning algorithms used to classify the various emotions. This chapter also contains data sets of emotions and a few key challenges in this field. For researchers with engineering backgrounds who are naive to this field, this chapter could be helpful.

INTRODUCTION

The human brain has billions of neurons that may fire in a particular brain area during the activity. The human brain generates various five signals, they are, Delta, Theta, Alpha, Beta, and Gamma. These signals have a unique frequency (Tangkraingkij, 2016). Beta signals have generated during emotions, which may be anger, aggression, happiness, sadness, upset, fear, confusion, pain, guilt, surprise, etc., More Emotions lead to various health issues like instability in BP, due to hypertension people may affect by

DOI: 10.4018/978-1-6684-5673-6.ch006

Table 1. Different brain lobes

S. No.	Name of the Lobe	Role
1	Frontal lobe	Controls cognition and memory. Speech and language
2	Temporal lobe	Hearing, recognizing the language, and forming memory.
3	Occipital lobe	Visual
4	Parietal lobe	Integrating sensory information, including touch, temperature, pressure, and pain

a disease called Hypertensive retinopathy, which is a type of retinal sickness (Chowdhary & Acharjya, 2017), abnormal Heart rate, and severe problems with brain disorders people. It is a possibility to mitigate those problems before getting into worsening. Recording brain signal accurately is more difficult due to the non-stationary behavior, noisy, and non-linear nature (Topic & Russo, 2021). EEG is used to read an electrical signal of the brain, which has a poor spatial resolution (Frey et al., 2013). Many researchers are facing the challenging task while capturing these signals. The fMRI is good in spatial resolution (Frey et al., 2013), so it is possible to get better accuracy in classifications if researchers consider both the EEG and fMRI together in analyses.

Parts of the Brain

The brain is a complex organ in a human. Mainly it has three parts. They are the Cerebrum which is the largest portion of the brain, the Cerebellum - its surface is called as cortex area and the third part is the Brain stem. The cerebrum is further divided into two hemispheres; the left and right hemispheres. Each hemisphere's responsibility to the body in the opposite direction; has four different lobes, namely the Temporal lobe, Frontal lobe, Parietal lobe, and occipital lobe. Each lobe has its responsibility. The role of the different brain lobes is shown in Table 1. (Jawabri & Sharma, 2021; Stuss & Benson, 2019).

Characteristics of Brain Wave

Two features are required to define any wave. These features are strength and frequency. The strength of the current or voltage range of neurons is from 0 to 200μv. The frequency ranges from 1 to 50 times/ Second. During any mental activity neurons will communicate with each other by electrochemical signals, these signals travel in entire brain areas with oscillation. This neuronal oscillation is called brain waves (Buskila et al., 2019). Based on the above mentioned two features the brain waves are divided into Delta (δ), Theta (θ), Alpha (α), Beta (β), and Gamma (γ) (Tangkraingkij, 2016). Each wave has its frequency. As per the brain states the particular wave has been generated. The Gamma wave is the fastest wave among all. And it is difficult to capture. Table 2 depicts the characteristics of the brain wave.

The delta is the slowest wave among all, the frequency of the delta wave is from 0.5 Hz to 4Hz; Walter introduced during the year 1936 the delta wave was introduced but announced it in 1963, generated during sleeping in the frontal brain region. Theta wave has a frequency between 4Hz to 8Hz was introduced by Wolter and Dovey in 1944; generated during a very relaxed mind in the brain region of the Parietal Lobe and Temporal Lobe. The frequency of an alpha wave is from 8Hz to 35Hz. Introduced by Berger in 1927; it is generated in the frontal and occipital lobes while the eyes are closed. Beta wave frequency between 12Hz to 35Hz, generated from the Frontal and Central lobes of the brain during awakened in

Table 2. Characteristics of the brain waves

S. No.	Wave Type	Frequency	States
1	Delta	<4	During sleeping
2	Theta	4-8	Deep Relaxed
3	Alpha	8-12	Eye closed
4	Beta	12-35	Eye open, High Awareness
5	Gamma	>35	Full concentration, during problem-solving

the high awareness state. Berger introduced beta signals also. And Gamma wave has a frequency greater than 35Hz. It is the fastest wave, difficult to capture, and generated during deep concentration like at the time of problem-solving time. Introduced by Jasper and Andrews (Venkata et al., 2021). Figure 1 depicts normal brain waves and their frequency.

The following line shows how brain wave descends from the brain signal during sleeping activity. Before falling asleep if a person reads a book for a few minutes (Beta), then keep down the book, Switch off the lights and then fall asleep (delta). The brain signals descend from Beta - alpha - theta - delta.

READING BRAIN SIGNALS

There are three major methods, Invasive, Semi Invasive, and non-invasive respectively (Kumar & Singh 2021). The first one requires surgery to implant the electrodes exactly into the brain, the second one is partially invasive which means the electrodes are placed under the skull and above the cortex area; ECoG (Electrocorticography), and the last one places the electrode just on the scalp (Koudelková et al., 2018). Non-invasive methods are preferable because not necessary to do any surgical process (Kumar & Singh 2021). EEG, fMRI, fNIRS, and MEG are the non-invasive type. For practical purposes, EEG is a suitable one, because it is portable, cost-effective, comparatively easy to use, and has a good temporal resolution (Alotaiby et al., 2015). The main benefit of using brain waves is the original emotion has generated directly from the brain and avoids expression from facials or gestures (Bhardwaj et al., 2015).

Origin of EEG and fMRI

Hans Berger invented Electroencephalogram (EEG) who was a German psychiatrist. 6th July 1924. Berger recorded the first EEG during neurosurgery to 17 years old boy. EEG is one of the non-invasive techniques that read the electrical activity of the brain (İnce et al., 2021). Now EEG has a crucial role in many fields like health care, decoding covert speech, BCI applications, emotion detections, diagnosing brain disorders, and brain-ID. In general EEG electrodes are placed on the scalp to record the brain wave. EEG is good at temporal resolutions, and poor in spatial resolutions, so it is difficult to get an accurate signal due to the spatial resolution problem. After many decades the problem has been resolved by introducing the fMRI technique.

Researchers invented fMRI (functional Magnetic Resonance Imaging), with good spatial resolutions. It was developed at Bell Laboratories by a team headed by Ogawa in 1990 (Ogawa et al., 1990)

Figure 1. Normal brain waves with their frequency. Source: (Siuly et al., 2016)

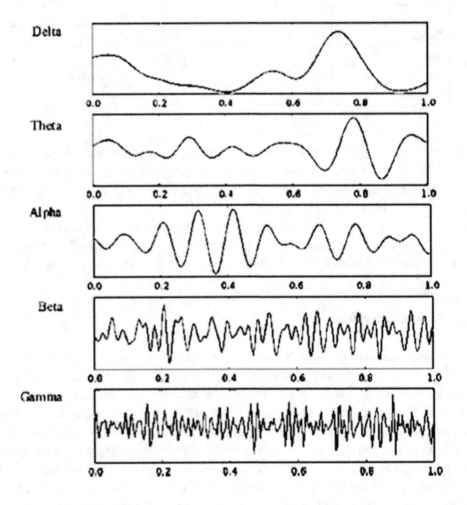

10-20 International Standard System

10-20 international standard electrodes are used to record brain activity. Channel selections and placing electrodes on the scalp is very important for the following reason. Too many electrodes which are irrelevant data may lead to overfitting problems, chances are more to miss the important features by selecting the wrong channels it may increase the computational complexity, and set up time will be reduced if limited relevant channels are selected in some applications (Alotaiby et al., 2015). Figure 2. 10-20 International electrodes' approximate locations depict the montage of the electrodes. The meaning of 10-20 is the distance between the neighbor electrodes is 10% or 20% from the front and back or left to right of the skull. (Suhaimi et al., 2020). Every electrode is labeled by a letter with a number. Letters F,

Figure 2. 10-20 International electrodes' approximate locations

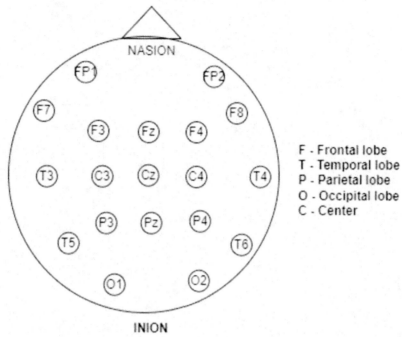

T, P, and O indicate the name of the lobe and C for the center of the brain. The number is marked as an odd number in the left hemisphere and an even number in the right hemisphere (Koudelková et al., 2018).

EMOTIONS STRUCTURE IN NEUROLOGY

Thalamus receives input from sensory input. The sensory inputs include the following sense, taste, touch, hearing, and vision. But not smell (Courtiol & Wilson 2015). The limbic system and the cortex receive information from the Thalamus. If the evaluated input is relevant to the goal which is evaluated by the limbic system then it sends the details to the body, cortex, and cognitive processes also. Human emotions are generated by Cortical and subcortical structures (Roxo et al., 2011).

Category of Emotions

The brain is responsible for controlling human emotions. The brain wave data is a kind of biological message, it will have emotional features, (Li et al., (2019). Emotions are the basic feelings of human beings; they may be positive or negative emotions (Fredrickson, 2004). Positive emotions are happiness, joy, love, surprise, etc., similarly negative emotions are anger, guilt, aggression, sadness, etc. elicits according to the current situation of any incident human. In early research, emotions are recognized through

Figure 3. Emotions structure in neurology

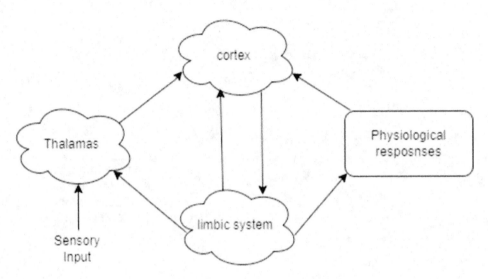

facial expressions, text, or gestures (Bhardwaj et al., 2015). Recent research shows that it is possible to recognize the different emotions from the brain wave through EEG.

Emotions in the Brain

Many neurological studies reported that there is a link between emotions and EEG signals. Among the four lobes, the neurons which are located in the Frontal lobe are activated more during emotions (Sarno et al., 2016). Positive emotions are from the left hemisphere and negative emotions are from the Right hemisphere (Lane et al., 2002). But for the facial expressions, the Positive emotions are from the right hemisphere and the negative emotions are from the left hemisphere. But still, it is an argument (Burgund, 2021). The temporal brain lobe generates more positive emotions in beta and gamma waves (Zheng et al., 2017). Most of the research was done on negative emotions.

Emotion Intelligence

A little research was available related to emotional intelligence. A model of emotional intelligence (EI) is generally unique for every individual. It refers to an ability to produce, identify, and understands the feeling of their own and others. The researchers recorded EEG signals in event-related potential. They showed that the theta and alpha signals activated more in emotional intelligence (Smith et al., 2018).

Figure 4. Relationship between artificial intelligence and deep learning

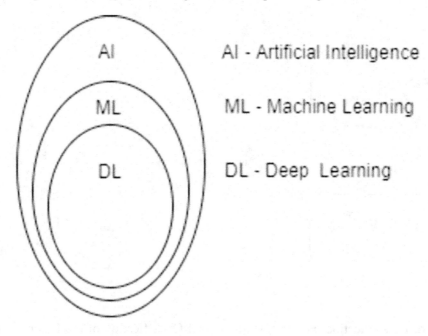

AI AND DEEP LEARNING IN EMOTION DETECTION

Deep learning is a technique that is the combination of Artificial Intelligence and Machine learning algorithm. And it is defined as a subset of machine learning. A small set of data is enough to train a model in machine learning. To train any model in deep learning required more data for better performance. Also, it avoids generalization issues. DL is not like machine learning, feature extraction and classification had done in a single phase.

Different Techniques of Sensing Emotion

Two approaches are used to analyze the emotions, namely Constructionist and Locations. The former approach requires more dimensions to study and classify emotions. Later the researchers assume that every emotion has a particular brain structure and pattern, but it is still a hypothesis, not yet proved by experiments. The Constructionist approach says that emotion comes from the brain's functional network interactions. In their studies, the brain activity reflects on three-dimensional models – Valence, Arousal, and Dominance (VAD) (Wyczesany & Ligeza, 2015).

In the last decades, the researcher used emotion detection in facial expressions or eye blinking as an image through a camera, thermal image by pulse rate, skin temperature, and, heat radiation.

One research shows that human emotion detection and classification using a traditional method like facial expression images using AI with deep learning. It was a challenging task for them to design an AI system. It has the potential to detect emotion from facial expressions. To do this mainly three major

Figure 5. Emotion sensing technique using camera and thermal images

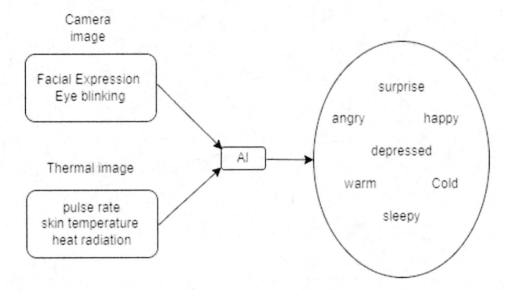

steps are need; Face detection, Feature extraction and Classification of the Emotions (Jaiswal et al., 2020). The author used Convolutional Neural Network because this model is suitable for image data as an input. A CNN is also called as ConvNet (Chowdhary & Acharjya, 2017).

Another research reveals that emotion recognition through speech signals. The author used two-stage approaches, one is feature extraction and another is a classification engine. Audio features are extracted and then selecting related parameters from the audio feature extraction. For the classification Support Vector Machine (SVM) was used (Aouani & Ayed, 2020).

Emotion recognition in Human voice and facial expressions has become highlighted research in recent years. It has both advantages and disadvantages. An advantage of facial expression is, reducing

Figure 6. Emotion classification in brain signals

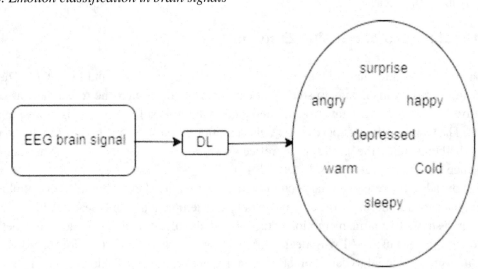

Figure 7. General framework of emotion classifications using deep learning

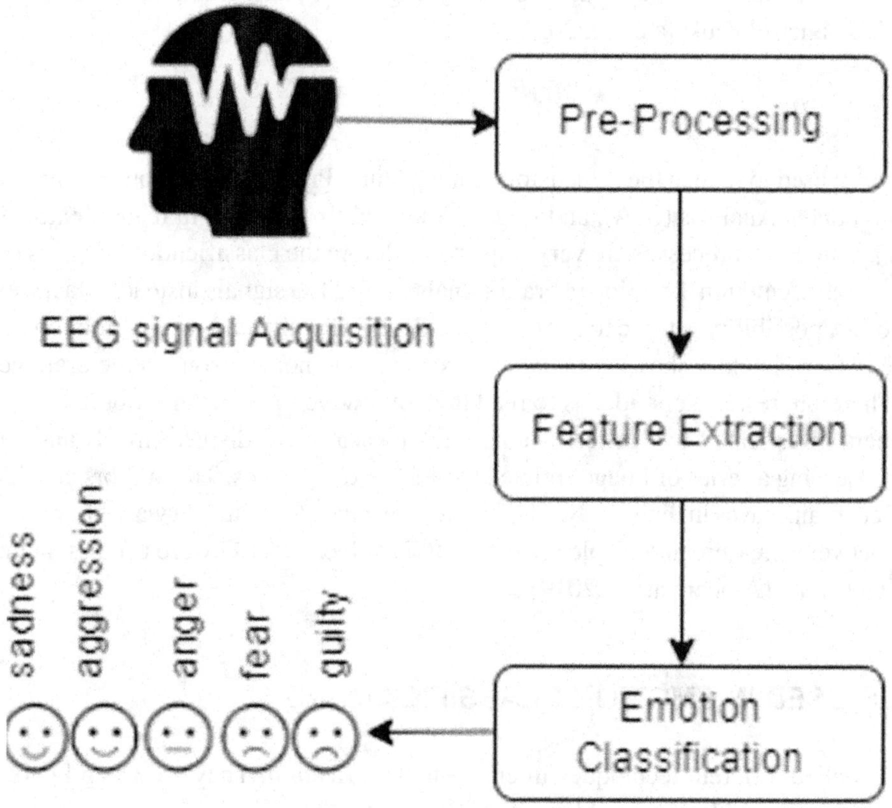

accidents by reading the facial expression of the driver. It is a challenge and hard task to recognize emotion in human voice due to different phonetic sounds in various languages. It required special software and was cost-effective.

PREREQUISITES:

Brain Signals are non-static and unique, while signal acquisition is not possible to get only the signals, they will be mixed with noises called non-brain signals (Al-Kadi et al., 2013). Before using the raw brain signal, a few important steps need to perform for better performance. They are Pre-processing and Feature extraction.

Pre-processing

Preprocessing means the removal of noises from the recorded brain signal. The noises may be generated by the brain while signal acquisition like eye blinking or movement in the body. Otherwise any electronic signals in the recording ambiance like mobile signal, or electrical motor sound (Venkata et al., 2021).

These should be eliminated from the raw brain signal. The pro-processing is also called signal normalization. BioSig free software tool is available for analyzing bio-signals. It has the potential to remove artifacts from EEG signals (Venkata et al., 2021).

Feature Extraction

Feature extraction is used to reduce the dimension of the feature. Principal Component Analysis (PCA), Independent Component Analysis (ICA), and Regression Analysis are used in feature extraction (Venkata et al., 2021). These two processes are very important. Before the classification, this has to be done.

The latest research is emotion detection in brain signals using EEG signals instead of facial expression or voice detection. A possibility is there to avoid the accident earlier by reading the emotion through the brain wave. The reason is before showing facial expressions and phonetic sounds the brain generates a related signal. Therefore researchers' idea is to read the brain wave to detect emotion.

The researchers investigated two different emotions; pleasure and displeasure. Brain waves were recorded while observing a series of images related to those two emotions. The authors considered only the Alpha and Beta brain waves in their study. The research result states that beta waves have the potential to discriminate between pleasure and displeasure. The PSD values of EEG were used as an input to the classifier LDA and KNN (Ameera at el., 2019).

TECHNIQUES USED IN EMOTION CLASSIFICATIONS

The researchers applied different techniques in emotion classification. They are Deep Learning Technique, Transfer Learning, and Ensemble Methods

Deep Learning Technique

Deep learning is an artificial neural network-based machine learning concept (Janiesch et al., 2021). It is a computational model with many layers that learns data representation. There is one input layer, one output layer, and at least one hidden layer between the input and output layers. Through a back-propagation algorithm, deep learning learns complicated structures from a large amount of data. It trains the model by changing the internal parameter from the previous layer (LeCun et al., 2015).

Deep Learning Algorithms Used in Classification of Emotions

Support Vector Machine (SVM) is a binary classifier. Linear and Non-linear SVM are available. Usually, linear SVM is used in high-dimensional data. Training is faster than the non-linear SVM (Chauhan et al., 2019). Most EEG application has high dimensional feature vectors. To classify the emotions SVM and K-Nearest Neighbor Algorithm (KNN) were used. It has been proved that in discriminating features in EEG data (Sha'abani et al., 2020). The researchers were used to classify the seven types of emotions in EEG signals using Linear Discriminant Analysis (LDA) and SVM (Bhardwaj et al., 2015). SVM has used not only in the EEG application, in other application also, a recent study showed the SVM classifier has given the best result while comparing the COVID-19 coughs and non-COVID-19 coughs in area under Receiver Operating Characteristic Curve (Goar et al., 2021).

Figure 8. Ensemble method

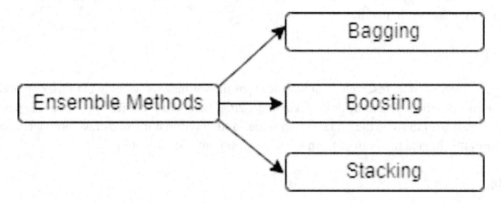

Transfer Learning

Transfer learning is a machine learning model where a model developed for a task is reused as the starting point for a model in a second task but to a similar problem. Transfer learning is applicable during a shortage in training data. Transfer learning consumes less time to train the target model and no need to scratch from the beginning.

Transfer learning influences the existing data collected from other subjects to create a model for a new individual with a slight adjustment in data. But sometimes using existing labeled data blindly leads to negative transfer learning that destroys the performance of the model, instead of enriching it. The researchers proposed a new framework in conditional transfer learning for positive transfer. The study shows that similar EEG signals get maximum transfer improvements in valence and arousal classification accuracy (Lin & Jung, 2017)

Ensemble Method

The ensemble method is a group classifier algorithm, which could be used to increase the generalization of a classifier. It is very difficult to get a good generalization from one classifier, but it is possible from the number of week-classifiers. The ensemble method was used in EEG emotion classification, because of its high accuracy and generalization (Li et al., 2022).

In recent years, researchers have shown interest in ensemble learning in addition to the traditional approach and deep learning approach in emotion classification and have given the best result using EEG signals (Chen et al., 2021). There are three ensemble methods are available. Boosting, bagging, and stacking, are all ensemble methods (Syarif et al., 2012).

Bagging

Bagging is well suited where the classifier algorithm was unstable. The bagging procedure is also called bootstrap aggregating. (Breiman, 1996). The bootstrapping method is used to form the statistical inferences (Efron & Tibshirani, 1994). This method was not new, it was introduced three decades before but was not familiar because of the lack of advanced modern computer technology. Anyway, the statistical method never changed, but the implementation has been changed because now the availability of modern computer technology. Bagging tries to solve the over-fitting issue. Takes homogeneous classifier algorithm and processes in parallel.

Boosting

Boosting is widely used by researchers; it has the capability of making a strong classifier by boosting a group of weak classifiers. It is more or less akin to bagging, except the classifier processes are performed consecutively. It tries to solve the under-fitting issue. Both ensemble methods take homogeneous classifier algorithms. In general, both of them are using voting for classification.

Stacking

This ensemble method is different from the above two types in two manners. The first difference is it takes a non-homogeneous classifier. The second difference is not using the voting process to get the best classifier result; instead, it performs the second level classification to predict the best classification result. The individual classifiers are called first-level classifiers. It gives the new feature representation to the next level, and the combined classifier is called the second-level classifier or meta-learner. The two-level of classifiers used to avoid over-fitting issues (Wolpert, 1992). The idea of stacking originated from Wolpert in 1992. The Wolpert idea was the first level of data contains more information (Breiman, 1996).

KEY CHALLENGES

The main challenges in emotion recognition using brain signals are the following. The primary challenge is that in the same emotion there is a different neuronal activity elicitation in each neuron. Another challenge is ignoring the interactions between multiple bands and channels; while collecting features of EEG signals either manually in the machine learning model or automatically by the deep learning model (Phan et al., 2021). And very limited public data sets are available. Few data sets have insufficient EEG data. The consequence is model leads into under-fit. There is a possibility to increase the insufficient EEG data by data augmentation (Chowdhary & Acharjya, 2017). So a model can produce good classification accuracy.

Available EEG Datasets for Emotion

Many researchers used SEED (Shanghai Jiao Tong University Emotion EEG Dataset) and DEEP (A Database for Emotion Analysis using Physiological signal) data sets, these two are public datasets.

The SEED dataset was first introduced by Zhang and Li in 2015. It contains EEG and Eye movement signals. It has been recorded from 15 healthy subjects while watching emotional movie clips (Xiang et al., 2015).

The DEEP data set was first introduced by Koelstra and others in 2012. It contains EEG and peripheral physiological signals from 32 healthy subjects. It was recorded at the time of watching music videos (Koelstra et al. 2012).

A DREAMER database is a multimodal database and the author recorded EEG and ECG signals while audio and visual stimuli. The Emotions such as valence, arousal, and dominance has been analyzed (Katsigiannis & Ramzan, 2017).

AMIGOS is A data set for Multimodal research of affect, personality & mood on an Individual or GrOupS. The AMIGOS dataset differs from the other two datasets (SEED and DEEP). Two sets of experiments they have done with individual subjects & group subjects were watching the short and long videos in a single trial classification of arousal and valence emotion (Miranda-Correa et al., 2018).

CONCLUSION

In recent years, in addition to the camera image and thermal image in emotion detection, the researchers' interest is brain signals using non-invasive devices like EEG and fMRI. But still, this is not yet deployed; because of the lack of data availability. In this chapter, the authors have given the details on where the researcher can access the SEED and DEEP data sets. Also given minute detail related to EEG, and the possible deep learning algorithm used in emotion classification. The author briefed the transfer learning and an ensemble method at the basic level.

REFERENCES

Al-Kadi, M. I., Reaz, M. B. I., & Ali, M. A. M. (2013). Evolution of electroencephalogram signal analysis techniques during anesthesia. *Sensors (Basel)*, *13*(5), 6605–6635. doi:10.3390130506605 PMID:23686141

Alotaiby, T., Abd El-Samie, F. E., Alshebeili, S. A., & Ahmad, I. (2015). A review of channel selection algorithms for EEG signal processing. *EURASIP Journal on Advances in Signal Processing*, *2015*(1), 1–21. doi:10.118613634-015-0251-9

Ameera, A., Saidatul, A., & Ibrahim, Z. (2019, June). Analysis of EEG spectrum bands using power spectral density for pleasure and displeasure state. *IOP Conference Series. Materials Science and Engineering*, *557*(1), 012030. doi:10.1088/1757-899X/557/1/012030

Aouani, H., & Ayed, Y. B. (2020). Speech emotion recognition with deep learning. *Procedia Computer Science*, *176*, 251–260. doi:10.1016/j.procs.2020.08.027

Bhardwaj, A., Gupta, A., Jain, P., Rani, A., & Yadav, J. (2015, February). Classification of human emotions from EEG signals using SVM and LDA Classifiers. In *2015 2nd International Conference on Signal Processing and Integrated Networks (SPIN)* (pp. 180-185). IEEE. 10.1109/SPIN.2015.7095376

Breiman, L. (1996). Bagging predictors. *Machine Learning*, *24*(2), 123–140. doi:10.1007/BF00058655

Breiman, L. (1996). Stacked regressions. *Machine Learning*, *24*(1), 49–64. doi:10.1007/BF00117832

Burgund, E. D. (2021). Left Hemisphere Dominance for Negative Facial Expressions: The Influence of Task. *Frontiers in Human Neuroscience*, *15*, 549. doi:10.3389/fnhum.2021.742018 PMID:34602999

Buskila, Y., Bellot-Saez, A., & Morley, J. W. (2019). Generating brain waves, the power of astrocytes. *Frontiers in Neuroscience*, *13*, 1125. doi:10.3389/fnins.2019.01125 PMID:31680846

Chauhan, V. K., Dahiya, K., & Sharma, A. (2019). Problem formulations and solvers in linear SVM: A review. *Artificial Intelligence Review*, *52*(2), 803–855. doi:10.100710462-018-9614-6

Chen, Y., Chang, R., & Guo, J. (2021). Emotion Recognition of EEG Signals Based on the Ensemble Learning Method: AdaBoost. *Mathematical Problems in Engineering*, *2021*, 2021. doi:10.1155/2021/8896062

Chowdhary, C. L., & Acharjya, D. P. (2017). Clustering algorithm in possibilistic exponential fuzzy C-mean segmenting medical images. In *Journal of Biomimetics, biomaterials and biomedical engineering* (Vol. 30, pp. 12–23). Trans Tech Publications Ltd. doi:10.4028/www.scientific.net/JBBBE.30.12

Courtiol, E., & Wilson, D. A. (2015). The olfactory thalamus: Unanswered questions about the role of the mediodorsal thalamic nucleus in olfaction. *Frontiers in Neural Circuits*, *9*, 49. doi:10.3389/fncir.2015.00049 PMID:26441548

Efron, B., & Tibshirani, R. J. (1994). *An introduction to the bootstrap*. CRC Press.

Fredrickson, B. L. (2004). The broaden–and–build theory of positive emotions. *Philosophical Transactions of the Royal Society of London. Series B, Biological Sciences*, *359*(1449), 1367–1377. doi:10.1098/rstb.2004.1512 PMID:15347528

Frey, J., Mühl, C., Lotte, F., & Hachet, M. (2013). *Review of the use of electroencephalography as an evaluation method for human-computer interaction*. arXiv preprint arXiv:1311.2222.

Goar, V. K., Yadav, N. S., Chowdhary, C. L., & Mittal, M. (2021). An IoT and artificial intelligence-based patient care system focused on COVID-19 pandemic. *International Journal of Networking and Virtual Organisations*, *25*(3-4), 232–251. doi:10.1504/IJNVO.2021.120169

İnce, R., Adanır, S. S., & Sevmez, F. (2021). The inventor of electroencephalography (EEG): Hans Berger (1873–1941). *Child's Nervous System*, *37*(9), 2723–2724. doi:10.100700381-020-04564-z PMID:32140776

Jaiswal, A., Raju, A. K., & Deb, S. (2020, June). Facial emotion detection using deep learning. In *2020 International Conference for Emerging Technology (INCET)* (pp. 1-5). IEEE.

Janiesch, C., Zschech, P., & Heinrich, K. (2021). Machine learning and deep learning. *Electronic Markets*, *31*(3), 685–695. doi:10.100712525-021-00475-2

Jawabri, K. H., & Sharma, S. (2021). Physiology, cerebral cortex functions. In *StatPearls* [internet]. StatPearls Publishing.

Katsigiannis, S., & Ramzan, N. (2017). DREAMER: A database for emotion recognition through EEG and ECG signals from wireless low-cost off-the-shelf devices. *IEEE Journal of Biomedical and Health Informatics*, *22*(1), 98–107. doi:10.1109/JBHI.2017.2688239 PMID:28368836

Koudelková, Z., Strmiska, M., & Jašek, R. (2018). Analysis of brain waves according to their frequency. *Int. J. Of Biol. And Biomed. Eng.*, *12*, 202–207.

Kumar, S., & Singh, S. K. (2021). *Brain Computer Interaction (BCI): A Way to Interact with Brain Waves*. Academic Press.

Lane, R. D., Nadel, L., & Kaszniak, A. W. (2002). Cognitive Neuroscience. *Cognitive Neuroscience of Emotion*, 407.

LeCun, Y., Bengio, Y., & Hinton, G. (2015). Deep learning. *Nature, 521*(7553), 436-444.

Li, R., Ren, C., Zhang, X., & Hu, B. (2022). A novel ensemble learning method using multiple objective particle swarm optimization for subject-independent EEG-based emotion recognition. *Computers in Biology and Medicine, 140*, 105080. doi:10.1016/j.compbiomed.2021.105080 PMID:34902609

Li, T. M., Chao, H. C., & Zhang, J. (2019). Emotion classification based on brain wave: A survey. *Human-centric Computing and Information Sciences, 9*(1), 1–17. doi:10.118613673-019-0201-x

Li, X., Zhang, P., Song, D., Yu, G., Hou, Y., & Hu, B. (2015). *EEG based emotion identification using unsupervised deep feature learning*. Academic Press.

Lin, Y. P., & Jung, T. P. (2017). Improving EEG-based emotion classification using conditional transfer learning. *Frontiers in Human Neuroscience, 11*, 334. doi:10.3389/fnhum.2017.00334 PMID:28701938

Miranda-Correa, J. A., Abadi, M. K., Sebe, N., & Patras, I. (2018). Amigos: A dataset for affect, personality and mood research on individuals and groups. *IEEE Transactions on Affective Computing, 12*(2), 479–493. doi:10.1109/TAFFC.2018.2884461

Ogawa, S., Lee, T. M., Nayak, A. S., & Glynn, P. (1990). Oxygenation-sensitive contrast in magnetic resonance image of rodent brain at high magnetic fields. *Magnetic Resonance in Medicine, 14*(1), 68–78. doi:10.1002/mrm.1910140108 PMID:2161986

Phan, T. D. T., Kim, S. H., Yang, H. J., & Lee, G. S. (2021). EEG-Based Emotion Recognition by Convolutional Neural Network with Multi-Scale Kernels. *Sensors (Basel), 21*(15), 5092. doi:10.339021155092 PMID:34372327

Roxo, M. R., Franceschini, P. R., Zubaran, C., Kleber, F. D., & Sander, J. W. (2011). The limbic system conception and its historical evolution. *TheScientificWorldJournal, 11*, 2427–2440. doi:10.1100/2011/157150 PMID:22194673

Sarno, R., Munawar, M. N., Nugraha, B. T., Sarno, R., Munawar, M., & Nugraha, B. (2016). Real-time electroencephalography-based emotion recognition system. *Int. Rev. Comput. Softw. IRECOS, 11*(5), 456–465. doi:10.15866/irecos.v11i5.9334

Sha'abani, M. N. A. H., Fuad, N., Jamal, N., & Ismail, M. F. (2020). kNN and SVM classification for EEG: A review. *InECC, E2019*, 555–565. doi:10.1007/978-981-15-2317-5_47

Siuly, S., Li, Y., & Zhang, Y. (2016). EEG signal analysis and classification. *IEEE Transactions on Neural Systems and Rehabilitation Engineering, 11*, 141–144.

Smith, R., Killgore, W. D., Alkozei, A., & Lane, R. D. (2018). A neuro-cognitive process model of emotional intelligence. *Biological Psychology, 139*, 131–151. doi:10.1016/j.biopsycho.2018.10.012 PMID:30392827

Stuss, D. T., & Benson, D. F. (2019). The frontal lobes and control of cognition and memory. In *The frontal lobes revisited* (pp. 141–158). Psychology Press. doi:10.4324/9781315788975-8

Suhaimi, N. S., Mountstephens, J., & Teo, J. (2020). EEG-based emotion recognition: A state-of-the-art review of current trends and opportunities. *Computational Intelligence and Neuroscience, 2020*. doi:10.1155/2020/8875426 PMID:33014031

Syarif, I., Zaluska, E., Prugel-Bennett, A., & Wills, G. (2012, July). Application of bagging, boosting and stacking to intrusion detection. In *International Workshop on Machine Learning and Data Mining in Pattern Recognition* (pp. 593-602). Springer. 10.1007/978-3-642-31537-4_46

Tangkraingkij, P. (2016). Significant frequency range of brain wave signals for authentication. *Software Engineering, Artificial Intelligence, Networking and Parallel Distributed Computing, 2015*, 103–113.

Topic, A., & Russo, M. (2021). Emotion recognition based on EEG feature maps through deep learning network. *Engineering Science and Technology, an International Journal, 24*(6), 1442-1454.

Venkata Phanikrishna, B., Pławiak, P., & Jaya Prakash, A. (2021). *A Brief Review on EEG Signal Pre-processing Techniques for Real-Time Brain-Computer Interface Applications*. Academic Press.

Wolpert, D. H. (1992). Stacked generalization. *Neural Networks, 5*(2), 241–259. doi:10.1016/S0893-6080(05)80023-1 PMID:18276425

Wyczesany, M., & Ligeza, T. S. (2015). Towards a constructionist approach to emotions: Verification of the three-dimensional model of affect with EEG-independent component analysis. *Experimental Brain Research, 233*(3), 723–733. doi:10.100700221-014-4149-9 PMID:25424865

Zheng, W. L., Zhu, J. Y., & Lu, B. L. (2017). Identifying stable patterns over time for emotion recognition from EEG. *IEEE Transactions on Affective Computing, 10*(3), 417–429.

Chapter 7
A Neural Network Approach to Increase Project Team Effectiveness Through Emotional Intelligence

Niranjan Rajpurohit
Jaipuria Institute of Management, Jaipur, India

Jevin Jain
NMIMS, India

Yash Agrawal
Intellibuzz TEM Pvt. Ltd., India

ABSTRACT

Artificial neural networks (ANNs) and their applications have revolutionized several industries and functions, including HR, in a short span of time. These state-of-the-art AI solutions build together or independently a more efficient way for the human resource managers to predict the potential success of an employee in his or her work team. Extant research has established the positive effect of emotional intelligence on team effectiveness. Emotional intelligence is playing an increasingly bigger role in determining one's success as an effective team member. People with higher EQ are better able to work in teams, adjust to the change, and are flexible in workplace. This chapter attempts to design a model, deploying neural networks, to aid in increasing project team effectiveness.

INTRODUCTION

The traditional perspective of Human Resource Management being a support function is being overcome by appreciation of the fact that HR is a business-oriented or strategic function (Hope-Hailey et al., 1997). Emerging strategic HRM practices are comprised of aligning the processes of Human Resource Manage-

DOI: 10.4018/978-1-6684-5673-6.ch007

ment with the objectives of the business in a company (Boxall et al., 2007). Traditional HR practices included collection of personal records of the workers as well as the information linked to them like the health benefits, review of performance, payroll, etc (Channi et al., 2022). In present scenario the functionality of HR has extended its edges and is playing a bigger role in a company. Human Resource has proven its ability of becoming a strategic partner by using the advantageous benefits of data analysis (Lawler et al, 2003). Such a growing potential and importance of Human Resource analysis is not just a theoretical matter, but also depends on the data of the people and needs a high level of expertise in data science (Njemanze, 2016).

In recent years, machine learning and artificial intelligence has taken a great leap forward. Analysis of data done on real time is made effective further by correctly using the tools of Artificial intelligence. Numerous companies such as UBS groups, Citigroup, Goldman Sachs, and other such companies use the software of AI for assessing traits such as Teamwork. These tools are helpful to predict the workers that can be highly successful in their job, or the best suitable employees for a specific profile. Such tools using Artificial Intelligence can be applied to analyze documents, resumes, video interviews, etc. to help in generating the important patterns linked to the employees (Oran, 2016).

AI uses technology of the brain of humans. Amazon used AI to make crucial decisions in its business in 2018. It employs algorithmic methods, which means that the collection, training and growth criteria are used based on various algorithms. Barbara (2018) found in his paper that AI technology is concerned with the cycle from sourcing to interviews. Wislow (2017) studied about the manner of using AI in HR, and it was made clear that AI reshapes the way companies handle their employees and create strategies that improve efficiency. AI can forecast the needs of workers and retention for employees in the organization because work can't be done manually, and that work can be done easily with the help of artificial intelligence. Today many businesses like such as Google, IBM, etc. use AI and have gained many benefits like easy access to information. AI can minimize the workload of HR managers and reduce time, as it helps in retrieve and picks, as well as granting leaves to workers in the company. Surve (2017) studied the problem for AI is Human-Robot Interaction (HRI). Yet Emotional Intelligence is not available for AI. It is the greatest downside of Human-Robot Interaction. Robots can only do the pre-instructing stuff.

Apart from the present scope of application of AI techniques in HR, there is a significant scope of use of these techniques in building and deploying agile teams. Today's complex business scenarios, with need for rapid and flexible response to change, require solutions through the collaborative efforts of agile teams. Standard methods used for the statistics like the Linear MDA (Multiple Discriminant Approaches), multivariate approaches, and univariate approaches etc. were based on assumptions made linearly along with the assumptions of normality that are complicated when applied to problems of real-time world. ANN and its peculiarity to resolve the complex issues as per its architecture, enables in identification of the combinations of the parameters involved, and also in case of large amount of data to select teams.

The chapter begins with exploring applications of AI in building effective teams. In subsequent sections it explores the convergence of the themes of EI and AI. It then deliberates on research methodology, data preparation and choice of intelligent models used. The results are discussed towards the end with conclusion and scope of future work.

BUILDING EFFECTIVE TEAMS USING AI

As per Smith and Katzenbach (2003), a team is defined as: "A small number of people with complementary skills, who are committed to a common purpose, performance goals, and approach for which they hold themselves mutually accountable." Most of the teams in both large scale and small-scale organization, in some way fit in the definition given above. Such an explanation helps in highlighting few elements of which a real team is comprised - their mutual accountability, common strategy or approach, common goals or purposes, their commitment, as well as the complementary skills (Smith and Katzenbach, 2003; Spatz, 2000). Another definition was presented by Hackman (1987, 1990) in two of his works, as various people, all with different jobs, who adaptively work together for achieving the specific common objectives. As per Salas and Baker (1997), a team can also be considered as two (or more) individuals with specific objectives assigned to them, performing certain tasks, and who co-ordinate and interact for achieving a common objective.

Team Effectiveness

Different researchers have come up with different explanations of the word - Team Effectiveness. Mohrman et al. (1995), explained the term team effectiveness, according to three main concepts: (a) Team performance - an extent to which the productive output of the group meets the consumer approvals, (b) Independent Functions - an extent till which the team members are reliant on one another, and (c) Satisfaction - that whether all the members are highly satisfied with the membership of team. Cohen et al. (1996) elaborated the concepts considering both work life quality and high performance of the employees. Such concept was drawn from the social and technical ideas, that state both these systems could be increased to promote the team effectiveness. Tannenbaum et al. (1996) stated that team effectiveness is a combination of the members' growth ability and the performance output which helps them to regenerate themselves. The above given definitions, along with other note-worthy explanations, also detail performance as a crucial factor.

Usually, when the team attains specific objectives, the team is considered to be efficient. But it's also a fact that teams are based effectively on accomplishments of goals which cannot consider any other aspects. Various research linked to the term team effectiveness result in different models. Hence, it is highly relevant for the researchers for examining different models of team effectiveness for determining the factors of team effectiveness which are used for developing the tools which can be applied to the research. In our research, we have used the model of team effectiveness as given by Rasker et al. (2001) which is comprised of 5-factors that result in effectiveness in teams. These factors will also act as the input/independent variables for the neural network proposed, along with the Employee Data. Situational aspects like time stress, uncertainty, and dynamism, arise externally and are impacted by the environment. Whereas the factors of an organization are determined externally of a team like the company's reward system and social support along with outlining the overall goals, missions as well as the objective of the project team.

For making sure that the missions of the team are easily achieved, a team must have a proper cohesion and structure, and also a better function of leadership for the whole project. In addition to this, every member of the team must have proper KSA- "Knowledge, Skills, and Attitude" to make sure all activities and tasks are efficiently and successfully accomplished. Finally, such types of models impose various factors related to task like load, interdependency, structure, and complexity, for the teams in achieving their objectives. Additionally, teamwork is something which ties all these factors together. It includes two types of behavioural activities like the activities related to the team and related to the tasks. (Rasker et al. 2001).

Artificial Neural Networks

The ANNs are a sort of information elaboration systems which are able to simulate the behaviour of a biological nervous system, similar to one present in the brain of a human, for the resolution of a specific problem. This definition of ANN shows that they are not an easy and common algorithm written by a programmer, but are instead information processing models capable of performing complex operations with a small and acceptable error.

Thus, Artificial Neural Networks are elaborative and mathematical models used for reproducing the behaviour of neurons for resolving non-linear and complex issues by using a simpler pattern of elements, which are connected with each other. This capability of learning these statistical as well as mathematical models, from experience, is a highly crucial and peculiar characteristic of the Artificial Neural Networks. However, such characteristic does not make the ANN capable of explicitly evaluating the mathematical connection in the output and given input variable. Hence ANN is a type of Black-Box system as it is not possible to univocally know how the outcomes are achieved, although it is trained as per a learning method using empirical data. Such ability helps the ANN in responding to the identified similar patterns but not identical to the trained ones.

Similar to biological networks, ANNs are composed of base elements that allow for the elaboration of all the information and data. These elements are called *artificial neurons* (or *neurons*), and they can be divided into different levels (layers): input, hidden, and output level. Each neuron of a specific layer can be linked to the ones of another layer by connections, similar to the biological synapses. This way, information is processed through the Network passing to the output layer from an input layer, thanks to the connection of neurons.

As the Artificial Neural Networks work as computing models attempting to simulate few of the biological NN properties, their structure is formed with numerous neurons connected together forming simple nodes to process all the information. Every neuron gets information as an input signal through an external stimulus or a node, it then locally processes it by a transfer function or by activating it, hence producing signals which are further sent to external output nodes. Even with a fact that to understand a single neuron is quite easy, several neurons interconnected to form a network becomes quite complex.

When developing an ANN, the first step is to choose among the different type of existing networks. Feed-forward networks are ANNs where the signal transfers to the output from an input in one-way only. There exist no loops of feedback, meaning that output from any layer has no impact of the same layer. These types of networks are straightforward in nature associating the output with its input. It is used extensively for pattern recognition. Whereas, Feedback Networks are the ones where the network is extremely complicated. It is also called dynamic type of network, stating that it has a continuously changing state till a point of equilibrium is reached. It stays on an equilibrium point till the changes in an input for new equilibrium state is achieved. For our problem, a Feedforward Network is more suitable. Feedforward network are presently used in a number of applications with higher rate of success. A learning process is an important step to be correctly evaluated and chosen because the effectiveness of ANN is mainly influenced on this process. Generally, the choice of the learning process depends on the kind of result or on the purposes expected by the Network. In Supervised learning, both input and target parameters have to be supplied to train the layers in a network. Due to the training algorithm, this data is used to modify the weights matrix of the connections, to minimize the error returned by the ANN. While in Unsupervised learning, only the input data is provided, therefore the weights of the connection matrix are modified using only this kind of information. For our problem, supervised learning is deemed fit.

Suitable Parameters of ANN for the Proposed Model

By defining input layer, along with an output layer and a set of hidden layers, we defined the whole ANN architecture, and it is generally known as MLP (the Multi-Layer Perceptron), also called a Feed Forward ANN pattern. The development of an ANN involves an optimum configuration of the following four elements in its architecture (Cybenko, 1989):

- The neuron present in every layer.
- Total layers
- Activation Function
- Training Algorithm used (as this helps in determining the final value of biases and weights)

Therefore, considering the pattern, a returned output through this Network (y) is calculated through the following equation:

Based on the output classes (High, Medium & Low) obtained from the Matching Index, best possible combination of the team members can then be selected for the desired team. The ANN output will assign a class for each employee, based on his suitability for the project team in question. We may then pick-up suitable number of employees from this class for the purpose of Team Selection.

Emotional Intelligence and its Impact on Team Effectiveness

Emotional Intelligence also called "EQ (Emotional Quotient)" is the ability of a person to recognize and reason with emotions. The skills involved in emotional intelligence include self-awareness, self-regulation, motivation, empathy, and social skills. Recently, it has become a buzz word in human resources departments, but researchers are saying that it is time emotional intelligence be taken seriously. There exist four different levels of emotions:

- Perceiving Emotions
- Reasoning with emotions
- Understanding Emotions
- Managing Emotions

Why EQ or Emotional Intelligence matters at workplace ? EQ affects our day-to-day decision-making process at workplace. Difference between people with High EQ and Low EQ can be seen below:
People with High EQ have:

- Make Better Decisions and Solve problems
- Keep cool under pressure
- Resolve conflicts

- Have greater empathy
- Listen, accept, and respect the constructive criticism

Whereas people with low EQ:

- Play the role of the victim or avoid taking responsibilities for errors
- Have passive or aggressive communication styles
- Refuse to work as a team
- Are overly critical of others or dismiss others' opinions

Hence, we can say that people who have high EQ are better able to work in teams, adjust to the change and be flexible in teams and workplace. Academic qualification won't matter, if the person doesn't have certain emotional qualities, he/she is unlikely to succeed. As the workplace continues to evolve, making room for new technologies and innovations, these qualities may become increasingly important.

As discussed earlier, A person with emotional intelligence has qualities like self-awareness, self-control, empathy, and social skills. These qualities help in deciding career that suits him/her. People with higher emotional intelligence have the ability to identify the needs of people who deal with them and therefore be able to maintain healthier relationships with them. The emotional intelligence of current employees is analysed on a regular basis to determine who possess the needed leadership potential. EQ is often one of the most important factors in the decision regarding pay rises and promotions.

The researchers from several studies conclude that Emotional Intelligence plays an important role as it is linked to every point in a work environment. Hence, to be successful and for company's growth emotional Intelligence plays a vital role.

Extent research has been done in order to find the effects of Emotional Intelligence on Team Effectiveness. Study revolves around the regression, correlation and means of emotional intelligence and team effectiveness. Author successfully shows positive effect. Correlation is 43%, mean value of emotional intelligence is 87.91 and mean value of team effectiveness is 35.38. Regressions value in author's study is at 19% which is quite significant. This proves Author's Hypothesis that there is a positive effect of Emotional Intelligence on team effectiveness.

Studies show that emotional intelligence influences team processes such as task conflict, relationship conflict and team effectiveness such as team performance, innovation, and cohesion. This study provides literature on emotional intelligence and intrateam conflict in several ways.

Firstly, the study proves a positive effect of emotional intelligence on team process and outcomes using relatively direct argument from role theory. Specifically, team emotional intelligence may help to clarify and establish members' roles in enhancing others' positive emotions and handling their negative emotions.

Second, the paper proceeds to find that team emotional intelligence is negatively associated with task conflict and relationships conflict. Author extends prior research, to separate the two conflicts as task conflicts is what causes relationship conflicts. It is arguable that task conflict directly or indirectly has a detrimental effect on team effectiveness. Author's study results show that team emotional intelligence plays a significant role in separating task conflict and relationship conflict and making them an individual variable.

Third, study identifies a link between two types of conflicts and team effectiveness. In this context, author's findings that the relationship between task conflict and team effectiveness based on team emotional intelligence is noteworthy. Mentioned results indicate that team emotional intelligence reduces the negative effects of relationship conflict on team cohesion. But authors are unable find significant effect of team emotional intelligence on relationship conflict, team performance.

Fourth, authors examined that team emotional intelligence affects team effectiveness. Results indicate that team emotional intelligence is positively related to team effectiveness. Until now, studies have shown only the effects of team emotional intelligence on performance. In this study, author shows that team emotional intelligence has positive effects on team performance, cohesion, and innovation.

Team emotional intelligence can give a channel to facilitate the exchange of ideas and information by fostering open discussion among members. This will contribute to innovation.

In sum, research findings have important theoretical implications for team emotional intelligence and conflict research. How emotional intelligence is positively related to team effectiveness.

RESEARCH METHODOLOGY

TF-IDF: TF-IDF (Term frequency-inverse document frequency) is a statistical measure that evaluates how relevant a word is to a document in a collection of documents. This is done by multiplying two metrics: how many times a word appears in a document, and the inverse document frequency of the word across a set of documents. It has many uses, most importantly in automated text analysis, and is very useful for scoring words in machine learning algorithms for Natural Language Processing .

TF-IDF was invented for document search and information retrieval. It works by increasing proportionally to the number of times a word appears in a document, but is offset by the number of documents that contain the word. So, words that are common in every document, such as this, what, and if, rank low even though they may appear many times, since they don't mean much to that document in particular.

TF-IDF for a word in a document is calculated by multiplying two different metrics:

- The term frequency of a word in a document. There are several ways of calculating this frequency, with the simplest being a raw count of instances a word appears in a document. Then, there are ways to adjust the frequency, by length of a document, or by the raw frequency of the most frequent word in a document.
- The inverse document frequency of the word across a set of documents. This means, how common or rare a word is in the entire document set. The closer it is to 0, the more common a word is. This metric can be calculated by taking the total number of documents, dividing it by the number of documents that contain a word, and calculating the logarithm.
- So, if the word is very common and appears in many documents, this number will approach 0. Otherwise, it will approach 1.

Multiplying these two numbers results in the TF-IDF score of a word in a document. The higher the score, the more relevant that word is in that particular document.

Determining how relevant a word is to a document, or TD-IDF, is useful in many ways, for example:

- **Information retrieval:-**TF-IDF was invented for document search and can be used to deliver results that are most relevant to what you're searching for. Imagine you have a search engine, and somebody looks for LeBron. The results will be displayed in order of relevance. That's to say the most relevant sports articles will be ranked higher because TF-IDF gives the word LeBron a higher score. It's likely that every search engine you have ever encountered uses TF-IDF scores in its algorithm.

- **Keyword Extraction:-**TF-IDF is also useful for extracting keywords from text. How? The highest scoring words of a document are the most relevant to that document, and therefore they can be considered *keywords* for that document.

Dataset contains large chunk of data. So, it is passed through different methods to extract the relevant features from the documents. Bags of Words is one of the methods. The data from datasets is passed through bags of words to get the relevant features that can be used to train the model. The output of bags of words is passed through TF-IDF to have a relevant and summarized data. Once we have our pre-processed data, the data is split for training and testing (usually 75% training, 25% testing). After splitting it passed to train the model (here Logistic Regression Model). Once we have trained and evaluated the model, we have our final model.

Employee created text data will be given as an input. The input would be a text of employees from various sources. Once, the input is provided the input goes through backend, where it provided to preprocessing and model objects. All the requires functions and objects are stored in model objects. Once the data is preprocessed it is provided to Model Building. Here the preprocessed data from the dataset and the data from backend is trained in Logistic Regression Model. Then the Output is provided to Backend and passed to frontend to display the category of news provided by the user.

Data Preparation

Data collected from over 15 teams was analyzed for the modeling. Considering that classification algorithms work with numerical data, textual data must be treated properly. Furthermore, having a deep understanding of the dataset allows to apply the methods of preprocessing to the problem of classification. Therefore, the emotion category dataset is pre-processed before it is given to the training mode.

1. **Stop Word Removal:** A stop word is a widely used term that has been configured to forget by a search engine, both when indexing search entries and when they are retrieved as a result of a search query. We wouldn't want these terms to take up space or precious computing time in our database. We can easily delete them for this, by saving a list of terms that you find to avoid terms.
2. **Bags of Words(BOW):** When modelling text with machine learning algorithms, the bag of words model is a way of representing text data. The bag of words model is simple to understand and apply, and has seen great success in issues like language modelling and classification of documents.
3. **TF-IDF:** TF-IDF stands for "Term frequency - Inverse Document Frequency." This is a technique for quantifying a word in texts, we usually measure a weight for each word that shows the meaning of the word in the text and corpus. This approach is a technique commonly used in Information Retrieval and Text Mining.

TF-IDF = Term Frequency (TF) * Inverse Document Frequency (IDF).

LOGISTIC REGRESSION

Logistic Regression model is trained with the preprocessed dataset of already classified emotion words. The model is divided into various stages where training and testing takes place. At first, the preprocessed words are fed to the model for training. The steps of preprocessing are repeated, and a list of words is generated. For the training array to be created the preprocessed words are compared and a training array of the length of words is generated.

In the logistic regression the constant (b0) moves the curve left and right and the slope (b1) defines the steepness of the curve. By simple transformation, the logistic regression equation can be written in terms of an odds ratio.

Similarly, training-tags array is generated which has the categories of the emotion headlines. The training and training-tags array is now given to the Logistic Regression and after iteratively learning the weights from the data the model converges and we get a final Logistic Regression model with the optimized learned weights that are most appropriate for our task.

This model after evaluation will be deployed and will be used in classifying emotions categories.

Naïve Bayes

Naïve Bayes classification algorithm is based on Bayes' Theorem. a Naive Bayes classifier assumes that the presence of a particular feature in a class is unrelated to the presence of any other feature. For example, some fruit might be considered to be an apple if it is red in colour, round in shape, and about 10 centimetres in diameter. Even if these features are dependant to each other or upon the existence of the other features, all of these properties independently contribute to the probability that this fruit is an apple and that is why it is known as 'Naive'.

Naive Bayes model is easy to build and particularly useful for very large data sets. Along with simplicity, Naive Bayes is known to outperform even highly sophisticated classification methods. Bayes theorem provides a way of calculating posterior probability $P(c|x)$ from $P(c)$, $P(x)$ and $P(x|c)$.

Where,

$P(c|x)$ is the posterior probability of class (c, target) given predictor (x, attributes).

$P(c)$ is the prior probability of class.

$P(x|c)$ is the likelihood which is the probability of predictor given class.

$P(x)$ is the prior probability of predictor.

Decision Tree

The decision tree is similar to a flowchart-like tree structure where the internal node represents a feature (or attribute), the branch represents the rule of thumb, and the node of each leaf represents the result. The highest node in the decision tree is known as the root node. It learns to distinguish on the basis of the value of the attribute. This flowchart-like structure helps you make decisions. Views similar to a flowchart diagram that easily mimics human-level thinking. That is why decision trees are easy to understand and interpret.

The tree resolution is a kind of white box ML algorithm. Share an internal decision-making concept, not found in the black box type of algorithms like Neural Network. Its training time is much faster compared to the neural network algorithm. The duration of the treatment decision is the function of the

Figure 1. Reading 1

```
Enter the sentence you want to test using logistic regression: I am feeling depressed today. Dont feel to work.
Actual sentence:  I am feeling depressed today. Dont feel to work.
Output is ['sadness']

Enter the sentence you want to test using naive bayes: I am feeling depressed today. Dont feel to work.
Actual sentence:  I am feeling depressed today. Dont feel to work.
Output is ['sadness']

Enter the sentence you want to test using decision tree: I am feeling depressed today. Dont feel to work.
Actual sentence:  I am feeling depressed today. Dont feel to work.
Output is ['sadness']
```

number of records and the number of symptoms in the data provided. Decision medicine is a method of distribution or non-parameter, which does not depend on the assumptions of distribution opportunities (Chowdhary et al., 2022). Decision trees can handle high-resolution data with good accuracy.

RESULTS AND DISCUSSIONS

Trained a model using NLP and ML algorithms to detect emotions from textual inputs. The model uses three ML algorithms for classifying emotions. Model used and their readings are given below:

- **Logistic Regression Classifier:**
  - Logistic regression train set Accuracy: 0.8577987051206593
  - Logistic regression test set result: Accuracy 0.6927966101694916
- **Naïve Bayes Classifier:**
  - Naive bayes train set Accuracy: 0.6723955267804591
  - Naive bayes test set Accuracy: 0.528954802259887
- **Decision Tree Classifier:**
  - Decision tree train set Accuracy: 0.9802236609770453
  - Decision tree test set Accuracy: 0.6076977401129944

From the above readings we can see that model using Logistic Regression is more efficient and accurate as compared to the model using Naïve Bayes or Decision Tree. We have proved this by giving all three models user data inputs and checked the observed and expected results.

A few of the readings have been highlighted below

Reading 1

User Input: "I am feeling depressed today. Don't feel to work."
  Expected Output: Sadness
  Observed Output:
  Discussion: We can see that all three models give the same expected output i.e., sadness.

Figure 2. Reading 2

```
Enter the sentence you want to test using logistic regression: I am feeling good because I am getting a promoted
Actual sentence:  I am feeling good because I am getting a promoted
Output is  ['joy']

Enter the sentence you want to test using naïve bayes: I am feeling good because I am getting a promoted
Actual sentence:  I am feeling good because I am getting a promoted
Output is  ['neutral']

Enter the sentence you want to test using decision tree: I am feeling good because I am getting a promoted
Actual sentence:  I am feeling good because I am getting a promoted
Output is  ['joy']
```

Reading 2

User Input: "I am feeling good because I am getting promoted"
   Expected Output: Joy
   Observed Output:
Discussion: We can see that except for Naïve Bayes, other two model which are Logistic Regression and Decision Tree give the same expected output. Due to probability theorem of Naïve Bayes, the result may vary depending upon the probability of word being used in different context.

Reading 3

User Input: "When stupid people push me during rush time in the city."
   Expected Output: Anger/Sadness
   Observed Output:

Figure 3. Reading 3

```
Enter the sentence you want to test using logistic regression: When stupid people push me during rush time in the city.
Actual sentence:  When stupid people push me during rush time in the city.
Output is  ['anger']

Enter the sentence you want to test using naïve bayes: When stupid people push me during rush time in the city.
Actual sentence:  When stupid people push me during rush time in the city.
Output is  ['sadness']

Enter the sentence you want to test using decision tree: When stupid people push me during rush time in the city.
Actual sentence:  When stupid people push me during rush time in the city.
Output is  ['anger']
```

Discussion: Here we have an interesting observation. Expected output for this input can be anger or sadness depending upon the context. But as different models use different algorithm for classification output may vary. Creating an association rule between context and user input will help the model to accurately classify the words with some pre-requisite meaning in use.

Figure 4. Reading 4

```
Enter the sentence you want to test using logistic regression: I feel useless. My job is boring.
Actual sentence:  I feel useless. My job is boring.
Output is  ['neutral']


Enter the sentence you want to test using naive bayes: I feel useless. My job is boring.
Actual sentence:  I feel useless. My job is boring.
Output is  ['neutral']


Enter the sentence you want to test using decision tree: I feel useless. My job is boring.
Actual sentence:  I feel useless. My job is boring.
Output is  ['neutral']
```

Reading 4

User Input: "I feel useless. My job is boring."

   Expected Output: Sadness

   Observed Output:

   Discussion: Here we see all three models fail to give expected output. This is because the efficiency of NLP and Machine Learning is limited to text inputs. This is opens doors to future work in integrating different primary sources of input and creating ae motion detector.

CONCLUSION

The Modelling as discussed by the authors will help establish the mediating influence of emotions on team effectiveness, on a real time basis. While the post facto analysis of a project team's effectiveness and its determinants has been the scope of research hitherto, the research design outlined by the authors will help in establishing the paths on a real time basis.

For a practising manager, the above model will have enormous utility as the manager will now be able to gauge the dominant team emotions on a real time basis, and thus would be able to intervene proactively. This will prove crucial in projects which have a short cycle and where agile methodology of project management is deployed.

LIMITATIONS AND FUTURE SCOPE

To have an even more accurate and reliable working model of emotion detection we can increase the number of inputs. Inputs which can be taken into considerations are:

- Image (CNN)
- EEG Signals (Bioengineering)
- Quantitative Data (Questionnaire Tests)

Combining two or more than two input model and then taking weighted average for the final output will make our model more accurate and reliable. As the number of inputs will increase the ANN will consist of more hidden layers.

Emotional recognition from EEG symptoms has made significant progress in recent years. Previous methods are usually performed on a time zone, a frequency domain, and a time frequency domain.

We suggest a face recognition method using a CNN model that removes facial features effectively. Compared with traditional methods, the proposed method can automatically learn the features of the pattern and reduce the imperfections caused by the artificial design features. The proposed method directly calculates the pixel value of the image by training the sample image data. Independent reading can completely detect the mysterious feature of the image. The training process for this proposed method uses proper weight initiation which has a significant impact on weight recovery. Our comprehensive experimental analysis shows that compared to previous texts, the proposed algorithm can improve the level of facial recognition of complex face to some degree. Compared to FRR-CNN and R-CNN models, the assembly speed of the proposed model is much faster in complex rear areas. Also, the proposed method reaches a higher level of recognition. Scanned faces can actually have a variety of sounds, such as facial expressions, body wraps, and blurring. To address these concerns, as a future project, we will investigate solid models that satisfy real-world situations. We will also focus on how to reduce the complexity of the network structure, and we will try to see the dynamics of 3D convolution technology.

Merging these two models of emotion detection we can get a better accurate and live emotion detection which can be used by organisation on real time basis.

A real-time emotional recognition algorithm using visual markers using an optical flow algorithm was developed to create a real-time sensory recognition system with minimal complexity (performance time, memory) using facial expressions and EEG symbols.

REFERENCES

Baker, D., & Salas, E. (1997). Team performance and assessment measurement: Theory, methods, and applications. Erlbaum.

Boxall, P. F., Purcell, J., & Wright, P. (2007). The goals of HRM. In Oxford Handbook of Human Resource Management. Oxford University Press.

Channi, H. K., Shrivastava, P., & Chowdhary, C. L. (2022). Digital Transformation in Healthcare Industry: A Survey. In *Next Generation Healthcare Informatics* (pp. 279–293). Springer. doi:10.1007/978-981-19-2416-3_16

Chowdhary, C. L., Khare, N., Patel, H., Koppu, S., Kaluri, R., & Rajput, D. S. (2022). Past, present and future of gene feature selection for breast cancer classification–a survey. *International Journal of Engineering Systems Modelling and Simulation*, *13*(2), 140–153. doi:10.1504/IJESMS.2022.123355

Cohen, S. G., Ledford, G. Jr, & Spreitzer, G. (1996). A predictive model of self-managing work team effectiveness. *Human Relations*, *49*(5), 643–676. doi:10.1177/001872679604900506

Cybenko, G. (1989). Approximation by superpositions of a sigmoidal function. *Mathematics of Control, Signals, and Systems*, *2*(4), 303–314. doi:10.1007/BF02551274

Hackman, J. R. (1987). *Handbook of Organizational Behavior.* Prentice-Hall.

Hackman, J. R. (1990). Groups that work (and those that don't): Creating conditions for effective teamwork. Jossey-Bass.

Hope-Hailey, V., Gratton, L., McGovern, P., Stiles, P., & Truss, P. (1997). A Chameleon Function? HRM in the '90s. *Human Resource Management Journal, 7*(3), 5–18. doi:10.1111/j.1748-8583.1997.tb00421.x

Katzenback, J. R., & Smith, D. K. (2003). The wisdom of teams. Harvard Business School Press.

Lawler, E. E. III, & Mohrman, S. A. (2003). HR as a Strategic Partner: What Does It Take to Make it Happen? *Human Resource Planning, 26*(5), 15.

Mohrman, S. A., Cohen, S. G., & Mohrman, A. M. (1995). *Designing team-based organizations: new forms for knowledge work.* Jossey-Bass.

Njemanze, I. (2016). *What Does Being a Strategic HR Business Partner Look Like in Practice?* Retrieved from Cornell University, ILR School site: http://digitalcommons.ilr.cornell.edu/student/101

Oran, O. (2016, June 7). *Wall Street hopes artificial intelligence software helps it hire loyal bankers.* Retrieved September 25, 2017, from https://www.reuters.com/article/us-banks-hiring-ai/wall-streethopes-artificial-intelligencesoftware-helps-it-hire-loyalbankers-idUSKCN0YT163

Rasker, P., van Vliet, T., van Den Broek, H., & Essens, P. (2001). *Team effectiveness factors: A literature review. TNO Technical report No.: TM-01-B007.*

Spatz, D. (2000). Team-building in construction. *Practice Periodical on Structural Design and Construction, 5*(3), 93–105. doi:10.1061/(ASCE)1084-0680(2000)5:3(93)

Surve, A. A. (2020). *Impact Of Artifical Intelligence In Human Resource Management* [Doctoral Dissertation]. University of Mumbai.

Tannenbaum, S., Beard, R., & Salas, E. (1992). Teambuilding and its influence on team effectiveness: An examination of conceptual and empirical developments. In *Issues, theory, and research in industrial/organizational psychology* (pp. 117–153). Elsevier Science. doi:10.1016/S0166-4115(08)62601-1

Van Pay, B. (2018). *How AI is reinventing HR.* Academic Press.

Wislow, E. (2017). *Top ways to use artificial intelligence in HR.* Academic Press.

Chapter 8
Deep Learning–Based Detection of Thyroid Nodules

Avani K. V. H.
BMS College of Engineering, India

Deeksha Manjunath
BMS College of Engineering, India

C. Gururaj
BMS College of Engineering, India

ABSTRACT

Thyroid nodule is a common disease on a global scale. It is characterized by an abnormal growth of the thyroid tissue. Thyroid nodules are divided into two types: benign and malignant. To ensure effective clinical care, an accurate identification of thyroid nodules is required. One of the most used imaging techniques for assessing and evaluating thyroid nodules is ultrasound. It performs well when it comes to distinguishing between benign and malignant thyroid nodules. But ultrasound diagnosis is not simple and is highly dependent on radiologist experience. Radiologists sometimes may not notice minor elements of an ultrasound image leading to an incorrect diagnosis. After performing a comparative study of several deep learning-based models implemented with different classification algorithms on an open-source data set, it has been found that ResNet101v2 gave the best accuracy (~96%), F1 score (0.957), sensitivity (0.917), etc. A simple and easy-to-use graphical user interface (GUI) has also been implemented.

INTRODUCTION

Conventional diagnostic and treatment procedures of diseases rely heavily on doctors'/clinicians' expert knowledge of the condition at hand. However, this diagnostic procedure has a significant flaw: its effectiveness relies highly on doctors' own experiences and intellect. As a result, diagnostic accuracy varies and is constrained. Image-based diagnosis procedures have become increasingly popular as digital technology has advanced, allowing clinicians to study abnormalities with organs beneath the skin and/

DOI: 10.4018/978-1-6684-5673-6.ch008

or deep within the human body. The diagnostic performance can be improvised with the use of imaging techniques. However, the ability and expertise of medical practitioners to exploit collected photos is still a factor. To address this issue, computer-assisted diagnostic systems were created to aid doctors in the prognosis and therapeutics process. The CAD systems, as their name implies, can be used for double verification, which is done to try to improve human diagnostic performance using a computer. This type of technology analyses and interprets medical images of various organs, such as Ultrasound scans. After the analysis is done, the classification output obtained helps doctors diagnose disorders.

The thyroid is an important organ in the human body that creates and produces vital hormones that regulate metabolism. It is located in the human neck. Thyroid disease has grown more crucial to diagnose and treat because of its vital role in the human body. The formation of nodules that cause thyroid cancer, as previously observed in prior studies, is a prevalent problem in the thyroid region. Thyroid nodules are anomalous lumps that grow on the human body's thyroid gland. Many reasons, including iodine deficiency, overgrowth of normal thyroid tissue, and thyroid cancer, can cause them. Thyroid nodules are usually segregated into two types based on their characteristics: benign (non-cancerous nodules) and malignant (cancerous nodules). Thyroid cancer is the most prevalent type of cancer, constituting 10% of all malignant tumours. Thyroid Cancer is a malignancy that occurs in the Endocrine System. Thyroid nodule detection has increased dramatically as several nodules are found by chance. The CAD classification of thyroid nodules can help the radiologist make an accurate diagnosis.

Clinically, evaluating thyroid nodules is difficult. Thyroid nodules are found out often by chance during neck diagnostic imaging and prevalence increases as a person ages. They are seen in 42–76% of adults. Many of thyroid nodules are considered non-cancerous, while 10% of them may be cancerous. Radioactive iodine therapy, thyroidectomy to prevent recurrence and death, immunotherapy or chemoradiotherapy may be recommended. Treatment for thyroid cancer varies based on the histological subtype, patient preference, and other factors as well as comorbidities. Ultrasound images are not particularly clear, which necessitates the use of a FNAB (invasive) procedure, which has unfavorable repercussions. For a cytological study of the nodule, a fine needle aspirate biopsy (abbreviated as FNAB) of the nodule might be obtained. Patients may have localized pain from FNABs, and while they are generally safe, there is a small risk of hematoma. The outcome of cytological analysis is uncertain in 20–30% of FNABs, which implies they do not always produce clinically meaningful data. The assessment of accidental Thyroid Nodules is usually performed by Sonography. Hypo-echogenicity, absence of a halo, micro-calcifications, firmness, intramodular flow, and a taller-than-wide form are some of the sonographic features of thyroid nodules that radiologists have recognized as suggestive indications of cancer (malignant).

Thyroid Imaging Reporting and Data System (TI-RADS)

TI-RADS is based on a five-point scale that assigns 0–3 points to each of the 5 Ultrasound features namely composition, echogenicity, shape, margin, and echogenic foci. A single score is generated due to the features composition, echogenicity, shape and margin due to mutually exclusive selections. The echogenic foci category might contain many features. The scores generated due to all features are added and the sum total obtained determines whether the nodule is harmless (TR1) or lethal (TR5). The TI-RADS score ranges from 1 to 5, nodules which have scores up to 3 can be classified as benign while nodules which have scores of more than 3 can be classified as malignant. The TR level, along with the nodule's maximal diameter, decides whether a Fine-Needle Aspiration Biopsy (FNAB) or no further action is recommended.

Figure 1. (a) Nodule of size 0.9cm small cystic spaces and considered benign (FN. Tessler et al., 2018).
Figure 1b: Nodule with significant cysts and considered malignant (FN. Tessler et al., 2018)

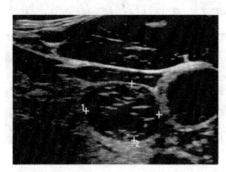 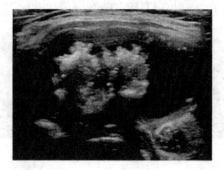

Composition

Nodules categorized as spongiform in ACR TI-RADS are not subjected to further feature assignment and are deemed as benign, requiring no further follow-up. If cystic components make up less than half of the nodule, it should not be considered benign. Furthermore, the existence of other characteristics such as peripheral calcifications or macrocalcifications, which are usually simple to spot, indicates that a nodule is not spongiform and may be malignant. Nodules with shadowing calcifications that prevent assessment of their architecture are presumed to be solid and must be investigated further.

Shape and Margin

The purpose is to see if the nodule has grown more front-to-back than side-to-side, indicating that it has crossed tissue planes and hence is suspicious. Nodules with a fully circular cross-section can also be found. The character of a nodule's interaction with surrounding intra- or extrathyroidal tissue is identified as its margin. If the nodule's solid component is angled into the surrounding tissue to any extent, the margin should be classed as lobulated or irregular, both of which are deemed safe. A pathognomonic sign of malignancy can be the invasion of the surroundings by extrathyroidal extensions. The same can be noticed in Figure 1a, 1b, 2a, 2b and 2c.

Echogenicity

The brightness of a thyroid nodule in comparison to the rest of the thyroid tissue is referred to as echogenicity. Hypoechoic nodules which are solid and not fluid filled are depicted by colors different from the surrounding thyroid tissue. When opposed to cystic or fluid-filled lesions, solid hypoechoic thyroid nodules have a higher risk of turning malignant. Other factors, such as size, may, however, suggest a nodule's likelihood of evolving into thyroid cancer. A fine-needle biopsy may be performed if a doctor feels a nodule is malignant for further investigation.

Deep learning-based techniques have lately been employed to solve various difficulties in medical image processing systems, thanks to technological advancements such as the back propagation algorithm, neural networks, and Graphics Processing Units (GPUs). Deep learning-based technology has had a lot

Figure 2. (a) Sonogram of a taller than wide Thyroid Cancer (FN. Tessler et al., 2018). Figure 2b. Sonogram that shows a Benign Nodule with smooth margin (arrows) (FN. Tessler et al., 2018). Figure 2c. Sonogram shows 2.0-cm Hypoechoic Thyroid Carcinoma (arrows) (FN. Tessler et al., 2018)

of success in detecting and classifying thyroid nodules (Chowdhary & Channi, 2022; Chowdhary & Srivatsan, 2022).

The rest of the chapter is organized as follows. Previous research works in the same area have been discussed briefly in Section 2 - Literature Survey. Section 3 - implementation - includes a detailed discussion of different approaches and technology used to classify thyroid nodules. The implementation of a simple Graphical User Interface (GUI) is included in Section 4. Section 5 comprises a detailed description of the evaluation metrics used. The results obtained on using different models, a comparative study of the different approaches used, the method that gave the best evaluation metrics values and the output obtained on using the GUI developed are analyzed and explained in Section 6. Section 7 concludes the authors' work with possible future research.

LITERATURE SURVEY

Deep learning techniques have been used extensively in the realm of healthcare research. This progress has undeniably positive consequences for society. The detection of thyroid nodules in ultrasound scan images is one such topic that has gotten a lot of attention throughout the world. The endeavour is further complicated by the need to categorise the nodules as benign or cancerous. Many research papers have been produced to accomplish this objective utilising various methods.

One method involves utilising standard neural networks to classify thyroid nodules in ultrasound pictures. Pre-trained GoogleNet and cost-sensitive random forest classifiers have been used (Chi et al., 2017). The elements of the nodule tissue texture itself, as well as the distinctions between textures from different tissues, are learned using a DCNN architecture. One of the disadvantages was the inclusion of fiducial markers added by radiologists to scan images, which degraded the learning process.

The use of feature vectors in conjunction with SVM or Fuzzy classifiers by H. Khachnaoui et al. yielded a good accuracy (H. Khachnaoui et al., 2018). Despite the great accuracy observed, the AdaBoost classifier was utilised with a limited amount of characteristics. The dataset in this study has a major disadvantage in that it does not sufficiently represent the actual population base in clinical practice. The ROIs (Region of Interests) identifying thyroid lesions are delineated by doctors rather than automatically discovered by the ultrasound CAD system, therefore the approach's efficacy is still dependent on physician experience.

In one of the experiments implemented by Vadhiraj et al. (2021) for image pre-processing and segmentation, the median filter and picture binarization was used achieving noise reduction in the raw scan pictures. Seven ultrasound picture features were extracted using the grey level co-occurrence matrix (GLCM). The support vector machine (SVM) and artificial neural network (ANN) classification methods were used in two different ways. The accuracy of ANN was 75 percent, respectively.

Some CAD systems provided a refined segmentation procedure with active outlines driven by local Gaussian distribution fitting energy before image characteristics were retrieved from thyroid ultrasound pictures, according to experimental data in the work of Q. Yu et al. (2017). For training purposes, the dataset did not include all forms of thyroid nodules. Both the ANN and the SVM models showed a high value in categorising thyroid node samples based on research of previous works. When the two techniques were integrated, the diagnosis of no cancerous nodes was missed. If both procedures indicated that a node was cancerous, the patient was to have a fine needle aspiration cytology (FNAC) test performed at the very least.

Nikhila et al. (2019) showed in their work a technique for extracting characteristics from ultrasound images based on the Residual U-net. Radiologists and clinicians can use computer-aided diagnosis (CAD) to increase diagnostic accuracy and reduce biopsy rates. In comparison to earlier models that used a lightweight model to optimize the feature extraction process for thyroid nodule classification, the proposed inception-v3 method had a 90% accuracy rate on validation data. The model had a greater accuracy than the Inception-v2 model. The most common way to diagnose thyroid gland problems is via an ultrasound scan. Radiologists and clinicians can use computer-aided diagnosis (CAD) to increase diagnostic accuracy and reduce biopsy rates.

For the categorization of thyroid nodules, Avola et al. (2021) in their work used the transfer learning method. They were able to achieve considerable results using a knowledge-driven learning and feature fusion strategy. They used an ensemble of experts obtained through transfer learning to investigate knowledge-driven techniques. The ensemble provides consultations to a DenseNet during its training, and the two components eventually interact to act as a CAD system. Their knowledge-driven approach is made up of three parts: a data augmentation and feature fusion phase that generates detailed nodule images. Transfer learning allows for a reduction in both the time and the quantity of samples required to properly train a network, making it suitable for the proposed ensemble, which is based on difficult-to-find medical images.

The classification of ultrasound pictures of thyroid nodules was improved in the DT. Nguyen et al.'s (2020) study by examining images in both the spatial (using deep learning) and frequency domains (using Fast Fourier Transform). To learn from data efficiently, a Convolutional Neural Network with several weighted layers is necessary. However, when the number of layers grows, the issue of vanishing gradients arises. CNN networks such as AlexNet and VGGNet, for example, have millions of parameters. DT. Nguyen et al. utilised a ResNet50-based network that has 50 weight layers in total. The size of the nodule had a significant impact on the classification outcome. Because the dataset was so small, utilising Binary Cross Entropy resulted in bias due to the dataset's imbalances. The Weighted Binary Cross Entropy approach which showed to be effective in reducing overfitting and bias in trained classifiers was employed.

Abdolali et al. (2020) published the first systematic review of CAD systems for thyroid cancer sonographic diagnosis in this publication. The advancement of machine learning has promoted the construction of complicated and comprehensive models for thyroid nodule sonographic diagnosis. The automatic parameterization of thyroid has been handled from many viewpoints (e.g. detection, segmentation, and

Figure 3. Block diagram representing End-to-End implementation

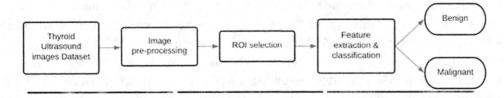

classification) utilising various approaches, as illustrated in this survey. This paper's categorization of approaches serves as a reference guide to the current techniques for analysing thyroid US pictures. To offer the necessary accuracy, more efficient machine learning models should include the anatomical context inherent to the thyroid gland.

Another research paper by W. Song et al. (2018), proposed a novel MC-CNN framework for thyroid nodule detection and classification on ultrasound images. With the goal of better identifying benign nodules from malignant nodules, as well as the complicated background, the new learning architecture allowed the detection and classification tasks to share commonly needed features. In order to achieve this goal, a multi-scale layer was included in the new learning architecture to increase the detection performance of thyroid nodules with scales that vary dramatically. As a result, the nodule candidates discovered were fed back into the spatial pyramid augmented by AlexNet to boost classification performance even further.

The above research papers have obtained accuracies of around 90% and moderate sensitivities and f1 scores. Sensitivity, which is one of the most critical evaluation metrics, indicates whether the model has fewer false negatives obtained on correct prediction of images of malignant nodules as malignant itself. Predicting images of malignant nodules as malignant itself is very crucial as if predicted as benign, the patient will not be given treatment immediately, hence worsening the condition. F1 scores and accuracies obtained in the previous works can be improved by using an efficient deep learning model with well-structured architecture and a classifier. This project can also be made accessible to the users by means of a GUI (Graphical User Interface) or an application, thus allowing them to analyse their scan images without the intervention of the medical staff.

IMPLEMENTATION

Block Diagram

The block diagram of the implementation is shown in Figure 3.

Dataset

The dataset used for the implementation of this project is The Digital Database of Thyroid Ultrasound Images (DDTI) which is a free and open-source database from Colombia's Universidad Nacional (L. Pedraza et al., 2015). A series of B-mode Ultrasound images are used to create the DDTI, which includes a thorough explanation and description of the diagnosis of suspected Thyroid Nodules by at least two qualified radiologists. DDTI has 299 cases of which 270 are of women and 29 are of men. DDTI has a

Figure 4. (a) Ultrasound Image of a Benign Thyroid Nodule – case number 600 (L. Pedraza et al., 2015).
Figure 4b. Ultrasound Image of a Benign Thyroid Nodule – case number 597 (L. Pedraza et al., 2015)

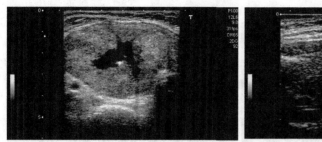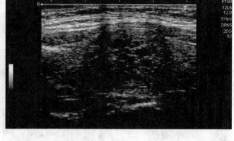

total of 347 photos. The cases included in the DDTI dataset are gathered by one of the largest diagnostic centres (for imaging) in Columbia - The IDIME Ultrasound Department. The Thyroid Ultrasound images saved in JPG format (without compressing) were obtained from video sequences taken by Ultrasound Devices. The devices used were the TOSHIBA Nemio 30 or the TOSHIBA Nemio MX. The nodule polygon and explanation of the diagnosis of the ultrasound image of each patient were recorded in a separate file of the format XML. TI-RADS - Thyroid Imaging, Reporting and Data System was used by experts to classify patients (FN. Tessler et al., 2017). For all five categories of Ultrasonography found in a nodule, points are given according to TI-RADS. More points are given to those features which contribute to a higher risk of malignancy. The sum of the points of all the categories gives the TI-RADS score. The score ranges from TI-RADS Score of 1 (harmless) to a TI-RADS score of 5 (destructive) (high suspicion of malignancy). The XML file includes a detailed explanation of the diagnosis of each patient based on the Ultrasound Image.

Examples of the images in the DDTI dataset.

Benign Thyroid Nodule

The XML file provided in the DDTI Dataset for Figure 4a states the following:

Case Number: 600

Gender: Female

Composition: Spongiform appearance

Echogenicity: Hyperechogenicity

Margins: Well defined smooth

Calcifications: Microcalcification

Tirads score: 2

The XML file provided in the DDTI Dataset for the Fig.4b states the following:

Case Number: 597

Gender: F

Composition: Predominantly Solid

Echogenicity: Iso Echogenicity

Margins: Well defined smooth

Calcifications: non

Tirads score: 2

ii. Malignant Thyroid Nodule

The XML file provided in the DDTI Dataset for the Fig.5a states the following:

Figure 5. (a) Ultrasound image of a Malignant Thyroid Nodule – case number 608 (L. Pedraza et al., 2015). Figure 5b. Ultrasound image of Malignant Thyroid Nodule – case number 612 (L. Pedraza et al., 2015)

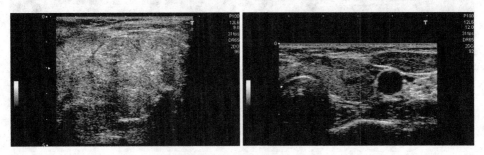

Case Number: 608
Gender: F
Composition: Solid
Echogenicity: Hypoechogenicity
Margins: Ill defined
Calcifications: Macrocalcification
Tirads score: 5
The XML file provided in the DDTI Dataset for the Figure 5b states the following:
Case Number: 612
Gender: F
Composition: Solid
Echogenicity: Hypoechogenicity
Margins: Well defined smooth
Calcifications: Microcalcification
Tirads score: 4c

As depicted in Figure 4a, 4b, 5a and 5b, there are regions of high intensity and regions of low intensity. The background (border areas with poor illumination and some additional artifacts) and the thyroid region (the inner brighter part that captures the details of the thyroid region) are the two primary parts of the acquired ultrasound thyroid images.

Figure 7 has a spongiform appearance as stated in the XML file provided. Spongiform appearance is due to the occurrence of very small cysts, similar to the fluid-filled spaces in a wet sponge. If the cystic components in the image are more than 50%, then the composition is said to be spongiform. An even, progressively curved interface characterizes a smooth margin which is found in the figure (FN. Tessler et al., 2018). Tissues which have a higher echogenicity are defined as hyperechogenic and are usually represented by higher pixel values (or intensity) in the ultrasound images. This image has a TI-RAD score of 2 because it has a hyperechogenicity (1 point) and microcalcifications (1 point).

Figure 8 has a predominantly solid composition which signifies that the nodules have small cystic components that take up less than 5% of the total volume. Predominantly solid can be considered as the case which has mixed cystic and solid composition (FN. Tessler et al., 2018). When the nodule's echogenicity is similar to that of the surrounding thyroid parenchyma, it is defined as iso echogenicity. The

TI-RAD score for iso echogenicity is 1 point and for the composition it is 1 point, hence, the TI-RAD score for this image is 2.

Figure 9 has a solid composition which indicates that the cystic components occupy a volume less than 5% of the total volume (FN. Tessler et al., 2018). Tissues with lower echogenicity are defined as hypoechogenic and are represented by lower intensity values (or lower pixel values), hence Hypoechogenicity is indicated by the darker portion in the image. Huge specks of calcium that can be observed inside a thyroid nodule or in the periphery (so-called eggshell/rim calcifications) as huge bright spots in an ultrasound image are called microcalcifications. The TI-RAD score for microcalcification is 1 point, for solid composition it is 2 points, for hypoechogenicity it is 2 points, hence the total TI-RAD score is 5 points.

Figure 10 is similar to that of figure 9 but the main difference is the calcifications which are clearly visible in the image. There are microcalcifications present in this image. The TI-RAD score for this figure is 2 points for hypoechogenicity, 2 points for solid composition making it a total of 4. The XML file for this figure states that the TI-RAD score is 4c which signifies the presence of highly suspicious nodules (50-85% risk of malignancy) (J. Sánchez et al., 2014).

The dataset has images which vary based on TI-RAD scores calculated by considering factors such as echogenicity, composition, echogenic foci (calcifications), margins and shape.

Image Loading and Pre-processing

The images were first loaded by iterating through the folders of the open-source CAS dataset using the OpenCV functions. The images were then split into training and testing images in the ratio 4:1. Keras functions were used for image pre-processing. The image loaded was of the format: width x height x channels.

Images obtained from the open-source CAS dataset (L. Pedraza et al., 2015) are of the size or resolution 560 x 360 (width x height). These images were resized to 256 x 256. For ImageNet scale networks, the rule of thumb is to use 256 x 256 sized images (Al-Shweiki, Jumana, 2021).

The images were then converted to numpy format which stores the images in height x width format using np.array() function.

If only structured data is used for a given data science or machine learning business problem, and the data obtained includes both categorical and continuous variables, most machine learning algorithms will not understand or be able to deal with categorical variables. When data is provided as a number rather than category to a model for training and testing, machine learning algorithms perform better in terms of accuracy and other performance measures. Since machine learning algorithms perform better with numeric values and mostly work exclusively with numeric values, the train and test labels of the train and test images are encoded respectively. The method used is called "label encoding". In python label encoding, the categorical value is replaced with a numeric value between 0 and the (number. of classes – 1). For example, if the categorical variable value comprises 3 unique classes, then the labels are encoded to a range of values between 0 and 2 – (0, 1, 2). Since the labels used in our project are benign and malignant (number of unique classes = 2), they are encoded to 0 and 1 respectively. Label Encoding is done for labels of both the training and testing images. For the implementation of Label Encoding, the LabelEncoder module from the preprocessing module from sklearn package was imported. fit and transform functions were then used to assign a numerical value to the categorical values.

Figure 6. US (Ultrasound) image of a thyroid nodule (L. Pedraza et al., 2015)

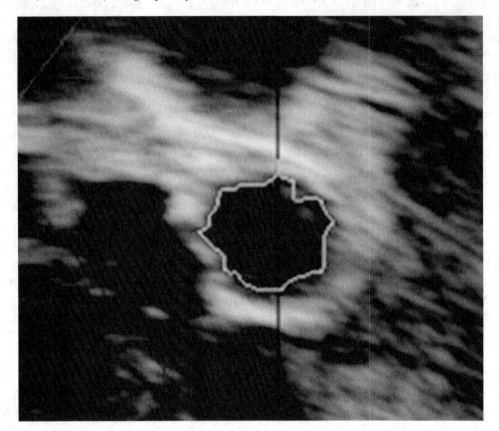

The pixel values of the images can have a value ranging from 0 to 256. The computation of high numeric values may get more complex when using the image as is and sending it through a Deep Neural Network. The complexity can be reduced by normalizing the numbers to a range of 0 to 1. Normalization is done by dividing all pixel values by 255 resulting in pixels in the range 0 to 1. These small values of pixels make computations easier.

The images were in the format (height, width, channels). But the neural network (based on ImageNet) accepts an input which is a 4-dimensional Tensor of the format batch size x height x width x channels. Hence, images need to be converted to batch format. As the matrix (input to the network) is required to be of the form (batchsize, height, width, channels), an extra dimension is added to the image at a particular axis (axis = 0). The extra dimension is added by using expand_dims() function where the axis parameter is set to 0. The axis parameter defines at what position the new axis should be inserted. axis = 0 signifies rows and axis = 1 signifies columns.

Region of Interest

Figure 6 shows an example of ultrasound images provided in the dataset for reference The area in green represents the nodule. The borders of the nodule have higher intensity (lighter shades – white) values compared to the surrounding background. This is how the nodule region is differentiated from the rest of the image.

Tissues with lower echogenicity are defined as hypoechogenic and are represented by lower intensity values (or lower pixel values), hence Hypoechogenicity is indicated by the darker portion in the image. Tissues which have a higher echogenicity are defined as hyperechogenic and are usually represented by higher pixel values (or intensity) in the ultrasound images indicated by the lighter portion of the image. When the nodule's echogenicity is similar to that of the surrounding thyroid parenchyma, it is defined as iso echogenicity that is there is not much difference in the pixel values or intensity.

Deep Learning Models

VGG 19

The dimensions of the input image are 224 by 224. A set of convolutional layers are used to process the image. The receptive field of the layers is small. VGG19 includes additional filters (convolutional) in one of the setups. This can be considered as a modification of the input channels wherein the modification is linear. Convolution stride which is a parameter that decides amount of movement is set as 1 pixel for thirty-three convolution layers. Input Spatial Padding (Convolutional layer) is set to the same value. After convolution, for the sake of preservation of Spatial Resolution this procedure is done. Part of the convolutional layers succeeded by max pooling layers (5 of them) constitute spatial pooling. For max-pooling over a 2 by 2-pixel window, the parameter responsible for movement in an image - stride is set to 2.

Three layers which are fully connected are added after convolutional layers (stack of layers). ImageNet Large Scale Visual Recognition Challenge known as ILSVRC is used for large-scale evaluation of algorithms. Due to the many deep convolutional layers in the VGG 19, it performs 1000-way ILSVRC Classification.

VGG-19 has several advantages, including the fact that it is a particularly suitable architecture for benchmarking on a specific job, and that pre-trained networks for VGG are simple to construct and understand. VGGNet, on the other hand, has two shortcomings. For starters, it is quite slow. VGG19 consumes large memory due to the number of nodes which are connected completely and its depths. Hence, implementation of VGG is a time-consuming process. Second, the network architectural weights are extremely substantial.

Residual Network (ResNet)

The idea behind a network with residual blocks as seen in Figure 7 is that each layer is fed to the network's next layer, as well as directly to the next layers, skipping a few layers in the process. Considerably deeper neural networks can be trained with residual blocks. Because it bypasses one or more levels in between, the connection (curve arrow) is known as a skip connection or shortcut connection. Because an identity function can be learnt from it, it's also known as identity connection. Instead of allowing layers to learn the underlying mapping, the network is allowed to fit the residual mapping. So, instead of say H(x), initial mapping, let the network fit, $F(x) = H(x) - x$ which gives $H(x) = F(x) + x$.

The benefit of including this type of skip connection is that any layer that degrades architecture performance will be bypassed by regularization. As a result, very deep neural networks can be trained

Figure 7. A Residual Block (KS Srujana et al., 2022).

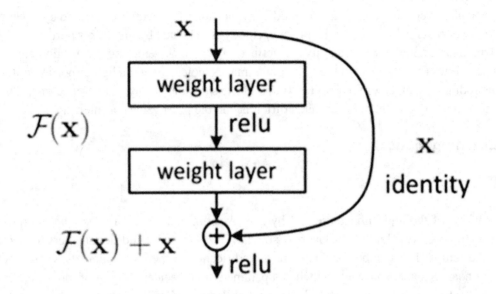

without the issues caused by vanishing/exploding gradients. The ResNet 101 architecture contains 101 layers of Deep Convolutional network. The ResNet-101 version 2 model is divided into several stages, each with its own convolution and identity block. There are multiple convolution layers in each convolution block, and many convolution layers in each identity block. There are around 45 million trainable parameters in the ResNet-101v2. The aforementioned explanation concludes that ResNet is faster than VGG19 and gives greater accuracy.

DenseNet

The fact that every layer is connected to every other layer is the reason that this architecture is given the name DenseNet. For L layers there are $(\frac{1}{2})*L*(L+1)$ connections which are direct. For each layer, the input includes preceding feature maps, and its feature maps are considered as the input for the succeeding layers. For a layer inside DenseNet, the input is a concatenation of feature maps of the previous layers. Due to this, the network is compact and less bulky thereby resulting in fewer channels, better computational and memory efficiency. pre-Activation Batch and ReLU constitute the basic architecture of DenseNet. They are used for each layer (composition) after which they are used for thirty-three convolutional layers with output feature maps of the number of channels. The same is noticed in Figure 8.

Some of the advantages of DenseNet over VGG and ResNet are as follows. Firstly, the error signal can be conveyed more directly to earlier tiers. As earlier layers can receive direct supervision from the final classification layer, this is a form of implicit deep supervision. Secondly, the number of parameters in ResNet is proportional to channels for each layer, but the number of parameters in DenseNet is proportional to channel multiplied to growth rate for each layer. Therefore, DenseNet is substantially smaller than ResNet. This aspect is very important in making the computation process easy and subsequently reducing the execution time. DenseNet performs well in the absence of sufficient training data.

Figure 8. DenseNet Architecture (Veena et al., 2021)

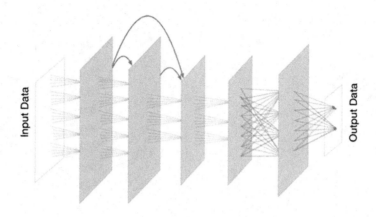

MobileNet

MobileNet is a convolutional neural network (CNN) for computer vision applications that is simple, efficient, and computationally light. Only the first layer is a full convolutional layer. All the other convolutional layers are depth wise and separable. Only the last layer is not followed by batch normalization and ReLU non-linearity as it does not have any non-linearity and is fully connected. It is followed by a softmax layer which is used for classification. For down sampling, for the first layer which is a full convolutional layer as mentioned previously, as well as for depth wise convolution, strided convolution is used. MobileNet consists of a total of 28 layers which includes depth wise and point wise convolutional layers considered separately as seen in Figure 9.

Some of the advantages of MobileNet are as follows. Firstly, the network size is reduced. Secondly, the number of parameters is decreased. Thirdly, it is faster in performance and lightweight. Finally, MobileNets are considered small, low-latency CNNs.

Figure 9. MobileNet Standard Architecture (Rahul et al., 2022)

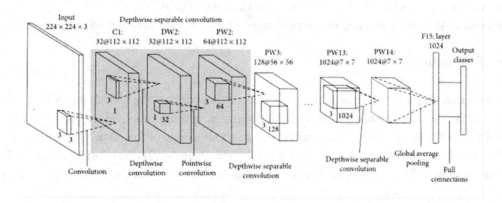

Figure 10. Architecture of Inception-Resnet-V2 (C.Gururaj et al., 2020)

Inception-Resnet-V2

The Convolutional Neural Network (CNN) Inception-ResNet-v2 which has been trained on over a million images from the ImageNet database is a 164-layer network. It can classify images into 1000 different object categories. As a result, the network has learned a variety of rich feature representations for a variety of images. The network takes a 299-by-299 image as input and outputs a list of estimated class probabilities. This is shown in Figure 10.

It's built on a foundation of the Inception structure and the Residual connection. Multiple sized convolutional filters are combined with residual connections in the Inception-Resnet block. The use of residual connections not only avoids the degradation issue caused by deep structures, but it also cuts training time in half.

Figure 18 shows the network's initial layers, which include three standard convolutional layers, a max-pooling layer, two convolutional layers, and another max-pooling layer. The network's next stage is inception convolution, which entails convoluting an input multiple times with different filter sizes for each convolution, then merging (stacking) the results and passing them on to the rest of the network (C.Gururaj et al., 2020).

The network then repeats inceptions and residuals a number of times, with some parts repeating 10 or 20 times until it reaches the end, when it uses dropout layers to randomly drop weights (make filter values equal to 0) to prevent overfitting. In addition, the second last layer is a fully connected layer that influences all neurons based on the learned information. Finally, a softmax layer is used to probabilistically distribute the scores to the final 1000 neurons (C.Gururaj et al., 2020).

The Inception-ResNet-v2 architecture outperforms previous state-of-the-art models in terms of accuracy.

Feature Extraction

Feature extraction for images is done using global feature descriptors like Local Binary Patterns (LBP), Histogram of Oriented Gradients (HoG), Color Histograms, and so on, as well as local descriptors like SIFT, SURF, and ORB. For these hand-crafted features, knowledge of the respective domain is a must.

But when using Deep Neural Networks like CNN, the Deep Neural Networks automatically learn features in a hierarchical manner from the images inputted. Lower layers learn low-level features like corners and edges, while intermediate layers learn colour, shape, and so on, and upper layers learn high-level features like objects present in the image.

By using the activations accessible before the network's last completely linked layer, CNN is employed as a Feature Extractor (that is, before the final softmax classifier). These activations will be used as a feature vector in a machine learning model (classifier) that learns to classify it further. This approach is ideally suited for Image Classification issues, where a pre-trained CNN might be used as a Feature Extractor - Transfer Learning - instead of training a CNN from start (which is time-consuming and difficult).

The pre-trained models are loaded from the Keras library's application module, and the model is built based on the user-specified configurations. Following this, the features are extracted from the user-specified layer in the ImageNet dataset-pre-trained model (Example, ResNet101V2).

ImageNet is a massive image database with about 14 million images. It was created by academics with the objective of doing computer vision research. In terms of scale, it was the first of its sort. ImageNet includes a hierarchy of images which are sorted and labeled. Machine Learning and Deep Neural both include training of machines using a large dataset of images. Machines must be able to extract useful features from these training images. Having learned these features, they can utilize these features to classify images and perform a variety of other computer vision tasks. Researchers can use the set of images provided by ImageNet to compare their models and algorithms.

Example of feature extraction implemented for ResNet101V2 Model:

Keras comes with a variety of models. Model Architecture and Model Weights are the two aspects of a trained model. Because the weights are big files, they are not included with Keras. On specifying weights='imagenet' in the model initialization, the imagenet weights file is imported. If weights is set to none, then the model does not use pretrained weights and weights are obtained on training the model from scratch using randomly initialized weights initially.

When loading a model, the "include top" parameter can be set to False, which means that the fully connected output layers of the model used to make predictions are not loaded, allowing for the addition and training of a new output layer. Input_shape = (SIZE, SIZE, 3) is the new output layer in this case. To exclude the default classifier of the respective model and include a classifier of our choice, the include top parameter is set to false.

Fitting the Classification Model or Algorithm – For Example, SVM:

From the svm module of the sklearn package, SVC (Support Vector Classifier) is imported.

The SVM (Support Vector Machine) Classifier is implemented using a kernel which is used to transform low dimensional space (of input data) into a higher dimensional space. It essentially converts a problem which is non-separable into a separable problem by adding a dimension. SVM is known for providing a good accuracy for problems that have non-linear separation. The classifier model is built using SVC with the parameter kernel as linear wherein a linear kernel is used as a dot product between values. The features extracted (for training and testing images) from the previous stage are used for training the classification algorithm by fitting it on them (features) using the class_model.fit() function.

Classification Algorithms

K Nearest Neighbours (KNN)

For both classification and regression, K-nearest neighbours (KNN), which is mostly a supervised learning approach, is adopted. KNN works in the following fashion: the Euclidean distance between the new data point (in this case an image) and the training data is calculated. Following this, if the distance is minimum between the new data point and one of the classes, then it is categorized into that class. The KNN model compares the new data set to the normal and malignant scans and labels it as one of the two based on the most similar properties. When there are two categories, and a new data point needs to be classified between the two categories, KNN may be required. KNN has a number of advantages, including a short calculation time, ease of implementation, adaptability (it may be used for regression and classification), and high accuracy.

XGBoost

'XGBoost stands for "Extreme Gradient Boosting." XGBoost is a tool for distributed gradient boosting that has been optimised to be versatile, fast, and portable. It uses a parallel tree boosting approach to rapidly and precisely solve a wide range of data science problems.

The XGBoost approach has shown to have numerous advantages over other classifiers. XGBoost is a faster algorithm than other algorithms due to its simultaneous and distributed processing. Both system optimization and machine learning methodologies were carefully considered when developing XGBoost. The goal of this library is to push computers to their processing limits in order to produce a library that is accurate.

AdaBoost

AdaBoost is the abbreviation for Adaptive Boosting. AdaBoost. It is one of the efficient boosting designs specifically for binate classification problems. It's also a fantastic location to learn about boosting algorithms. It is adaptive that subsequent classifiers are modified in support of occurrences misclassified by previous ones. Outliers and noisy data can make it vulnerable.

Across various cycles, AdaBoost attempts to build a sole composite strong learner. It compiles all the weak learners at one instance to create a strong learner. During every single round of iteration in the training process, a new weak learner is appended to the ensemble, and the weighting vector is changed to pivot on cases that were misclassified in previous rounds. This results in the outperformance of the classifier than the weak learner classifiers in terms of accuracy. The most significant advantages of AdaBoost include low generalisation error, easy implementation, ability to work with a wide range of classifiers, and doesn't require any parameter adjustments. Because this technique is susceptible to outliers, it necessitates close scrutiny of the data.

Decision Tree

Decision Tree is one of the approaches for supervised learning that is used most commonly to solve classification issues. The nodes of the tree depict the attributes of the dataset, branches characterize decision rules, and the conclusion is given by the leaf nodes in this tree-structured classifier.

The significant constituents present in a decision tree include leaf nodes and decision nodes. The output of the decisions of the tree characterizes leaf nodes which further does not contain any branches. On the other hand, the decision nodes have the functionality to make any decision regarding the problem and further contain many branches. Some of the drawbacks of this classifier is: The decision tree is complicated since it has many tiers/layers. It may have an overfitting problem. The computational complexity is increased as additional class labels are added in the decision tree. However, these decision trees also have significant benefits which include Decision Trees are designed/developed to reflect and parallel the conventional human thinking abilities when making decisions. This aspect makes them comprehensible.

Support Vector Machine (SVM)

Support Vector Machine, abbreviated as SVM, is one of the most widely adopted methods for supervised learning and more specifically for classification issues. The SVM algorithm's sole purpose is to determine the optimum line, also called a decision boundary. This is used to easily group or categorize a new data point in n-dimensional space containing different categories. The ideal boundary distinguishing different classes is termed as the hyperplane. SVM helps in choosing the extreme points that assist in creating the hyperplane. These extreme cases are called support vectors.

Making a straight line between two classes is how a simple linear SVM classifier works. That is, all of the data points on one side of the line will be assigned to one category, while the data points on the other side will be assigned to a different category. This implies that there may be an endless number of lines from which to choose. The linear SVM algorithm is superior to other algorithms such as k-nearest neighbors because it selects the best line to classify the data points. It selects the line that divides the data and is the farthest distant from the closest data points. This may be fine for data that is linearly distributed.

The reason for utilization of SVMs is that they can uncover intricate associations between the data without requiring to perform a lot of manual modifications. When working with smaller datasets that contain thousands of features, SVM is the best solution compared to any other classifiers.

The pros of SVM are: It is very effective for datasets with multiple features like the medical data. It saves memory by using only a subset of training data points which are called support vectors present in the decision function. However, the downsides of SVM include: if the frequency of features is greater than the number of data points, then over-fitting may be the consequence. Because of the long training time, it works best with tiny sample sets. On noisy datasets with overlapping classes, it's less effective.

Prediction

After the network is loaded and initialized, the next step involves using the model.predict() function. The predict function is used on the features obtained from the test images. The output vector obtained from model.predict() consists of the encoded labels which is difficult for humans to comprehend. Hence, the output is decoded to convert the encoded labels back to the original categorical values which can be easily understood by the user. Decoding of the encoded labels is implemented using the inverse_transform method. The encoded labels 0, 1 are hence decoded to give benign and malignant. This stage gives the final output in the Detection and Classification of Thyroid Nodules into Malignant and Benign Nodules.

EVALUATION

Evaluation Metrics

The capability of a predictive model is quantified by Evaluation Metrics. This usually entails training a model on a dataset, then using the model to generate predictions on a holdout dataset that was not used during training and comparing the predictions to the predicted values in the holdout dataset. Metrics for classification problems include comparing the expected class label to the predicted class label or interpreting the problem's predicted probabilities for class labels. The selection of a model, as well as the data preparation procedures, is a search issue led by the evaluation metric. The results of any experiment are quantified using a metric.

Accuracy

Model accuracy can be defined as the frequency or number of classifications a deep learning model correctly predicts by the total number of predictions made by it. It is a quantitative factor for analyzing the performance of a deep learning model. It is one the most significant metrics that has to be accounted for or considered.

$$Accuracy = \frac{True\,Positive}{(True\,Positive + True\,Negative)}\,x100\,Eqn.$$

(1)

Confusion Matrix

A Confusion matrix is an N-by-N matrix adopted to evaluate the performance of a deep learning model, where N represents the number of target classes present. The matrix attempts to compare the correct target values with those predicted by the classification model. Confusion matrix depicts ways in which a model becomes ambiguous when making predictions. Large values across the diagonal and small values off the diagonal characterize a good matrix (model). Measuring or finding the confusion matrix gives us a clearer idea of the model performance and the different kinds of errors generated by it.

Components of Confusion Matrix:

a. True Positive (TP): A true positive is an outcome where the model correctly predicts the positive class.
b. False Negative (FN): A false negative is an outcome where the model incorrectly predicts the negative class.
c. False Positive (FP): A false positive is an outcome where the model incorrectly predicts the positive class.
d. True Negative (TN): A true negative is an outcome where the model correctly predicts the negative class.

Sensitivity or Recall or False Positive Rate

Sensitivity is defined as the ratio of true positives to the actual positives in the data. The ability of a test to correctly identify patients with a condition is referred to as sensitivity.

If a model has high sensitivity, it implies that the model will have fewer false negatives which is crucial when the model is used for the detection of a medical condition.

$$\text{Sensitivity} = \frac{True\ Positive}{\left(True\ Positive + False\ Negative\right)} \text{Eqn.} \tag{2}$$

Specificity

Specificity is defined as the proportion of actual negatives, which get predicted as the negative. The fraction of actual negatives that were predicted as negatives is known as specificity (or true negative). This means that a part of true negatives will be predicted as positives, which could be referred to as false positives. This fraction is also known as a True Negative Rate (TNR). The product of specificity (true negative rate) and false positive rate is always one. If a model has high specificity, it implies that it is good at predicting True Negatives.

$$\text{Specificity} = \frac{True\ Negative}{\left(True\ Negative + False\ Positive\right)} \text{Eqn.} \tag{3}$$

Precision

The precision is one of the evaluation metrics defined as the ratio between the number of positive data points correctly classified to the total number of data points classified as positive correctly or incorrectly.

The precision tends to be smaller if the deep learning model makes very less positive classifications or multiple wrong correct (positive) classifications. In contrast, the precision tends to be high when the developed classification model makes few incorrect Positive classifications or multiple correct positive classifications.

$$\text{Precision} = \frac{True\ Positive}{\left(True\ Positive + False\ Positive\right)} \text{Eqn.} \tag{4}$$

F1 Score

The harmonic mean between precision and recall is termed as F1 Score. It is mainly used as a measure to evaluate performance of a deep learning model. F1-score is employed when False Negatives and False Positives are more significant. One of the options to address class imbalance issues is to utilize more accurate metrics, such as the F1 score, which consider not only the number of prediction mistakes made by the model but also the type of errors made.

$$\text{F1 Score} = \frac{True\ Positive}{True\ Positive + 0.5\left(False\ Positive + False\ Negative\right)} \text{Eqn.} \tag{5}$$

Negative Predictive Value (NPV)

The negative predictive value is defined as the proportion of predicted negatives that are real negatives. It reflects the probability that a predicted negative is a true negative. It expresses the likelihood that a predicted negative is indeed a true negative.

$$NPV = \frac{True\ Negative}{(True\ Negative + False\ Negative)} Eqn. \qquad (6)$$

False Positive Rate (FPR)

The false-positive rate is based on how many actual negatives the model predicted incorrectly. This metric is complementary to the true positive rate, or recall.

The FPR is best explained as the probability of falsely rejecting the null hypothesis which is one of the important terms in the medical diagnostic domain. The false-positive rate is one of the metrics used to assess how well machine learning models perform when applied to classification issues. Lesser the false positive rate, better is the deep learning model.

$$FPR = \frac{False\ Positive}{Total\ no.of\ Negatives} = \frac{False\ Positive}{(False\ Positive + True\ Negative)} Eqn. \qquad (7)$$

False Negative Rate (FNR)

The false-negative rate measures the percentage of false negatives against all negative predictions. This metric is complementary to the true negative rate.

Lesser the false negative rate, better and more accurate is the deep learning model.

$$FNR = \frac{False\ Negative}{Total\ no.of\ Positives} = \frac{False\ Negative}{(False\ Negative + True\ Positive)} Eqn. \qquad (8)$$

False Discovery Rate (FDR)

FDR is the (expected) proportion of false positives among all variables called significantly.

The False Discovery Rate (FDR) is the percentage of hypotheses incorrectly believed to be true. A test that passes the acceptability criteria based on threshold is referred to as a 'discovery'. The FDR is useful since it calculates how enriched the accepted discoveries are for actual discoveries.

Figure 11. Graphical User Interface

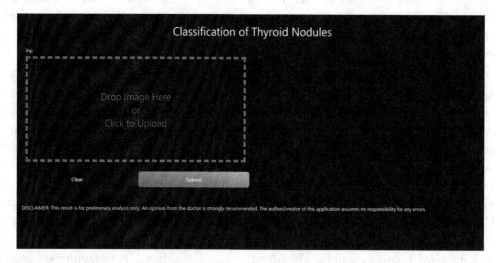

$$FDR = \frac{False\ Positive}{\left(False\ Positive + True\ Negative\right)} Eqn.$$ (9)

Receiver operating characteristic curve (ROC)

A ROC curve is a plot that evaluates the performance of a deep learning classification model over all categorization levels. The parameters plotted in this curve include True and False Positive Rate

TPR vs. FPR at different categorization levels is plotted on the ROC curve. As the threshold of the classification is reduced, multiple data points are classified as positive, which results in an increase in both False and True Positives. A ROC curve is depicted in the figure below.

Area Under the Curve (AUC)

AUC stands for area under the curve, ROC Curve to be specific. As the name suggests, it evaluates a 2-dimensional area of the ROC Curve. The AUC gives the outline of the ROC curve and further determines the ability to distinguish or segregate different classes given to the implemented classifier. Which means that it tends to give a better view of how the model distinguishes between the present positive and negative classes. The greater the AUC, more accurate is the deep learning model.

GRAPHICAL USER INTERFACE (GUI)

A user interface or computer program that facilitates interaction or communication between people and electronic devices like computers, phones etc. via visual indicators, and symbols is called Graphical User Interface.

The Figure 11 is a simple Graphical User Interface that has been implemented with Gradio (Python package). Using Gradio, it is possible to easily generate customizable UI (User Interface) components for a machine learning model, any API, or any function using only a few lines of code. The GUI can be either embedded into the Python notebook or the URL provided by Gradio can be opened by anyone.

Gradio is implemented using the function. Interface (). The user is prompted to upload or drag an ultrasound scan image that is to be classified. Internally, the image inputted by the user is first resized to the dimensions 256 x 256 in order to maintain uniformity of it with the pre-processed source images. The images are in the format (height x width x channels). But the neural network (based on ImageNet) accepts an input which is a 4-dimensional Tensor of the format batch size x height x width x channels. Hence, a dimension was added to the resized image. Following this, features are extracted by using. predict () function and the deep learning-based model. These features are then used by the classifier to predict whether the ultrasound image (provided by user) consists of a benign or malignant thyroid nodule. The obtained classification output is then displayed. The output displayed will be red if the output is 'MALIGNANT' and green if the output is 'BENIGN'. A link which when clicked opens a new tab with more information about the classification is also displayed. A file with the same contents is also displayed, when the user clicks on it, the file gets downloaded. The user can use either the link or download the file to view more information about TI-RADS Classification.

RESULTS

Confusion Matrix and Evaluation Metrics

The following results are obtained when SVM is used as the classifier shown in Figure 12 a through e and Table 1.

Comparative Study of Results Obtained from all the Models Implemented

The F1 score is a metric for how accurate a model is on a given data set. Therefore, a higher F1 score implies that the model gives a more accurate classification output. From the Fig.13 a through e it is visible that the Resnet-101V2 model has the highest F1 score.

If a model has high sensitivity, it implies that the model will have fewer false negatives which is crucial when the model is used for the detection of a medical condition. Resnet-101V2 has the highest sensitivity, hence it is the best model that can be applied for the detection and classification of thyroid nodules. If a model has a high Negative Predictive Value, when it classifies an ultrasound image as negative (or benign in this case), then the probability of the nodule in the image actually being benign is high. Since Resnet-101V2 has the highest Negative Predictive Value, this model can be trusted most to give an accurate negative (benign) output. A low value of False Negative Rate implies that the model classifies an image which is actually positive (or malignant) as negative (benign) rarely. Resnet-101V2 having the lowest value of False Negative Rate can be considered as the best model suited for the Detection and Classification of Thyroid nodules. The Resnet-101V2 which is 101 layers deep provides the highest accuracy of 95.83%.

Figure 12. Confusion Matrices of DL models

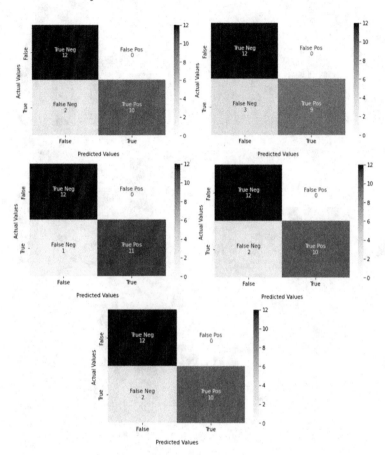

Table 1. Table showing the evaluation metric values obtained for all the deep learning models

	VGG19	DenseNet-169	Resnet-101 V2	MobileNet	Inception-Resnet-V2
Sensitivity	0.834	0.75	0.916	0.833	0.833
Specificity	1.0	1.0	1.0	1.0	1.0
Precision	1.0	1.0	1.0	1.0	1.0
Negative Predictive value	0.857	0.8	0.923	0.857	0.857
False positive rate	0.0	0.0	0.0	0.0	0.0
False negative rate	0.167	0.25	0.833	0.166	0.166
False discovery rate	0.0	0.857	0.0	0.0	0.0
F1 score	0.909	87.5	0.956	0.909	0.909
Overall Accuracy	91.667	91.667	95.833	91.666	91.666

Figure 13. Bar graphs of various evaluation metrics of all DL models

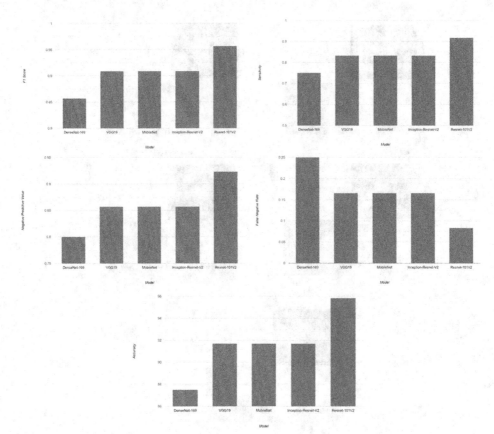

Comparative study of F1 scores of Different Classifiers for each Model Implemented

The F1 score is a metric for how accurate a model is on a given data set shown in Figure 14 a through e and Table 2. Therefore, a higher F1 score implies that the model gives a more accurate classification output.

ROC Curve (The Receiver Operator Characteristic Curve) and AUC (Area under the Curve)

ROC is used mainly for binary classification problems. The AUC summarises the ROC curve and determines a classifier's ability to discriminate across classes. The ROC Curves are obtained for different models implemented with SVM as the classifier. The same can be observed in Figure 15 a through e and Table 3.

Figure 14. Comparison of F1 scores of different classifiers for each DL model

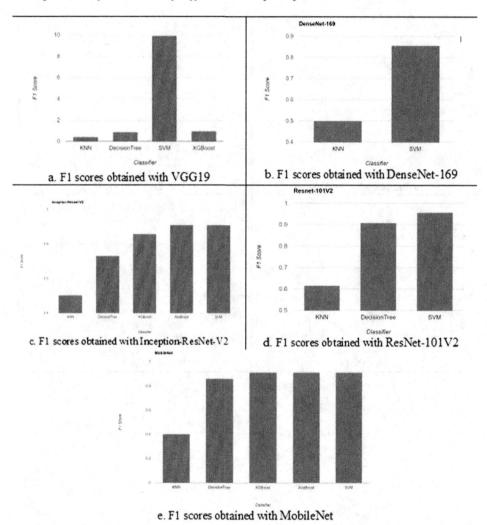

a. F1 scores obtained with VGG19

b. F1 scores obtained with DenseNet-169

c. F1 scores obtained with Inception-ResNet-V2

d. F1 scores obtained with ResNet-101V2

e. F1 scores obtained with MobileNet

Table 2. Table showing the F1 Scores of the deep learning models with different classifiers

	VGG19	DenseNet-169	Resnet-101 V2	MobileNet	Inception- Resnet-V2
KNN	0.5	0.5	0.615	0.4	0.4
Decision Tree	0.736	1.0	0.909	0.857	0.857
SVM	0.909	0.857	0.956	0.909	0.909
XGBoost	0.857	1.0	1.0	0.909	0.956
AdaBoost	0.909	1.0	1.0	0.909	1.0

Figure 15. ROC Curves for different DL models

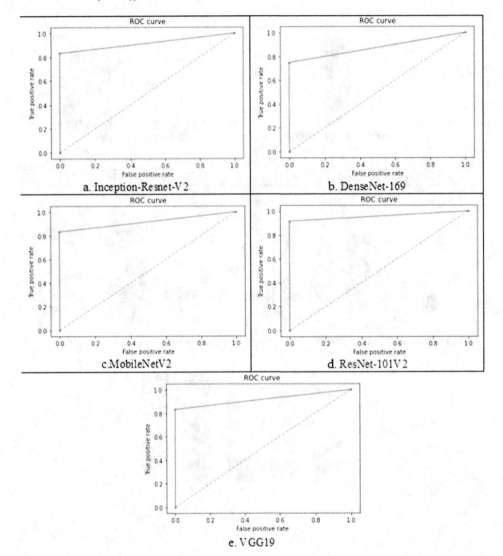

Table 3. Table showing the AUC values obtained corresponding to various DL models

DL model	AUC
Inception-Resnet-V2	0.916
DenseNet-169	0.875
MobileNet	0.916
VGG-19	0.916
ResNet-101 V2	0.958

Graphical User Interface

Figure 16. GUI giving for the output for Benign Nodule

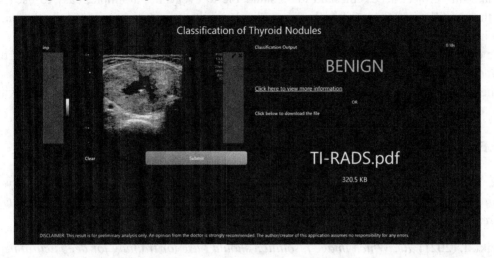

CONCLUSION AND FUTURE SCOPE

A comparison study of different Deep Learning Based models and Classifiers for the Detection and Classification of thyroid nodules into benign and malignant nodules has been done.

One of the challenges faced was the lack of a good GPU configuration. This was overcome by using Google Colab which an open-source platform specifically used for notebooks is written in python. Colab makes it very easy to use Keras and TensorFlow libraries.

Figure 17. GUI giving for the output for Malignant Nodule

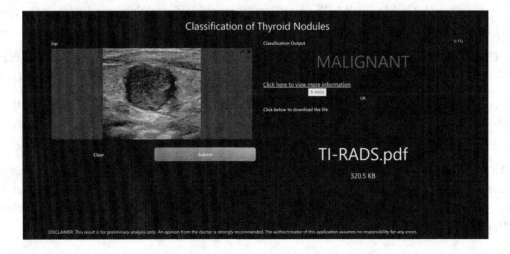

After performing a comparative study of different models and classifiers, it was found that ResNet-101v2 gave the best accuracy - 95.83%, F1 score - 0.957 and Sensitivity - 0.917 when used with the classifier SVM.

To make this project accessible and understandable to everyone, a simple, easy to use GUI that displays the classification output after the user uploads an ultrasound scan image of the thyroid nodule has been implemented.

Usage of real-time datasets acquired from hospitals would help improve the accuracy of the classification output given by our model.

Another enhancement that could be made to this project is by implementing it on hardware with GPU.

REFERENCES

Abdolali, Shahroudnejad, Hareendranathan, Jaremko, Noga, & Punithakumar. (2020). *A systematic review on the role of artificial intelligence in sonographic diagnosis of thyroid cancer: Past, present and future.* CoRR abs/2006.05861.

Al-Shweiki, J. (2021). *Re: Which Image resolution should I use for training for deep neural networks?* ResearchGate.

Avola, D., Cinque, L., Fagioli, A., Filetti, S., Grani, G., & Rodolà, E. (2021). *Knowledge-Driven Learning via Experts Consult for Thyroid Nodule Classification.* ArXiv, abs/2005.14117.

Chi, J., Walia, E., Babyn, P., Wang, J., Groot, G., & Eramian, M. (2017). Thyroid Nodule Classification in Ultrasound Images by Fine-Tuning Deep Convolutional Neural Network. *Journal of Digital Imaging, 30*(4), 477–486. doi:10.100710278-017-9997-y PMID:28695342

Chowdhary, C. L., & Channi, H. K. (2022). Deep Learning Empowered Fight Against COVID-19: A Survey. In *Next Generation Healthcare Informatics* (pp. 251–264). Springer. doi:10.1007/978-981-19-2416-3_14

Chowdhary, C. L., & Srivatsan, R. (2022). *Non-invasive Detection of Parkinson's Disease Using Deep Learning.* Academic Press.

Fernández Sánchez, J. (2014). TI-RADS classification of thyroid nodules based on a score modified regarding the ultrasound criteria for malignancy. *Revista Argentina de Radiología, 78*(3), 138–148.

Gururaj, C., & Tunga, S. (2020). AI based feature extraction through content based image retrieval. *Journal of Computational and Theoretical Nanoscience, 17*(9-10), 4050–4054. doi:10.1166/jctn.2020.9018

Khachnaoui, H., Guetari, R., & Khlifa, N. (2018). A review on Deep Learning in thyroid ultrasound Computer-Assisted Diagnosis systems. *2018 IEEE International Conference on Image Processing, Applications and Systems (IPAS)*, 291-297. 10.1109/IPAS.2018.8708866

Nayak, Holla, Akshayakumar, & Gururaj. (2021). Machine Learning Methodology toward identification of Mature Citrus fruits. In Computer Vision and Recognition Systems using Machine and Deep Learning Approaches IET Computing series vol. 42. The Institution of Engineering and Technology. doi:10.1049/PBPC042E_ch16

Nguyen, D. T., Kang, J. K., Pham, T. D., Batchuluun, G., & Park, K. R. (2020, March 25). Ultrasound Image-Based Diagnosis of Malignant Thyroid Nodule Using Artificial Intelligence. *Sensors (Basel)*, *20*(7), 1822. doi:10.339020071822 PMID:32218230

Nikhila, Nathan, Ataide, Illanes, Friebe, & Abbineni. (2019). Lightweight Residual Network for The Classification of Thyroid Nodules. *IEEE EMBS*.

Pedraza, L., Vargas, C., Narvaez, F., Duran, O., Munoz, E., & Romero, E. (2015). An open access thyroid ultrasound-image database. *Proceedings of the 10th International Symposium on Medical Information Processing and Analysis*.

Rahul, Uppunda, Sumukh, Vinayaka, & Gururaj. (2022). Self-Driving Car using Behavioral Cloning. In Fundamentals and Methods of Machine and Deep Learning: Algorithms, Tools and Applications. Wiley Publications. doi:10.1002/9781119821908.ch16

Song, W., Li, S., Liu, J., Qin, H., Zhang, B., Zhang, S., & Hao, A. (2018). Multitask cascade convolution neural networks for automatic thyroid nodule detection and recognition. *IEEE Journal of Biomedical and Health Informatics*, *23*(3), 1215–1224. doi:10.1109/JBHI.2018.2852718 PMID:29994412

Srujana, K. S., Kashyap, S. N., Shrividhiya, G., Gururaj, C., & Induja, K. S. (2022). Supply Chain Based Demand Analysis of Different Deep Learning Methodologies for Effective Covid-19 Detection. In *Innovative Supply Chain Management via Digitalization and Artificial Intelligence* (pp. 135–170). Springer. doi:10.1007/978-981-19-0240-6_9

Tessler, F. N., Middleton, W. D., & Grant, E. G. (2018, April). Thyroid Imaging Reporting and Data System (TI-RADS): A User's Guide. *Radiology*, *287*(1), 29–36. doi:10.1148/radiol.2017171240 PMID:29558300

Tessler, F. N., Middleton, W. D., Grant, E. G., Hoang, J. K., Berland, L. L., Teefey, S. A., Cronan, J. J., Beland, M. D., Desser, T. S., Frates, M. C., Hammers, L. W., Hamper, U. M., Langer, J. E., Reading, C. C., Scoutt, L. M., & Stavros, A. T. (2017). ACR thyroid imaging, reporting and data system (TI-RADS): White paper of the ACR TI-RADS committee. *Journal of the American College of Radiology*, *14*(5), 587–595. doi:10.1016/j.jacr.2017.01.046 PMID:28372962

Vadhiraj, V. V., Simpkin, A., O'Connell, J., Singh Ospina, N., Maraka, S., & O'Keeffe, D. T. (2021). Ultrasound image classification of thyroid nodules using machine learning techniques. *Medicina*, *57*(6), 527. doi:10.3390/medicina57060527 PMID:34074037

Yu, Q., Jiang, T., Zhou, A., Zhang, L., Zhang, C., & Xu, P. (2017). Computer-aided diagnosis of malignant or benign thyroid nodes based on ultrasound images. *European Archives of Oto-Rhino-Laryngology*, *274*(7), 2891–2897. doi:10.100700405-017-4562-3 PMID:28389809

Chapter 9
Emotion–Based Human–Computer Interaction

Sujigarasharma K.
https://orcid.org/0000-0003-0982-8739
School of Information Technology and Engineering, Vellore Institute of Technology, Vellore, India

Rathi R.
https://orcid.org/0000-0002-3903-2099
School of Information Technology and Engineering, Vellore Institute of Technology, Vellore, India

Visvanathan P.
School of Information Technology and Engineering, Vellore Institute of Technology, Vellore, India

Kanchana R.
Computer Science and Engineering, Vel Tech Ranganathan Dr.Sagunthala R&D Institute of Science and Technology, Chennai, India

ABSTRACT

One of the important aspects of human-computer interaction is the detection of emotions using facial expressions. Emotion recognition has problems such as facial expressions, variations of posture, non-uniform illuminations, and so on. Deep learning techniques becomes important to solve these classification problems. In this chapter, VGG19, Inception V3, and Resnet50 pre-trained networks are used for the transfer learning approach to predict human emotions. Finally, the study achieved 98.32% of accuracy for emotion recognition and classification using the CK+ dataset.

INTRODUCTION

Today's most challenging question about human-computer interaction is how to make computers more user-friendly using intelligent user interfaces. The design of recent human-machine interfaces should take this to promote more natural and human-like interaction (Acharjya & Chowdhary, 2018). Emotions are the user effects and have been recognized as the most essential methods by which people can

DOI: 10.4018/978-1-6684-5673-6.ch009

communicate with one another. The significance and potential of emotions and sentimental interfaces given using human emotions are becoming increasingly desirable in intelligent user interfaces, such as human-robot interactions. To provide an effective user interface and take advantage of the user's emotions, the user's emotional state must be identified or observed in various ways considering a variety of methods such as facial emotions, speech or words, and facial gestures. Facial emotions are the major mode of human communication and hence it is the consequence of the messages being communicated. Facial attachments, nonuniform illuminations, position variations, and other such factors all pose obstacles in the field of emotion recognition. The conventional method for facial emotion detection has the drawback of extracting features and classification analysis. To this issue, research people are more interested in deep learning techniques.

Deep learning has proven to be an extremely useful technique over the last few decades due to its ability to manage a large number of data. (LeCun et al., 2015) Hidden layers are gaining popularity over standard methods in pattern recognition from small input images, such as handwritten numeral identification. In a Deep neural learning network, a convolutional neural network (CNN) is widely used. CNN is the most popular model for the image domain because of its intrinsic structure. According to the researcher (Ravi, 2018), pre-trained CNN components of facial expression recognition have been presented. The parameters are taken using a VGG19 network. The research was carried out on CK+ and JAFFE databases, with 91.15%, and 91.75% of accuracy, correspondingly. The author (Shaha et al., 2018) uses transfer learning techniques of a VGG19 pre-trained network for image classification. This chapter trains the CNN model with the CK+ Dataset and classifies emotions based on extracted features. Resnet50, VGG19 and Inception V3 networks have been trained on ImageNet in this chapter. The pre-trained network model is used in an initial point of the model, using Transfer Learning if the domain was the same. This chapter describes the objective, results, comparisons, and conclusion.

RELATED WORK

The authors (Ozdemir et al., 2019) suggested a LeNet architecture-based facial detection system. This study makes use of a combined KDEF and JAFFE dataset The Haar cascade package is being used to filter the emotion recognition. This task was accomplished with an accuracy of 95.40%.

The authors (Jyostna & Veeranjaneyulu, 2019) demonstrated how to deal with different situations using a CNN. VGG16 and SVM classifier is deployed for extracting features. The algorithm had an 82.27% of accuracy without face detection and 87.16% of accuracy with face detection on the CK+ database. The author (Fan et al., 2018) presented recognising emotional expressions for the multi-region CNN method, as indicated in this paper. The sub-networks provided the attributes derived from the eyes, mouth and nose. To estimate emotions, the ratings over the sub-networks are integrated.

In this article (Wang et al., 2019) collect the most number of data. Here they used FER2013, CK +, JAFFE and SFEW datasets to test the model. The databases RAF- DB and AFEW 7.0 have been used in this study. The authors (Sreelakshmi & Sumithra, 2019) created an emotion identification system based on the MobileNet V2 architecture. The model is evaluated on real-time images and obtains an accuracy of 90.15%. Resnet50 and VGG16 facial expression recognition were exhibited as the state of the science.

To achieve the highest accuracy they used the CNN model and the SVM classifier. As stated the author (Roopa, 2019) suggests using the Inception V3 model to detect facial expressions. This model used the KDEF database, to achieve an accuracy of 35%.

In this study (Yldz et al., 2020) using the ImageNet database, Some improvement processes were carried out on pre-trained convolutional neural network models using the ImageNet database. ResNet, VGG19, Xception and MobileNet are the models used here. When the results are compared, it is clear that the MobileNet model achieves the highest accuracy value. The author (Bae et al., 2020) employed an ANN as a classifier in this experiment. After fine-tuned, Inception V3 has an accuracy of 85.5%.

This chapter is organised as follows. Initially, we discussed the Emotion detection process and then the CNN transfer learning model is discussed. Followed by that results and analysis is carried out for the CK+ dataset. Finally, the chapter ends with a comparison of different transfer learning techniques discussed and a conclusion

EMOTION DETECTION PROCESS

This chapter mainly concentrates on different pre-trained networks based on CNN for detecting face emotions. Presently, Human emotion extraction is becoming increasingly important in affective computing.

Figure 1. Emotion Detection Process

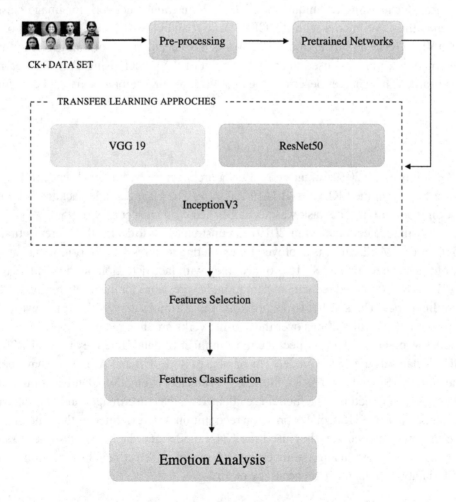

Figure 1 illustrates the Emotion Detection Process Diagram. The model predicts the basic emotions of anger, fear, sadness, happiness, surprise, and disgust. In this process Input image from the CK+ dataset is pre-processed before being fed into the retained network. While in the pre-trained networks, the image is sensed by the pre-trained network. Image resizing is the first step in the process. In this process resizes the input images to the pre-trained model's image size. The CK + dataset images have a resolution of (640 x 490) and 24bit colour. Resnet50 and VGG19 have (224 x 224) inputs and Inception V3 has (299 x 299) inputs. As a result, images were resized based on the pre-trained CNN module's input image size. Then, The pre-trained CNN layers were frozen except for the fully-connected layers. In the last, the trained data was updated for the fully connected layer and classified according to the emotions.

CK+ Database

This model is capable of recognizing seven basic emotions as follows:

- Happy
- Sad
- Angry
- Surprise
- Disgust
- Fear
- Neutral

The Cohn-Kanade (CK+) database has 123 different subjects ranging in gender, natality and ages from 18 to 50 years old from the 593 video sequences. (Lucey et al., 2010) Each video recognises a Happy, Sad, Angry, Surprise, Disgust, Fear and neutral facial expressions, captured at (640 x 480) or (640 x 490)resolution and 30 fps. **Figure 2** shows a sample prediction of differential expression. The CK+ database is mainly used in emotion detection and classification methods.

Figure 2. Different Expressions

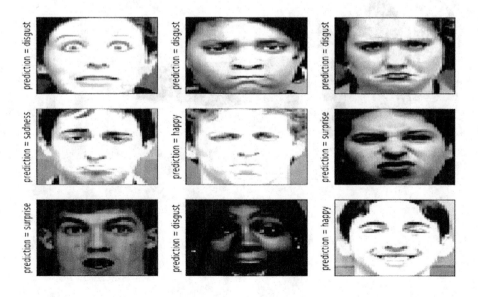

CONVOLUTIONAL NEURAL NETWORKS

Over the past few decades, pattern detection domain ranging the image processing that is advanced made by CNN. Parameters, CNNs have more advantages in Artificial neural networks. The developers and achievement are considered as the biggest models inspired by academics to prove by CNN with various tasks that the more important. To insert into some other way, thus they could not have spatial prosperities when deploying a facial gestures detection model, no need to worry about the face adjustment in the images. What matters is that they are detected, no matter where they are in the environment. The capacity of CNN to extract abstract features when input propagates deeper levels is another important feature. (Fuan et al., 2017) For example, in character classification, the edge may be recognised in the early layers, followed by simpler layers forms in the second layers, and finally higher level attributes such as faces in the third layers.

Visual Geometry Group (VGG19)

Both high-level and low-level image features are extracted by VGG19 layer by layer. The image classification is recognised and achieved the best accuracy demands. The most important identification method is divided into a collection of data, pre-processing the data, training the model, and testing the model. (Zhou et al., 2020) The six important structures are made by VGG19 and all the structures are connected in fully-connected layers and convolutional layers with multiple models.

The convolutional layer has the size of (3 x 3), and the input has a size of (224 x 224 x 3). **Figure 3** depicts the VGG19 architecture. A (224 x 224) RGB image has been submitted to this network. This means that the matrix is in the form (224, 224,2). The most pre-processing method is done to subtract the average (RGB) values of each pixel is considered to the entire training dataset. This allowed covering

Figure 3. VGG19 Architecture

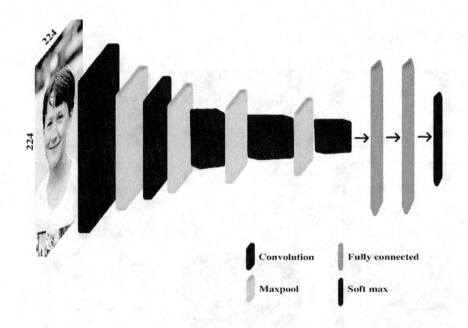

the entire concept of the image. Max pooling ran a (2 x 2) pixel window on Side 2. Implementing the three number of layers with fully-connected layers, the two are 4097 in size, then 1000 channel layer for 1000 way ILSVRC classification and the last layer is the SoftMax function.

Inception V3

Inception Networks (Google Net) has proven to most computationally structured, the network is produced by the parameters in the economics of cost in occurred. The Inception V3 Network is modified, which must be accepted to ensure that the advantages of computational are not. The Inceptionv3 architecture has been reused in a variety of applications and is frequently "pre-trained" from ImageNet. As a result of the unpredictability of the new network's efficiency, adapting an Inception network for different use cases becomes a problem, so Inception V3 optimisation has introduced the different approaches for easier modification to loosen limitations. (Wang et al., 2020) The more important techniques used in this model, are dimension reduction, factorized convolution, and regularisation.

Figure 4. Inception V3 Architecture

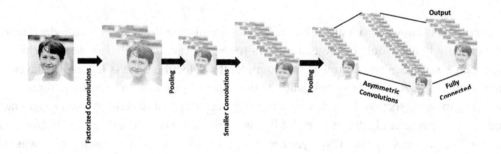

The architecture of the Inception v3 network (**Figure 4**) is built in stages as described below.

Factorized Convolutions

In the network number of the frameworks is reduced and the computational performance is also reduced. So that efficient network also controlled

Smaller Convolutions

Replacing the large coil with a smaller coil will speed up your workout. Suppose a (5 x 5) filter has 25 parameters. The two (3 x 3) filters that replace the (5 x 5) convolution have only 18 (3 x 3 + 3 x 3) parameters instead.

Auxiliary Classifier

Auxiliary classifiers are small CNNs that are inserted between layers during training, and the losses incurred add to the losses in the main network. In GoogLeNet, helper classifiers were used for deeper networks, but in Inception v3, helper classifiers act as normalizations.

Asymmetric Convolutions

A (3x3) fold can be replaced with a (1x3) fold followed by a (3x1) fold. The advanced asymmetric convolution is slightly higher than the number of frameworks with the (3x3) convolution replaced by a (2x2) convolution.

Grid Size-Reduction

The reduction of the grid size is usually done by a pooling operation. However, more efficient methods have been proposed to address computational cost bottlenecks.

ResNet50

ResNet, an compression for Residual Network. It is a type of neural network. In the deep neural network, we normally bundle some of the extra layers to resolve a complicated problem. Which is used to improve the performance and accuracy. for example, the detecting edge is learned by layer one, the identifying texture is learned by layer two, and the detecting object is learned by layer three, and so on with the case of image detection. However, a maximum deep dimension is discovered in the traditional CNN model. (Deshpande et al., 2021) The plot below depicts the error percentage on training and testing data for a 20 layer network and a 56 layer network. The testing data and training data which has 20 layers of the network is lower than the 56 layers of the network in the error percentage. It implies that adding more layers to a network degrades its performance. This could be attributed to the optimization function, network initialization, and, most importantly, the vanishing gradient problem. It could happen due to overfitting, but the error per cent of the 56-layer network is worse on both training and testing data, which does not happen when the model is overfitting.

Resnet50 Architecture (Figure 5) includes the following elements, A layer is formed by convolutions of 64 different kernels with a kernel size of (7 x 7), all with strides of size 2 and a stride length of 2 with the highest pooling. Thus the following convolution is a (1 x 1.64) kernel, led by a (3 x 3.64) kernel, and finally a (1 x 1.256) kernel. This process is repeated three times. so that there will be a total of 9 layers in this step. Then there is the (1 x 1.128) kernel, followed by the (3 x 3.128) kernel, and finally the (1 x 1.512) kernel. Here the total number of layers contains 12, which is performed four times in this process. They are (1 x 1.256) kernels, (2 x 3.256) kernels, and (1 x 1.1024), which make the total of 18 layers by repeating 6 times. After repeating the (1 x 1.512) kernel, which had two, (3 x 3.512), and (1 x 1.2048) layers, three times to get a total of nine layers. The fully connected tier moves with 1000 nodes, to get one tier the softmax function is used for considering the medium pool. The activation function and the maximum/average pooling layer are ignored. As these layers are added together, to get a CNN with 50 layers.

Figure 5. ResNet50 architecture

Layer name	Output size	18-Layer	34-Layer	50-Layer	101-Layer	152-Layer
Conv1	112 x 112	7x7, 64, stride 2				
Conv2x	56 x 56	3x3 max pool, stride 2				
		$\begin{bmatrix} 3 \times 3,64 \\ 3 \times 3,64 \end{bmatrix} \times 2$	$\begin{bmatrix} 3 \times 3,64 \\ 3 \times 3,64 \end{bmatrix} \times 3$	$\begin{bmatrix} 1 \times 1,64 \\ 3 \times 3,64 \\ 1 \times 1,256 \end{bmatrix} \times 3$	$\begin{bmatrix} 1 \times 1,64 \\ 3 \times 3,64 \\ 1 \times 1,256 \end{bmatrix} \times 3$	$\begin{bmatrix} 1 \times 1,64 \\ 3 \times 3,64 \\ 1 \times 1,256 \end{bmatrix} \times 3$
Conv3x	28 x 28	$\begin{bmatrix} 3 \times 3,128 \\ 3 \times 3,128 \end{bmatrix} \times 2$	$\begin{bmatrix} 3 \times 3,128 \\ 3 \times 3,128 \end{bmatrix} \times 4$	$\begin{bmatrix} 1 \times 1,128 \\ 3 \times 3,128 \\ 1 \times 1,512 \end{bmatrix} \times 4$	$\begin{bmatrix} 1 \times 1,128 \\ 3 \times 3,128 \\ 1 \times 1,512 \end{bmatrix} \times 4$	$\begin{bmatrix} 1 \times 1,128 \\ 3 \times 3,128 \\ 1 \times 1,512 \end{bmatrix} \times 8$
Conv4x	14 x 14	$\begin{bmatrix} 3 \times 3,256 \\ 3 \times 3,256 \end{bmatrix} \times 2$	$\begin{bmatrix} 3 \times 3,256 \\ 3 \times 3,256 \end{bmatrix} \times 6$	$\begin{bmatrix} 1 \times 1,256 \\ 3 \times 3,256 \\ 1 \times 1,1024 \end{bmatrix} \times 6$	$\begin{bmatrix} 1 \times 1,256 \\ 3 \times 3,256 \\ 1 \times 1,1024 \end{bmatrix} \times 23$	$\begin{bmatrix} 1 \times 1,256 \\ 3 \times 3,256 \\ 1 \times 1,1024 \end{bmatrix} \times 36$
Conv5x	7 x 7	$\begin{bmatrix} 3 \times 3,512 \\ 3 \times 3,512 \end{bmatrix} \times 2$	$\begin{bmatrix} 3 \times 3,512 \\ 3 \times 3,512 \end{bmatrix} \times 3$	$\begin{bmatrix} 1 \times 1,512 \\ 3 \times 3,512 \\ 1 \times 1,2048 \end{bmatrix} \times 3$	$\begin{bmatrix} 1 \times 1,512 \\ 3 \times 3,512 \\ 1 \times 1,2048 \end{bmatrix} \times 3$	$\begin{bmatrix} 1 \times 1,512 \\ 3 \times 3,512 \\ 1 \times 1,2048 \end{bmatrix} \times 3$
	1 X 1	Average pool, 1000-d fc, SoftMax				
FLOPs		1.8×10^9	3.6×10^9	3.8×10^9	7.6×10^9	11.3×10^9

RESULTS AND ANALYSIS

The results of the VGG19, InceptionV3 and ResNet50 model's performance metrics show a Specificity, Sensitivity, Precision, Accuracy and F1 score. True-positive (TP), True-negative (TN), False-positive (FP) and false-negative (FN) metrics are used to perform the calculation.

Accuracy

The proportion of correct samples to the total number of samples is defined as accuracy.

$$Accuracy = \frac{(TN + TP)}{(TN + TP) + (FN + FP)}$$

Sensitivity

Sensitivity is defined as the ratio of true-positive cases to total true-positive and false-negative cases.

$$Sensitivity = \frac{TP}{(TP + FN)}$$

Specificity

Specificity is defined as the ratio of correctly predicted positive cases to correctly predicted positive and false-positive cases.

$$Specificity = \frac{TN}{(TN + FP)}$$

Precision

Precision is defined as the ratio of true-positive cases to total predicted positive cases.

$$Precision = \frac{TP}{(TP + FP)}$$

F1 Score

The F1 score is a weighted average of sensitivity and precision. An F1 score indicates that the model result is better at predictions.

$$F1\,Score = 2 \times \left(\frac{Precision \times Sensitivity}{(Precision + Sensitivity)} \right)$$

VGG19

The VGG19 model is more accurate to predict neutral emotions and less accurate in predicting happy emotions. **Table 1** displays the performance metrics of the proposed model using VGG19. **Figure 6** depict the accuracy and **Figure 7** depict the loss. According to the computation, the F1 score of the VGG19 model is **84.15**, and the accuracy is **96.91%**.

Inception V3

The InceptionV3 model's performance metrics are displayed in **Table 2.** According to the computation, the F1 score is **77.68**, and when using a pre-trained InceptionV3 model, the accuracy is **95.8%**. **Figure 8** depict the accuracy and **Figure 9** depict the loss of InceptionV3.

Resnet50

The ResNet50 model's performance metrics are displayed in Table 3. According to the computation, the F1 score is 92.61, and when using a pre-trained Resnet50 model, the accuracy is 98.32%.

Figure 10 depict the accuracy and Figure 11 depict the loss of Resnet50.

Table 1. Performance Matrix by using the VGG19

Emotions	TP	TN	FP	FN	Sensitivity	Specificity	Precision	F1 Score	Accuracy
Happy	23	113	12	0	1.00	0.90	0.66	0.79	0.92
Sad	4	139	0	5	0.44	1.00	1.00	0.62	0.97
Angry	16	127	1	4	0.80	0.99	0.94	0.86	0.97
Surprise	47	101	0	0	1.00	1.00	1.00	1.00	1.00
Disgust	28	115	1	4	0.88	0.99	0.97	0.92	0.97
Fear	8	137	1	2	0.80	0.99	0.89	0.84	0.98
Neutral	6	140	1	1	0.86	0.99	0.86	0.86	0.99
Average %					82.52%	98.19%	90.14%	84.15%	96.91%

Table 2. Performance Matrix by using the InceptionV3

Emotions	TP	TN	FP	FN	Sensitivity	Specificity	Precision	F1 Score	Accuracy
Happy	20	110	12	1	0.95	0.90	0.63	0.75	0.91
Sad	5	135	1	2	0.71	0.99	0.83	0.77	0.98
Angry	12	122	2	5	0.71	0.98	0.86	0.77	0.95
Surprise	40	99	2	2	0.95	0.98	0.95	0.95	0.97
Disgust	24	110	2	5	0.83	0.98	0.92	0.87	0.95
Fear	5	139	2	2	0.71	0.99	0.71	0.71	0.97
Neutral	3	138	1	3	0.50	0.99	0.75	0.60	0.97
Average %					76.67%	97.42%	80.79%	77.68%	95.80%

Table 3. Performance Matrix by using the Resnet50

Emotions	TP	TN	FP	FN	Sensitivity	Specificity	Precision	F1 Score	Accuracy
Happy	20	120	3	1	0.95	0.98	0.87	0.91	0.97
Sad	6	135	0	1	0.86	1.00	1.00	0.92	0.99
Angry	17	125	2	1	0.94	0.98	0.89	0.92	0.98
Surprise	43	100	0	3	0.93	1.00	1.00	0.97	0.98
Disgust	28	112	1	2	0.93	0.99	0.97	0.95	0.98
Fear	8	135	1	0	1.00	0.99	0.89	0.94	0.99
Neutral	7	139	1	1	0.88	0.99	0.88	0.88	0.99
Average %					92.82%	99.09%	92.77%	92.61%	98.32%

Figure 6. VGG16 accuracy

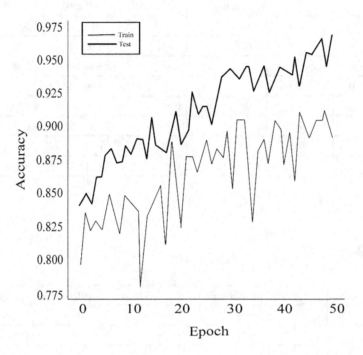

Figure 7. VGG16 loss

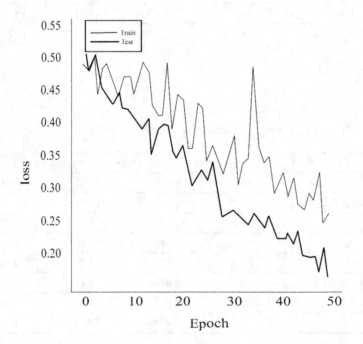

Figure 8. InceptionV3 accuracy

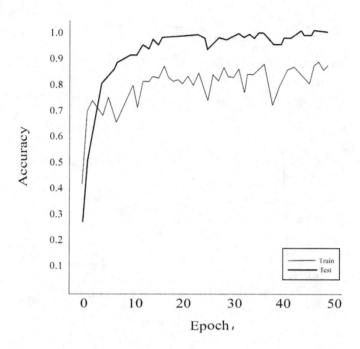

Figure 9. InceptionV3 loss

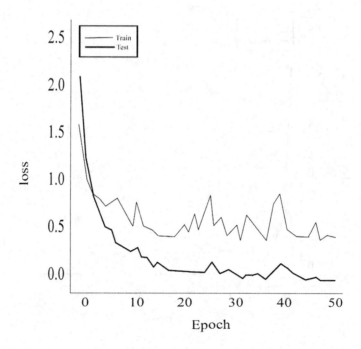

Figure 10. ResNet accuracy

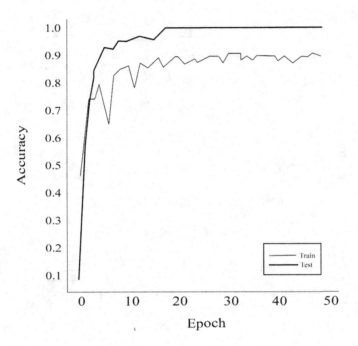

Figure 11. ResNet loss

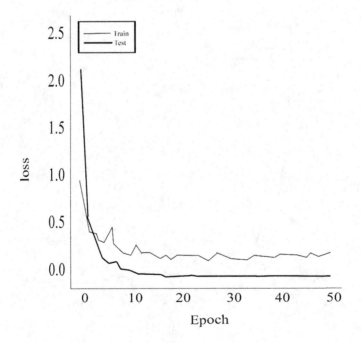

COMPARISON WITHIN PROPOSED METHODS

This chapter discussed different networks with VGG19, Inception and ResNet50. Comparison and the result obtained for all networks are described in Table 4. The Resnet50 has the highest sensitivity, specificity, precision, F1 score, and accuracy among the different networks used in this chapter. VGG19 has the second-highest accuracy among all models. The least accurate network was Inception v3. Resnet50 network performs the best accuracy with 98.32% in all three networks.

Table 4. Comparison within proposed methods

Network	Sensitivity	Specificity	Precision	F1 Score	Accuracy
VGG19	82.52%	98.19%	90.14%	84.15%	96.91%
Inception V3	76.67%	97.42%	80.79%	77.68%	95.80%
ResNet50	92.82%	99.09%	92.77%	92.61%	98.32%

CONCLUSION

In this chapter, different transfer learning models are used for facial emotion recognition. Here we used VGG19, ResNet50 and Inception V3 pre-trained convolutional neural networks which are trained in the ImageNet database for facial emotion recognition. CK+ dataset is used to test the model. The accuracy achieved in the VGG19, Inception V3, and Resnet50 models is 96.91%, 95.80%, and 98.32% respectively. When compared with other pre-trained models Resnet50 achieved the highest accuracy.

REFERENCES

Acharjya, D. P., & Chowdhary, C. L. (2018). Breast cancer detection using hybrid computational intelligence techniques. In *Handbook of Research on Emerging Perspectives on Healthcare Information Systems and Informatics* (pp. 251–280). IGI Global. doi:10.4018/978-1-5225-5460-8.ch011

Bae, J., Kim, M., & Lim, J. S. (2020, October). Feature Extraction Model Based on Inception V3 to Distinguish Normal Heart Sound from Systolic Murmur. In *2020 International Conference on Information and Communication Technology Convergence (ICTC)* (pp. 460-463). IEEE. 10.1109/ICTC49870.2020.9289317

Deshpande, A., Estrela, V. V., & Patavardhan, P. (2021). The DCT-CNN-ResNet50 architecture to classify brain tumors with super-resolution, convolutional neural network, and the ResNet50. *Neuroscience Informatics*, *1*(4), 100013. doi:10.1016/j.neuri.2021.100013

Fan, Y., Lam, J. C., & Li, V. O. (2018, October). Multi-region ensemble convolutional neural network for facial expression recognition. In *International Conference on Artificial Neural Networks* (pp. 84-94). Springer. 10.1007/978-3-030-01418-6_9

Fuan, W., Hongkai, J., Haidong, S., Wenjing, D., & Shuaipeng, W. (2017). An adaptive deep convolutional neural network for rolling bearing fault diagnosis. *Measurement Science & Technology*, *28*(9), 095005. doi:10.1088/1361-6501/aa6e22

Jyostna Devi, B., & Veeranjaneyulu, N. (2019). Facial emotion recognition using deep cnn based features. *International Journal of Innovative Technology and Exploring Engineering*, *8*(7).

LeCun, Y., Bengio, Y., & Hinton, G. (2015). Deep learning. *Nature, 28*(521), 7553.

Lucey, P., Cohn, J. F., Kanade, T., Saragih, J., Ambadar, Z., & Matthews, I. (2010, June). The extended cohn-kanade dataset (ck+): A complete dataset for action unit and emotion-specified expression. In *2010 IEEE Computer Society Conference on Computer Vision and Pattern Recognition-Workshops* (pp. 94-101). IEEE.

Ozdemir, M. A., Elagoz, B., Alaybeyoglu, A., Sadighzadeh, R., & Akan, A. (2019, October). *Real time emotion recognition from facial expressions using CNN architecture. In 2019 medical technologies congress (tiptekno)*. IEEE.

Ravi, A. (2018). *Pre-trained convolutional neural network features for facial expression recognition.* arXiv preprint arXiv:1812.06387.

Roopa, N. (2019). Emotion Recognition from Facial Expression using Deep Learning. *International Journal of Engineering and Advanced Technology.*

Shaees, S., Naeem, H., Arslan, M., Naeem, M. R., Ali, S. H., & Aldabbas, H. (2020, September). Facial emotion recognition using transfer learning. In *2020 International Conference on Computing and Information Technology (ICCIT-1441)* (pp. 1-5). IEEE.

Sreelakshmi, P., & Sumithra, M. D. (2019). Facial Expression Recognition robust to partial Occlusion using MobileNet. *International Journal of Engineering Research & Technology (Ahmedabad)*, *8*(06).

Theckedath, D., & Sedamkar, R. R. (2020). Detecting affect states using VGG16, ResNet50 and SE-ResNet50 networks. *SN Computer Science*, *1*(2), 1–7. doi:10.100742979-020-0114-9

Wang, C., Chen, D., Hao, L., Liu, X., Zeng, Y., Chen, J., & Zhang, G. (2019). Pulmonary image classification based on inception-v3 transfer learning model. *IEEE Access: Practical Innovations, Open Solutions*, *7*, 146533–146541. doi:10.1109/ACCESS.2019.2946000

Yıldız, G., & Dizdaroğlu, B. (2020, October). Traffic Sign Recognition via Transfer Learning using Convolutional Neural Network Models. In *2020 28th Signal Processing and Communications Applications Conference (SIU)* (pp. 1-4). IEEE. 10.1109/SIU49456.2020.9302399

Zhou, J., Yang, X., Zhang, L., Shao, S., & Bian, G. (2020). Multisignal VGG19 network with transposed convolution for rotating machinery fault diagnosis based on deep transfer learning. *Shock and Vibration*, *2020*. doi:10.1155/2020/8863388

Chapter 10
A Study of Human Interaction Emotional Intelligence in Healthcare Applications

Vanmathi C.
Vellore Institute of Technology, India

Mangayarkarasi R.
(iD) https://orcid.org/0000-0003-3088-6001
Vellore Institute of Technology, India

Prabhavathy P.
Vellore Institute of Technology, India

Hemalatha S.
Vellore Institute of Technology, India

Sagar M.
Vellore Institute of Technology, India

ABSTRACT

A human's words, facial expressions, gestures, tone of voice, and even keyboard force can all be used in conjunction with artificial intelligence technologies to perform emotion intelligence (EI) identification. The development of artificial emotional intelligence has made it possible for people and robots to interact in a manner that is more natural, similar to the way that humans engage with one another. The expansion of the internet of things and wearable technology has a positive impact on the development of emotion detection software in the healthcare sector. This system contributes to society by making use of many forms of technology. There is always going to be a trade-off between price and functionality. The development of software with emotional intelligence relies on the collection of extensive datasets and the development of reliable modelling techniques. This chapter uses case studies, computing, and AI-based research methods to analyze emotional intelligence systems and their effects on human-computer interaction in the healthcare sector.

DOI: 10.4018/978-1-6684-5673-6.ch010

INTRODUCTION

Examples of what might be included in the definition of emotional intelligence include the capacity to manage one's behavior, deal with challenging social situations and make decisions that lead to beneficial results. Emotional intelligence can also be measured by one's ability to make good decisions that lead to positive outcomes. There is a correlation between the amount of stress that a person feels in their line of work and the level of emotional intelligence that they possess as a professional. According to the explanation of the term "emotional intelligence" offered by the American psychologist Daniel Goleman (Goleman, 2011), the concept of emotional intelligence is comprised of five primary aspects that are essential to its development. Self-awareness, motivation, social skills, the capacity to self-regulate, and empathy are some of the components that make up emotional intelligence. A collection of emotional, social, and relational skills that leads the way to perceive, grasp, and express oneself; connect with others; manage interpersonal exchanges; deal with obstacles, and make effective and meaningful use of emotional knowledge. Figure 1 illustrates the most important aspects of emotional intelligence after they have been broken down into the parts from which they are composed. Numerous studies have been carried out, and the findings of these investigations indicate that high emotional intelligence is accountable for ninety per cent of top performers. People who experience a greater number and range of happy emotions perform at a higher level with fewer errors. These people also report feeling happier overall. This is because they have a more optimistic perspective on life. Compassion is a crucial component of the professional connection; resonance and rapport are expressions of caring, and individuals who are participating in the connection share optimism and positive feelings with one another. The benefits of having an EI intern increase in direct proportion to the level of difficulty of the task that is being performed. This is because having an EI intern minimizes the cost of treatment and legal fees. If the EI is higher, then there is less room for careless practice, which means that the diagnostic accuracy will be higher as a direct result of this. People who practice EI can feel less anger and other unpleasant emotions, which in turn leads to a rise in the effectiveness of teams and the productivity of groups. The use of EI leads to increases in cognitive health and welfare, as well as memory and performance, which are all boosted as a result of the application of EI.

Researchers are more conscious that emotions play a significant role in the design process as well. Researchers in human-computer interaction (HCI) and design are now looking at the distinctions of emotion and how it affects our behavior. As a relatively new area of study, this is heartening news, and there are numerous promising directions in which it might go from here. Emotional research in the field of HCI is inherently interdisciplinary. For example, researchers are interested in the perception and synthesis of emotional expressions on the face and body, as well as how emotions affect information processing and decision-making processes. HCI Emotional Intelligence in Healthcare is discussed in detail in this chapter. It finds and analyses the underlying causes of a wide range of problems.

This chapter gives insights on HCI Emotional Intelligence in healthcare. It identifies the various challenges and also analyzed the deeper level of the issues. The chapter starts with an introduction to emotional intelligence, the role of HCI in emotional intelligence followed by the impact of HCI EI in healthcare, technology impact and its influences on healthcare workers and patients. Finally discussed the future of EI in healthcare and followed by a conclusion.

Figure 1. Five areas of Emotional Intelligence.

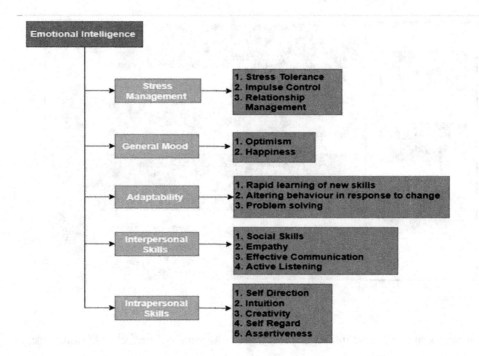

EMOTIONAL INTELLIGENCE IN HEALTHCARE

The idea that emotional intelligence (EI) is necessary for both mental health and the effective practice of medicine is gaining traction as a topic of conversation in a variety of healthcare-related professions, including those related to medicine. This is because the concept suggests that EI is required for both the efficient practice of medicine and the maintenance of mental health. The field of healthcare, much like a great number of other occupations (Fariselli et al., 2008) is a complicated and demanding sector of work in which social ties are of the biggest significance. [Case in point:] The healthcare sector is a difficult place to work because of the many high-stakes issues, the rapid speed, and the complicated linkages. This is true for the industry in general, as it is true for many other demanding industries as well. Medical practitioners have a large emotional and relational burden, which they need to carefully manage to offer patients the best possible treatment while working in these settings. It would appear that EI is a necessary component in this "game" of achieving a balance between stimuli that are in direct opposition to one another. Emotional intelligence has been linked to alleviating the negative impacts of stress, which is contrary to the findings of several studies, which found that stress was connected with decreased performance and emotional intelligence was linked to mitigating the negative effects of stress.

It has been demonstrated that there is a direct and significant positive association between emotional intelligence and job engagement and task balance. This correlation is favorable as well as significant. The workers at EI healthcare reported feeling even greater satisfaction in their jobs and a marked improvement in their ability to maintain a good balance between their personal and professional life. Figure 2 is an illustration of the link and communication that occurs between patients, members of the healthcare staff, and the management of the healthcare system. The illustration also shows the many

Figure 2. Emotional Intelligence in Healthcare

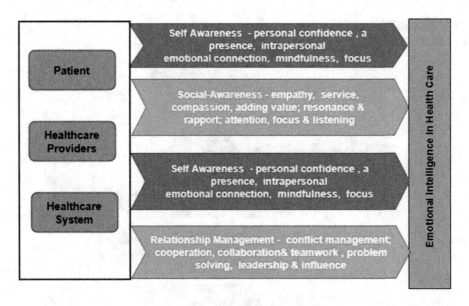

various components of emotional intelligence that are important in the field of healthcare, and it does it in an easy-to-understand way.

The level of emotional intelligence among a range of professionals, most notably students, has been shown to have decreased, according to a study that was carried out not too long ago (Khan et al., 2021). The research was carried out not too long ago. The article provides a synopsis of the findings of seventy separate studies that were conducted among college students in Western countries between the years 2003 and 2018 and published in a study article that was distributed by the Journal of Personality. The studies were carried out between 2003 and 2018. Emotional intelligence (EI), according to research that was only just issued by the World Economic Forum, is one of the top ten characteristics that will be necessary for Industry 4.0 and higher. This is the case for a few reasons: first, it is required to cultivate positive traits; second, emotional intelligence is a critical talent for people who will be working in the workplace in the future; and third, it is necessary to cultivate positive characteristics.

Computing in Healthcare

Affective computing, often known as artificial emotional intelligence, is the name given to the type of computing technology that was developed specifically for emotional intelligence. Professor Rosalind Picard is credited for establishing the AC (Picard, 2003) lab at the MIT Media Lab in the year 1995. The laboratory employed cameras, microphones, and physiological sensors to collect reactions to determine feelings; based on the data that was gathered, the robots responded. In today's world, the competence of a machine when it comes to reviewing data might help to identify contentious details that some humans would miss. The field of artificial emotional intelligence is concerned with the technologies that are used to gather human emotions by analyzing data from the following variables: facial expressions, motions, voice modulation, and pressure measured through keystrokes, amongst other things, to determine the state of the emotion and react upon it. There is active participation from a large number of business vendors in the creation of better products.

The program that detects emotions known as Affectiva assists advertisers in increasing the value of their sales. To obtain information on the customer's experience with the product, the candidate program analyses a video clip of the customer and watches their facial expressions in real-time. Microsoft has a team that is solely devoted to the research and development of technologies aimed at improving emotional intelligence and general well-being (Chowdhary, 2022). The artificial emotional intelligence system used by Cogito, which was meant to respond to customer service calls, identifies the caller's mood and adapts its response based on that mood. Cogito was created to handle customer support calls. Companion Mx offers an app for monitoring emotions, which analyses a recording phone call to assess the state of the user's mood as well as their level of anxiousness. The wearable device known as BioEssence was developed at the MIT Media Lab. It monitors the wearer's pulse rate to determine their level of stress and annoyance. People who suffer from autism, and have difficulty understanding the emotional thoughts and feelings of others, have a strong demand for the technology known as artificial emotional intelligence (AEI). They would benefit greatly from having a technology on their person that could read other people's thoughts before responding.

Impact of EI on Healthcare

Stress is an issue that has been discussed at length among medical students on numerous occasions, and it has been found that the majority of medical students suffer high levels of stress (Birks et al., 2009). The majority of the students are confronted with difficulties associated with the course material, a new environment, and new members, in addition to the financial, emotional, and social difficulties associated with spending their first time away from home. Additional significant sources of stress for students studying healthcare include the acquisition of practical clinical skills as well as the emotions that are required to treat a patient (Chowdhary et al., 2021). There is a correlation between stress and greater rates of anxiety, depression, and the use of drugs and alcohol among healthcare students, as well as attrition. Emotional intelligence (EI) is becoming increasingly relevant in the workplace, as indicated by the altering role of the manager and scientific research associating emotional intelligence with performance results. EI is the capacity to handle the feelings of others sensitively and thoughtfully. In addition to that, it entails the capability of retaining one's motivation, passion, and emotional steadiness. Medical Students can accurately identify, communicate, comprehend, and integrate their feelings. It would appear that EI acts as a stress stabilizer in this scenario, at least on some level. On the other hand, the effect appeared to be substantially less pronounced at times when there were generally higher levels of stress (Panigrahi et al., 2021).

Intelligent Health (Rubeis, 2022) iHealth is seen as a chance for greater real-time self-monitoring, as well as the integration of assessment inside a hospital setting. It enhances decision-making, and as a result, personalized treatment can be provided. The EMA has proven to be a useful instrument for assessing the symptoms of patients as well as other behavioural characteristics. The EMA will help provide accurate predictions, prevent illness, reduce the number of hospitalizations, and improve self-management. Concerns relating to privacy should be addressed by the establishment of regulations that are unambiguous and apply everywhere. The primary concern here is one of policy. The gathering and analysis of data can be utilized not just to categorize persons but also to standardize behaviour. One sort of prejudice that may have become more prevalent in the use of data and the acceptance of its judgement is known as confirmation bias and automation bias. According to the findings of the analysis, iHealth can provide more individualized care; yet, it also poses several ethical difficulties. The primary reasons for this are issues of bias and privacy related to individuals' data.

Burnout (Năstasă et al. 2015) investigates the possibility of an emotional intelligence connection between medical professionals and nurses. The symptoms of the illness can be broken down into three distinct stages: emotional weariness, depersonalization, and personal accomplishment. For the sake of this definition, emotional tiredness is described as the experience of experiencing less energy and having blurry eyesight when it comes to emotions, as a result of feeling that one's emotions are being ripped out at work. Depersonalization is the process of destroying personal relationships, which can lead to feelings of dependence on others, negative feelings about oneself, self-doubt, and cynicism, among other undesirable outcomes. One's ability to have a pessimistic view of their self-assessment, which will ultimately limit their potential, is a personal accomplishment. The achievement that nurses and other support workers, such as administrative assistants, have attained compares favourably to that of doctors. Women are more likely to suffer from burnout syndrome than males. When compared to male participants, female healthcare workers report higher levels of weariness and personal success. Male subjects report higher levels of depersonalization.

The capabilities model was designed to interpret emotional intelligence to measure the capacity of cognitive intelligence. Burnout may act as a negative pole for employees due to emotional tiredness, and depersonalization, or it may act as a positive pole, which is the emotional intelligence where people adapted to an adverse situation. Either way, it may act as a negative pole for the employees. The research focuses on two different kinds of psychological assessments, namely the Maslach Burnout Inventory (MBI) and the Emotional Intelligence Scale (EIS). These tests were administered to a total of 120 healthcare professionals, including female and male doctors and nurses. When estimating burnouts, the Cronbach alpha coefficient is utilized, which resulted in high scales for internal consistency (0.93 in MBI), even though there are 25 separate qualities. The Emotional Intelligence Scale (EIS) utilized 33 characteristics (based on the Lickert scale), and the student's emotional intelligence was measured at the beginning and end of the school year. This resulted in the highest 0.86 Cronbach alpha index. According to the findings, the symptoms of burnout are more prevalent in females, including emotional tiredness and a sense of personal success. On the other hand, depersonalization is more prevalent in males.

The purpose of this study is to provide evidence that demonstrates the efficacy of EI as a safeguard against burnout (Arnone et al., 2019). The most important findings imply that physicians and nurses who work in emergency departments are more likely to experience burnout and that emotional intelligence plays a significant part in the process of recovering from burnout. Both of them are exhibiting a strong and negative association with each other at the same time (Bebarta et al., 2021). They feel that it is essential to provide training that focuses on developing emotional intelligence in healthcare professionals and that the development of emotional intelligence among healthcare workers is important for personal achievement among healthcare employees.

The association that has been maintained between the Emotional Intelligence (EI) of physicians and doctors and the satisfaction of their patients is the topic of this paper, which describes the relationship. The research demonstrated both a high level of accuracy as well as a significant association between the aforementioned two characteristics. An additional intriguing finding about the findings is that the EI of female practitioners was seen to be higher than that of male practitioners. Because of these findings, medical professionals will be able to improve their EQ skills and provide patients with higher-quality care. According to the findings, it is advised that medical professionals receive training in EI to make the most of their EI talents in addition to their clinical skills to better understand and manage the emotions of their patients.

Another study examining the relationship between job satisfaction and gender discrimination in employee benefits was carried out among health care employees in the Delhi NCR area of India (Srivastava et al., 2021). The replies received from 260 professionals working in health care are analyzed using conventional tools. Both linear and moderated regression were utilized in the process of testing the hypotheses. The data suggest that the components of EI have a significant influence on the levels of JS that health care workers experience. The findings of the moderated regression showed that gender has a significant role in determining the connection between EI and JS. To provide patients with better quality health care facilities, the EI construct is a vital component to have.

An investigation into employee engagement and levels of job satisfaction among administrative staff in Malaysian institutions of higher learning (Alam, 2009) was conducted. According to the findings of the study, the abilities of workers in general and emotional intelligence, in particular, have a significant bearing on the success of workplace goals and, as a consequence, on the degree to which individuals feel satisfied in their jobs. The evidence to support this assertion has not yet been objectively studied at all levels of workers and their job positions in a variety of industrial contexts, therefore this argument continues to be difficult to prove. This research attempts to bridge the gap by investigating the factors that contribute to positive work attitudes, behaviors, and outcomes in public sector organizations among university employees who do not teach and have high levels of emotional intelligence. As a consequence of this, people give their best effort in the workplace so that they can continue to enjoy their jobs. At University Perlis Malaysia, 120 of the non-teaching staff members' emotional intelligence was evaluated using a Likert scale with five points. Using correlation statistics, it was found that EI, in all three of its elements (evaluation, use, and regulation), was strongly and positively connected with work satisfaction. According to the results of the linear regression analysis, the EI dimensions can accurately predict levels of job satisfaction.

This article presents the findings of a study on internet fixation, a mental syndrome that has been shown to cause substantial harm to a cohort of students studying to become healthcare professionals (Sharp et al., 2020). The evaluation of emotional intelligence, preparedness to use mobile technology, and internet addiction among young people are the topics of the questionnaire. Both Pearson's correlation Coefficient and hierarchal regression are utilized in the analysis of the gathered data. According to the findings of the survey, a sizeable proportion of students studying to become healthcare professionals overused and made unnecessary use of the internet. Addiction to the internet showed a negative correlation with emotional intelligence and readiness to apply mobile learning. It is vital to test children who are addicted to the Internet with the right screening instruments, as well as to implement key preventative strategies. In addition, the right actions need to be taken to cultivate emotional intelligence and mobile learning skills, as well as to minimize internet addiction to some degree.

To get the most out of their performance, surgeons and other medical professionals should be aware of their feelings as well as those of their patients. EI is not to be confused with IQ in any way, shape, or form because it is something that can be taught and is always being improved upon. When assessing emotional intelligence, both validated self-reporting questionnaires and multi-rater evaluations are utilized. It has been suggested that performance can be measured, in addition to serving as a criterion for selecting a person to get training and a potential predictor of burnout in the future. It has been proposed that EI become a required part of the curriculum and training of modern surgeons as well as other medical professionals.

Figure 3. EI Healthcare triangle and its benefits

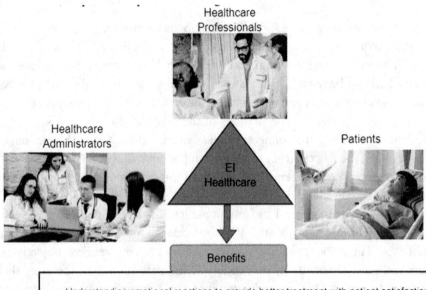

The research uses a multivariate statistical method to conduct a factor analysis to investigate the EI of the COVID 19 pandemic to achieve efficient relationship management among medical professionals (Baghcheghi & Koohestani, 2022). Relationship management is one of the fundamental competencies that health care practitioners are expected to possess. This involves being self-aware, being able to manage oneself, and being aware of situations and the people in those situations to maintain cordial and productive relationships over an extended period. They must obtain training in how to do self-emotional assessments because a significant portion of their job comprises dealing with the emotional responses of these stakeholders, such as anger, fear, and hopelessness. The findings that were deduced from the analysis, in conjunction with formal and informal conversations with medical professionals, led to the conclusion that social and learning skills, such as the ability to resolve conflicts, build relationships, learn quickly, and comprehend organizations, are essential.

The study assists practitioners in improving their EI abilities, which ultimately leads to improved healthcare. According to the study, health care professionals who have clinical experience and the ability to observe patients' emotions should receive training in emotional intelligence (EI). Figure 3 illustrates all of the numerous advantages of employing EI in the medical field, coupled with a picture of a triangle.

TECHNOLOGY AND EI HEALTHCARE

Human Emotions can be influenced by Technology. Various HCI research addresses emotion in a variety of ways based on a variety of purposes has been analyzed in this article. Artificial intelligence (AI) is currently in use to optimize surgical schedules, System reads past data and depending on future needs it will optimize its schedule to reach maximum and efficient use of resources. AI is also used to reduce time, by effectively scheduling appropriate resources needed reducing the time needed to transfer the patient from the Emergency room to the normal ward by scheduling according to priority which reduced waiting time making sure the emergency room remains vacant for emergencies. Diagnosis also can be done by taking inputs from experts around the world, hence making hospitals a global point of contact making sure that inputs from experts are utilized in deciding for the patient.

An investigation on how Machines are starting to get capacities to detect and perceive human inclination, to answer it with better abilities so that pessimistic sentiments are more averse to raise and to have different abilities that can be utilized to help individuals create and survey different capacities and ways of behaving that add to the ability to appreciate individuals on a deeper level. The study (Picard, 2008) engages in man-made consciousness analysts have zeroed in on giving machines, etymological and numerical intelligent thinking capacities, displayed after the exemplary semantic also, numerical intelligent insights. This paper portrays new exploration that is giving machines (counting programming specialists, mechanical pets, work stations, from there, the sky is the limit) abilities of the ability to understand people on a profound level. Machines have for quite some time had the option to show up as though they have enthusiastic sentiments, however, presently machines are likewise being customized to realize when and how to show feeling in manners that empower the machine to seem sympathetic or in any case genuinely astute. Machines are currently being provided with the capacity to detect and perceive articulations of human feelings like interest, pain, and joy, with the acknowledgement that such correspondence is crucial for assisting machines with picking more accommodating and less exasperating conduct.

The research examines the profitability the government or insurances gain by investing in improving people's EI and health care expenditures impacts (Pivec, 2006) The concept of Emotional intelligence accounts for the idea that people differ in the ways they deal with interpersonal or intrapersonal skills. They discuss the three levels of emotional intelligence and particularly focus on one level, trait. The participants who are from the Mutual Benefit Society in Belgium were asked to present their age, sex and education and their Emotional intelligence was evaluated with the Profile of Emotional Competence. They considered both the dependent variable Expenditure and the independent variable Emotional Intelligence score and applied a logarithmic transformation to obtain the elasticity coefficient. Based on the elasticity coefficient obtained the results were produced. Ultimately the results stated that it would be important to increase people's EI and approximately, improving EI by 1% would decrease health care expenditure by 1% and priority should be given to people with low educational levels.

The recent attempts at emotional regulations with the help of technology in various fields such as medical, gaming and fashion. Various examples of how emotions are involved in technology use are shown and also different root causes of arising emotions have been listed. The research discusses a workshop, CHI 2022 (Wadley et al., 2022) where the goal is to create a community of researchers who will collaborate on future research and construct a framework and research agenda that will guide continuing HCI work on emotion. It lists the various sessions of the workshop, and the pre and post-workshop plans. This workshop aims to bring together interested scholars to assess current research on emotion in HCI and speculate on future directions. This study describes a stress recognition experiment in human-computer interaction in which Thirty-one healthy volunteers completed five challenging HCI activities while having their skin conductance signals measured. 15 typical computer users were asked to identify unpleasant computer interactions in pre-experiment interviews and those activities reported as stressful, were selected as the most commonly. Seven prominent machine learning classifiers were used to assess the obtained skin conductance signals. This high level of precision highlights the use of physiological signals for stress identification in the context of common HCI activities. Furthermore, the findings enable us to begin integrating the specialized stress identification mechanism into PhysiOBS, a previously suggested software tool that assists researchers and practitioners in evaluating user emotional experiences.

Computer-based intelligence intends to make and foster insightful frameworks (Kolski et al., 2020). It is valuable to understand that both AI and HCI need to consider individuals who will be associated with the utilization of the innovation being created. On one side, AI endeavors to impersonate the person and excuse their ways of behaving to construct different kinds of smart frameworks, together with robots. HCI attracts to comprehend the person to more readily adjust machines to further develop wellbeing, Productivity and solace insight. Man-made intelligence centers on interior components of a levelheaded insight. All things being equal, HCI centers on principal peculiarities of communication among individuals and the devices, which they made and use. The goal of this study is to figure out what design requirements emotional robots have. This research proposes an instructional Robotics framework that incorporates Emotional Intelligence throughout the learning process. These robots can help children with particular educational challenges like autism spectrum diseases.

Users' interactions with computing gadgets increasingly resemble human-human interactions (Mukeshimana et al., 2017). Emotion recognition in Human-Computer Interaction attempts to make interaction easier and wiser, resulting in more natural interaction. This paper provides a quick overview of the current scenario of multimodal emotion recognition research in Human-Computer Interaction (HCI). Emotion recognition as a research topic, its application in Human-Computer Interaction, as well as its obstacles and prospects are discussed. As a conclusion of a study, a proposal for designing a multimodal emotion recognition analyzer is reported. Human emotion is expressed in a variety of ways. Information fusion approaches are required for an autonomous multimodal emotion recognizer. Integration of emotion recognition in human-computer interaction has increased the value of intelligent tutoring systems and healthcare systems in everyday life.

EI in Bigdata

The necessity of determining Emotional intelligence (EI) is essential to track the mental health of self as well as the people surrounding us. Classifying various emotions assists any individual to interpret others' thoughts and responses. There is a lot of factors influencing our emotional intelligence, it can be described as the intellectual ability a person learns from their ancestral or developed life period. Big data analytics is a kind of analytics that, comes to complex applications, predictive models, statistical algorithms. The objective of this research (Mikolajczak et al., 2010) is to portray the importance of big data analytics in emotional intelligence detection. Emotion recognition detection benefited from big data, as the technology has an ample amount of data regarding the interpretation of human emotions along with the presence of artificial intelligence. Many aspects need to consider apart from facial expression and tone of voice, the parameter heart rate is a good factor that may influence emotion detection. To make the system to be more précises, it needs support from deep learning methods, due to its ability in handling a huge number of samples. AI act as the most promising factor in the big data cycle, data aggregation, storage, and retrieving the various form of data from distinct sources which demand proper data, context, action, goal and risk management. AI can choose the correct data types, along with possible connections established among the samples in the datasets and infer knowledge using natural language processing. AI techniques are quite useful for data preparation tasks, designing data models, and data exploration. Similar to humans, AI can learn the error pattern while learning.

Most probably, data were collected through a questionnaire. Emotional intelligence considers four different traits: Empathy, the perceived way, and the way of expressing emotions and relationships (Smith et al., 2008). By collecting together, they indicate the knowledge of own as well as other's emotions. And the correlation score between the empathy factors the emotional intelligence is more useful to become a self-aware person and helps to use emotionality in a balanced way and respond compassionately in a different context. Thus, the integration of Artificial Intelligent big data provides a robust and good tool for developing emotional intelligence detection systems.

EI HCI and Decision-Making Healthcare

The decision-making to the knowledge part of the robot advisors design is provided by this work (Morana et al., 2020). This research work focused on such a way to concentrate on the factors influencing the investment choices of users through the Chabot of Robo-advisor. Robo-advisors in this work is meant to suggest financial recommendations to private households at a low cost. In this research, 183 lab experiments have been conducted examining the various design levels of a Robo-advisor that might counteract the absence of human involvement and the outcomes are documented. As a consequence, it was attempted to arrive at the trust of users to follow its recommendations. Thus, the authors claim that the observed social communication by users was influenced by the anthropomorphic design. And this is expected to have a positive implicit influence on the plausibility to follow the recommendations.

Blair et al. (2021) attempted to make an interactive system to participate in the conversation about the allegations of algorithmic systems. To implement this, the authors proposed a chain of participating mechanisms for the development of algorithmic techniques. During this process, a framework for a live investigation of these concerns was provided. The outcomes are compiled into a group of best customs to occupy human beings on these themes. This work is also a solution for machine learning and artificial intelligence systems without the presence of human beings.

Recently, Alnuaim et al. (2022) aimed at developing an HCI-based emotion detection system in the journey of detecting emotions in the human voice with the help of artificial intelligence methods (Alnuaim et al., 2022) In the evolution, various sound analysis methods have been built, yet it was highly impossible to deliver an emotional study in a live speech. Also, it is very difficult to merge the results from several professions concerned with emotion recognition. It was planned to detect 8 unique emotions including neutral, calm, happy, sad, angry, fearful, disgusted, and surprised moods. In this particular study, the Ryerson Audio-Visual Database of Emotional Speech and Song (RAVDESS) open-source dataset was used. A Multilayer perceptron classifier was proposed for this purpose and overall accuracy of 81% was attained.

THE FUTURE OF EI IN HEALTHCARE

Emotional intelligence is one of the most important factors in achieving greatness in individual and organizational endeavors, including the selling of products and services, marketing, and the happiness of customers. Consequently, the development of an artificial emotional intelligence tracker is necessary to achieve complete automation of human mental and physical functions. Artificial emotional intelligence

(AEI) blends artificial and emotional intelligence. According to the statistics (Makridakis, 2017), approximately 52 per cent of consumers utilize AI-enabled digital devices to improve the quality of their lifestyle. The next revolution in artificial intelligence technologies will be the development of artificial emotional intelligence. The task of integrating empathy or the ability to discern human feelings is a difficult one. Voice and facial expression analysis are two methods that can be used by the AEI software to help medical professionals diagnose mental conditions such as dementia and depression (Celani et al., 1999) This article explores the difficulties that arise when attempting to read the facial expressions of people who have autism. Understanding the facial expressions of people who have autism is made easier by the application of deep learning techniques, which provide positive outcomes. A deep learning model was developed by the authors of (Ahmed et al., 2022) to analyze the facial expressions of people with autism. The accuracy of the categorization is 95 per cent, and it is achieved through the employment of the CNN-based models MobileNet, Xception, and InceptionV3. Another issue that can arise with this kind of program when it is deployed in a real-time setting is one that, in many instances, is not investigated. Interpreting facial expressions using ResNet50 and VGG19 as described in (Tamilarasi & Shanmugam, 2020; Jahanara, & Padmanabhan; 2021generates a system with an accuracy value of 89 per cent and 84 per cent, respectively. In this case, the software (Tamilarasi & Shanmugam, 2020; Jahanara, & Padmanabhan; 2021) is tested in a real-time setting, whereas the software (Tamilarasi & Shanmugam, 2020; Jahanara, & Padmanabhan; 2021are not deployed in real-time; hence, there may be a large number of factors that need to be incorporated to gain higher accuracy.

There are a variety of applications for EI affective computing in the healthcare industry, and there is room for further development in this arena. By automatically recording the user's emotional states through the use of human-computer interaction tools, emotional intelligence can be applied to cognitive computing to provide superior assistance in the field of healthcare. However, there is no question that it will be successful in the future and encourage scholars to work in this area.

CONCLUSION

One of the numerous benefits of applying AI technology in the healthcare industry is that it can optimize big data sets that are kept in complex systems. Furthermore, these involve both machines and people and require a system that is more stochastic and less deterministic than a traditional assembly line. As a result, to handle these types of variation, one would require a robust system that learns from its mistakes and optimizes the algorithm to make it better each time it is used. The future of healthcare will be determined by how well we learn from and apply data. The data acquired in the past can be used to make accurate predictions about some life-threatening conditions, which in turn can save lives. Therefore, the accumulation of data and the appropriate use of that data will be necessary to endow systems with emotional intelligence. Early diagnosis is possible thanks to the convergence of data science, artificial intelligence (AI), machine learning, and appropriate point-of-care testing. Adopting A.I. will make the process simpler for patients; they will no longer be required to wait for confirmation from hospital authorities. Additionally, once a patient is discharged from the emergency room, a normal ward bed will be automatically reserved and assigned to that specific patient, turning the system into one that is patient centric. EI is critically important in both the process of making healthcare a patient-centered system and the optimization of all processes related to healthcare.

REFERENCES

Ahmed, Z. A., Aldhyani, T. H., Jadhav, M. E., Alzahrani, M. Y., Alzahrani, M. E., Althobaiti, M. M., Alassery, F., Alshaflut, A., Alzahrani, N. M., & Al-Madani, A. M. (2022). Facial Features Detection System To Identify Children With Autism Spectrum Disorder: Deep Learning Models. *Computational and Mathematical Methods in Medicine, 2022*. doi:10.1155/2022/3941049 PMID:35419082

Alam, M. M. (2009). The relationships between emotional intelligence and job satisfaction: Empirical findings from a higher education institution in Malaysia. *Journal of Health Care Professionals and Social Sciences, 5*(2), 124–139. doi:10.46745/ilma.jbs.2009.05.02.04

Arnone, R., Cascio, M. I., & Parenti, I. (2019). The role of Emotional Intelligence in health care professionals' burnout. *European Journal of Public Health, 29*(Supplement_4), ckz186–ckz553. doi:10.1093/eurpub/ckz186.553

Baghcheghi, N., & Koohestani, H. R. (2022). The predictive role of a tendency toward mobile learning and emotional intelligence in Internet addiction in healthcare professional students. *Journal of Advances in Medical Education & Professionalism, 10*(2), 113. PMID:35434145

Bebarta, D. K., Das, T. K., Chowdhary, C. L., & Gao, X. Z. (2021). An intelligent hybrid system for forecasting stock and forex trading signals using optimized recurrent FLANN and case-based reasoning. *International Journal of Computational Intelligence Systems, 14*(1), 1763–1772. doi:10.2991/ijcis.d.210601.001

Birks, Y., McKendree, J., & Watt, I. (2009). Emotional intelligence and perceived stress in healthcare students: A multi-institutional, multi-professional survey. *BMC Medical Education, 9*(1), 1–8. doi:10.1186/1472-6920-9-61 PMID:19761603

Blair, K., Hansen, P., & Oehlberg, L. (2021, June). Participatory Art for Public Exploration of Algorithmic Decision-Making. In *Companion Publication of the 2021 ACM Designing Interactive Systems Conference* (pp. 23-26). 10.1145/3468002.3468235

Celani, G., Battacchi, M. W., & Arcidiacono, L. (1999). The understanding of the emotional meaning of facial expressions in people with autism. *Journal of Autism and Developmental Disorders, 29*(1), 57–66. doi:10.1023/A:1025970600181 PMID:10097995

Chowdhary, C. L. (2022). Agile Supply Chain: Framework for Digitization. In *Innovative Supply Chain Management via Digitalization and Artificial Intelligence* (pp. 73–85). Springer. doi:10.1007/978-981-19-0240-6_5

Chowdhary, C. L., Alazab, M., Chaudhary, A., Hakak, S., & Gadekallu, T. R. (2021). *Computer Vision and Recognition Systems Using Machine and Deep Learning Approaches: Fundamentals*. Technologies and Applications. Institution of Engineering and Technology.

Fariselli, L., Freedman, J., Ghini, M., & Valentini, F. (2008). *Stress, emotional intelligence, and performance in healthcare*. Academic Press.

Goleman, D. (2011). The brain and emotional intelligence: New insights. *Regional Business*, 94-95.

Jahanara, S., & Padmanabhan, S. (2021). *Detecting autism from the facial image*. Academic Press.

Khan, M., Minbashian, A., & MacCann, C. (2021). College students in the western world are becoming less emotionally intelligent: A cross-temporal meta-analysis of trait emotional intelligence. *Journal of Personality, 89*(6), 1176–1190. doi:10.1111/jopy.12643 PMID:33872392

Kolski, C., Boy, G. A., Melançon, G., Ochs, M., & Vanderdonckt, J. (2020). Cross-fertilisation between human-computer interaction and artificial intelligence. In *A guided tour of artificial intelligence research* (pp. 365–388). Springer. doi:10.1007/978-3-030-06170-8_11

Makridakis, S. (2017). The forthcoming Artificial Intelligence (AI) revolution: Its impact on society and firms. *Futures, 90*, 46–60. doi:10.1016/j.futures.2017.03.006

Mikolajczak, L., Bodarwe, K., Laloyaux, O., Hansenne, M., & Nelis, D. (2010). Association between frontal EEG asymmetries and emotional intelligence among adults. *Personality and Individual Differences, 48*(2), 177–181. doi:10.1016/j.paid.2009.10.001

Morana, S., Gnewuch, U., Jung, D., & Granig, C. (2020). The Effect of Anthropomorphism on Investment Decision-Making with Robo-Advisor Chatbots. ECIS.

Mukeshimana, M., Ban, X., Karani, N., & Liu, R. (2017). Multimodal emotion recognition for human-computer interaction: A survey. *System, 9*, 10.

Năstasă, L. E., & Fărcaş, A. D. (2015). The effect of emotional intelligence on burnout in healthcare professionals. *Procedia: Social and Behavioral Sciences, 187*, 78–82. doi:10.1016/j.sbspro.2015.03.015

Panigrahi, R., Borah, S., Bhoi, A. K., Ijaz, M. F., Pramanik, M., Jhaveri, R. H., & Chowdhary, C. L. (2021). Performance assessment of supervised classifiers for designing intrusion detection systems: A comprehensive review and recommendations for future research. *Mathematics, 9*(6), 690. doi:10.3390/math9060690

Picard, R. W. (2003). Affective computing: Challenges. *International Journal of Human-Computer Studies, 59*(1-2), 55–64. doi:10.1016/S1071-5819(03)00052-1

Picard, R. W. (2008). *Toward machines with emotional intelligence*. Academic Press.

Pivec, M. (Ed.). (2006). *Affective and emotional aspects of human-computer interaction: game-based and innovative learning approaches* (Vol. 1). IOS Press.

Rubeis, G. (2022). iHealth: The ethics of artificial intelligence and big data in mental healthcare. *Internet Interventions: the Application of Information Technology in Mental and Behavioural Health, 28*, 100518. doi:10.1016/j.invent.2022.100518 PMID:35257003

Sharp, G., Bourke, L., & Rickard, M. J. (2020). Review of emotional intelligence in health care: An introduction to emotional intelligence for surgeons. *ANZ Journal of Surgery, 90*(4), 433–440. doi:10.1111/ans.15671 PMID:31965690

Smith, L. M., Heaven, P. C. L., & Ciarrochi, J. (2008). Trait emotional intelligence, conflict communication patterns, and relationship satisfaction. *Personality and Individual Differences, 44*(6), 1314–1325. doi:10.1016/j.paid.2007.11.024

Srivastava, S., Misra, R., Pathak, D., & Sharma, P. (2021). Boosting Job Satisfaction Through Emotional Intelligence: A Study on Health Care Professionals. *Journal of Health Management*, *23*(3), 414–424. doi:10.1177/09720634211035213

Tamilarasi, F. C., & Shanmugam, J. (2020, June). Convolutional neural network-based autism classification. In *2020 5th International Conference on Communication and Electronics Systems (ICCES)* (pp. 1208-1212). IEEE. 10.1109/ICCES48766.2020.9137905

Wadley, G., Kostakos, V., Koval, P., Smith, W., Webber, S., Cox, A., . . . Slovák, P. (2022, April). The Future of Emotion in Human-Computer Interaction. In *CHI Conference on Human Factors in Computing Systems Extended Abstracts* (pp. 1-6). 10.1145/3491101.3503729

Chapter 11
To What Extent Can Multidisciplinary Artificial Intelligence Applications Enhance Higher Education?
Open and Distance E–Learning in South Africa

Nomvula J. Ndhlovu
University of South Africa, South Africa

Leila Goosen
iD https://orcid.org/0000-0003-4948-2699
University of South Africa, South Africa

ABSTRACT

In order to provide readers with an overview of, and summarize, the content of this chapter, the purpose is stated as answering the primary research question: To what extent can multidisciplinary artificial intelligence in education (AIED) applications enhance higher education teaching and learning at an open and distance e-learning (ODeL) institution in South Africa? It is important to note that this is done against the background of multidisciplinary applications of deep learning-based artificial emotional intelligence.

Anyone, who had "been frustrated asking questions of Siri or Alexa", and then were annoyed at the tone-deaf responses from the digital assistant, "knows how dumb these supposedly intelligent assistants are, at least when it comes to emotional intelligence" (Krakovsky, 2018, p. 18).

DOI: 10.4018/978-1-6684-5673-6.ch011

INTRODUCTION

Emotions and intelligence are co-related phenomena; therefore, emotions must be taken into consideration when designing towards true intelligence. Emotional intelligence has emerged as an important area of research in Artificial Intelligence (AI), while in a comprehensive *review* on the performance assessment of supervised classifiers for designing intrusion detection systems, Panigrahi et al. (2021, p. 1) indicated that supervised learning and pattern recognition was another "crucial area of research in" image processing, information retrieval, intrusion detection systems, knowledge engineering and medical imaging. Numerous algorithms had been designed to cover a wide range of such complex real-life application domains. Emotion recognition and mining tasks are often limited by the availability of manually annotated data. Several information and communication technologies (ICTs) are being used towards attaining emotional intelligence acceleration and augmentation. Like this book, the chapter will present emerging trends related to research in this field, about emerging trends with regard to technologies and tools used to simplify and streamline the formation of deep learning for system architects and designers. As part of this book, the chapter is designed to serve as a preferred reference for research and development. Machines may never need all the emotional skills that people have. There is, however, evidence that machines require at least some of these skills to appear intelligent when interacting with people.

Zawacki-Richter et al. (2019, p. 3) stated that although the field of artificial intelligence originated "from computer science and engineering," it was "strongly influenced by other disciplines such as" cognitive science, economics, neuroscience and philosophy. Therefore, AI is an interdisciplinary and Industry 5.0 a multidisciplinary research area respectively.

Higher education institutions are moving along towards the digital revolution, where artificial intelligence in education had been transformed by being influenced by not only what is taught, but also how it is taught (Roll & Wylie, 2016). The University of South Africa (UNISA) is a leading Open and Distance e-Learning (OeDL) institution in Africa, with student enrollment of over 400 000 students. UNISA is situated in Pretoria, the capital city of South Africa. South Africa is a developing country with its challenges. Teaching and learning is one of the core areas of business for the university. As a distance education provider, it is important that the university improve its offerings to students that are geographically separated.

Innovative educational technologies had revolutionized and played an active role in teaching and learning methods (Fahimirad & Kotamjani, 2018), as the presence of technological tools or applications can improve the former, providing vast opportunities to the education world. The new wave of technologies, including "developments in the 'smart classroom' as a new frontier" in the age of the smart university, as examined in the article by Kwet & Prinsloo (2020, p. 510), had evolved into using applications in teaching and learning in higher education. The evolution in terms of shifting priorities in education not only changed the way in which things are done, but also the use of these technologies to make the work environment a better place (Roll & Wylie, 2016). With digitized learning content, the distance in terms of geography, space, and time are mitigated, providing students with the freedom to choose suitable learning path and training goals. Students can actively access study materials, as well as interact with their lecturers, at any time, using computers or smartphones. The development of online learning systems helps students save time, effort and costs.

Artificial intelligence is one of the leading applications of Information Systems (IS). It offers modern knowledge in terms of understanding the nature of human intelligence and how it stimulates smart computational intelligence that is limited to processing information, but it does not have the ability to understand what it is processing.

AI is being applied in many different ways and different contexts. Artificial intelligence applications are important for educational institutions and universities, to help with the large amount of data that need be processed in real time. "The field of education is a place where artificial intelligence is poised to make big changes. The implementation of" Artificial Intelligence in Education (AIED) has several benefits for students and educators (Sadiku, Musa, & Chukwu, 2022, p. 5), where it can be used to stimulate innovative teaching with the purpose of improving learning outcomes (Holmes, Bialik, & Fadel, 2019). By design, intelligent technology is a method, which uses knowledge to achieve concrete purposes efficiently. Knowledge and research are increasingly shaping the use of technology through artificial intelligence for educational purposes (Kwet & Prinsloo, 2020).

Target Audience

Like the target audience of this book, the chapter is designed so that it can serve as a preferred reference in the libraries of academic institutions, research and development centers, departments of business, computer and information sciences, organizations dealing with artificial emotional intelligence, and data science/artificial intelligence firms developing products in the domain of emotional intelligence.

Recommended Topics

Based on the recommended topics provided for the book, this chapter will especially focus on the following:

- Components and Characteristics of Emotional Intelligence
- Emotional Artificial Intelligence and the Internet of Things (IoT)
- Machine/Deep Learning Approaches for Artificial Emotional Intelligence
- Benefits and Challenges of using Deep Learning in Emotional Intelligence
- Sustainable Emotional Intelligence
- The Role of Machine/Deep Learning in Emotional Intelligence
- Bio-Physiological Sensors in Emotion Recognition
- The Application of Emotional Intelligence in Business Process Management
- Emotional Intelligence in the Era of Industry 4.0

Organization of the Chapter

Against the background of multidisciplinary applications of deep learning-based artificial emotional intelligence, a literature review will be provided, along with a focus on the issues, problems, threats, etc. applicable to this study. Solutions and recommendations to counter the issues, problems, threats, etc. presented are then discussed. After future research directions are considered, the conclusion follows.

Objective

As part of the book, this chapter aims to explore artificial intelligence applications in emotional intelligence, including machine learning and deep learning. Like this book, the chapter will present up-to-date technologies and solutions to aspects regarding the applications of artificial intelligence in emotional intelligence. Therefore, as part of this book, the chapter further aims to address training needs in research and the scientific community.

In a study of an ODeL institution in South Africa, the *purpose* was to answer the primary research question: To what extent can multidisciplinary artificial intelligence in education applications enhance teaching and learning in higher education?

The next section will situate the study reported on in this chapter against the background of multi-disciplinary applications of deep learning-based artificial emotional intelligence.

BACKGROUND

This section of the chapter will provide broad *definitions* and discussions of the topic of the extent to which multidisciplinary artificial intelligence applications can enhance higher education, and incorporate the views of others (in the form of a *literature review*) into the discussion to support, refute, or demonstrate the authors' position on the topic.

Components and Characteristics of Emotional Intelligence

In an employee perspective on emotional intelligence or artificial intelligence, Emotional Intelligence (EI and emotional intelligence were used interchangeably in the journal article on hospitality marketing and management by Prentice et al. (2020, p. 377)) as a "personal intelligence and artificial intelligence", which is referred to as a machine intelligence, are indicated as having "been popular in the relevant *literature* over the last two decades."

According to White & Katsuno (2022), artificial emotional intelligence referred to technologies that perform, recognize or record affective states. Taking artificial emotional intelligence beyond East and West in an internet policy *review,* White & Katsuno (2022, p. 6) compared "the formation of the field of affective computing, originating mainly in America and Europe, with approaches to emotional robotics and affective engineering" towards drawing "out the significance of certain cultural differences in *defining* artificial emotional intelligence".

Similar to some of the research on technology-supported teaching and learning methods for educators offered in Goosen (2019), the journal article on affective computing by Abdollahi et al. (2022, p. 1) presented recent research on a pilot study "integrating artificial emotional intelligence in a" socially assistive robot (Ryan) and studied the effectiveness of the robot in engaging with older adults.

An article that showed that legal intelligence through artificial intelligence required emotional intelligence and proposed a new competency model for the 21st century legal professional by Carrel (2018, p. 1153) acknowledged that the profession was "not replacing emotional intelligence with artificial intelligence but" was, instead, creating complimentary intelligence, which relied on both.

Emotional Artificial Intelligence and the Internet of Things

A journal article on chemical and pharmaceutical sciences *reviewing* the Internet of Things and its applications in healthcare by Singh et al. (2017, p. 447) suggested that the Internet of Things was "a buzzword in the computing and" technological worlds. The IoT could change the way human beings live their lives by making it more convenient and 'smarter'. The IoT also "has the capability to add intelligence" to real world objects and allow these to communicate with each other. The IoT further provides "common infrastructure through which different devices can be connected and communicate smartly", including such areas as sensor networks, Internet Protocol (IP), Radio Frequency Identification (RFID) and Wireless Fidelity (Wi-Fi).

Since the birth of Industry 5.0, it had been "poised to harness extreme automation". A journal article on integrative biology by Özdemir & Hekim (2018, p. 65) called for measures related to Industry 5.0, which can democratize knowledge co-production by making sense of Big Data, together with artificial intelligence, the Internet of Things and a next-generation technology policy, as well as "building on the new *concept* of symmetrical innovation."

"Industry 5.0 is based on the synergy between humans and autonomous machines." According to Aslam et al. (2020, p. 2), the article by Nahavandi (2019) further added that innovation in the era of the Internet of Things and Industry 5.0 required an Absolute Innovation Management (AIM) framework. For increased production, "however, Industry 5.0 is more focused on" information.

Artificial Intelligence in Education

The next subsection, as was done by Holmes et al. (2019, p. 13), will provide a "brief background to artificial intelligence" and "interested readers will find more information about the origins and development of AI and its various techniques". According to Holmes et al. (2019, p. 1), artificial intelligence "is arguably *the[1]* driving technological force of the first" decades of the 21st "century, and will transform virtually every industry, if not human endeavors at large." At the center of curriculum redesign, AI both holds promises and have implications for teaching and learning, as it can be used to develop a curriculum that improves online tutoring services, teaching processes, as well as learning processes to enhance teaching and learning at the university.

Since the field of artificial intelligence is interdisciplinary in its formation (see introduction section), there is little agreement among AI researchers on a common *definition* and understanding of AI and intelligence in general. In an introduction to a special issue discussing artificial intelligence, Haenlein & Kaplan (2019, p. 5) indicated that artificial intelligence is commonly *defined* as the ability of a system "to interpret external data correctly, … learn from such data, and" use such learning "to achieve specific goals and tasks through flexible adaptation."

In a bibliometric analysis with a latent semantic approach and against the background of computers in human behavior, according to Shen and Ho (2020, p. 1), Technology-Enhanced Learning (TEL) in higher education described information and communication technologies in terms of "the outcomes of teaching and learning. Its adoption in higher education" was an advance aimed towards designing, developing and evaluating socio-technical innovations, which will support and enhance the "learning practices of both individuals and" organizations (Shen & Ho, 2020, p. 2). It is expected that in this digital era, users of the system be digitally literate, as most educational activities are presented using digital applications. The use of technology provides support to teachers and students and mediate educational activities for improved learning outcomes. The online journal article on distance education and e-learning by Halili (2019) supported the opinion that technological advancements in education 4.0 could accelerate teaching and learning processes and improve students' learning experiences. Teachers can save lessons and teaching materials that students can access anytime, anywhere via these educational applications.

The exploratory *review* of artificial intelligence in education information by Lameras & Arnab (2021, p. 1) to empower teachers "attempted to gather evidence from the *literature* by shedding light on the emerging phenomenon of" *conceptualizing* "the impact of artificial intelligence in education." In terms of the tools of artificial intelligence in education, in particular, the paper by Lameras & Arnab (2021) attempted to contemplate questions around what is meant by artificial intelligence in education?

The assumption by many is that artificial intelligence in education refers to students being taught by robot teachers, but the reality is simpler. Yet, it still has the potential to be transformative (Holmes et al., 2019). AIED applications refer to the use of artificial intelligence "technologies or application programs in educational settings" towards facilitating teaching and learning (Hwang, Xie, Wah, & Gašević, 2020, p. 1).

Against the background of educational technologies and society, Chen et al. (2022, p. 28) considered two decades of communication between students "and instructors, based on 47 publications in the International Journal of Artificial Intelligence in Education (IJAIED) in 1994, 2004, and 2014." The latter authors continued to cite e.g., the articles by Hwang et al. (2020) and Chen et al. (2020) – see next section of this chapter – as well as the journal article on artificial intelligence in education by Roll & Wylie (2016, p. 582), who aspired "to achieve measurable improvement in … aspects beyond the scope of the tutored environment."

In an international journal article on innovation studies reflecting on a twenty-year data-driven historical analysis of educational research, Guan ert al. (2020, p. 134) retrieved over 400 research articles on the application of AI innovation in education and Deep Learning (DL) techniques in teaching. According to Guan et al. (2020, p. 135), the AIEd applications, which are available today include student-oriented, instructor-oriented and institutional system-oriented AIEd. These applications can help to monitor students' progress so that the student can be provided with more support when there is a need. The latter authors further indicated that student-oriented AI enabled "students to study a subject domain, in an adaptive or personalized learning management system and an instructor-oriented tool can automate tasks such as administrative procedures, assessments, plagiarism detection and" the provision of feedback.

The international journal article on educational technologies in higher education by Zawacki-Richter et al. (2019, p. 1) sought "to provide an overview of research on AI applications in higher education through a systematic *review*" and also asked where the educators were?

As tuition is one of the three core areas of business at UNISA, student-centeredness and flexible learning are among the approaches used by the university towards improvement. In an international journal article on learning and development *reviewing* the application of artificial intelligence in teaching and learning in educational contexts, Fahimirad & Kotamjani (2018, p. 107) agreed that recently, along with advancements related to artificial intelligence, institutions in higher education had begun "to make effective changes in the core design of" their learning offering. The latter authors also supported the idea that artificial intelligence had such potential.

The purpose of the study reported on by Chen et al. (2020, p. 75264) "was to assess the impact of" AI on education, premised "on a narrative and framework for assessing AI identified from a" *review.*

In their scoping *review* of artificial intelligence, computers and education, Su and Yang (2022, p. 1) indicated that artificial intelligence "tools are increasingly being used in the field of early childhood education (ECE) to enhance learning and development among young children".

A journal article on educational technology and society by Devedžić (2004, p. 29) explored "the fundamental roles as well as practical impacts of" AI, as well as "Web Intelligence (WI) in the context of" AIED research.

"Building super intelligent systems in education" can revolutionize teaching and learning (Malik, Tayal, & Vij, 2019, p. 407).

"As for the results of" the study reported on in the journal article on innovation in educational and cultural research by Bali et al.i (2022, p. 146), in its application, artificial intelligence in" higher education/universities has had both positive and negative impacts on the relationships between intelligence and learning, as well as the perceived relationships between educators and students, when it was carried out.

The following section of the chapter will present the authors' perspective on the issues, problems, threats, etc., as these relate to the main theme of the book.

MAIN FOCUS OF THE CHAPTER

Issues, Problems, Threats

This section of the chapter will present the authors' perspective on the issues, problems, threats, etc., as these relate to the main theme of the book, Multidisciplinary Applications of Deep Learning-Based Artificial Emotional Intelligence, and arguments supporting the authors' position. It will also compare and contrast with what had been, or is currently being, done as it relates to the specific topic of the chapter, on the extent to which multidisciplinary artificial intelligence applications can enhance higher education.

According to Chowdhary et al. (2020), image processing techniques have been crucial in analyzing and resolving issues related to segmentation and feature extraction in medical imaging for the last two decades. Other fields where such issues might occur could also include e.g., meteorology or brain diagnostics (Chowdhary et al., 2021).

As part of a systematic *review*, Chowdhary & Acharjya (2020) indicated that medical imaging was a process or technique used to find and analyze diseases. As example of the latter, the earlier international journal article on healthcare information systems and Informatics by Chowdhary & Acharjya (2016, p. 38) specified that the diagnosis of cancer had been "of prime concern in recent years." However, such medical images often "contain uncertainties due to various factors". The latter article therefore recommended a hybrid scheme for breast cancer detection using an intuitionistic fuzzy rough set technique.

In the context of educational technologies and society, Huang et al. (2021) looked at research issues with regard to the applications of artificial intelligence in language education.

The international journal article on image, graphics and signal processing by Khan & Debnath (2020, p. 19) addressed problems related to the identification of "certain human behavior such as distraction" from video streams using artificial emotional intelligence "and also predicting the pattern of" these. The latter article thus proposed "an artificial emotional intelligent or emotional AI algorithm to detect any change in visual attention for individuals."

According to the international journal article on evaluation and research in education by Rachmawati et al. (2021, p. 676), "Industry 5.0 is a new era initiated by the Japanese government … . The emergence of industry 5.0 was caused by the failure of industry 4.0", upon which "Japan finally came up with its idea to develop the industry 5.0 era to balance technology and" resolutions related to social problems.

In a journal article on applied science and engineering, Chowdhary et al. (2019, p. 691) showed that one "of the biggest problems faced regarding images in various fields" was the generation of a meaningful description for a particular image, i.e., the "caption for the image. The images are being used for numerous purposes" and the latter authors therefore offered an experimental assessment of a beam search algorithm for the improvement in image caption generation.

"The enormous growth in internet usage has led to the development of different malicious software posing serious threats to computer security" (Khare, et al., 2020, p. 1). The various computational activities possible led the latter authors (Khare et al., 2020) to develop a spider monkey optimization (SMO) and deep neural network (DNN) hybrid classifier model for intrusion detection. "It is therefore vital that all cyber users be aware of the cyber risks and threats and know how to address or avoid" such cyber threats (Kritzinger, Loock, & Goosen, 2019, p. 477). Through the lens of 21st century learning skills and game-based learning, lecture notes in computer science and the proceedings of the 43rd conference of the Southern African Computer Lecturers' Association (SACLA) are showing that computer lecturers are using their institutional Learning Management System (LMS) for ICT education in the cyber world (Goosen & Naidoo, 2014). A paper in the proceedings of a South African international conference on educational technologies further indicated that such technologies could be implemented for an Information and Communication Technologies for Development (ICT4D) Massive Open Online Course (MOOC) in the 21st century (Goosen 2015).

"Considering the increasing importance of" artificial intelligence in education and the absence regarding application and theory gaps during the rise of artificial intelligence in education, Chen et al. (2020, p. 1) "analyzed 45 articles in terms of annual distribution, leading journals, institutions," etc. with regard to artificial intelligence, computers and education.

Panigrahi et al. (2021, p. 1) indicated that despite "an enormous array of supervised classifiers, researchers are yet to recognize a robust classification mechanism that accurately and quickly classifies the target dataset, especially in the field of intrusion detection systems (IDSs)."

Whilst AIEd had "been around for about 30 years, it" was still unclear how educators can take "pedagogical advantage of it on a broader scale, and how it can actually impact meaningfully on teaching and learning in higher education" (Zawacki-Richter et al., 2019, p. 1).

The article by Kwet and Prinsloo (2020, p. 510) provided "a *conceptual* map of the scope and limitations of smart classrooms".

In the proceedings of the international conference on computer science and artificial intelligence, Salam et al. (2017) investigated strategic barriers to the effective integration of ICT in the public schools of Pakistan.

Toward artificial emotional intelligence for cooperative social human–machine interaction, Erol (2019, p. 234) specified that the "aptitude to identify the emotional states of others and" respond to exposed emotions was "an important aspect of human social intelligence." When it comes to the age of artificial emotional intelligence, Schuller & Schuller (2018, p. 38) also pointed out that emotions "and emotional intelligence are not" considered to form part of the aspects related to human intelligence, which are represented by computers in AI. Creativity is further "still largely lacking in AI," as well as emotional and social intelligence.

Ndhlovu & Goosen (2021) indicated the need for re-envisioning and restructuring e-learning through engagement with underprivileged communities with regard to the impact of effectively using ICTs to facilitate teaching and learning in classrooms (Libbrecht & Goosen, 2015).

Machine/Deep Learning Approaches for Artificial Emotional Intelligence

In terms of software practice and experience, Parimala, et al. (2021, p. 550) showed that social media played a vital role in the analysis of "the actual emotions of people" during and after a disaster, while sentiment analysis was a method for the detection of a pattern from emotions and feedback. The latter authors therefore carried out a spatiotemporal-based sentiment analysis on tweets for **risk** assessment of an event using a deep learning approach.

A research anthology on artificial intelligence applications in security by Chowdhary, Darwish and Hassanien (2021) pointed out that such deep learning refers to scientific algorithms, which are customized for use in a particular assignment.

With regard to Chief Executive Officer (CEO) emotions and firm valuation in initial coin offerings, the strategic management journal article by Momtaz (2021, p. 558) was "accompanied by artificial emotional intelligence software for implementation in … a novel artificial emotional intelligence (henceforth, emotion AI) approach."

Benefits and Challenges of using Deep Learning in Emotional Intelligence

Technology brings many opportunities to learn and teach more effectively and to contribute to the process of knowledge construction.

Since the education sector was "associated with highly dynamic business environments" that were "controlled and maintained by information systems, recent technological advancements" led to a competitive environment having been created, since most of the universities need to use technology to offer their classes (Owoc, Sawicka, & Weichbroth, 2019, p. 37). Hence, the benefits, challenges, strategies, criteria and guidelines for the selection and implementation of AI applications need to be considered in terms of enhancing educational environments (Goosen, 2004). Owoc, et al. (2019) further specified that the competitiveness of Higher Education Institutions (HEIs) depended strongly on increasing effective learning methods and was supported by artificial intelligence technologies and tools in education.

The paper by Akinwalere & Ivanov (2022, p. 1) aimed to evaluate the challenges and opportunities related to artificial intelligence within higher education.

The chapter by Bolton et al. (2020, p. 99) investigated the security aspects of an empirical study into the impact of digital transformation via unified communication and collaboration technologies on the productivity and innovation of a global automotive enterprise. The latter authors also indicated that large "automotive Original Equipment Manufacturers (OEM), such as General Motors (GM), face unique challenges in transforming their enterprises into the IoT and Industry 4.0 age, due to their scale and broad dependency on global supply chain and product partnerships."

The journal article on industrial integration and management by Javaid et al. (2020, p. 507) "identified and studied significant challenges faced in the context of Industry 5.0", as well as the supportive features and potential applications of Industry 5.0, which can be "helpful for the COVID-19 pandemic."

In addition, and also related to another one of the recommended topics discussed in this chapter, Sustainable Emotional Intelligence, to counter the challenges faced, the article by Nahavandi (2019, p. 1) presented "several developments achieved by researchers for use in Industry 5.0".

Sustainable Emotional Intelligence

The paper by Pedro et al. (2019, p. 4) reflected on some of the challenges and opportunities, as well as risks related to artificial intelligence "in education for sustainable development" and preparing students for an artificial intelligence-powered context.

Against the background of sustainable cities and society Bhattacharya et al. (2021, p. 1) suggested that since "December 2019, the coronavirus disease (COVID-19)" pandemic outbreak had caused many deaths "and affected all sectors of human life. With" the gradual progression of time, however, a survey on deep learning and medical image processing for/during the coronavirus (COVID-19) pandemic was needed.

With regard to the sustainability and applications of artificial intelligence, teachers "have the main responsibility of teaching in" relation to any academic and administrative roles of artificial intelligence in education (Ahmad, Alam, Rahmat, Mubarik, & Hyder, 2022, p. 1).

In the proceedings of the 26th conference of the Southern African Association for Research in Mathematics, Science and Technology Education (SAARMSTE), Goosen (2018a) explained how **sustainable** and inclusive quality education could be achieved through research-informed practice on information and communication technologies.

The Role of Machine/Deep Learning in Emotional Intelligence

In terms of research **issues** in, **the roles of**, **challenges** related to, and a vision for, artificial intelligence, computers and education, Hwang, et al. (2020, p. 3) stated that the integration of artificial intelligence into education are opening up new opportunities towards vastly improving "the quality of teaching and learning". Various platforms can be used to support online learning. In the process, quality education can be achieved through the integration of technological applications. Hwang, et al. (2020, p. 3) further indicated that the implementation of artificial intelligence-based systems offered much promise towards enhancing learning performance and the experiences of students, as well as assisting teachers in advancing their teaching practice.

Bio-Physiological Sensors in Emotion Recognition

In the context of **sensors**, the majority of imaging techniques used "symmetric and asymmetric cryptography algorithms" towards encrypting "digital media. Most of the research" work contributed to the *literature* focused "primarily on the Advanced Encryption Standard (AES) algorithm for encryption and decryption." The paper by Chowdhary et al. (2020, p. 1) proposed an analytical study of hybrid techniques for image encryption and decryption.

Also against the background of sensors, the "herpesvirus, polyomavirus, papillomavirus, and retrovirus families are associated with breast cancer. More effort" was needed towards assessing "the role of these viruses in the detection and diagnosis of breast cancer cases" (Chowdhary, Mittal, Pattanaik, & Marszalek, 2020, p. 1). Addressing this gap, the latter authors recommended an efficient segmentation and classification system for medical images using intuitionist possibilistic fuzzy C-mean clustering and fuzzy support vector machine (SVM) algorithms.

Research Questions

At an open and distance e-learning institution in South Africa, the study reported on in this chapter aims to establish the extent to which multidisciplinary artificial intelligence in education applications can enhance teaching and e-learning in higher education.

The following research questions were therefore considered:

1. What is the role of multidisciplinary artificial intelligence applications in higher education?
2. Which multidisciplinary artificial intelligence applications are used for teaching and e-learning in higher education?
3. What effect do these applications have on users?
4. To what extent can these applications enhance teaching and e-learning in higher education?

Reasons Why the Researchers are Interested in the Topic

The authors would like to understand how multidisciplinary artificial intelligence applications can be used to enhance teaching and learning at an open and distance and e-learning university, where throughput is of importance. There is a need to explore the effect of these applications on users.

Expected Contribution of the Study

The authors hope to learn more about the role of artificial intelligence and its impact on higher education. Student support is key to the improvement of throughput. Innovative strategies used by teachers can also stimulate e-learning in the interest of enhanced teaching enabling students to contribute to the growth of the South African economy.

The researchers would also like to contribute to the teaching and learning body of knowledge, through an understanding of the solutions and recommendations related to artificial intelligence in education for an open and distance e-learning environment.

The next section of the chapter will discuss solutions and recommendations to counter the issues, problems, threats, etc., presented in this section.

SOLUTIONS AND RECOMMENDATIONS

Solutions

Technology brings positive learning experiences and solutions to students and improvements for teachers to use during instruction.

With regard to one of the recommended topics discussed in this chapter, Benefits and Challenges of using Deep Learning in Emotional Intelligence, at the 11th international conference on educational and information technologies, Qin & Wang (2022, p. 62) explored feasible solutions related to the proposed benefits and challenges of "the application of artificial intelligence in education".

The Application of Emotional Intelligence in Business Process Management

Also related to another of the recommended topics discussed in this chapter, *Emotional Intelligence in the Era of Industry 4.0*, the chapter by Bolton et al. (2021b, p. 151), on an empirical study into the impact on innovation and productivity towards the post-COVID-19 era digital transformation of an automotive enterprise, indicted that their earlier chapter (Bolton, Goosen, & Kritzinger, 2021a) pointed to solutions and recommendations to counter "*management* challenges *in the* digital *era* by analyzing the impacts *of Industry 4.0* in modern *business*" *process management* environments. Digital communication is also "increasingly vital in *Industry 4.0* and" IoT-enabled *business process management* (Bolton et al., 2020, p. 100).

Emotional Intelligence in the Era of Industry 4.0

The article by Nahavandi (2019) discussed a human-centric solution with regard to Industry 5.0.

The chapter on the integration and implementation of the internet of things through digital transformation and the impact of these on productivity and innovation by Bolton et al. (2021c, p. 86) established "background context on the development of the technologies associated with the Internet of Things and how it overlaps with other emerging digital paradigms, such as *Industry 4.0*."

The earlier paper by Bolton et al. (2016, p. 1) provided "background context on the development of IoT technologies and how these developments overlap with industry, enabling revolutionary changes such as *Industry 4.0* and the advent of the Industrial Internet."

Methodology to be Followed

As was done in the study on educational technologies in distance education reported by Goosen & Mukasa-Lwanga (2017), qualitative perspectives will be obtained based on data collected from the students, teachers and curriculum designers at the University of South Africa, preferably in the College of Human Sciences. A structured questionnaire will be sent to their email addresses.

Availability of Data

A survey questionnaire will be used to collect data from participants. The study reported on in this chapter will attempt to obtain results that can be generalized. Data will be analyzed using SPSS software.

Recommendations

Branch & Burgos (2021) recommended radical solutions in terms of digital transformation strategies for Latin American universities related to artificial intelligence and technology 4.0 in higher education.

In line with the subsequent section, Panigrahi et al. (2021) offered recommendations for future research directions in the context of the performance assessment of supervised classifiers for designing intrusion detection systems.

The following section of the chapter will discuss future and emerging trends and provide insight about the future of the theme of the book, Multidisciplinary Applications of Deep Learning-Based Artificial Emotional Intelligence, from the perspective of the chapter focus. The viability of a paradigm, model, implementation issues of proposed programs, etc., may also be included in this section. Future research directions within the domain of the topic, on the extent to which multidisciplinary artificial intelligence applications can enhance higher education, will finally be suggested.

FUTURE RESEARCH DIRECTIONS

Chowdhary et al. (2015) appeared in proceedings on emerging trends in networks and computer communications, while at an international conference on emerging trends in information technology and engineering, Reddy et al. (2020, p. 1) indicated that as technologies and digitization grow, there was a huge surge in the "digital storage of health records." In line with one of the recommended topics discussed in this chapter, the important role of machine learning in "uncovering patterns existing in these" was also mentioned. The latter paper looked at an ensemble-based machine learning model for diabetic retinopathy classification.

The chapter by Bolton et al. (2022a) discussed emerging trends with regard to technologies for innovation and productivity management in the automotive industry in terms of the impact of digital transformation on communication. Also in terms of the impact of digital transformation, the chapter by Bolton et al. (2022b) detailed challenges and emerging trends regarding strategies for a global automotive enterprise towards the post COVID-19 era.

With regard to digital transformation in the education industry, Burns (2018) suggested five emerging trends in the context of the future of work.

In terms of the roles of artificial intelligence in education, McArthur et al. (2005, p. 42), in their journal article on educational technologies, looked at the progress, which had been made at the time, and future prospects for artificial intelligence in education. It then used a "summary to project various future applications of AI--and advanced technology in general--to education, as" well as in the classroom.

Also in the context of artificial intelligence in education, but much more recently, Goksel & Bozkurt (2019, p. 224) provided current insights and future perspectives related to research on learning in the age of transhumanism. "It is still a field in its infancy, but" even though artificial intelligence had only become a reality a short while ago, it now forms part of everyday routines and is penetrating every aspect of every-ones' lives, including education.

"Like many researchers in other countries," the chapter by Flogie & Aberšek (2022, p. 97) showed the contribution of artificial intelligence in education training environments to *active learning* theory and practice, which will likely "increase in the future, in the way that education is taught and delivered to" students. The number of trans-disciplinary and cross-disciplinary approaches to action research and *action learning* for e-schools, community engagement, and ICT4D are therefore likely to continue growing (Goosen, 2018b).

Haenlein and Kaplan (2019) also provided a brief history of the past, present and future of artificial intelligence. "With the rapid development of technology in the digitalization era, *Industry 4.0* became a terminology", which referenced "research and development in the field of technology" future service in industry 5.0 (Al Faruqi, 2019, p. 67).

"In fact, in the industry 5.0 era resilience is needed by individuals to face various challenges in the future." The article by Rachmawati et al. (2021, p. 676) therefore considered the prevalence of academic resilience in social science students when facing the industry 5.0 era.

With regard to key technologies, which featured within *Industry 4.0* architectures, future "Industry 4.0 environments will have increasing demands on communication supporting requirements of ubiquitous, real time and simultaneous system to system, machine to machine and people to machine/system communication and collaboration" (Bolton et al., 2021c, p. 89).

A book on the 'heart of the machine' and the future in a world of artificial emotional intelligence by Yonck (2020, p. viii) indicated that in "this future age of artificial emotional intelligence", a group of technologies, which "can read and respond to" emotional states meant that this field was "well on its way to transforming".

As the *ethical* "concerns of AI in education were also not" part of the scope of the study by Ahmad, et al. (2022, p. 8), future research directions could include these. Ensuring research integrity and the *ethical* management of data in the context of e-schools and community engagement (Goosen, 2018c) and *ethical* information and communication technologies for development solutions for MOOCs could be considered (Goosen, 2018d).

Chowdhary et al. (2021) suggested future research directions in intelligent retrieval and cognitive deep learning. Finally, the paper by Pedro, et al. (2019, p. 4) reflected on future research "directions for AI in education".

Whilst it had "been around for about thirty years" (Akinwalere & Ivanov, 2022, p. 1), according to various international reports cited by Zawacki-Richter et al. (2019, p. 1), AIEd is still "one of the currently emerging" trends in fields related to educational technologies. Huang, et al. (2021) also considered emerging trends related to the applications of artificial intelligence in language education. Finally, Malik, et al. (2019, p. 407) provided an analysis of the emerging trends related to the role of artificial intelligence in education and teaching, which led to certain findings and conclusions on intelligent computing techniques.

The next section of the chapter will provide a discussion of the overall coverage of the chapter and concluding remarks.

CONCLUSION

Against the background of the "many applications in the field of sciences such as" biology, Loria (2022, p. 2) came to the conclusion "that artificial intelligence is very helpful … in order to exceed the current marginal improvements in the" role of artificial intelligence in modern education.

REFERENCES

Abdollahi, H., Mahoor, M., Zandie, R., Sewierski, J., & Qualls, S. (2022). Artificial emotional intelligence in socially assistive robots for older adults: A pilot study. *IEEE Transactions on Affective Computing*, 1. doi:10.1109/TAFFC.2022.3143803

Ahmad, S. F., Alam, M. M., Rahmat, M., Mubarik, M. S., & Hyder, S. I. (2022). Academic and Administrative Role of Artificial Intelligence in Education. *Sustainability*, *14*(3), 1101. doi:10.3390u14031101

Akinwalere, S. N., & Ivanov, V. (2022). Artificial Intelligence in Higher Education: Challenges and Opportunities. *Border Crossing*, *12*(1), 1–15. doi:10.33182/bc.v12i1.2015

Al Faruqi, U. (2019). Future service in industry 5.0. *Jurnal Sistem Cerdas*, *2*(1), 67–79. doi:10.37396/jsc.v2i1.21

Aslam, F., Aimin, W., Li, M., & Ur Rehman, K. (2020). Innovation in the era of IoT and industry 5.0: Absolute innovation management (AIM) framework. *Information (Basel)*, *11*(2), 1–24. doi:10.3390/info11020124

Bali, M. M., Kumalasani, M. P., & Yunilasari, D. (2022). Artificial Intelligence in Higher Education: Perspicacity Relation between Educators and Students. *Journal of Innovation in Educational and Cultural Research*, *3*(2), 146–152. doi:10.46843/jiecr.v3i2.88

Bhattacharya, S., Maddikunta, P. K., Pham, Q. V., Gadekallu, T. R., Chowdhary, C. L., Alazab, M., & ... . (2021). Deep learning and medical image processing for coronavirus (COVID-19) pandemic: A survey. *Sustainable Cities and Society*, *65*, 65. doi:10.1016/j.scs.2020.102589 PMID:33169099

Bolton, A., Goosen, L., & Kritzinger, E. (2016). Enterprise Digitization Enablement Through Unified Communication and Collaboration. *Proceedings of the Annual Conference of the South African Institute of Computer Scientists and Information Technologists*. ACM. 10.1145/2987491.2987516

Bolton, A., Goosen, L., & Kritzinger, E. (2021b). An Empirical Study into the Impact on Innovation and Productivity Towards the Post-COVID-19 Era: Digital Transformation of an Automotive Enterprise. In L. C. Carvalho, L. Reis, & C. Silveira (Eds.), *Handbook of Research on Entrepreneurship, Innovation, Sustainability, and ICTs in the Post-COVID-19 Era* (pp. 133–159). IGI Global. doi:10.4018/978-1-7998-6776-0.ch007

Bolton, A., Goosen, L., & Kritzinger, E. (2021c). The Integration and Implementation of the Internet of Things Through Digital Transformation: Impact on Productivity and Innovation. In P. Tomar (Ed.), Integration and Implementation of the Internet of Things Through Cloud Computing (pp. 85-112). IGI Global.

Bolton, A., Goosen, L., & Kritzinger, E. (2022b). Challenges and Emerging Strategies for a Global Automotive Enterprise Towards a Post COVID-19 Era: The Impact of Digital Transformation. In *Challenges and Emerging Strategies for Global Networking Post-COVID-19 (pp. 76-109)*. IGI Global. doi:10.4018/978-1-7998-8856-7.ch005

Bolton, A. D., Goosen, L., & Kritzinger, E. (2021a). Unified Communication Technologies at a Global Automotive Organization. In M. Khosrow-Pour (Ed.), *Encyclopedia of Organizational Knowledge, Administration, and Technologies* (pp. 2592–2608). IGI Global. doi:10.4018/978-1-7998-3473-1.ch179

Bolton, A. D., Goosen, L., & Kritzinger, E. (2022a). Emerging Technologies for Innovation and Productivity Management in the Automotive Industry: Impact of Digital Transformation on Communication. In *Emerging Technologies for Innovation Management in the Software Industry (pp. 60-85)*. IGI Global. doi:10.4018/978-1-7998-9059-1.ch003

Bolton, T., Goosen, L., & Kritzinger, E. (2020). Security Aspects of an Empirical Study into the Impact of Digital Transformation via Unified Communication and Collaboration Technologies on the Productivity and Innovation of a Global Automotive Enterprise. Communications in Computer and Information Science, 1166, 99-113.

Branch, J. W., & Burgos, D. (2021). *Radical Solutions for Digital Transformation in Latin American Universities: Artificial Intelligence and Technology 4.0 in Higher Education.* Springer.

Burns, M. (2018). *Digital Transformation In The Education Industry: 5 Trends.* Retrieved from https://www.digitalistmag.com/future-of-work/2018/05/10/5-digital-transformationtrends-in-education-industry-06164785

Carrel, A. (2018). Legal intelligence through artificial intelligence requires emotional intelligence: A new competency model for the 21st century legal professional. *Ga. St. UL Rev, 35,* 1153.

Chen, L., Chen, P., & Lin, Z. (2020). Artificial intelligence in education: A review. *Institute of Electrical and Electronics Engineers Access, 8,* 75264–75278. doi:10.1109/ACCESS.2020.2988510

Chen, X., Xie, H., Zou, D., & Hwang, G. J. (2020). Application and theory gaps during the rise of Artificial Intelligence in Education. *Computers and Education: Artificial Intelligence, 1.*

Chen, X., Zou, D., Xie, H., Cheng, G., & Liu, C. (2022). Two Decades of Artificial Intelligence in Education. *Journal of Educational Technology & Society, 25*(1), 28–47.

Chowdhary, C. L., & Acharjya, D. P. (2016). A hybrid scheme for breast cancer detection using intuitionistic fuzzy rough set technique. *International Journal of Healthcare Information Systems and Informatics, 11*(2), 38–61. doi:10.4018/IJHISI.2016040103

Chowdhary, C. L., & Acharjya, D. P. (2020). Segmentation and feature extraction in medical imaging: A systematic review. *Procedia Computer Science, 167,* 26–36. doi:10.1016/j.procs.2020.03.179

Chowdhary, C. L., Darwish, A., & Hassanien, A. E. (2021). Cognitive Deep Learning: Future Direction in Intelligent Retrieval. In Research Anthology on Artificial Intelligence Applications in Security (pp. 2152-2163). IGI Global.

Chowdhary, C. L., Goyal, A., & Vasnani, B. K. (2019). Experimental assessment of beam search algorithm for improvement in image caption generation. *Journal of Applied Science and Engineering, 22*(4), 691–698.

Chowdhary, C. L., Mittal, M., Pattanaik, P. A., & Marszalek, Z. (2020). An efficient segmentation and classification system in medical images using intuitionist possibilistic fuzzy C-mean clustering and fuzzy SVM algorithm. *Sensors (Basel), 20*(14), 3903. doi:10.339020143903 PMID:32668793

Chowdhary, C. L., Muatjitjeja, K., & Jat, D. S. (2015). *Proceedings of Emerging Trends in Networks and Computer Communications '15.* Academic Press.

Chowdhary, C. L., Patel, P. V., Kathrotia, K. J., Attique, M., Perumal, K., & Ijaz, M. F. (2020). Analytical study of hybrid techniques for image encryption and decryption. *Sensors (Basel), 20*(18), 5162. doi:10.339020185162 PMID:32927714

Devedžić, V. (2004). Web intelligence and artificial intelligence in education. *Journal of Educational Technology & Society, 7*(4), 29–39.

Erol, B. A., Majumdar, A., Benavidez, P., Rad, P., Choo, K. K., & Jamshidi, M. (2019). Toward artificial emotional intelligence for cooperative social human–machine interaction. *IEEE Transactions on Computational Social Systems*, *7*(1), 234–246. doi:10.1109/TCSS.2019.2922593

Fahimirad, M., & Kotamjani, S. S. (2018). A review on application of artificial intelligence in teaching and learning in educational contexts. *International Journal of Learning and Development*, *8*(4), 106–118. doi:10.5296/ijld.v8i4.14057

Flogie, A., & Aberšek, B. (2022). Artificial intelligence in education. In O. Lutsenko & G. Lutsenko (Eds.), *Active Learning: Theory and Practice* (pp. 97–118). doi:10.5772/intechopen.96498

Goksel, N., & Bozkurt, A. (2019). Artificial intelligence in education: Current insights and future perspectives. In *Handbook of Research on Learning in the Age of Transhumanism* (pp. 224–236). IGI Global. doi:10.4018/978-1-5225-8431-5.ch014

Goosen, L. (2004). *Criteria and Guidelines for the Selection and Implementation of a First Programming Language in High Schools*. Potchefstroom Campus: North West University.

Goosen, L. (2015). Educational Technologies for an ICT4D MOOC in the 21st Century. In D. Nwaozuzu, & S. Mnisi (Ed.), *Proceedings of the South Africa International Conference on Educational Technologies* (pp. 37 - 48). Pretoria: African Academic Research Forum.

Goosen, L. (2018a). Sustainable and Inclusive Quality Education Through Research Informed Practice on Information and Communication Technologies in Education. In L. Webb (Ed.), *Proceedings of the 26th Conference of the Southern African Association for Research in Mathematics, Science and Technology Education (SAARMSTE)* (pp. 215 - 228). Gabarone: University of Botswana.

Goosen, L. (2018b). Trans-Disciplinary Approaches to Action Research for e-Schools, Community Engagement, and ICT4D. In T. A. Mapotse (Ed.), *Cross-Disciplinary Approaches to Action Research and Action Learning* (pp. 97–110). IGI Global. doi:10.4018/978-1-5225-2642-1.ch006

Goosen, L. (2018c). Ethical Data Management and Research Integrity in the Context of e-Schools and Community Engagement. In C. Sibinga (Ed.), *Ensuring Research Integrity and the Ethical Management of Data* (pp. 14–45). IGI Global. doi:10.4018/978-1-5225-2730-5.ch002

Goosen, L. (2018d). Ethical Information and Communication Technologies for Development Solutions: Research Integrity for Massive Open Online Courses. In C. Sibinga (Ed.), *Ensuring Research Integrity and the Ethical Management of Data* (pp. 155–173). IGI Global. doi:10.4018/978-1-5225-2730-5.ch009

Goosen, L. (2019). Research on Technology-Supported Teaching and Learning for Autism. In L. Makewa, B. Ngussa, & J. Kuboja (Eds.), *Technology-Supported Teaching and Research Methods for Educators* (pp. 88–110). IGI Global. doi:10.4018/978-1-5225-5915-3.ch005

Goosen, L., & Mukasa-Lwanga, T. (2017). Educational Technologies in Distance Education: Beyond the Horizon with Qualitative Perspectives. In U. I. Ogbonnaya, & S. Simelane-Mnisi (Ed.), *Proceedings of the South Africa International Conference on Educational Technologies* (pp. 41 - 54). Pretoria: African Academic Research Forum.

Goosen, L., & Naidoo, L. (2014). Computer Lecturers Using Their Institutional LMS for ICT Education in the Cyber World. In C. Burger, & K. Naudé (Ed.), *Proceedings of the 43rd Conference of the Southern African Computer Lecturers' Association (SACLA)* (pp. 99-108). Port Elizabeth: Nelson Mandela Metropolitan University.

Guan, C., Mou, J., & Jiang, Z. (2020). Artificial intelligence innovation in education: A twenty-year data-driven historical analysis. *International Journal of Innovation Studies, 4*(4), 134–147. doi:10.1016/j.ijis.2020.09.001

Haenlein, M., & Kaplan, A. (2019). A brief history of artificial intelligence: On the past, present, and future of artificial intelligence. *California Management Review, 61*(4), 5–14. doi:10.1177/0008125619864925

Halili, S. H. (2019). Technological advancements in education 4.0. *The Online Journal of Distance Education and E-Learning, 7*(1), 63-69.

Holmes, W., Bialik, M., & Fadel, C. (2019). *Artificial intelligence in education: Promises and Implications for Teaching and Learning*. Center for Curriculum Redesign.

Huang, X., Zou, D., Cheng, G., Chen, X., & Xie, H. (2021). Trends, research issues and applications of artificial intelligence in language education. *Journal of Educational Technology & Society, 24*(3), 238–255.

Hwang, G. J., Xie, H., Wah, B. W., & Gašević, D. (2020). Vision, challenges, roles and research issues of Artificial Intelligence in Education. *Computers and Education: Artificial Intelligence, 1*.

Javaid, M., Haleem, A., Singh, R. P., Haq, M. I., Raina, A., & Suman, R. (2020). Industry 5.0: Potential applications in COVID-19. *Journal of Industrial Integration and Management, 5*(04), 507–530. doi:10.1142/S2424862220500220

Khan, R., & Debnath, R. (2020). Human distraction detection from video stream using artificial emotional intelligence. *International Journal of Image, Graphics and Signal Processing, 10*(2), 19–29. doi:10.5815/ijigsp.2020.02.03

Khare, N., Devan, P., Chowdhary, C. L., Bhattacharya, S., Singh, G., Singh, S., & Yoon, B. (2020). SMO-DNN: Spider monkey optimization and deep neural network hybrid classifier model for intrusion detection. *Electronics (Basel), 9*(4), 692. doi:10.3390/electronics9040692

Krakovsky, M. (2018). Artificial (emotional) intelligence. *Communications of the ACM, 61*(4), 18–19. doi:10.1145/3185521

Kritzinger, E., Loock, M., & Goosen, L. (2019). Cyber Safety Awareness – Through the Lens of 21st Century Learning Skills and Game-Based Learning. *Lecture Notes in Computer Science, 11937*, 477–485. doi:10.1007/978-3-030-35343-8_51

Kwet, M., & Prinsloo, P. (2020). The 'smart' classroom: A new frontier in the age of the smart university. *Teaching in Higher Education, 25*(4), 510–526. doi:10.1080/13562517.2020.1734922

Lameras, P., & Arnab, S. (2021). Power to the Teachers: An Exploratory Review on Artificial Intelligence in Education. *Information (Basel), 13*(1), 14. doi:10.3390/info13010014

Libbrecht, P., & Goosen, L. (2015). Using ICTs to Facilitate Multilingual Mathematics Teaching and Learning. In *Mathematics Education and Language Diversity* (pp. 217–235). Springer.

Loria, A. A. (2022, January 20). *The Role of Artificial Intelligence in Modern Education.* Retrieved from https://www.depedbataan.com/resources/4/the_role_of_artificial_intelligence_in_modern_education.pdf

Malik, G., Tayal, D. K., & Vij, S. (2019). An analysis of the role of artificial intelligence in education and teaching. In *Recent Findings in Intelligent Computing Techniques* (pp. 407–417). Springer. doi:10.1007/978-981-10-8639-7_42

McArthur, D., Lewis, M., & Bishary, M. (2005). The roles of artificial intelligence in education: Current progress and future prospects. *Journal of Educational Technology, 1*(4), 42–80.

Momtaz, P. P. (2021). CEO emotions and firm valuation in initial coin offerings: An artificial emotional intelligence approach. *Strategic Management Journal, 42*(3), 558–578. doi:10.1002mj.3235

Nahavandi, S. (2019). Industry 5.0—A human-centric solution. *Sustainability, 11*(16), 4371. doi:10.3390u11164371

Ndhlovu, N. J., & Goosen, L. (2021). Re-Envisioning and Restructuring E-Learning Through Engagement With Underprivileged Communities: The Impact of Effectively Using ICTs in Classrooms. In C. Bosch, D. J. Laubscher, & L. Kyei-Blankson (Eds.), *Re-Envisioning and Restructuring Blended Learning for Underprivileged Communities* (pp. 66–87). IGI Global. doi:10.4018/978-1-7998-6940-5.ch004

Owoc, M. L., Sawicka, A., & Weichbroth, P. (2019, August). Artificial intelligence technologies in education: benefits, challenges and strategies of implementation. *International Federation for Information Processing (IFIP) International Workshop on Artificial Intelligence for Knowledge Management* (pp. 37-58). Cham: Springer.

Özdemir, V., & Hekim, N. (2018). Birth of industry 5.0: Making sense of big data with artificial intelligence, "the internet of things" and next-generation technology policy. *OMICS: A Journal of Integrative Biology, 22*(1), 65–76. doi:10.1089/omi.2017.0194 PMID:29293405

Panigrahi, R., Borah, S., Bhoi, A. K., Ijaz, M. F., Pramanik, M., Jhaveri, R. H., & Chowdhary, C. L. (2021). Performance assessment of supervised classifiers for designing intrusion detection systems: A comprehensive review and recommendations for future research. *Mathematics, 9*(6), 690. doi:10.3390/math9060690

Parimala, M., Priya, R. S., Reddy, M. P., Chowdhary, C. L., Poluru, R. K., & Khan, S. (2021). Spatio-temporal-based sentiment analysis on tweets for risk assessment of event using deep learning approach. *Software, Practice & Experience, 3*(51), 550–570. doi:10.1002pe.2851

Pedro, F., Subosa, M., Rivas, A., & Valverde, P. (2019). *Artificial intelligence in education: Challenges and opportunities for sustainable development.* United Nations Educational, Scientific and Cultural Organization.

Prentice, C., Dominique Lopes, S., & Wang, X. (2020). Emotional intelligence or artificial intelligence– an employee perspective. *Journal of Hospitality Marketing & Management, 29*(4), 377–403. doi:10.10 80/19368623.2019.1647124

Qin, H., & Wang, G. (2022, January). Benefits, Challenges and Solutions of Artificial Intelligence Applied in Education. In *11th International Conference on Educational and Information Technology (ICEIT)* (pp. 62-66). IEEE. 10.1109/ICEIT54416.2022.9690739

Rachmawati, I., Multisari, W., Triyono, T., Simon, I. M., & da Costa, A. (2021). Prevalence of Academic Resilience of Social Science Students in Facing the Industry 5.0 Era. *International Journal of Evaluation and Research in Education, 10*(2), 676–683. doi:10.11591/ijere.v10i2.21175

Reddy, G. T., Bhattacharya, S., Ramakrishnan, S. S., Chowdhary, C. L., Hakak, S., & Kaluri, R. (2020, February). An ensemble based machine learning model for diabetic retinopathy classification. *International conference on emerging trends in information technology and engineering (ic-ETITE)* (pp. 1-6). IEEE. 10.1109/ic-ETITE47903.2020.235

Roll, I., & Wylie, R. (2016). Evolution and revolution in artificial intelligence in education. *International Journal of Artificial Intelligence in Education, 26*(2), 582–599. doi:10.100740593-016-0110-3

Sadiku, M. N., Musa, S. M., & Chukwu, U. C. (2022). Artificial Intelligence in Education. *International Journal of Scientific Advances, 2*(1), 5–11.

Salam, S., Jianqiu, Z., Pathan, Z. H., & Lei, W. (2017, December). Strategic barriers in the effective integration of ICT in the public schools of Pakistan. In *Proceedings of the International Conference on Computer Science and Artificial Intelligence* (pp. 169-172). New York: ACM. 10.1145/3168390.3168422

Schuller, D., & Schuller, B. W. (2018). The age of artificial emotional intelligence. *Computer, 51*(9), 38–46. doi:10.1109/MC.2018.3620963

Shen, C. W., & Ho, J. T. (2020). Technology-enhanced learning in higher education: A bibliometric analysis with latent semantic approach. *Computers in Human Behavior, 104*, 104. doi:10.1016/j.chb.2019.106177

Singh, B., Bhattacharya, S., Chowdhary, C. L., & Jat, D. S. (2017). A review on internet of things and its applications in healthcare. *Journal of Chemical and Pharmaceutical Sciences, 10*(1), 447–452.

Su, J., & Yang, W. (2022). Artificial intelligence in early childhood education: A scoping review. *Computers and Education: Artificial Intelligence, 3*.

White, D., & Katsuno, H. (2022). Artificial emotional intelligence beyond East and West. *Internet Policy Review, 11*(1).

Yonck, R. (2020). *Heart of the machine: Our future in a world of artificial emotional intelligence.* Arcade.

Zawacki-Richter, O., Marín, V. I., Bond, M., & Gouverneur, F. (2019). Systematic review of research on artificial intelligence applications in higher education–where are the educators? *International Journal of Educational Technology in Higher Education, 16*(39), 1–27. doi:10.118641239-019-0171-0

ENDNOTE

[1]   Emphasis as in original.

Chapter 12
Google Play Store Apps:
Data Analysis and Popularity Predictions Using Artificial Emotional Intelligence

Parvathi R.
Vellore Institute of Technology, Chennai, India

Pattabiraman V.
iD https://orcid.org/0000-0001-8734-2203
Vellore Institute of Technology, Chennai, India

ABSTRACT

The Google Play Store is one of the most well-known and widely used Android app stores. On the Play Store, there is a lot of new information not only by the developers of the programme but also by the users who provide reviews and ratings. All of this information may be used to provide valuable insight into app popularity, which can be quite beneficial to app creators. The authors used a Google Play Store raw data collection from the Kaggle website. The data set includes a variety of features that can be used to forecast app success. Many classifier models are used to predict the popularity of apps in this study and determined which one give the best results. In the classification model, user reviews are added as a numerical feature. This feature has been found to considerably improve classification accuracy. Surprisingly the social aspects have a significant impact on the popularity of an app are also considered in this study.

INTRODUCTION

With around 5 million apps, the Google Play Store is said to be the world's largest digital distribution channel for Android apps. User given ratings and reviews are crucial for the feedback and favourable ratings entice people to become more interested in the items or services. In the Google Play Store, the majority of apps have received higher ratings, instilling trust in users. However, one of the key reasons for their success is that approximately 81 percent of the apps are free.

DOI: 10.4018/978-1-6684-5673-6.ch012

People have been starting to use mobile phones more and more over the years, which is another reason why the app development industry is seeing immense success. With all this data available in the Google Play Store, there is enormous scope for data related research.

This word contains feature extraction from a longitudinal app analysis in this study to determine whether an app will be successful or not. Data extraction, data cleaning, data visualization, feature extraction, and prediction utilizing various models are the five steps of our analysis. To begin with, we extract the data from the Kaggle website and do the necessary cleaning. After this process, and visualize this dataset using various plots to better understand it. The feature extraction stage is the next critical step in determining which features assist us in predicting the app's popularity. Finally, several classification algorithms are applied to the dataset to evaluate which algorithm or machine learning model gives the highest percentage of accuracy (Chowdhary, 2011; Chowdhary & Channi, 2021). Finally, there is a discussion on the reasons for the highest accuracy.

Huge amounts of data get added to the app stores everyday. This includes not only the information about a given app contributed by the developers, but also the reviews and ratings contributed by users. It is quite interesting to conduct analysis on this data as it can give important insight about the popularity of an app launched on the play store. This kind of analysis was seen in the following studies.

In their study, Businge et al. (2019) and others observed that not only social but also technical factors played a major role in determining an app's popularity. They tried to find relationships between the code available on GitHub for these apps and the ratings available for these apps. It was, however, observed that these technical factors had little role in the prediction of App popularity. The ratings available in the Google Play Store still play a major role in evaluating the success of the app. Overall, it was concluded in this study that the available social factors are a much better feature for App prediction than the technicalities of an App.

In other different kinds of studies done by researchers, including the one by Monett & Stolte (2016), they try to evaluate different prediction models available for predicting App success. These models, however, use the user response available in the form of rating out of 5 from the available dataset of customer reviews of mobile apps. This numeric attribute plays a major role in determining App success. These prediction models use ratings with other attributes available in the dataset to make predictions for App success. All of these studies have revealed a key conclusion - rating out of 5 is an important feature and is also closely related to user reviews as observed in performing the sentiment analysis of these textual data.

This work categorized as follows: Chapter 1 discussed about the Introduction about the problem motivation, problem statement, Literature survey with various National and Internation publications related to the problem statement are discussed in the Chapter 2. Chapter 3 introduces about the different algorithms used in the work and Chapter 4 elaborates about the system architecture used in this work. Chapter 5 discuss about the implementation like preprocessing, feature extraction, prediction, sentiment analysis and Chapter 6 deals with result and discussion of the implementation. Chapter 7 describes about the conclusion.

LITERATURE SURVEY

Sentiment Analysis is an important attribute as it gives more insight into customer behaviour and a subjective review of the customer to the App (Philip et al., 2003). Similar to this work, was the work done by Suresh and others (Chumwatana, 2015; Suresh & Urolagin, 2020; Kumari & Singh, 2016; Hanyang,

2019). They chose specific reviews giving out major details and reflecting high polarity and combined them with other attributes. These were then used to predict the popularity of the Apps.

Similar to the above approaches, a recent study by Suleman et al. (2019) looked into the application of machine learning algorithms to a dataset covering attributes including, the size of an app, the type of App, the category of App, the numbers of downloads and user reviews, the Android version of the app and finally the content rating to calculate a Rank (Hu et al.,2019). This rank more specifically determines the Rank of a given App in a bucket of similar Apps. Popular classification algorithms like Naive Bayes classifier, decision tree classifier, linear regression, k-means clustering, logistic regression, k-nearest neighbors, support-vector machine and artificial neural networks were chosen for this purpose.

Some more studies conducted on different App stores have used a similar approach (Sarro et al., 2018; Aslam & Ashraf, 2014; Kumari & Singh, 2016). The authors looked into other popular App stores apart from the Google play App store. Studies done in Samsung Android stores have gathered raw features and information available about the apps to come up with similar prediction mechanisms. Some more research done on the BlackBerry-World-App store, has used similar kinds of data. Important features have been congregated and assembled into quantitative vectors to be used in predicting the success of Apps.

Another important consideration could be the emojis used by the users in their reviews. Some authors, like Martens et al. (2017) and Kumari & Singh (2016) has tried to represent these emojis numerically to aid in prediction. Every emoji gives a specific score based on the emotion that it is generally used to convey. Emojis expressing happiness, content, excitement, and positivity were grouped into one category, and emojis expressing negativity, distress, anger, and sadness were grouped into another category. During sentiment analysis of user reviews, it was found that this addition seemed to be useful.

The studies mentioned above have given some interesting and unusual insights. However, it is found that these studies have not included sentimental analysis (Buche et al., 2013) as a part of their prediction model. This work also includes sentiment analysis as a numeric feature as a part of the prediction model. Various Machine Learning algorithms and different sentiment analysis methods are incorporated in the following chapter.

ALGORITHMS

Decision Tree

The decision tree is easy to understand and is analogous to the human decision-making process. Nonlinear patterns can be captured easily. Balanced the data set before generating the model to avoid a biased tree. Decision trees can handle ambiguity in both construction and classification procedures. Each of the internal node data is separated by a decision rule. The Gini index as a cost function is used to evaluate splits in the data set. It is computed by subtracting one from the total squared probability of each class. The Gini index is used for the larger divisions, whereas information gain is used for the smaller partitions with distinct values, and is more difficult to apply. The most significant disadvantage of decision trees is that the splits they produce at each node are optimised for the data set to which they are fitted. Other forms of data are rarely separated in this way. However, the system will generate a huge number of these decision trees, turned in slightly different ways, and combine their predictions (Zhang et al., 2021).

Random Forest

Random Forest uses the supervised learning approach. It is ensemble learning based because this can integrate many different classifiers to resolve complicated problems, thereby increasing the accuracy. A Random Forest is like an improved version of a decision tree. By dividing the dataset into smaller divisions and constructing decision trees for those divisions, and taking the average, the performance improves. It is a collection of many decision trees merged to give improved prediction results. Accuracy will be greater if more trees are combined. This also prevents overfitting. All variables are subject to random forest regression. The random forest findings tell us the relative relevance of the variables and their impact on popularity. The Mean Square Error is used to evaluate the results of the random forest regression (Bhattacharyya et. al.,2021).

Logistic Regression

Logistic Regression is used for two-class classification machine learning methods. Here the binary classification data set is carried out. The outcome, or target variable, is a variable that can accept the values of either 0 or 1. It differs from linear regression in terms of the target, which is categorical in this case. As a result, the Sigmoid function is used in logistic regression for binary categorization. If the curve moves towards infinity in the positive direction, then the output is considered as 1, whereas if the curve moves towards infinity in the negative direction, then the output is considered as 0. By the concept of step function if the output of a sigmoid is greater than 0.5 then it is treated as 1 whereas if it is less than 0.5 it is considered as 09 (Yang & Li, 019)

Gaussian Naive Bayes

Given the value of the class variable, naive Bayes is a supervised learning approach. This algorithm uses the principle of Bayes' theorem in which there is presumption of conditional independence between all the available feature pairs. Conditional feature distributions are disassociated, each distribution can be estimated separately as 1-D. The mean and the Standard Deviation are the two factors that determine the Gaussian distribution of a series. Using the Gaussian Distribution Function, estimate the chance that the value x will occur using the mean value of the series and its standard deviation, as illustrated if the input values from the series instead of x (Hung-Ju et.al.,2022).

K Nearest Neighbours

Both classification and regression predicting tasks can benefit from the use of a K closest neighbor classifier. It works by computing the distance between the points and then selecting the k closest neighbours. If the value of k is less, then low bias and high variance. A higher K value, on the other hand, will result in smoother decision boundaries, which means reduced variance but more bias.

Estimating the test error rate by excluding a section of the training set from the fitting procedure is an alternate and wiser approach. The validation set is a subset that can be utilized to choose the proper level of flexibility for our algorithm. In this work, k-fold cross validation is used on this data set. K-fold cross-validation is used for dividing the data into k divisions or the folds of roughly similar size at random. The same is applied to the remaining k-1 folds by considering the first one for validating. After

Figure 1. Architecture Diagram

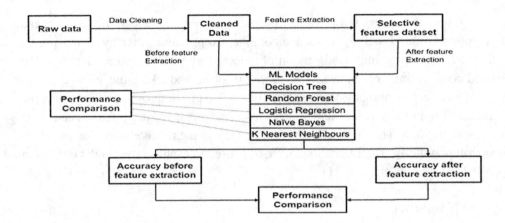

that, the classification rate is calculated on the observations and used as a validation set. This procedure yields k test error estimates, which are then averaged Zhang (2016). The architectural details and the implementation with result are discussed in the following sections.

ARCHITECTURE DIAGRAM

The extracted data is used to make App popularity predictions before and after feature extraction and sentiment analysis, and the results are compared. Moreover, this work tries to find the best performing algorithm by comparing the accuracy of all the prediction models. The complete methodology is shown in Figure 1.In the implementation phase, the data cleaning, Data Visualization and Sentiment Analysis are carried out in the next session.

IMPLEMENTATION

Data Extraction

Google Play Store raw data collected from the Kaggle website is used in this work. This information was gathered from the Google Play Store.

Data Cleaning

Data cleaning is critical when putting raw data into a more usable format. Completeness and compatibility can be improved by going through the cleaning process. The raw data contains a lot of useless information. It could also aid in determining the consistency of the values. Data can also be incomplete, meaning that some values are missing. Text preparation is needed to overcome large computational times and stop words always tend to reduce the accuracy of the predicted results. Stemming, lowercase conversion, punctuation, and omitting terms are all part of the preprocessing process.

Figure 2. Top 10 categories of apps installed

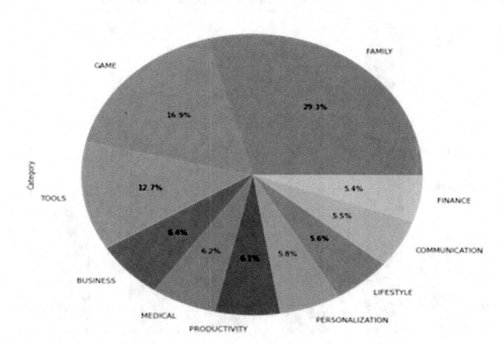

Data Visualization

There are several features in this data collection that can be used to analyze it. Plots such as bar graphs and pie graphs aid in better visualizing the dataset and obtaining the necessary information about the main features required for prediction.

As shown in Figure 2, family and gaming are the most popular categories of all the apps that are being installed from the Play Store. This indicates that apps in the gaming and family categories are more popular, and therefore, apps in these areas have a higher probability of success.

The top five genres of the Google Play Store, as shown in Figure 3, are Tools, Entertainment, Education, Business, and Medical.

Figure 4 shows that only 7.4 percent of paid applications are available. The bulk of paid apps are under a dollar. As a result, its popularity is unaffected by this feature

Figure 5 shows that practically all apps (almost 81 percent) are accessible to people of all ages, with only 0.03 percent restricted to adults 18 and over.

Figure 6 shows that the average rating is quite high when using the popularity feature, ranging between 4.2 and 5.0. Considering the data for each category with a rating of more than or equal to 4.0, which was the most highly regarded. This will aid in developing a better model.

As seen in Figure 7, the social networking apps are definitely the ones with the most reviews. The apps with the best ratings are Facebook and WhatsApp.

Figure 3. Top 5 genres of apps installed

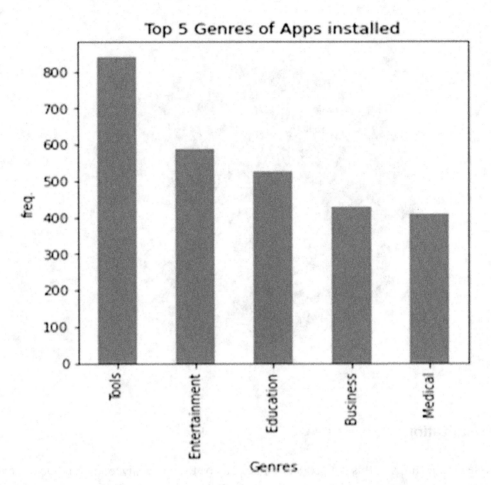

Feature Extraction

A variety of features to check which one influences whether or not an app is also analyzed. The correlation table between downloads and other features to determine which apps would generate the most money. Installs and reviews have a strong inverse correlation, as seen in Figure 8. This is understandable given that popular apps receive more reviews. There is no link between installs and other characteristics such as size, rating, or price. Also, there is no link between rating and price. The installation of an app is used to show the popularity of an app because it is independent and not correlated with any other parameters.

Analyzing the sentiments of Playstore reviews can reveal a lot about an app's problems or customers' experiences. Furthermore, the app reviews indicate that reviews play a key influence in determining whether or not the app is effective. Taking user ratings for all apps, analyzing them, and including them as a feature can aid in improved prediction. Natural Language Processing is used to do sentiment analysis of user reviews. The sentiment for each app is calculated and used as one of the main factors in the prediction.

Figure 4. Distribution of paid vs. free apps installed

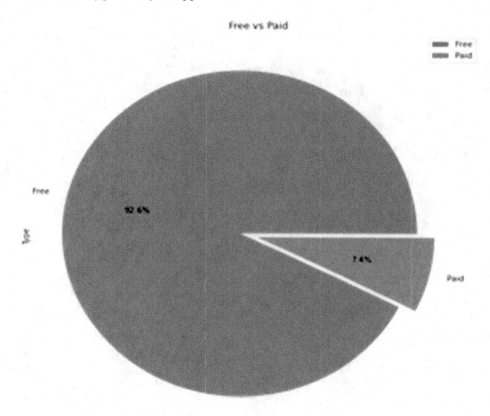

Prediction using ML Models

The feature number of installs is used to determine whether or not the app is successful in this analysis. If the number of installs for a given app exceeds the threshold limit, it will be classified as successful; if it falls below that, it will be classified as unsuccessful.

In this work, variety of machine learning models were used to make this prediction, including Decision Trees, Random Forests, Logistic Regression, Naive Bayes, and K Nearest Neighbors(Thiviya et a.., 2019). The accuracy of all of the models is analyzed to see which one is the most accurate, as well as whether or not, including sentiment as a feature can improve the prediction results. Out of the total apps, 9064 apps are used for training and 1776 apps are used for testing.

Before Sentimental Analysis

Table 1 shows that the decision tree gives better results in predicting whether an app is successful or not, and Naive Bayes has the least performance among all other models.

Figure 5. App distribution based on content rating

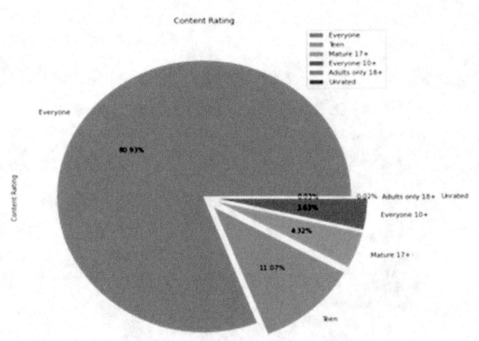

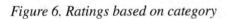

Figure 6. Ratings based on category

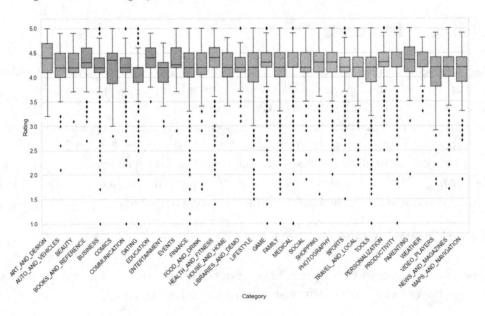

Figure 7. Apps with most reviews

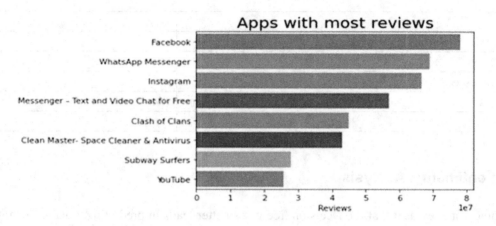

Figure 8. Correlation between all the features

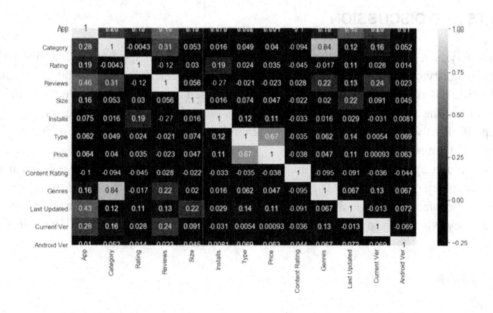

Table 1. Accuracy of algorithms before Sentimental Analysis

Algorithm	Accuracy
Decision Tree	82%
Random Forest	77%
Logistic Regression	64%
Naive Bayes	62%
K Nearest Neighbours	74%

Table 2. Accuracy of algorithms after Sentimental Analysis

Algorithm	Accuracy
Decision Tree	89%
Random Forest	85%
Logistic Regression	87%
Naive Bayes	77%
K Nearest Neighbours	80%

After Sentimental Analysis

From table 2 it is evident that the Decision tree gives better leads in predicting whether an app is successful or not whereas Naive Bayes has the least performance among all other models.

RESULTS AND DISCUSSION

From this analysis, it was found that there was no correlation between app features like size, rating, and price. The majority of apps were in the tool genres, such as Entertainment, Education, Business, and Medical. Models classified the apps into two categories based on our findings: successful and failed.

Furthermore, the app's reviews indicate that reviews play a key influence in determining whether or not the app is effective. Adding review sentiment for all apps, analyzing them, and including them as a feature aided in improved prediction.

The decision tree gave the highest accuracy of 89 percent, and the Gaussian Naive Bayes model gave the lowest accuracy of 75 percent . The decision tree worked well since it needed to make a decision based on a critical feature: the number of installs. The Gaussian Naive Bayes, on the other hand, had the lowest accuracy, which was to be expected given that it presupposes an object attribute independence.

CONCLUSION

Various classification algorithms are executed on this data and found that the Decision tree gave the highest accuracy of prediction. The decision tree is also not only relatively easy to visualize and comprehend, but also fairly simple to implement. It is also faster and saves computational power. Many classifier models were evaluated to predict the popularity of apps in this study and determined which one gave the best results. Number of installs as a deciding factor of whether or not an App could be labeled successful. If an App had at least a hundred thousand installs, model classified it as a successful App. There could be several other ways of labeling success of an App that could be explored. The dataset contains a lot of information and can be used to make several other valuable predictions. This predictions could be insightful to App developers, advertisers, researchers and also users in general.

REFERENCES

Aslam, S., & Ashraf, I. (2014). Data mining algorithms and their applications in education data mining. *International Journal (Toronto, Ont.), 2*(7).

Bhattacharya, S., Maddikunta, P. K. R., Pham, Q. V., Gadekallu, T. R., Chowdhary, C. L., Alazab, M., & Piran, M. J. (2021). Deep learning and medical image processing for coronavirus (COVID-19) pandemic: A survey. *Sustainable Cities and Society, 65,* 102589. doi:10.1016/j.scs.2020.102589 PMID:33169099

Buche, A., Chandak, D., & Zadgaonkar, A. (2013). *Opinion mining and analysis: a survey.* arXiv pre-print arXiv:1307.3336.

Businge, J., Openja, M., Kavaler, D., Bainomugisha, E., Khomh, F., & Filkov, V. (2019, February). Studying android app popularity by cross-linking github and google play store. In *2019 IEEE 26th International Conference on Software Analysis, Evolution and Reengineering (SANER)* (pp. 287-297). IEEE. 10.1109/SANER.2019.8667998

Chowdhary, C. L. (2011). Linear feature extraction techniques for object recognition: Study of PCA and ICA. *Journal of the Serbian Society for Computational Mechanics, 5*(1), 19–26.

Chowdhary, C. L., & Channi, H. K. (2022). Deep Learning Empowered Fight Against COVID-19: A Survey. In *Next Generation Healthcare Informatics* (pp. 251–264). Springer. doi:10.1007/978-981-19-2416-3_14

Chumwatana, T. (2015). *Using sentiment analysis technique for analyzing Thai customer satisfaction from social media.* Academic Press.

Hu, H., Wang, S., Bezemer, C. P., & Hassan, A. E. (2019). Studying the consistency of star ratings and reviews of popular free hybrid Android and iOS apps. *Empirical Software Engineering, 24*(1), 7–32. doi:10.100710664-018-9617-6

Kumari, N., & Singh, S. N. (2016, January). Sentiment analysis on E-commerce application by using opinion mining. In 2016 6th International Conference-Cloud System and Big Data Engineering (Confluence) (pp. 320-325). IEEE. doi:10.1109/CONFLUENCE.2016.7508136

Martens, D., & Johann, T. (2017, May). On the emotion of users in app reviews. In *2017 IEEE/ACM 2nd International Workshop on Emotion Awareness in Software Engineering (SEmotion)* (pp. 8-14). IEEE. 10.1109/SEmotion.2017.6

Monett, D., & Stolte, H. (2016, September). Predicting star ratings based on annotated reviews of mobile apps. In *2016 Federated Conference on Computer Science and Information Systems (FedCSIS)* (pp. 421-428). IEEE. 10.15439/2016F141

Philip, B., Trevor, H., Christopher, M., & Shivakumar, V. (2003). An exploration of sentiment summarization. In *Proceedings of AAAI* (pp. 12-15). AAAI.

Sarro, F., Harman, M., Jia, Y., & Zhang, Y. (2018, August). Customer rating reactions can be predicted purely using app features. In *2018 IEEE 26th International Requirements Engineering Conference (RE)* (pp. 76-87). IEEE. 10.1109/RE.2018.00018

Suleman, M., Malik, A., & Hussain, S. S. (2019). Google play store app ranking prediction using machine learning algorithm. *Urdu News Headline, Text Classification by Using Different Machine Learning Algorithms, 57*.

Suresh, K. P., & Urolagin, S. (2020, January). Android App Success Prediction based on Reviews. In *2020 International Conference on Computation, Automation and Knowledge Management (ICCAKM)* (pp. 358-362). IEEE. 10.1109/ICCAKM46823.2020.9051529

Thiviya, T., Nitheesram, R., Srinath, G., Ekanayake, E. M. U. W. J. B., & Mehendran, Y. (2019). *Mobile Apps' Feature Extraction Based On User Reviews Using Machine Learning*. Academic Press.

Yang, Z., & Li, D. (2019, July). Application of logistic regression with filter in data classification. In *2019 Chinese Control Conference (CCC)* (pp. 3755-3759). IEEE. 10.23919/ChiCC.2019.8865281

Zhang, N., Gupta, A., Chen, Z., & Ong, Y. S. (2021). Evolutionary machine learning with minions: A case study in feature selection. *IEEE Transactions on Evolutionary Computation*.

Zhang, Z. (2016). Introduction to machine learning: K-nearest neighbors. *Annals of Translational Medicine, 4*(11), 218. doi:10.21037/atm.2016.03.37 PMID:27386492

Chapter 13
Providing the Population With Medical Services in the Context of Emotional Intelligence:
Evidence of Russian Regions

Iuliia Pinkovetskaia

https://orcid.org/0000-0002-8224-9031

Ulyanovsk State University, Russia

ABSTRACT

The purpose of study was to evaluate the indicators characterizing the development of the healthcare system in the regions of Russia. The study used official statistical information on the activities of medical organizations located in all 82 regions of Russia for 2020. The density functions of the normal distribution were used as models. The research showed that on ten thousand people living in the region are an average of 48 doctors, 85 hospital beds, 289 patients who were served daily in organizations engaged in outpatient treatment. These indicators are higher than in many other countries, which creates prerequisites for the development of emotional intelligence in the Russian healthcare sector. In most regions the salary in the healthcare sector did not differ significantly from the average salary in the corresponding region. The proposed methodological approach and the results obtained have a scientific novelty, since the assessment of regional features of medical care in the regions of Russia has not been carried out before.

INTRODUCTION

In recent years, improving the efficiency of healthcare has become a key aspect of the development of national economies. In a number of studies, for example (Preston, 2007; Shkolnikov et al., 2019), it has been observed that there is a strong positive correlation between the health of the population of countries and their gross domestic product. Higher income is the chief criteria in countries with better health than in countries with lower health status. The state of health is an important characteristic of human potential, therefore, the improvement of the health system plays an important role in public policy (Milcent, 2016;

DOI: 10.4018/978-1-6684-5673-6.ch013

Durrani, 2016; Al-Hanawi et al., 2019; Britto et al., 2018). The healthcare system of modern countries is aimed at ensuring an optimal return on the resources spent, as well as preserving the health of the population. The problem of healthcare efficiency is especially relevant today in the context of the COVID-19 pandemic (Haldane et al., 2021; Chubarova, 2021; Karan & Wadhera, 2021). The COVID-19 pandemic affected most countries and demanded an increase in the role of healthcare as a system that ensures the security and survival of the nation, as well as the internal stability of modern economies.

Russia currently has the Healthcare Development Strategy for the period up to 2025 (2022), which includes an assessment of the current state, challenges and threats to the development of the healthcare system, defines the goal, main tasks, priority areas, mechanisms for implementing the development of healthcare (Reddy et al., 2020Chowdhary & Acharjya, 2020;). In addition, the activities included in the National Project "Healthcare" are carried out in parallel (On national goals and strategic objectives, 2022), aimed at improving the availability of medical care, improving its quality and comfort. Among other things, it is planned to create an optimal network of medical organizations in cities and villages, including in hard-to-reach territories of Russia. It is important for the Government and regional authorities to understand the processes taking place in the field of medical care. Without which it is impossible to effectively manage the health sector and achieve the goals set.

Contemporary researchers have been attracted by the importance of regional characteristics of the activities of medical organizations (Karani, 2014; Lacouz & Midler, 2021; Sokanto & Bruise, 2021). Our research contributes to the study of these problems using the example of the Russian regions.

Some of the modern scientific studies draw attention to the fact that the quality of medical services and patient satisfaction largely depends on the emotional intelligence of healthcare workers. Articles by the following authors have been devoted to this problem (Kadadi & Shankargouda, 2020; Kaya et al., 2018). Doctors and nurses show increased sensitivity to the needs and emotions of the patient (Weng et al., 2008). This improves medical care and patient care, as well as solves their psychological problems in critical situations (Borges et al., 2019). It should be noted that emotional intelligence is conditioned by direct contacts between medical workers and patients (Durkin et al., 2019).

The purpose of our study was to evaluate the indicators characterizing the development of the healthcare system in the regions of Russia. It should be noted that the increase in the volume of medical care to the population creates prerequisites for the development of such an urgent phenomenon as emotional intelligence. The paper is aimed at obtaining a certain empirical and methodological contribution to understanding the peculiarities of the development of the healthcare system in Russia. This contribution consists in the fact that the author's method of modeling the evaluation of indicators characterizing the availability of inpatient and outpatient treatment, the availability of qualified medical personnel and the level of remuneration of doctors and nurses in all regions of Russia is proposed. The empirical contribution is related to the determination of averages and standard deviations by regions of the corresponding indicators. In addition, regions with maximum and minimum values of these indicators were identified.

The structure of this work is as follows. The second section provides an overview of recent scientific publications on the problem of healthcare development in Russia. The methodology, initial data and design of the study are described in the third section. The fourth section presents the results of the development of mathematical models and evaluation of their quality. The fifth section discusses the results of the study and verification of the formulated hypotheses. The sixth section describes the contribution analysis of the study. The seventh section offers conclusion. The eighth section shows future studies. Then bibliographic references are provided.

Table 1. Scientific publications on the problems of the health care system in Russia

Authors	Problems in the study
1	2
Travnikova, Shubina (2020)	The dynamics of changes in indicators characterizing the provision of medical care in Russia for the period from 1970 to 2019 is considered. The number of people who received medical care on an outpatient basis, as well as the number of hospital beds in inpatient medical organizations were considered as indicators.
Reprintseva (2020)	The analysis of changes in the number of hospital beds in Russia for the period from 2005 to 2018 was carried out. It is shown that this indicator has been decreasing over the years. At the same time, there was a tendency to increase the number of beds per hospital, that is, the enlargement of hospitals.
Rakova (2021)	The dynamics of changes in 2010-2019 of such an indicator of the Russian healthcare system as the average number of patients who visited outpatient polyclinic organizations per day is considered. It is concluded that over the years under review, the values of this indicator have increased by eight percent.
Posentseva et al. (2020)	The analysis of the average salary of doctors and nurses of medical organizations in the Central Federal District of Russia for 2018 was carried out. A significant differentiation of this indicator by region is shown, depending on the level of economic development and financial indicators of the regions.
Lazareva (2021)	The use of indicators such as the number of doctors and nurses, as well as the number of hospital beds to characterize the system of medical care in Russia is substantiated.
Ivanov, Suvorov (2021)	An assessment of the number of hospital beds and the number of doctors in Russia was carried out. It is concluded that given the large size of the territory and the uneven settlement of the population, it seems appropriate to increase these indicators, that is, an extensive development of healthcare. According to the authors, this is the only way to ensure the availability of medical care for the entire population.
Dubina (2021)	The financial aspects of the development of medical organizations in the regions of Russia are considered. It is proposed to use as a key indicator a coefficient reflecting the ratio of wages of employees employed in the medical sector and the average for the region. In order to improve the quality of medical care and its accessibility, it is proposed to ensure a priority increase in the salaries of medical workers.
Shishkin et al. (2017)	It is proved that there are significant differences in the availability of medical care in different regions due to the differentiation of state funding per inhabitant of the region.
Vlasova (2021)	Trends in the development of the healthcare system in 2015-2019 are considered on the example of the Kursk region. The dynamics of the number of doctors and hospital beds is given. The influence of the level of socio-economic development of the region on these indicators is shown.
Zyukin (2020)	The main results of the processes of optimization of the healthcare industry in Russia for the period from 2016 to 2018 are considered. It is concluded that in this period there was an increase in the availability of outpatient treatment due to an increase in the number of relevant organizations. The possibilities of providing services in primary health care organizations, as well as disease prevention, have increased. It is proposed to use the number of visits per day as an indicator characterizing the activities of these organizations.
Belyaev (2021)	The strategic directions of healthcare development in the regions of Russia are considered. It is shown that in order to ensure the availability of medical services, it is necessary to increase the number of nurses in the healthcare sector.

Source: The table is compiled by the author on the basis of the information provided in the Russian science citation index

BACKGROUND

A number of scientific publications have been was devoted to the problems of assessing the level of healthcare in Russia and its regions in recent years. A brief description of the most interesting of these publications is given in table 1.

Based on the information given in Table 1, it can be stated that the problem of studying the level of development of the healthcare system in Russia has received considerable attention in scientific publications. Most of the publications were devoted to the analysis of problems in the country as a whole. In addition, some publications have addressed the issues of medical care in certain regions. At the same time, in our opinion, sufficient attention has not been paid to the problem of a comprehensive assessment of regional features characteristic of the activities of organizations in the health sector. As the main indicators characterizing the current health care system, the following have been proposed in publications: for outpatient organizations - the daily number of patient visits; for inpatient organizations - the number of hospital beds; the number of medical personnel; the number of nurses; the ratio of salaries of health workers and average salaries by region. Most of the studies of Russian scientists have been devoted to these indicators. An analysis of published scientific papers allowed us to conclude that it seems logical to use relative indicators to compare the values of indicators by region, since regions differ significantly in the number of economic entities, population, size and location. Taking this into account, it seems appropriate to study the problem of medical care precisely taking into account relative indicators.

MAIN FOCUS OF THE CHAPTER

In this work examines the indicators characterizing the organization of healthcare in the regions of Russia. These indicators are:

- number of hospital beds per ten thousand people living in the region (indicator 1);
- daily number of visits to outpatient clinics for ten thousand people living in the region (indicator 2);
- number of doctors per ten thousand people living in the region (indicator 3);
- number of nurses per ten thousand people living in the region (indicator 4);
- ratio of salaries of doctors and nurses to the average salary in the region (indicator 5).

The process of research comprises of five steps. At the first step, information was collected on the activities of all healthcare organizations located in the regions of Russia in 2020. Databases of initial data were formed characterizing the total number of visits to outpatient organizations by patients in each of the regions, the number of hospital beds in inpatient medical organizations in each of the regions, the number of certified doctors who operate in each of the regions, the number of professional nurses in each of the regions, the amount of costs for paying salaries to doctors and nurses in each of the regions. In addition, information was collected on the numbers population, as well as on average wages for the entire circle of employees in each of the regions. At the second step, the values of the above five indicators were calculated for each of the regions. At the third step, mathematical models were developed and the distribution of indicators by region was estimated. At the fourth step, the average values of indicators for the regions of Russia were determined, as well as the ranges in which the values of these indicators are for most of them. At the fifth step, regions were identified that were characterized by the maximum and minimum values of indicators according to data for 2020.

The study used official statistical information of the Federal Service of State Statistic (2022).

In this study, the following hypotheses were tested:

hypothesis 1 - in most regions of Russia, the values of the first four indicators are largely similar to the corresponding values in economically developed modern countries;

hypothesis 2 - the values of the fifth indicator in the regions of Russia are significantly lower compared to the corresponding values of indicators in economically developed modern countries;

hypothesis 3 - the values of all five indicators characterizing the development of medical care differ by region, but the coefficients of variation for each of these indicators are not very large (that is, they do not exceed 33%);

hypothesis 4 - the regions in which the maximum and minimum values of each of the five indicators are noted are located in different federal districts. That is, the territorial location of the regions does not affect the maximum and minimum values of the indicators.

The evaluation of the values of the five considered indicators was carried out on the basis of mathematical modeling of the initial empirical data. As models, we used the density functions of the normal distribution, the method of developing which for estimating the values of relative indicators was proposed by the author. Some aspects of using the methodology are given in the paper (Pinkovetskaia et al., 2021). The number of medical organizations, doctors and nurses working in different regions is large. This, as well as the presence of various factors affecting the formation of health system indicators, indicates the probabilistic (stochastic) nature of the formation of the values of the five indicators we are considering in different regions. Indicators are formed under the influence of two types of factors, the first of which determines the similarity of the values of indicators in these regions, and the second - their differentiation. The first type of factors leads to the fact that the indicators are grouped near a certain average value for all regions. The second type of factors determines the degree of variation in the values of indicators. At the same time, deviations of indicators for specific regions from the average value can be either decreasing or increasing. This assumption is based on the multidirectional action of factors of the second type. This phenomenon confirms the possibility of considering the density function of the normal distribution as a function approximating the frequency of distribution of the values of the indicators discussed in this article.

The study of phenomena and processes whose parameters are formed as a result of the combined influence of many factors acting additively and independently of each other can be carried out using the law of normal distribution (Orlov, 2004). It follows from Chebyshev's theorem (Kramer, 1999) that individual random variables can have a significant spread, and their arithmetic mean is relatively stable. This theorem, also called the law of large numbers, establishes that the arithmetic mean of a sufficiently large number of independent random variables loses the character of a random variable. Thus, the values of the sets indicators of medical organizations, the number of doctors and nurses are random variables that can have a significant spread, but it is possible to predict what value their arithmetic mean will take. In accordance with Lyapunov's theorem, the distribution law of the sum of independent random variables approaches the normal distribution law if the following conditions are met: all variables have finite mathematical expectations and variances, and none of the values differs sharply from the others. The above conditions are met for the values of the indicators considered by us for the aggregates of the objects considered by us in different regions. As Gmurman (2003) points out, the law of distribution of the sum of independent random variables approaches the normal fairly quickly (even with the number of terms on the order of ten). As already noted, the number of medical organizations, doctors and nurses in all regions without exception is very large, that is, the above requirement is met in all regions.

Distribution functions are used to describe both continuous and discrete quantities (Wentzel, 2010). The probability density is a derivative of a non-decreasing function, so it is non-negative over the entire range of variations. The distribution density function contains complete information about the random variable. The main numerical characteristics describing a specific random variable are:

- characteristics of the position of a random variable on the numerical axis (mode, median, mathematical expectation). It should be noted that for the density functions of the normal distribution, these three characteristics are equal to each other;
- the characteristic of the spread of a random variable near the average value is called the standard deviation. The variance of a random variable is used to calculate it;
- coefficients of asymmetry and kurtosis, which are equal to zero for a normal distribution.

The graph of the density function of the normal distribution is a symmetrical unimodal bell-shaped curve, the axis of symmetry of which is a vertical drawn through a point that is the center of symmetry of the density function of the normal distribution.

The general form of the density function of the normal distribution is as follows:

$$y(x) = \frac{A}{\sigma \times \sqrt{2\pi}} \cdot e^{\frac{-(x-m)^2}{2 \times \sigma^2}}$$, where A - coefficient of model; x - the indicator whose distribution we

are studying; m - the average value of the indicator for all observed objects; σ - the mean square (standard) deviation.

The development of mathematical models describing the distribution of indicators using the density functions of the normal distribution is based on the construction of appropriate histograms. With a large number of empirical source data (more than 40), it is advisable to group these data by intervals for the convenience of information processing. To do this, the range of indicator values is divided into a certain number of intervals. The number of intervals should be chosen in such a way that, on the one hand, the diversity of the indicator values is taken into account, and on the other hand, the regularity of the distribution depends to a small extent on random effects.

When considering distribution density functions describing indicators in regions, the number of intervals ranges from 7 to 9. Each interval must contain at least five elements, and only two elements are allowed in extreme intervals.

Based on the constructed histograms, models are developed, that is, the density functions of the normal distribution are estimated. It seems reasonable to perform calculations with a different number of intervals during a computational experiment. Thus, when analyzing indicators by regions of the country, we can consistently consider three density functions of the normal distribution corresponding to histograms with the number of intervals 7, 8 and 9. The choice of the function that best approximates the initial data is carried out in accordance with the criteria below.

In the course of computational experiments, the results of empirical observations are approximated and the parameters (characteristics) of the distribution functions of random variables are estimated.

To assess the quality of the achieved functions, i.e. the level of approximation of empirical data, we used the well-known and well-proven statistical tests of Pearson, Kolmogorov-Smirnov and Shapiro-Wilk (criteria of agreement).

The variance analysis of indicators for regions with minimum and maximum values of indicators, carried out at the fifth step of the study for each of the indicators, was based on the ANOVA method (Ostertagova & Ostertag, 2013). The procedure of univariate variance analysis included determining the ratio of intergroup variance to intragroup variance for these two groups of regions. The analysis of variance allowed us to check how much the variance caused by the difference between the groups was greater compared to the variance caused by intra-group variability.

Table 2. Calculated values of criteria. Source: The data in the table are based on the results of calculated functions.

Indicators	Kolmogorov-Smirnov test	Pearson test	Shapiro-Wilk test
number of hospital beds per ten thousand people living in the region	4.01	0.06	0.96
daily number of visits to outpatient clinics for ten thousand people living in the region	4.48	0.08	0.96
number of doctors per ten thousand people living in the region	2.10	0.04	0.97
number of nurses per ten thousand people living in the region	2.51	0.06	0.97
ratio of salaries of doctors and nurses to the average salary in the region	0.20	0.02	0.99

In the course of the computational experiment, mathematical modeling was carried out on the basis of empirical data. The models that describe the distributions ($y_1 ; y_2 ; y_3 ; y_4 ; y_5$) of the five indicators ($x_1 ; x_2 ; x_3 ; x_4 ; x_5$) across 82 regions are shown below. Number of hospital beds per ten thousand people living in the region is $y_1(x_1) = \dfrac{1025.17}{12.76 \times \sqrt{2\pi}} \cdot e^{-\frac{(x_1 - 84.74)^2}{2 \times 12.76^2}}$ (1). Daily number of visits to outpatient clinics for ten thousand people living in the region is $y_2(x_2) = \dfrac{3895.21}{52.06 \times \sqrt{2\pi}} \cdot e^{-\frac{(x_2 - 288.99)^2}{2 \times 52.06^2}}$ (2). Number of doctors per ten thousand people living in the region is $y_3(x_3) = \dfrac{820.43}{9.49 \times \sqrt{2\pi}} \cdot e^{-\frac{(x_3 - 48.35)^2}{2 \times 9.49^2}}$ (3). Number of nurses per ten thousand people living in the region $y_4(x_4) = \dfrac{1230.57}{15.64 \times \sqrt{2\pi}} \cdot e^{-\frac{(x_4 - 106.98)^2}{2 \times 15.64^2}}$ (4). Ratio of salaries of doctors and nurses to the average salary in the region $y_5(x_5) = \dfrac{4.61}{0.07 \times \sqrt{2\pi}} \cdot e^{-\frac{(x_5 - 1.03)^2}{2 \times 0.07^2}}$ (5).

The quality of functions (1)-(5) we tested using such criteria: Kolmogorov-Smirnov, Pearson and Shapiro-Wilk. Calculated values of criteria are given in Table 2.

Information given in column 2 of Table 2 showed that all calculated values are less than the critical value by the Kolmogorov-Smirnov test (0.174) at significant level equal 0.05. Data in column 3 are less than critical value of Pearson criterion (9.49). Data in column 4 exceed critical value 0.93 Shapiro-Wilk test with significant level of 0.01. Thus, the computational experiment showed that all developed functions have high quality.

At the next step of the study, we made estimation of discussing indicators on the base of achieved functions. The values of the indicators, the average by regions, are shown in column 2 of Table 3. The average values were determined on the base of functions (1)-(5). The third column of Table 3 indicate the standard deviations for discussing indicators. The values of the indicators characterizing the upper and lower boundaries of the intervals corresponding to the majority of regions are shown in column 4.

Table 3. Values of indicators characterizing organization of healthcare in the regions of Russia. Source: The calculations are carried out by the author on the basis of functions (1)-(5).

Indicator numbers	Average values	Standard deviation	Values for most regions
1	2	3	4
number of hospital beds per ten thousand people living in the region	84.74	12.76	71.98-97.50
daily number of visits to outpatient clinics for ten thousand people living in the region	288.99	52.06	236.93-341.05
number of doctors per ten thousand people living in the region	48.35	9.49	38.86-57.84
number of nurses per ten thousand people living in the region	106.98	15.64	91.34-122.62
ratio of salaries of doctors and nurses to the average salary in the region	1.03	0.07	0.96-1.10

We calculate the lower limits as the difference between the average value and the standard deviation, and we calculate the upper limits as the sum of the average value and the standard deviation.

The above information shows the possibility of assessing the indicators characterizing the activities of regional health systems in Russia, based on the use of density functions of the normal distribution.

The next step was to identify the regions in which the maximum and minimum values of each indicator were marked. In this case, the maximum values are those that exceed the upper limits of the ranges specified in column 4 of Table 3, and the minimum values are those that are less than the lower limits of the specified ranges.

The results of this analysis are shown in Table 4. Along with the lists of regions, this table also shows the values of indicators by region, as well as which of the federal districts the regions belong to.

In the above lists of regions, the territorial location is indicated in column 4 of Table 4, that is, the federal districts in which these regions are located are described. The analysis shows that the regions with the maximum and minimum values of each of the five indicators are located in different federal districts. That is, the maximum and minimum values of the indicators are not determined by the territorial location of the regions. Consequently, the forth hypothesis was confirmed.

Then the so-called ANOVA analysis was carried out. At the same time, for each of the considered indicators, the values of indicators for two groups of regions were compared, respectively, with the maximum and minimum values of indicators. The results of the ANOVA analysis are shown in Table 5. It contains statistical estimates for each of these groups of regions, which are described below. At the same time, the first and second rows of the table show, respectively, the average values of indicators for groups of regions with maximum and minimum values. The third and fourth lines show differences for each of the groups of regions with maximum and minimum values of indicators. The fifth line shows the intergroup estimates for groups of regions with maximum and minimum values of indicators. The sixth line shows the difference within the groups of regions with maximum and minimum values. The seventh, eighth and ninth rows of the table demonstrate the results of ANOVA quality testing.

An analysis of the data presented in Table 5 shows that for groups of regions characterized by maximum and minimum values of indicators, there are relatively small differences within each group. This indicates that each of these groups includes regions with small differences in the values of indicators.

Table 4. Characteristics of regions with maximum and minimum indicator values. Source: Developed by the author on the basis of data from Table 3.

Indicators	Region	Value	Federal district
1	2	3	4
	With maximum values of indicators		
	Trans - Baikal territory	97.51	Far East
	Murmansk region	103.56	North-West
	republic of Tyva	106.72	Siberian
	Magadan region	110.43	Far East
	Kamchatka territory	111.84	Far East
	Sakhalin region	115.22	Far East
	Jewish Autonomous region	116.17	Far East
	Chukotka Autonomous	128.89	Far East
number of hospital beds per ten thousand people living in the region	With minimum values of indicators		
	republic of Ingushetia	48.71	North-Caucasus
	Leningrad region	59.56	North-West
	Chechen republic	62.94	North-Caucasus
	republic of Tatarstan	63.93	South
	republic of Adygea	67.92	South
	Belgorod region	69.49	Central
	republic of Dagestan	70.03	North-Caucasus
	Moscow	71.61	Central
	With maximum values of indicators		
	Chuvash republic	345.4	Privolzskiy
	Udmurt republic	346.4	Privolzskiy
	Lipetsk region	353.2	Central
	St. Petersburg	354.6	North-West
	republic of Khakassia	354.9	Siberian
	Vladimir region	361.6	Central
	Novgorod region	396.3	North-West
	Arkhangelsk region	401.8	North-West
	Komi Republic	407.0	North-West
	Magadan region	440.8	Far East
	Chukotka Autonomous	487.6	Far East
daily number of visits to outpatient clinics for ten thousand people living in the region	With minimum values of indicators		
	Chechen republic	181.2	North-Caucasus
	republic of Crimea	186.9	South
	Sevastopol	188.6	South
	republic of Ingushetia	200.3	North-Caucasus
	Kabardino-Balkar republic	221.3	North-Caucasus
	Perm region	228.5	Privolzskiy
	Karachay-Cherkess republic	229.4	North-Caucasus
	Tomsk region	229.4	Siberian
	Krasnodar territory	231.6	South
	Stavropol territory	234.4	South
	With maximum values of indicators		
	republic of Sakha	60.3	Far East
	Astrakhan region	62.1	South
	Magadan region	62.4	Far East
	Sakhalin region	64.6	Far East
	Moscow	69.9	Central
	republic of North Ossetia - Alania	69.9	North-Caucasus
	Chukotka Autonomous	73.7	Far East
	St. Petersburg	89.3	North-West
number of doctors per ten thousand people living in the region	With minimum values of indicators		
	Kurgan region	28.9	Ural
	Chechen Republic	32.2	North-Caucasus
	Pskov region	32.4	North-West
	Vologda region	36.1	North-West
	Republic of Mari El	36.4	Privolzskiy
	Vladimir region	36.5	Central
	Kostroma region	36.9	Central
	Leningrad region	37.1	North-West
	Jewish Autonomous region	37.6	Far East
	Rostov region	38.7	South

continued on following page

Table 4. Continued

Indicators	Region	Value	Federal district
	With maximum values of indicators		
	Altai republic	123.1	Siberian
	Ulyanovsk region	123.2	Privolzskiy
	Arkhangelsk region	125.2	North-West
	Murmansk region	130.1	North-West
	Tyumen region	130.1	Ural
	republic of Sakha	135.4	Far East
	Sakhalin region	139.7	Far East
	Chukotka Autonomous	142.5	Far East
	Komi republic	143.6	North-West
	republic of Tyva	147.6	Siberian
	Magadan region	154.2	Far East
number of nurses per ten thousand people living in the region	With minimum values of indicators		
	Leningrad region	71.5	North-West
	Sevastopol	76.0	South
	Chechen republic	80.4	North-Caucasus
	Moscow region	81.3	Central
	Kaliningrad region	82.8	North-West
	Primorsky territory	84.1	Far East
	republic of Ingushetia	86.6	North-Caucasus
	Rostov region	87.6	South
	Tomsk region	88.7	Siberian
	republic of Dagestan	89.9	North-Caucasus
	Moscow	90.3	Central
	Krasnodar territory	91.1	South
	With maximum values of indicators		
	republic of Tyva	1.10	Siberian
	Chuvash republic	1.10	Privolzskiy
	Kaliningrad region	1.10	North-West
	Novgorod region	1.11	North-West
	republic of Ingushetia	1.13	North-Caucasus
	Pskov region	1.15	Central
	Penza region	1.15	Privolzskiy
	Altai republic	1.15	Siberian
	Moscow region	1.17	Central
	republic of Kalmykia	1.21	South
	Sevastopol	1.21	South
	With minimum values of indicators		
	Trans - Baikal territory	0.88	Far East
	Krasnoyarsk territory	0.90	Siberian
	Magadan region	0.91	Far East
	Astrakhan region	0.93	South
	Lipetsk region	0.93	Central
	Kostroma region	0.93	Central
ratio of salaries of doctors and nurses to the average salary in the region	Ryazan region	0.94	Central
	Kemerovo region	0.94	Siberian
	Vologda region	0.95	North-West
	Republic of Mari El	0.95	Privolzskiy
	Krasnodar Territory	0.95	South
	Arkhangelsk region	0.95	North-West
	Tomsk region	0.95	Siberian
	Oryol region	0.96	Central
	Stavropol Territory	0.96	South
	Murmansk region	0.96	North-West

The average values for groups of regions with maximum values of indicators differ significantly from the average values for groups of regions with minimum values. The difference between the groups of regions with maximum and minimum values is much greater than the difference typical for each of the groups for all the considered indicators. The data given in Table 5 show that for each of the indicators considered in the article, there are significant differences between groups of regions with maximum values and minimum values. This follows from the fact that the ratio between intergroup and intra group

Table 5. Statistical characteristics describing groups of regions with maximum and minimum values of indicators. Source: Calculated by the author on the basis of ANOVA analysis

Nº	Statistical characteristics	Indicator 1	Indicator 2	Indicator 3	Indicator 4	Indicator 5
1	Average for regions with maximum values of indicators	111.29	386.33	69.03	135.88	1.14
2	Average for regions with minimum values of indicators, %	64.27	213.16	35.28	84.19	0.94
3	Variance for regions with maximum values	88.63	2096.20	88.86	109.62	0.002
4	Variance by regions with minimum values	56.25	455.54	9.44	37.11	0.001
5	Variance between groups of regions with maximum and minimum values	8843.34	157074.26	5061.00	15334.22	0.281
6	Variance inside groups of regions with maximum and minimum values	72.44	1319.05	44.18	71.64	0.001
7	Fisher criterion	122.08	119.08	114.55	214.04	291.52
8	Critical value according to the Fisher criterion	4.60	4.38	4.49	4.32	4.24
9	Significance level	less 0.001	less 0.001	less 0.001	less 0.001	less 0.001

deviations for each of the indicators given in the seventh row of the table is much greater than one. These ratios represent the calculated values of the Fisher criterion, which are greater than the tabular values of this criterion given in the eighth row of the table. It is necessary to note that the significance level is less than 0.001, that is, with a probability of 99.9%, there are significant differences characteristic of groups of regions with maximum and minimum values of indicators. Thus, the statistical characteristics of the ANOVA analysis based on intergroup differences, namely on the Fisher criteria and the significance level, showed the high quality of the estimates obtained.

SOLUTIONS AND RECOMMENDATIONS

The analysis of the data given in the second table allows us to characterize the level of development of the healthcare system in the regions of Russia. The average value of the first indicator for the regions of Russia, namely the number of hospital beds per ten thousand people living in the region in 2020 was almost 85. For most regions, this indicator was in the range from 72 to 97. The values of the indicator in the regions of Russia were lower than in Japan (128) and the Republic of Korea (124), close to the values of similar indicators in Germany (79) and Austria (72). It should be noted that the values of the first indicator in Russia were higher compared to most economically developed European countries, in which the corresponding indicators took values from 21 to 68, the USA (28), Canada (25) and China (48) (OECD, 2021).

The average value of the second indicator for the regions of Russia in 2020, namely the daily number of visits to outpatient clinics for ten thousand people living in the region was 289. In most regions, the values of this indicator ranged from 237 to 341.

The average value of the third indicator for the regions of Russia in 2020, namely the number of doctors per ten thousand people living in the region was 48. For most regions, the values of this indicator were in the range from 39 to 58. In the same interval there were values of similar indicators for such European countries as Austria (54), Norway (51), Lithuania (46), Germany (45), Spain (44), Sweden (43), Denmark (42), Czech Republic (41), Italy (40), Iceland (39). In other economically developed European countries, the values of the indicators were slightly lower and ranged from 30 to 38. It should also be noted that the number of doctors per ten thousand people in China was 22, in the USA - 26 and Canada - 28.

The average value of the fourth indicator for the regions of Russia in 2020, namely the number of nurses per ten thousand people living in the region was 107. For most regions, the values of this indicator were in the range from 91 to 123. According to European medical statistics, higher values of similar indicators (compared to the regions of Russia) were observed only in three countries: Finland (143), Germany (132) and Ireland (129) (Eurostat, 2022). In five European countries, the values of the indicators are in the same range as most Russian regions. The values of the indicator in these countries are as follows: Luxembourg - 117, Sweden - 109, France - 108, Slovenia - 101, Denmark - 101. In other European countries, the values of the indicators vary from 33 to 78.

The above data indicate that the first hypothesis was confirmed.

Comparative analysis of the average values of the third and fourth indicators indicates that the ratio of the number of nurses and the number of doctors in Russia in 2020 was 2.2. That is, the number of nurses was more than twice the number of doctors. It should be noted that similar values of this ratio were observed in countries such as Estonia, Romania, Ukraine and Tajikistan (World health statistics, 2020). The highest values (more than 6) of the ratio of the number of nurses and doctors in the European region were observed in countries such as Belgium and Norway. Relatively high values of this ratio (from 4 to 5) were in Switzerland, Ireland and Luxembourg. In some countries, the number of nurses was not much (less than twice) higher than the number of doctors. These countries include Lithuania, Austria, Portugal, Bulgaria, Italy, Spain, Slovakia, Latvia.

The average value of the fifth indicator for the regions of Russia in 2020, namely the ratio of salaries of doctors and nurses to the average salary in the region was 1.03. For most regions, the values of this indicator were in the range from 0.96 to 1.10. Consequently, in most regions of Russia, the average salary in the healthcare system differed slightly from the salary level of all employees in the regions as a whole. It should be noted that in the US healthcare system, wages were almost one and a half times higher than the average salary of all employees in the country, and in Germany and France, medical workers received a third higher salary compared to the average for these countries (SalaryExplorer, 2022). Thus, the second hypothesis was confirmed.

The data of the second table allows us to conclude about the differentiation of the values of indicators by region. The degree of variation of each of the indicators was analyzed. For this purpose, we used the standard deviations indicated in column 3. The variation indices are as follows: for the first indicator – 15%, for the second indicator - 18%, for the third indicator - 20%, for the fourth indicator - 14%, for the fifth indicator - 7%. This analysis showed that in the regions under consideration, the level of differentiation of the values of all five indicators was below 33%, that is, not very significant. Consequently, the third hypothesis was confirmed.

FUTURE RESEARCH DIRECTIONS

Further research can be aimed at determining trends and patterns of changes in the indicators considered in this work over the following years. In addition, an assessment of the indicators of medical care in individual municipalities belonging to each of the regions of Russia is of particular interest. For such an assessment, a methodological approach based on the development of density functions of the normal distribution, which is given in this paper, can be used.

CONCLUSION

Our research makes a theoretical and practical contribution to the study of the problem of healthcare development in modern countries on the example of Russia. The theoretical contribution is connected with the development and application of the author's methodology for assessing relative indicators characterizing the availability of inpatient and outpatient medical care, the availability of doctors and nurses. The methodology is based on the use of mathematical models representing normal distribution functions. The obtained functions describe the regional distribution of the five indicators under consideration. They can be used as tools in subsequent research on the problem under consideration. The practical contribution of our research is based on obtaining new knowledge about the health systems that have developed in the regions of Russia. Such knowledge is necessary for the Government and regional public administration bodies. In addition, they are of interest to society, the population, as well as to medical professionals. It should be noted that to date, a comprehensive study of the regional characteristics of medical care provided to the population in Russia has not been conducted. Therefore, the comparative analysis by region is of great practical importance.

Our research has allowed us to obtain new and original conclusions, given below. It showed that for every ten thousand people living in the regions, there are an average of 85 hospital beds. In organizations engaged in outpatient diagnosis and treatment of diseases, 289 patients in average were served daily for every ten thousand people living in the regions. There were 48 doctors in average with special medical education working in the healthcare system for ten thousand residents of the regions. The number of nurses exceeded the number of doctors by 2.2 times. There were 107 nurses in average per ten thousand residents in the regions of Russia. The analysis showed that in most regions the average salary in the healthcare sector did not differ significantly from the average salary in the corresponding region.

The average values of the first four indicators for the regions of Russia were approximately at the same level as in economically developed European countries. The values of the fifth indicator for the regions of Russia were significantly lower compared to the countries of the European Union and the United States.

There was a certain differentiation of the values of the five indicators under consideration by region. At the same time, this differentiation was not very significant, since the coefficients of variation in the values of the indicators did not exceed 20%. The regions that were characterized by the maximum and minimum values of the five indicators under consideration were identified. Comparative analysis has shown that the territorial location of the regions does not affect the maximum and minimum values of the indicators.

The purpose of this study, related to the assessment of indicators characterizing the development of the healthcare system in the regions of Russia, has been achieved. The following conclusions have scientific novelty and originality. The study examined five indicators characterizing the provision of medical care in specialized organizations, the availability of certified doctors and nurses in the regions, as well as the level of remuneration of these specialists achieved in 2020. A method for estimating these five indicators using the density functions of the normal distribution is proposed. Based on the proposed methodology, the distribution of these indicators in 2020 across 82 regions of Russia was estimated.

The practical significance of the study for state and regional authorities is to take into account the peculiarities of the development of the healthcare system in the regions of Russia. The results of the work can be used in the activities of federal and regional structures related to the organization of medical care to the population and the justification for allocating additional resources to regions with a low level of medical care. Taking into account the small values of the fifth indicator in Russia in comparison with economically developed countries (indicated above), further development of the healthcare system in Russia, in our opinion, should be associated with an increase in the level of remuneration of medical personnel.

The new knowledge gained is of interest and can be used in educational programs of higher education in the relevant specialties. The methodology proposed in the study can be used by countries with a large number of territorial entities to conduct a comparative analysis of indicators.

The empirical data used in this study characterized the healthcare system in all 82 regions of Russia without exception. Consequently, our study had no limitations, that is, the sample in question coincided with the general population. The information used fully corresponded to the actual state of the healthcare system in Russia, since it was based on official statistical data, which by the end of 2020 were provided by all medical organizations located in each of the regions.

REFERENCES

Al-Hanawi, M. K., Khan, S. A., & Al-Borie, H. M. (2019). Healthcare human resource development in Saudi Arabia: Emerging challenges and opportunities - a critical review. *Public Health Reviews*, *40*(1), 1–16. doi:10.118640985-019-0112-4 PMID:30858991

Belyaev, S.A. (2021). Development of strategic development measures healthcare institutions. *Regional Bulletin, 1*(57), 5-7.

Borges, E., Fonseca, C., Baptista, P., Leite Queiros, C. M., & Baldonedo-Mosteiro, M. (2019). Compassion fatigue among nurses workingon an adultemergencyandurgent care unit. *Revista Latino-Americana de Enfermagem*, *27*, e3175. doi:10.1590/1518-8345.2973.3175 PMID:31596410

Britto, M., Fuller, S., Kaplan, H., Kotagal, U., Lannon, C., Margolis, P., Muething, S., Schoettker, P., & Seid, M. (2018). Using a network organisational architecture to support the development of Learning. *Healthcare Systems. BMJ Quality & Safety*, *27*(11), 937–946. doi:10.1136/bmjqs-2017-007219 PMID:29438072

Chowdhary, C. L., & Acharjya, D. P. (2020). Segmentation and feature extraction in medical imaging: A systematic review. *Procedia Computer Science*, *167*, 26–36. doi:10.1016/j.procs.2020.03.179

Chubarova, T.V. (2021). Effective healthcare as a condition for the reproduction of human potential: modern challenges for social policy. *Economic Security, 4*(3), 607–628.

Dubina, Y.Y. (2021). On approaches to assessing the cost effectiveness of the development of the health-care sector. *State and Municipal Administration. Scientific Notes, 1,* 263-267.

Durkin, J., Usher, K., & Jackson, D. (2019). Embodying compassion: A systematic review of the views of nurses and patients. *Journal of Clinical Nursing, 28*(9-10), 1380–1392. doi:10.1111/jocn.14722 PMID:30485579

Durrani, H. (2016). Healthcare and healthcare systems: Inspiring progress and future prospects. *mHealth, 2*(3), 1–9. PMID:28293581

Eurostat: Healthcare personnel statistics - nursing and caring professionals. (2022). https://ec.europa.eu/eurostat/statistics-explained/index.php?title=Healthcare_personnel_statistics_-_nursing_and_caring_professionals

Federal Service of State Statistic. (2022). https://rosstat.gov.ru/folder/13721

Gmurman, V. (2003). *Theory of probability and mathematical statistics.* Higher School.

Haldane, V., De Foo, C., Abdalla, S. M., Jung, A.-S., Tan, M., Wu, S., Chua, A., Verma, M., Shrestha, P., Singh, S., Perez, T., Tan, S. M., Bartos, M., Mabuchi, S., Bonk, M., McNab, C., Werner, G. K., Panjabi, R., Nordström, A., & Legido-Quigley, H. (2021). Health systems resilience in managing the COVID-19 pandemic: Lessons from 28 countries. *Nature Medicine, 27*(6), 964–980. doi:10.103841591-021-01381-y PMID:34002090

Ivanov, V.N., & Suvorov, A.V. (2021). Modern problems of the development of Russian healthcare. Part 1. *Problems of Forecasting, 6*(189), 59-71.

Kadadi, S., & Bharamanaikar, S.R. (2020). Role of Emotional Intelligence on in Healthcare Industry. *Drishtikon: A Management Journal, 11*(1), 1-37.

Karan, A., & Wadhera, R. (2021). Healthcare System Stress Due to Covid-19: Evading an Evolving Crisis. *Journal of Hospital Medicine, 16*(2), 127–135. doi:10.12788/jhm.3583 PMID:33523798

Karani, F. (2014). Spatial heterogeneity of the US healthcare organization in the context of reform. *American Journal of Economics and Control Systems Management, 4*(2), 47-54.

Kaya, H., Senyuva, E., & Bodur, G. (2018). The relationship between critical thinking and emotional intelligence in nursing students: A longitudinal study. *Nurse Education Today, 68,* 26–32. doi:10.1016/j.nedt.2018.05.024 PMID:29883912

Kramer, H. (1999). *Mathematical methods of statistics.* University Press.

Lacouz, I., & Midler, G. (2021). Antique US Government and State Health. *American Journal of Law & Medicine, 47*(1), 104–122.

Lazareva, N.V. (2021). Resource potential of the healthcare system. *Problems of improving the organization of production and management of industrial enterprises: Interuniversity collection of scientific papers, 1,* 32-37.

Milcent, C. (2016). Evolution of the Health System. Inefficiency, Violence, and Digital Healthcare. *China Perspectives (Online), 4*(4), 39–50. doi:10.4000/chinaperspectives.7112

OECD: Health at a Glance 2021: OECD Indicators. (2021). OECD Publishing. doi:10.1787/ae3016b9-

On national goals and strategic objectives of the development of the Russian Federation for the period up to 2024. (2022). Decree of the President of the Russian Federation dated 07.05.2018 No. 204. http://www.consultant.ru/document/cons_doc_LAW_335693/

Orlov, A. (2004). *Econometrica.* Exam.

Ostertagova, E., & Ostertag, O. (2013). Methodology and Application of One-way ANOVA. *American Journal of Mechanical Engineering, 1*(7), 256–261.

Pinkovetskaia, I., Nuretdinova, Y., Nuretdinov, I., & Lipatova, N. (2021). Mathematical modeling on the base of functions density of normal distribution. *Revista de La Universidad del Zulia, 12*(33), 34–49. doi:10.46925//rdluz.33.04

Posentseva, Y. S., Mustenko, N. S., & Khomutinnikov, A. D. (2020). Analysis of Health System Efficiency: Main Trends of Development and Prospects of Modernization. *Proceedings of the Southwest State University. Series: Economics, Sociology and Management, 10*(3), 123-139.

Preston, S. H. (2007). The changing relation between mortality and level of economic development. *International Journal of Epidemiology, 36*(3), 484–490. doi:10.1093/ije/dym075 PMID:17550952

Rakova, T. V. (2021). On the state of the Russian healthcare system before the coronavirus pandemic. *Azimuth of scientific research. Economics and Management, 10*(2), 267–269.

Reddy, G. T., Bhattacharya, S., Ramakrishnan, S. S., Chowdhary, C. L., Hakak, S., Kaluri, R., & Reddy, M. P. K. (2020, February). An ensemble based machine learning model for diabetic retinopathy classification. In *2020 international conference on emerging trends in information technology and engineering (ic-ETITE)* (pp. 1-6). IEEE.

Reprintseva, E. (2020). Assessment of indicators of the development of the hospital healthcare network in Russia. *Regional Bulletin, 7*(46), 83-85.

SalaryExplorer. (2022). http://www.salaryexplorer.com/

Shishkin, S. V., Sheiman, I. M., Abdin, A. A., Boyarsky, S. G., & Sazhina, S. V. (2017). *Russian healthcare in the new economic conditions: challenges and prospects. Report of the Higher School of Economics on the problems of the development of the healthcare system.* Publishing House of the Higher School of Economics.

Shkolnikov, V., Andreev, E., Tursun-zade, R., & Leon, D. (2019). Patterns in the relationship between life expectancy and gross domestic product in Russia in 2005–15: A cross-sectional analysis. *Lancet: Public Health, 4.*

Sokanto, G. L., & Bruise, S. (2021). Regional policy for health care reform in the United States. Administration approaches from Obama to Trump. *American Review of Public Administration, 51*(2), 62–77.

The Healthcare Development Strategy of the Russian Federation for the period up to 2025. (2022). http://www.kremlin.ru/acts/news/60708

Travnikova, D.A., & Shubina, E.Y. (2020). Analysis and evaluation of the dynamics of indicators of the development of the Russian healthcare system. *Issues of Sustainable Development of Society, 10,* 142-149.

Vlasova, O.V. (2021). Trends in the development of the region's of the healthcare system in the current socio-economic conditions. *Science and Practice of Regions, 3*(24), 47-51.

Weng, H. C., Chen, H. C., Chen, H. J., Lu, K., & Hung, S. Y. (2008). Doctors' emotional intelligence and the patient-doctor relationship. *Medical Education, 42*(7), 703–711. doi:10.1111/j.1365-2923.2008.03039.x PMID:18588649

Wentzel, E. (2010). *The theory of probability.* KnoRus.

World health statistics 2020: Monitoring health for the SDGs, sustainable development goals. (2020). World Health Organization.

Zyukin, D.A. (2020). On the results of the resource optimization process in the healthcare system. *Politics, Economics and Innovation, 6*(35), 1-7.

Chapter 14
The Effect of Emotional Intelligence Applications on the Lifestyle of the Elderly

Zahra Alidousti Shahraki

iD https://orcid.org/0000-0002-5027-7919

University of Isfahan, Iran

Mohsen Aghabozorgi Nafchi

Shiraz University, Iran

ABSTRACT

Today, many changes have been seen in the life of people in society with the development of new technologies. For example, developing various new communication platforms and applications such as social networks has been able to affect the lifestyle and communication of people in different age groups. The elderly are one of the most important sections of society, and other age groups have been affected by new applications and social networks in recent years. One of the important issues that should be considered for the elderly people is to provide a suitable environment to improve their quality of life because they are one of the most vulnerable groups in society who, due to old age and various diseases, don't have this power to do their daily routine, and this affects their moods. So, designing new intelligence applications for improving their emotional intelligence can play an important role to facilitate their work and communications. In this chapter, the authors discuss new artificial intelligence applications that can control the emotional intelligence of the elderly.

INTRODUCTION

The ability to think in the elderly is reduced due to disorders in their minds, so it can be provided as a way to understand the feelings of older people using intelligent patterns and identify their decisions by analyzing. Recognizing their facial expressions can improve their quality of life. It can help them to

DOI: 10.4018/978-1-6684-5673-6.ch014

make decisions by using deep learning algorithms. Also, cognitive science algorithms with the help of using artificial intelligence applications can help to identify their emotions.

The purpose of this chapter is to take a broader view of these people and to introduce and identify their abilities, emotions, and differences from other groups, as well as their inability to do their own thing, which leads to low self-esteem and self-confidence. Providing programs and applications that can provide an easier life for these people are discussed. By examining their problems, it will introduce and provide solutions to solve their problems.

In the following sections, the researchers will discuss the impact of emotional intelligence on culture and mood and intelligent tools that can detect different conditions of the elderly with artificial intelligence techniques and work in different situations that need help. The important issue that is mentioned in this chapter is the effect of emotional intelligence on the mental and emotional condition of people. Older people have problems with their daily activities due to old age and lack of concentration. It is examined how emotional intelligence can help to increase concentration and strengthen their mental and emotional condition. Some issues have also been discussed and the role of emotional intelligence in controlling pandemic conditions has been investigated. In general, this chapter has been able to examine the various factors that cause changes in the living conditions of the elderly and by providing solutions to researchers to remind them that this can be done by designing special programs and applications to improve living conditions for the elderly. In the future, researchers can determine the positive or negative points of the presented models in the future by accurately implementing the mentioned cases. By implementing the mentioned models, the intensity of the influence of various factors such as age or gender may be effective. Therefore, new models and new applications can be designed and built according to the specific conditions of each elderly person. The problems and trends presented in each chapter are expressed by examining its positive or negative points. Each topic is presented according to the age and geographical conditions that can affect the elderly.

At the end of the chapter, it is concluded that different methods and programs of artificial intelligence can improve the lifestyle of different sections of society, especially the elderly, by controlling emotional intelligence applications.

Emotional Intelligence

Emotional intelligence (EQ) and intellectual ability are two important factors in the success of people in life. Each of these factors alone is not enough to achieve success. Having an intelligence quotient (IQ) helps to succeed in exams, but it is possible to control stress and overcome challenges in life, as well as to establish effective communication between people with no intelligence at all. Making informed decisions is due to emotional intelligence. It seems that with proper training and education, two criteria of EQ and IQ should be strengthened in people. Weakness is one of these criteria can cause problems in people's lives. The elderly are no exception to this condition, and strengthening their emotional intelligence will play a significant role in their lives.

Emotional Intelligence, Well-Being and Self-Aware

High emotional intelligence can help to better understand the environment and increase well-being. On the other hand, using intelligence and practical models can help to increase people's emotional intelligence. Increasing emotional intelligence changes the ability to understand and make better decisions and therefore the living conditions. People who increase their emotional intelligence cope better with changing life situations. Also, having the ability to become self-aware in challenging situations as a result of unwanted feelings can avoid a mitigated error. Errors can be prevented by using tools to identify challenging situations. Identifying vulnerable situations by intelligence algorithms can prevent mistakes. It is possible to understand unknown feelings and help a person who is injured or has momentary feelings in critical situations using intelligent tools in the direction of self-awareness. Having a large data set of people's conditions and emotions and designing an intelligent model can help a person who has different emotions in different situations to make decisions.

Emotional Intelligence and Body Language

More than half of our communication is made through body language. So, paying attention to the subject is extremely important. That's where your emotional intelligence comes in. Body language is a tool for conveying emotions. Emotions can be controlled by using intelligence applications that can feel and understand body language and help to the relationship.

The elderly cannot easily express their needs due to disorders in the brain and old age. By understanding their feelings that are due to pain or illness, they can be helped in times of need. By using machine learning, it can be gained a more accurate understanding of pain or need in the elderly and help meet their needs. Also, face recognition is a tool for understanding a person's moods and emotions and can be used with precise patterns to understand facial expressions and identify what the person needs.

Emotional Intelligence and Culture

The existence of cultural differences and their role in the behaviors of the elderly is a challenging issue that causes differences in emotionally intelligent applications. Categorizing and clustering people's emotions as well as categorizing different behavioral cultures in the elderly creates large data that needs more management. The elderly with different physical differences and diseases, as well as cultural differences that can be caused by climate change create a challenging program. It requires managing accurate emotional intelligence.

APPLICATIONS OF AI IN EMOTIONAL INTELLIGENCE

AI and Body Language

Behaviors, emotions, and thoughts can be sent both consciously and unconsciously. They can be displayed through gestures, illustrators, facial expressions, eye movement, posture, tension and touch. Artificial intelligence methods can analyze behaviors and thoughts, and as a result, using the imaging of different situations makes it easier to better understand emotions. Emotional intelligence patterns can help to improve the quality of cognition of each individual in different situations.

Accurate knowledge of people's emotions can help their health. Patterns of facial color and skin-color recognition at different times and in different emotions that are created for each person can show that they recognize the symptoms of a person's disease. Especially, emotional intelligence is accurately assessed in real times by using smart applications for the elderly.

It's important to say that designing and implementing intelligent robots which can understand and analyze emotional intelligence are able to help control people's emotional intelligence. Robots that can make better decisions in emergencies by recognizing facial expressions and understanding the physical differences of the elderly can create a milestone point in the emotional intelligence industry. These tools help the elderly and other people with physical or mental disabilities to have a higher quality of life.

AI and Childhood

Dependence and emotional connection between people are formed from childhood. These connections cause the formation of emotional intelligence in people. Older people become dependent on them because of the emotional intelligence they learned from childhood.

According to Walker et al. (2022), the degree of dependence of people and the extent of their emotional feelings are related to emotional intelligence. Therefore, it can be considered that the method of education and training of each person from childhood affects the behavior, personality, mood of that person until adulthood and also causes emotional growth and increases or decreases emotional intelligence. With the studies that are done, the percentage of emotional intelligence can be calculated accurately. As a result, more attention can be paid to the upbringing and development of the child. The amount of anger and anxiety of everyone or even the amount of patience of each person that causes emotional growth has a direct effect on the emotional intelligence. So, finding new patterns from childhood of elderly people with the help of AI technologies can play an important role to increase the emotional intelligence of them.

In Puspitasari et al. (2022), the relationship between emotional intelligence and the environment in schools is studied. This study has shown that the environment can affect students' emotional intelligence. It is likely that older individuals with emotional intelligence disorders have experienced abnormal behaviors by educators during childhood and their school because personality development is shaped in school. These behaviors cause problems with self-esteem and decision-making, etc. By designing a questionnaire, older people can be asked about anomalies or bad events and the memories they have from childhood. The authors can conclude that the personality disorders and disorders of individuals are due to misbehavior. That has occurred since childhood especially in the school and school environment.

AI and Driving

Having high emotional intelligence can affect the behavior of people while driving. Studies in Ahmed et al. (2022), show that drivers, who behave better while driving, have higher emotional intelligence than other drivers. It seems that appropriate action can be taken in this regard. This should be done in such a way that when issuing a driver's license, people are tested for emotional intelligence percentage, and people who get a higher percentage have a license to get a license. Since a large part of the mortality rate of people in society constitutes traffic accidents, so checking the health of people and especially the health of their behavior is important. Thoughts and distractions cause people to make hasty and irrational decisions while driving, which can lead to accidents. Therefore, an accurate diagnosis of mental health should be considered. Older people also have less patience due to old age, which causes accidents while driving. Accurate identification of emotional intelligence for older people can ensure the health of their driving life.

AI and Mental Illness

An important point to consider in the lifestyle of the elderly is their mental illness. Older people, because of their prejudice or personality, may show double standards and try not to show their mental problems. A borderline personality disorder is known as an emotionally unstable personality disorder as in records of National Collaborating Centre for Mental Health (UK. (2009). This disease is known as an emotional personality disorder. This disease occurs more despite fear and feelings of emptiness and isolation. According to the symptoms reported in this disease, it seems that this disease increases with adulthood and aging. To prevent the development of this disease among people, strategies should be adapted to changes in people's lifestyles.

In Khosravi et al. (2022), the prevalence of borderline personality disorder (BPD) in the elderly has been declining. It seems that nowadays this problem should be increasing due to the loneliness and isolation of people. Intelligent methods can be used to accurately calculate the percentage of people with this or other diseases. Using intelligence applications can be an important point that records the percentage in case of changes and disturbances in their situations. Also it can analyze the rate of changes during days and by recording specific symptoms. Deep learning algorithms can record better results of people's status on smart watches or smart apps that a person uses. Suicide is a warning sign for today's society that it occurs due to personality disorders in individuals. Statistics show that the incidence of suicide among the elderly is decreasing but a lot of adults in the world is suicide (Bruce & Pearson, 2022). This is a significant alarm for communities. This suicide occurs due to various factors. The main source is a lack of control of emotional intelligence among the elderly. Controlling the emotional intelligence of the elderly by a therapist can reduce the number of victims. The use of smart therapists can help them whenever and wherever they are disturbed. Careful and principled planning can be done for this action. Designing intelligent applications is necessary to assess the mental condition of people at any time and in case of mental and personality changes. Also, it is necessary to present the principles and instructions of the therapist to them live. It seems that this action can make a big change in the situation for them.

In Vaishnavi et al. (2022), several learning machine techniques are examined to accurately assess the mental health of each person. Each technique determines a different percentage of change using its own factors. It's an important point that the criteria should be changed and reviewed according to the living environment of each person and their different age groups. The percentage of error in each benchmark is related to the data set. The data analysis method should be selected by examining the correct technique because having mental health and emotional and social health in the elderly has a great impact on their quality of life. It seems that the techniques and criteria should be considered for the elderly. Combining several patterns of artificial intelligence and changing the criteria can have a favorable result for this age group.

As mentioned in Kim et al. (2017), diagnosing depression among the elderly is a difficult task. The elderly have difficulty understanding symptoms such as isolation, depression, and lack of purpose. They think that it is a physical problem. In Kim & Sohn (2022), a model has been proposed that can identify the physical and mental symptoms of the elderly. Designing smart homes can help the elderly (Saragadam et al., 2022, Gadekallu et al., 2022). The use of smart applications and devices in the home environment can provide space for better diagnosis of the elderly. Smart devices must detect signal changes in the physical and mental state of the elderly.

AI and Care Issues

The work environment also affects the behavioral performance of nurses. Many older people live in nursing homes because of loneliness and disability. Nurses have an important role in controlling and managing the behavior of the elderly. Mouse et al. (2016) Nurses are in a stressful and busy environment and these conditions affect the control of their own behavior. According to a study (Najafpour et al., 2020), nurses' work environment is directly related to the emotional intelligence of the elderly. To control these conditions, designing programs and intelligent software that can perform some of the work and activities of nurses automatically can play an important role in reducing nurses' fatigue. Providing intelligent machine learning algorithms to provide food or health care and medicine to the elderly can lead to a useful management and thus increase emotional intelligence and improve the quality of life of the elderly.

The work-life and mental health of nurses is an important part of work health in the environment. Providing the necessary facilities and welfare in the workplace can reduce the fatigue and stress of nurses (Havaei et al., 2022). In nursing workplaces, a healthy environment for patients and nurses should be provided by providing welfare facilities. Today, with the development of technology, artificial intelligence applications can be used. Designing robots that can do some work with nurses can help nurses' well-being. Caring for the elderly in a hospital or nursing home is an important part that requires patience and emotion management. To obtain results in this case, artificial intelligence devices can be used in several wards of hospitals or multi-ward nursing homes. The wards, medical centers, and intensive care can be used the intelligent models if there is positive feedback. Due to the different emotional intelligence that exists in different age groups, the review and feedback of the results should be related only to the same age group. Then the change in environmental conditions should occur only for the same group.

In (Ganskaia & Abaimov, 20222), it deals with the application of artificial intelligence in inpatient care. Patient care includes setting patients' bedtime, timely diagnosis of medication for the patient, and so on. By giving instructions to intelligent machines, patients can be helped to improve patients by using machine learning patterns. As stated in (Ganskaia & Abaimov, 2022), adjusting the sleep time can play a significant role in health. The elderly, like patients, need to be cared for, and changes in their bedtime can cause mood swings or behaviors. Health control in different situations using a learning machine can help to control their emotions and moods.

Improved Prediction is used as a new model in machine learning to diagnose trauma in older adults (Morris et al., 202). The age of each elderly person and alertness help in the correct diagnosis. The machine learning pattern can help accurately assess the situation and help diagnose a person's health after a trauma.

Machine learning techniques can help to reduce the risk in the elderly. Predictive algorithms can help identify people at risk by identifying their symptoms. Using research (do Nascimento et al., 2022), reducing mobility in the elderly has a significant role in causing their problems. Immobility causes overweight, bone changes, and the inability to bend or lift the elderly. According to the studies, the age of people can also help in early diagnosis. It seems that by combining several learning machine algorithms, a higher percentage of people with physical injuries can be identified early and help their health and longevity.

AI and Cognitive Science

Cognitive science can help to diagnose the condition of the elderly. The connection between cognitive science and linguistics can help improve the quality of life of the elderly. Elderly people who have difficulty speaking and lack speech can use smart devices to accurately express their feelings and needs. Artificial intelligence programs that use voice processing can help to understand the needs of the elderly by recording the voice of the elderly and processing speech errors correctly. Semantics can lead to a correct understanding of a person's content along with voice processing. The use of semantic algorithms reduces cognitive errors and helps to improve the levels of their abilities.

Designing and implementing artificial emotional intelligence is a complex process. It should be done by studying neuroscience and processing brain function (Uden & Guan, 2022). Cognitive sciences in this field can also help to achieve the desired results. At present, the discussion of cognitive sciences and human brain processing is accompanied by extensive studies. A new perspective on artificial intelligence is opened by studying artificial intelligence and artificial brain processing. Artificial neuroscience must be able to understand semantics. Although this process may seem very complex, it will revolutionize artificial intelligence.

Exercises and activities that promote relaxation of the mind can play an important role in reducing depression in the elderly (Yuniartika et al, 2022). In smart homes, by detecting the elderly in a timely manner, techniques that create peace of mind can be used. Learning applications help to educate people to decrease stress and depression.

In Samosir et al. (2022), it is examined the impact of the disease base on sex. According to statistics, the mental health of each person varies according to whether they are male or female in each age group. This result can be significant in the case of designing smart applications. Also, the gender of the elderly is also considered. The use of artificial intelligence technologies in smart homes should be different according to the gender criteria of each elderly person. Therefore, in all conditions, the clustering technique should be used. Clustering algorithms help to classify people based on several criteria. Different criteria in each age group with different gender of each person get different results.

Deep neural networks can also help diagnose mental disorders or mental health in the elderly. It is diagnosed by a person's emotional health by using this algorithm (Fei et al., 2022). Deep neural algorithms help to diagnose facial expressions and body movements. By changing the organs of the body, the level of emotional intelligence can be determined.

In (Cai, 2022), it is discussed the impact of social participation on the cognitive abilities of older people. It is discussed the fact that social participation can have different effects on cognitive issues in different age groups. The elderly refuse to be present in the community due to their physical and mental problems. Their non-participation can cause disorders in their speech and hearing systems and psychological problems. Examining different criteria and factors can help to solve this problem. Using intelligent methods or artificial intelligence hardware that can help to treat their disorders increases social vitality in the elderly and improves their quality of life.

AI, EQ, AND CORONA-VIRUS

Corona-virus had many negative effects on the living system of people all over the world. Quarantine caused economic, scientific, cultural, and educational crises in societies. Cultural and educational problems reduced social interactions between individuals. Each age group was affected according to its specific circumstances. The elderly were more vulnerable due to the severe decline in social communication as well as the inability to use smartphones to communicate online socially (Martins Van Jaarsveld, 2020). These injuries will continue for a long time.

As the risk of corona-virus disease decreases, it is continued to see a decrease in social interactions and psychological damage to individuals. In this regard, serious solutions must be identified to eliminate these injuries. With the decline of social communication, the emotional intelligence of the elderly has also been affected. The inability to communicate, lack of self-confidence and frustration, and fear of loneliness are issues that arose for the elderly in this crisis.

According to the study of spiritual well-being on the standard of living of people in the days of Corona (Baykal et al., 2022), it can be concluded that people who have a higher level of spirituality than other people are less likely to suffer from mental crises. A high spiritual level can be achieved by having a strong sense of creation as well as by performing meditation movements. Now that this issue has been addressed, more serious decisions can be made to prevent future crises. By using advanced deep learning applications and intelligence software, it can help to raise the level of the spiritual well-being of individuals. Given that the elderly are also at risk, applications should be designed in such a way as to increase the level of the spiritual health of the elderly.

As discussed in the use of artificial intelligence tools and applications in the management and control of emotional intelligence, an important point is also examined in (Morales Rodríguez et al., 2020). This is a negative impact of smartphones on emotional intelligence. In fact, it is discussed the use of intelligent tools to manage emotional intelligence in different situations and argued that the use of machine learning algorithms can control emotional intelligence in different places and times, including fear and lack of self-confidence and isolation is there to help. But it must also be seriously considered that these days, smartphones alone have caused isolation among different people in society. Social communication occurs through social networks, and especially in the Corona pandemic, social communication was limited to voice and video calls on social networks and distance learning. Therefore, there is coordination and management between these two issues. People should be divided into different age groups, and for each age group, a different emotional intelligence control program should be designed through smartphones. Young people and students who use social networks more should simultaneously control and manage emotional intelligence and control the use of social networks. Elderly people who use fewer smart tools due to a lack of interest in social networks and a lack of interest in smartphones should use other techniques to create social interactions and increase emotional intelligence. Designing smart devices that do not require direct use by the elderly can be a good option for this age group. Using voice processing and signal processing of the elderly, as well as semantics processing the movements of the elderly, can provide various training to prevent the reduction of emotional intelligence in the elderly.

In addition to these issues that should be considered, mobile addiction is a topic of study. Mobile addiction is caused by the isolation and loneliness of people in the modern world. Not having access to social networks for a few hours' causes fear and apprehension among people. This can affect emotional intelligence. People who spend many hours a day on social media are more vulnerable. Lack of internet connection endangers the mental health of these people. Momentary stress causes serious damage to the health of the mind and body. Investigating this issue is very complicated. Encouraging people to reduce their use of social media and news, as well as encouraging people to use smartphones, as well as designing smart apps for the well-being of people's lives are conflicting issues. It seems that providing solutions for the proper use of smartphones in a way that does not cause addiction to mobile phones are important issues that should be considered in the design of smart applications. All the mentioned challenges can be explained for each age group. Each age group has different challenges in Internet addiction according to their circumstances. Elderly people also need smart applications due to their high need to control health issues. Therefore, providing a solution to increase their emotional intelligence along with managing them for mobile addiction are challenging issues that should be studied with clustering algorithms and deep learning.

AI, EQ, AND SPEECH RECOGNITION

Speaking is an important part of communication. Designing and implementing programs that can cover communication using speech emotion recognition is an important turning point for dialogue between people. It is designed and implements a speech recognition system (Stavrianos et al., 2022). This system is designed to communicate between the patient and the doctor. This pattern can also be used to communicate between the elderly and other age groups. Using machine learning in this template can help to accurately identify communications and information.

By designing a multidimensional system, the elderly are helped to automatically recognize their different emotions. All six emotions, which include disgust, anger, fear, joy, sadness, and surprise, are defined as different situations, and automatic voice and video recognition in the system can help the elderly (Sreevidya et al., 2022). This system can help the elderly to diagnose and control emotional intelligence because it includes all the senses in a multidimensional way. Data clustering, which includes different senses and audio and visual abilities of the elderly, can play a significant role in the implementation of the program. Combining different patterns of signal processing and audio and video processing with machine learning patterns can provide a good system for the elderly.

Also, convolutional neural networks (CNN) have been used to detect sound and images. Image processing can help identify facial expressions in the elderly. Recognizing emotions using face image processing results makes it more accurate to recognize emotions. Each emotion can be placed in different layers. It seems that by designing a multi-layered model, it is possible to identify and classify different situations and needs of each elderly person in different situations according to different emotions. This model can be a good start for designing and implementing an accurate model. Recognizing the needs of each elderly person using facial expressions helps to improve their quality of life. Eye movement can estimate the needs of each person in different situations. A wider multi-layered pattern is designed by moving the eye along with different facial expressions.

AI, EQ, AND RELATIONSHIP

Emotional intimacy and emotional arousal between people is one of the potential pleasures that cause sexual experience between people. Natural emotions trigger emotional conversations and then conversations and sexual activity. Emotional intelligence can be examined in this field. It is a questionable issue if having a high emotional intelligence among people causes intimacy and sexual activity among people or not. Emotional intelligence evokes strong emotions. These emotions, if not properly controlled, can lead to emotional emotions that may lead to abnormalities in society. In any case, the elderly, because of the experience of these feelings of intimacy and sex that they had, should be able to respond to this need in old age. Understanding their needs correctly using emotional intelligence can help them to have this experience in old age.

Using artificial robots or artificial dolls can provoke emotional emotions. These days, the proliferation of artificial dolls has led to different experiences of emotional emotions among people (Belk, 2022).

With the spread of artificial dolls, artificial emotions will become popular and a new branch of emotional intelligence called artificial emotional intelligence will be created. Relationships between artificial dolls and robots with humans cause changes and challenges. If human desire and the relationship between human emotional intelligence and artificial dolls increase, it will reduce human emotional relationships with humans. In this situation, there is a fundamental change in the definition of different types of intelligence. To take a closer look at this issue, it is needed to look at a lot of information about human emotional intelligence when communicating emotionally with robots and dolls. Facial expressions should be examined using machine learning patterns. A challenging topic that may be explored in the coming decades is the study of emotional intelligence in dolls and artificial robots. Robots can be designed that can use machine learning to understand and analyze data and test their emotional intelligence in different situations. This is a challenging issue; however, it may be a little worrying for communities and human relationships. Communication between humans decreases and each human makes meaningful connections with a robot. So it must be likely that emotional intelligence will undergo a major transformation. The definition of emotional intelligence changes and is divided into different branches. The meaning of communication changes and the emotions between robots and humans change. The advantages and disadvantages of this challenge must be considered. Deep learning patterns will change, and it will faced a great challenge in terms of communication. This will happen in the coming decades. Semantic patterns will change in relation to human-human and human-robot and robot-robot.

Elderly people with different emotional intelligence have different conditions than other people. Implementing artificial emotional intelligence for the elderly will make changes in their lifestyle. Designing artificial dolls that can arouse their emotional intelligence makes them feel lonely away from the elderly. Also, artificial dolls designed by machine learning and semantics in different situations can help the elderly in their health. Taking medicine is one of the important points that the elderly forget when they are alone. Determining the time of taking medicine by using dolls and artificial robots can help the elderly.

Making decisions using emotional intelligence will help seniors do their jobs. Elderly people make poor decisions because of reduced brain function or Alzheimer's or other factors. Artificial intelligence can make decisions by analyzing the situation of the elderly who suffer from mental isolation. Management of this decision is by combining machine learning patterns and clustering of the brain and neuroscience. Introducing semantic algorithms in linguistics can help in speech recognition. Elderly people with speech disorders can achieve a comfortable lifestyle by designing linguistic robots.

The elderly may not be able to communicate well with artificial emotional devices. They see this as a violation of their privacy. Therefore, in order to use intelligent emotional tools, it is necessary to use linguistic models that understand the speech of the elderly and find out whether the elderly are in a good mental condition or not. Linguistics can interpret a person's speech. If the speech change is positive, it indicates that the elderly tend to communicate with the emotional robot. If the change in speech style has a negative result, the robot should have a better choice in making decisions by controlling artificial emotional intelligence and correct diagnosis.

In (Goda et al., 2020), it examined the differences between communication in the elderly with cognitive impairment and the normal elderly. The study found that the elderly with cognitive impairment were poor at making decisions and communicating with robots. According to the results of this study, it seems that the use of graph algorithms should be applied in the division of the elderly. Identifying the differences between the elderly based on the differences can present an intelligent program suitable for each elderly person. Routing algorithms can also be used to find the shortest way to reach the goal with the best performance. Graphs techniques can improve the diagnosis of each elderly person according to their different lifestyle. Each path has different results. By reviewing and analyzing the results, the best path is determined. Based on the best path, special smarts applications are designed for them. All these efforts are to achieve the well-being of life for these people.

The important point presented in the (Alloghani et al., 2022) is about the risk of privacy and data security, as well as the correct criterion in clarifying legal issues in terms of communication between smart devices and individuals. Statistics and information about their privacy should be used in machine learning processes as well as image and audio processes to obtain results on patients' conditions and ways to improve them. The issue of data security, if carefully and transparently addressed in applications and robots, can encourage older people to work together to more use smart tools like smartphones.

The (Abdollahi et al., 2022) examines the social robot. The robot communicates with the elderly in both empathetic and non-empathetic ways. The results of the study showed that the empathetic robot was able to reduce the rate of depression among the elderly. Talking and showing emotion on the robot's face, which includes showing a smile or eye movement, can create a positive feeling in the elderly. This feeling causes no isolation and the feeling of rejection away from the elderly. It can increase life expectancy. An issue that should be considered in the development of a social empathetic robot is the feeling of greater understanding of the elderly. Recognizing the facial expressions of the elderly by an empathetic robot can change the type of conversation between them. The empathetic robot must be able to change the shape of its face according to the position and behavior of the elderly person. With this technique, a strong feeling is created between the robot and the elderly, and the feeling of loneliness is significantly reduced. This issue of Ryan's perception of emotion should be explored. The limitation of using social robots is the lack of understanding of emotions and conversation. Cognitive science and speech science can help develop the Ryan robot (Abdollahi et al., 2022). The processing audio and video signals from the elderly in the robot's brain can deepen the conversation and increase the feeling of empathy.

Empathy creates a good feeling and a positive attitude. This feeling also causes self-care. Therefore, creating a positive attitude that results from empathy among the elderly also helps in their health care (Podhorecka et al., 2022). Empathy evokes emotional intelligence, and according to the explanations given in the previous articles, the stimulation of various intelligence causes vitality and avoidance of isolation.

A very interesting point that has been examined in (Zhang et al., 2022) is the analysis of the percentage of empathy with the physical elements. In this study, the role of using elements and their attractiveness using colors, etc. in creating strong empathy has been positively mentioned. According to these results, it can be pointed out that if intelligent applications and robots that are designed to create empathy use attractive colors, they will have a greater impact on meeting the need for empathy and creating a positive attitude in the elderly. In designing and producing video content for the elderly, the coloring technique can have a strong effect on creating empathy.

As the authors talked about empathy and its effect on positive feelings, it is also discussed the effect of social networks on sympathy. Social networks can increase sympathy (Albashrawi et al., 2022). According to (Zhang et al., 2022) which was about the effect of color on the feeling of empathy, it can be argued that the design of social networks and robots and applications with attractiveness also increase sympathy. This feeling increases the level of well-being more in the elderly. Learning machines can play an important role in this regard. Understanding the needs of the elderly using machine learning algorithms helps to better design smart applications. If the level of need of the elderly is measured at different times, designing a program that can strengthen the level of empathy and sympathy at the same time will be of great help to the elderly.

The research (Juncos-Rabadán & Iglesias, 1994) examines the effect of age on language decline. Elderly people suffer from erosive changes in their linguistic levels, such as phonology, morphology, lexicon, syntax and semantics, with dementia. These changes disrupt communication. This can lead to isolation and depression among them. This communication disorder causes communication problems between humans and robots and artificial dolls. It can be inferred that the elderly have lower emotional intelligence than the younger age group. Therefore, designing a system that can help the elderly increase their language level can have positive results.

Bilingualism plays an important role in reducing the damage of intellectual isolation (Nanchen et al., 2017). Studies show that people who are bilingual or interact with a second language are less likely to suffer from mental retardation. This can have a great effect on encouraging people to learn a second language. Older people who have learned a second language are more likely to communicate and less likely to be lonely. Educational applications can expand education according to different age conditions.

Studies in a specific age group and a specific area have shown that a group of people suffer from communication disorders (Konadath et al., 2017). The percentage of people with this problem varies according to their gender. This research can be a good start to investigating the exact cause of this communication disorder. Creating a happy atmosphere and creating a strong communication space by using smart applications or designing a smart city can make a significant difference in these people. By examining the changes made, other age groups, as well as other areas, can be examined. This study can be extended to identify and eliminate the cause of communication disorders.

An important point that can be continued in the discussion is to examine the difference between emotional intelligence among the elderly who naturally suffer from old age and mental isolation or the elderly who have suffered from physical disabilities from birth or due to injury during their lifetime. In fact, the two groups have different emotional intelligence. The study of the degree of mental isolation and the percentage of decreased libido between these two groups should be done with criteria related to each group. And certainly, the design of intelligent systems should be done for each age group with its own conditions. Clustering these groups of people with their own criteria requires big data algorithms. A strong database is needed to design and implement the desired algorithm. So it is likely that machine learning can reduce this amount of data. Learning algorithms can reduce large amounts of data in the first step. By recognizing the type of elderly person according to the initial condition, the learning machine eliminates a large number of criteria. In the following, the authors will examine this issue.

AI AND EQ IN THE DISABLED ELDERLY

About 15 percent of the world's population is reported to live with one or more debilitating diseases. Of these, approximately 46% of the elderly, including those 60 years of age and older, have a disability. The rate of this disability is from moderate to severe.

Indeed, the world's aging population and the increasing risk of disability in the elderly are leading to a further increase in the population affected by disability. Based on data from the World Population: 2015 Survey (United Nations, 2015), the number of older people has grown significantly in recent years in most countries and regions. According to forecasts, between 2015 and 2030, the number of people aged 60 or over in the world is estimated to be 56%. According to studies, the rate of disability increases among the elderly due to the accumulation of health risks throughout life - the presence of injury or chronic illness.

People with disabilities face various obstacles, including environmental factors. Which makes them less involved in all aspects of life? Older people have the most vulnerable people in the community. To improve the quality of life of this group of people, solutions must be provided so that a significant percentage of people in the world are not deprived of the right to life. These days, smart devices can play a significant role in improving the quality of life of the elderly with disabilities. Having conversations between them reduces the tendency to isolate. By designing smart grids, the vulnerability of these people can be significantly reduced.

People with disabilities may have an eye area or an imbalance in walking or an inability to hear, etc. They also have some problems in doing their daily chores such as bathing, toilet, dressing. Vulnerable or disabled people are cared for by health centers or disability homes. The people have their own special care due to the injuries they have. Different plans are made to improve the welfare of these people. The level of emotional intelligence in these people varies according to the level of harm they have. As mentioned in the previous topics, emotional intelligence includes fear, happiness, anger, and so on. Each person with a disability has more or less more than one specific emotional intelligence depending on their level of disability. An intelligent system that can control the level of emotional intelligence of these people can help to create welfare conditions for them. By controlling the emotional intelligence of vulnerable people, they can be informed about medical centers in situations where they need help. People with disabilities may physically harm themselves by changing their mental state due to their sense of exclusion from society. Prompt diagnosis of these people can prevent them from being harmed in a timely manner. People with disabilities who have difficulty walking are at greater risk. Detecting their physical movements using intelligent algorithms that control these people prevents the occurrence of the event.

Using neural network algorithms, it becomes easier to detect the movement of the human body and the speed of movement. Examination of the direction of movement of the human hip joint and the rate of change in physical position can be predicted (Foroutannia et al., 2022). By recognizing the initial position of the hip joint and the angle of movement of the limbs, it is possible to predict which next movement and direction of movement will go. Implementing an intelligent application that can instantly assess the human condition is a great help to people with disabilities. Predicting the movement of people and changing the angle of movement can help disabled people. If the change in movement is large, it can indicate the occurrence of a problem or landslide.

the machine learning algorithm can detect changes in the arteries (Hsiu et al., 2022). These changes indicate the presence of dementia in individuals. Pulse wave analysis using deep learning can help diagnose cognitive status. Changes in cognitive status cause changes in people's emotional intelligence. These changes, which are due to arterial changes in dementia, can be examined. Providing solutions in these situations can control the changes and help improve the individual's condition.

Mental disability is also one of the issues that can be investigated in the elderly with disabilities. Diagnosing a mental disability accurately is more difficult than diagnosing a physical disability. The type of physical disorder can be determined by a number of criteria in the speed of movement of the elderly person or the change in his body positioned. Diagnosing mental illness requires a more complex process. Diseases such as Alzheimer's or epilepsy or MS that have similar symptoms to dizziness may be more difficult to diagnose. Alzheimer's disease is a mental illness caused by a disorder in the nervous system.

Most people with Alzheimer's are elderly. Early diagnosis of this disease can improve a large number of patients. In (Gulapalli et al., 2022), the model has proposed to reduce the diagnosis of Alzheimer's in individuals and tries to work on speech-related signals based on the processing of speech signals. It seems that this algorithm can detect other diseases related to dementia such as Down syndrome and so on. Diagnosis of these mental illnesses can have a positive effect on the condition of patients with mental disorders. By making positive changes in the condition of the elderly, their emotional intelligence is stabilized and their quality of life is improved.

As mentioned in the description, in any case, the diagnosis of the type of disease should be done with powerful intelligent tools. There may be a percentage of error in diagnosing the exact type of disease in the elderly. It is hoped that studies and strong research can significantly improve people's lives with significant growth. Establishing social justice in the world is an important task that all organizations have a responsibility to do.

CONCLUSION

Changes in people's lifestyles also cause changes in people's physical and mental conditions. Helping to improve living conditions by using smart tools causes positive changes in people's lifestyles. Emotional intelligence is an important part of people's mental states, which includes different types of intelligence such as fear, anger, happiness, and so on. If emotional intelligence is well managed, it will prevent physical and mental injuries to people. Elderly people that constitute a large part of society may experience crisis and negative feelings in their lives for various reasons such as old age or physical or mental disorders caused by illness or aging. In this chapter, the researcher examined the living conditions of the elderly and the role of emotional intelligence in their quality of life. Emotional intelligence due to changes in people's living conditions should be managed using modern methods in people. The use of intelligent applications that are designed using deep learning patterns can detect their emotional intelligence in different situations where the elderly are, and offer special solutions in case of changes that cause negative changes.

Accurate diagnosis of physical and mental problems of the elderly using artificial intelligence models makes the emotional intelligence of people under control. The elderly can not control their emotional intelligence due to their special circumstances. Therefore, controlling emotional intelligence online using artificial intelligence applications can help the elderly. Introducing new solutions in designing intelligent methods helps to improve the quality of life of the elderly. The purpose of this study is to investigate the different living conditions of the elderly and also to investigate the causes of emotional intelligence in the elderly. The solutions provided help the smart application to play an effective role in controlling emotional intelligence in any situation of the elderly. Certainly controlling emotional intelligence creates personality (mental-physical) stability and therefore improves the living conditions of the elderly. It is suggested that authors and researchers in the future implement different sections of the chapter and analyze each section according to the specific circumstances of each elderly. Different parameters and variables can cause positive or negative changes on any algorithm. These changes can improve or weaken the performance of the application. Therefore, the implementation of the given opinions should be done carefully on the conditions of each age group.

REFERENCES

Abdollahi, H., Mahoor, M., Zandie, R., Sewierski, J., & Qualls, S. (2022). Artificial emotional intelligence in socially assistive robots for older adults: A pilot study. *IEEE Transactions on Affective Computing*, 1. doi:10.1109/TAFFC.2022.3143803

Ahmed, J., Ward, N., Otto, J., & McMahill, A. (2022). How does emotional intelligence predict driving behaviors among non-commercial drivers? *Transportation Research Part F: Traffic Psychology and Behaviour*, *85*, 38–46. doi:10.1016/j.trf.2021.12.013

Albashrawi, M., Yu, J., Binsawad, M., & Asiri, Y. (2022). Moving to Digital-Healthy Society: Empathy, Sympathy, and Wellbeing in Social Media. *Pacific Asia Journal of the Association for Information Systems*, *14*(2), 6.

Alloghani, M., Thron, C., & Subair, S. (2022). Cognitive Computing, Emotional Intelligence, and Artificial Intelligence in Healthcare. In *Artificial Intelligence for Data Science in Theory and Practice* (pp. 109–118). Springer. doi:10.1007/978-3-030-92245-0_5

Baykal, E. (2022). The Relationship Between Spiritual Well-Being and Life Satisfaction During COVID-19. In Handbook of Research on Interdisciplinary Perspectives on the Threats and Impacts of Pandemics (pp. 425-443). IGI Global.

Belk, R. (2022). Artificial Emotions and Love and Sex Doll Service Workers. *Journal of Service Research*. doi:10.1177/10946705211063692

Bruce, M. L., & Pearson, J. L. (2022). Designing an intervention to prevent suicide: PROSPECT (prevention of suicide in primary care elderly: collaborative trial). *Dialogues in Clinical Neuroscience*. PMID:22033641

Cai, S. (2022). Does social participation improve cognitive abilities of the elderly? *Journal of Population Economics*, *35*(2), 591–619. doi:10.100700148-020-00817-y

do Nascimento, C. F., de Moraes Batista, A. F., Duarte, Y. A. O., & Chiavegatto Filho, A. D. P. (2022). Early identification of older individuals at risk of mobility decline with machine learning. *Archives of Gerontology and Geriatrics*, *100*, 104625. doi:10.1016/j.archger.2022.104625 PMID:35085986

Fei, Z., Yang, E., Yu, L., Li, X., Zhou, H., & Zhou, W. (2022). A Novel deep neural network-based emotion analysis system for automatic detection of mild cognitive impairment in the elderly. *Neurocomputing*, *468*, 306–316. doi:10.1016/j.neucom.2021.10.038

Foroutannia, A., Akbarzadeh-T, M. R., & Akbarzadeh, A. (2022). A deep learning strategy for EMG-based joint position prediction in hip exoskeleton assistive robots. *Biomedical Signal Processing and Control*, *75*, 103557. doi:10.1016/j.bspc.2022.103557

Gadekallu, T. R., Srivastava, G., Liyanage, M., Iyapparaja, M., Chowdhary, C. L., Koppu, S., & Maddikunta, P. K. R. (2022). Hand gesture recognition based on a Harris hawks optimized convolution neural network. *Computers & Electrical Engineering*, *100*, 107836. doi:10.1016/j.compeleceng.2022.107836

Ganskaia, I., & Abaimov, S. (2022). *Before and After: Machine learning for perioperative patient care.* arXiv preprint arXiv:2201.08095.

Havaei, F., Ji, X. R., & Boamah, S. A. (2022). Workplace predictors of quality and safe patient care delivery among nurses using machine learning techniques. *Journal of Nursing Care Quality, 37*(2), 103–109. doi:10.1097/NCQ.0000000000000600 PMID:34593739

Goda, A., Shimura, T., Murata, S., Kodama, T., Nakano, H., & Ohsugi, H. (2020). Psychological and Neurophysiological Effects of Robot Assisted Activity in Elderly People With Cognitive Decline. *Gerontology & Geriatric Medicine, 6.* doi:10.1177/2333721420969601 PMID:33241078

Gulapalli, A. S., & Mittal, V. K. (2022). Detection of Alzheimer's Disease Through Speech Features and Machine Learning Classifiers. In *Intelligent Sustainable Systems* (pp. 627–639). Springer. doi:10.1007/978-981-16-6309-3_59

Hsiu, H., Lin, S. K., Weng, W. L., Hung, C. M., Chang, C. K., Lee, C. C., & Chen, C. T. (2022). Discrimination of the Cognitive Function of Community Subjects Using the Arterial Pulse Spectrum and Machine-Learning Analysis. *Sensors (Basel), 22*(3), 806. doi:10.339022030806 PMID:35161551

Juncos-Rabadán, O., & Iglesias, F. J. (1994). Decline in the elderly's language: Evidence from cross-linguistic data. *Journal of Neurolinguistics, 8*(3), 183–190. doi:10.1016/0911-6044(94)90025-6

Khosravi, M., & Hassani, F. (2022). From emotional intelligence to suicidality: A mediation analysis in patients with borderline personality disorder. *BMC Psychiatry, 22*(1), 1–11. doi:10.118612888-022-03891-6 PMID:35361178

Kim, J. Y., Liu, N., Tan, H. X., & Chu, C. H. (2017). Unobtrusive monitoring to detect depression for elderly with chronic illnesses. *IEEE Sensors Journal, 17*(17), 5694–5704. doi:10.1109/JSEN.2017.2729594

Kim, J., & Sohn, M. (2022). Graph Representation Learning-Based Early Depression Detection Framework in Smart Home Environments. *Sensors (Basel), 22*(4), 1545. doi:10.339022041545 PMID:35214446

Konadath, S., Chatni, S., Lakshmi, M. S., & Saini, J. K. (2017). Prevalence of communication disorders in a group of islands in India. *Clinical Epidemiology and Global Health, 5*(2), 79–86. doi:10.1016/j.cegh.2016.08.003

Martins Van Jaarsveld, G. (2020). The effects of COVID-19 among the elderly population: A case for closing the digital divide. *Frontiers in Psychiatry, 11,* 1211. doi:10.3389/fpsyt.2020.577427 PMID:33304283

Morales Rodríguez, F. M., Lozano, J. M. G., Linares Mingorance, P., & Pérez-Mármol, J. M. (2020). Influence of smartphone use on emotional, cognitive and educational dimensions in university students. *Sustainability, 12*(16), 6646. doi:10.3390u12166646

Morris, R. S., Tignanelli, C. J., deRoon-Cassini, T., Laud, P., & Sparapani, R. (2022). Improved prediction of older adult discharge after trauma using a novel machine learning paradigm. *The Journal of Surgical Research, 270,* 39–48. doi:10.1016/j.jss.2021.08.021 PMID:34628162

Mousavi, M., Parvin, S., Farid, F., Bahrainian, A., & Asghanejad Farid, A. (2016). Evaluation of emotional intelligence training efficiency aimed at improving the quality of life, reducing symptoms of anxiety and depression among the elderly in Tehran nursing home. *Journal of Fundamentals of Mental Health*, *18*(Special Issue), 520–526.

Najafpour, J., Keshmiri, F., Rahimi, S., Bigdeli, Z., Niloofar, P., & Homauni, A. (2020). Effect of emotional intelligence on the quality of nursing care from the perspectives of patients in educational hospitals. *Journal of Patient Safety & Quality Improvement*, *8*(1), 37–43.

Nanchen, G., Abutalebi, J., Assal, F., Manchon, M., Démonet, J. F., & Annoni, J. M. (2017). Second language performances in elderly bilinguals and individuals with dementia: The role of L2 immersion. *Journal of Neurolinguistics*, *43*, 49–58. doi:10.1016/j.jneuroling.2016.09.004

National Collaborating Centre for Mental Health. (2009). Borderline personality disorder: Treatment and management. British Psychological Society.

Podhorecka, M., Pyszora, A., Woźniewicz, A., Husejko, J., & Kędziora-Kornatowska, K. (2022). Empathy as a Factor Conditioning Attitudes towards the Elderly among Physiotherapists—Results from Poland. *International Journal of Environmental Research and Public Health*, *19*(7), 3994. doi:10.3390/ijerph19073994 PMID:35409677

Puspitasari, R., Budimansyah, D., Sapriya, S., & Rahmat, R. (2022, January). The Influence of Emotional Intelligence, Moral Intelligence and Intellectual Intelligence on Characters Caring for the Environmental School Students in the Perspective of Civic Education. In *Annual Civic Education Conference (ACEC 2021)* (pp. 343-348). Atlantis Press. 10.2991/assehr.k.220108.062

Samosir, F. J., Hulu, V. T., Julpa, A., & Sinurat, Y. T. (2022). Mental Health Exploration And Screening In Adults And Elderly Age Groups. *International Journal of Health and Pharmaceutical*, *2*(1), 29–35.

Saragadam, N., Koushmitha, S., Arun, Y. N. K., & Chowdhary, C. L. (2022). Data Protection Using Multiple Servers for Medical Supply Chain System. In *Innovative Supply Chain Management via Digitalization and Artificial Intelligence* (pp. 195–207). Springer. doi:10.1007/978-981-19-0240-6_11

Sreevidya, P., Veni, S., & Ramana Murthy, O. V. (2022). Elder emotion classification through multimodal fusion of intermediate layers and cross-modal transfer learning. *Signal, Image and Video Processing*, *16*(5), 1–8. doi:10.100711760-021-02079-x PMID:35069919

Stavrianos, P., Pavlopoulos, A., & Maglogiannis, I. (2022). Enabling Speech Emotional Intelligence as a Service in Homecare Platforms. In *Pervasive Healthcare* (pp. 119–144). Springer. doi:10.1007/978-3-030-77746-3_9

Uden, L., & Guan, S. (2022). Neuroscience and Artificial Intelligence. In Handbook of Research on New Investigations in Artificial Life, AI, and Machine Learning (pp. 212-241). IGI Global. doi:10.4018/978-1-7998-8686-0.ch009

Vaishnavi, K., Kamath, U. N., Rao, B. A., & Reddy, N. S. (2022). Predicting Mental Health Illness using Machine Learning Algorithms. *Journal of Physics: Conference Series*, *2161*(1), 012021. doi:10.1088/1742-6596/2161/1/012021

Yuniartika, W., Anwar, S., Kamil, A. R., & Herlinah, L. (2022). The effectiveness of yoga therapy to reduce the level of depression among elderly in the community. *Jurnal Ners dan Kebidanan Indonesia, 9*(4).

Walker, S. A., Double, K. S., Kunst, H., Zhang, M., & MacCann, C. (2022). Emotional intelligence and attachment in adulthood: A meta-analysis. *Personality and Individual Differences, 184*, 111174. doi:10.1016/j.paid.2021.111174

Zhang, J., Wen, X., & Whang, M. (2022). Empathy evaluation by the physical elements of the advertising. *Multimedia Tools and Applications, 81*(2), 2241–2257. doi:10.100711042-021-11637-x

Chapter 15
Deep Learning Methods for Modelling Emotional Intelligence

Neelu Khare
Vellore Institute of Technology, India

Brijendra Singh
ⓘ https://orcid.org/0000-0003-2608-3388
Vellore Institute of Technology, India

Munis Ahmed Rizvi
Vellore Institute of Technology, India

ABSTRACT

Machine learning and deep learning play a vital role in making smart decisions, especially with huge amounts of data. Identifying the emotional intelligence levels of individuals helps them to avoid superfluous problems in the workplace or in society. Emotions reflect the psychological state of a person or represent a quick (a few minutes or seconds) reactions to a stimulus. Emotions can be categorized on the basis of a person's feelings in a situation: positive, negative, and neutral. Emotional intelligence seeks attention from computer engineers and psychologists to work together to address EI. However, identifying human emotions through deep learning methods is still a challenging task in computer vision. This chapter investigates deep learning models for the recognition and assessment of emotional states with diverse emotional data such as speech and video streaming. Finally, the conclusion summarises the usefulness of DL methods in assessing human emotions. It helps future researchers carry out their work in the field of deep learning-based emotional artificial intelligence.

INTRODUCTION

The term Emotional Intelligence (EI) is referred to as the capability to distinguish emotions, to recognize

DOI: 10.4018/978-1-6684-5673-6.ch015

Figure 1. Components of Emotional intelligence

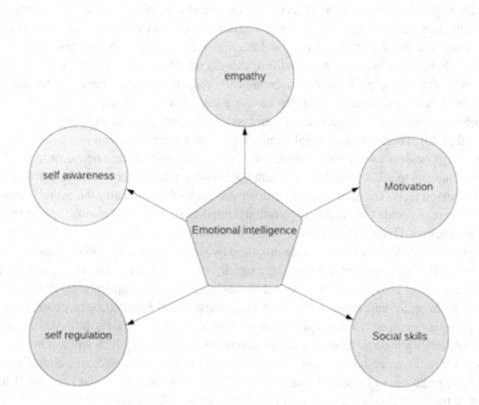

the context of emotion and its associations with the behaviour and expression of the person. Determining the cause of emotions, and interpreting the problem can be solved on basis of the determining emotions. EI considers perceiving the observation of emotion, relating emotion-associated thoughts, interpreting, deriving the motive behind emotions, and regulating emotions (Dollmat & Abdullah, 2021).

Emotional intelligence is defined as "the capacity to reason about emotions, and of emotions to enhance thinking. It includes the abilities to accurately perceive emotions, to access and generate emotions to assist thought, to understand emotions and emotional knowledge, and to reflectively regulate emotions to promote emotional and intellectual growth" (Mayer et al. 2004). Emotions are important because humans can communicate with people (Ekman et al., 2002). Facial expressions are crucial in identifying an individual's emotions. These expression talks a lot about an individual as it possesses diversities. Extracting the information from the facial expressions is not an easy task. Automated recognition of facial emotions using different sensor devices is very much required in various applications. Therefore, it is necessary to develop a system using artificial intelligence techniques which will capture human emotions and facial expressions effectively. Hence, it is an open challenge among the research community. Emotions can also be recognized using the voice of an individual using a device (Schuller et al. 2003). Deep learning-based train models can detect the voice of the person and predict the feeling of a person and his mental state.

Emotional programming is a field where engineers collect data related to different facial expressions, speech, and videos and identify and interpret the emotions of an individual in different situations. Further, the deep learning model is trained using the collected data to predict human emotions. These emotions help individuals to behave with others at their workplace and help humans to act intelligently to make healthy coordination with colleagues and friends. The most significant kind of natural human relationship involves emotion in a significant way. Emotional intelligence is used to process most aspects of human experience, including how we handle difficulties, express our feelings, and communicate with others. A person with emotional intelligence can communicate, empathize with others, and be both self- and socially aware. It has been demonstrated that having a high level of emotional intelligence helps students succeed academically, managers finish their tasks, and managers lead their teams more efficiently (Prentice et.al 2020). Therefore, emotional intelligence is important to human life.

Human beings possess two types of mind, one is emotional and another one is rational. A rational mind enables humans to think to make intelligent decisions. On the other hand, the emotional mind is about what a person feels. These two minds complement each other and carry the overall personality of a person. One cannot decide based on either a rational mind or an emotional mind. The challenge here is to incorporate these two bits of intelligence of mind to develop an intelligent system that reflects human behaviour. However, different definitions are proposed by various researchers in the literature (Alnuaim et al., 2022).Emotion Recognition is becoming a rapidly rising research field. The various application domains are exploiting emotion recognition techniques, such as game applications, health monitoring, and care, online shopping, and various online service applications like the cab, beauty care, home service, home appliance servicing, etc. Emotion plays a vital role in human life, it affects the psychological state of a person in a different situation. Emotions are a response to the stimulus which will last in a few minutes or seconds. As a result, a person, experiences feelings, and emotions, which can be classified into three labels: positive, negative, and neutral based on the feeling oneself in a particular situation (Lu, 2021)?

The rest of the book chapter is organized as follows: Section 2 depicts the overview of deep learning and its methods and their applicability in analyzing emotional intelligence. Different deep learning models, design, their implementation with results and discussions are described in Section 3.In Section 4, and conclusion is presented.

BACKGROUND

Deep Learning

Deep learning is a subsection of artificial intelligence that aims to enhance the accuracy and exploits data features and diverse algorithms to reflect the way humans learn and adapt things. It is based on the artificial neural network where multiple layers are used to process a huge amount of data and progressively extract potential features from the data.

A feed-forward neural network with more than three hidden layers is considered a deep neural network (DNN). Figure 2 illustrates the deep neural network architecture. DNN contains three layers, namely input, hidden, and output layers (Khare, N., Devan. Et.al 2020). The data can be fed through the input layer and processed via hidden layers to the output layer in the network. The number of input units in the input layer must be equal to the input features in the data. The next is the hidden layer, in a deep learning structure it is possible to include an additional hidden layer, which helps to handle diverse and high dimensional large, which leads to better convergence (Laddha et al., 2022; Sharma et al., 2022; Sharma & Kumar, 2022; Rautela et al., 2022). The hidden layer maps the input vector from the input

Figure 2. Deep Neural Network Architecture (Dollmat, K. S and Abdullah, N. A. 2021)

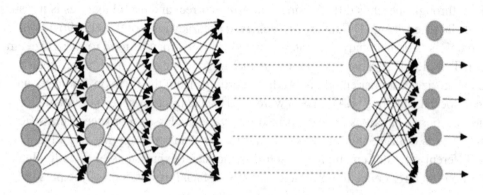

layer with some random weights, and bias which can be adjusted as learning progresses in the network. Similar to the input layer, the number of output units in the output layer must be equal to the number of classes present in the data.

Convolutional Neural Networks

CNN is a deep learning method also referred to as ConvNet, which will accept an image as an input, and assigns learning parameters to the objects of an image. It is majorly used in the image processing field for classifying images. CNN has less overhead of data pre-processing as compared to other types of classification algorithms. CNN has the capabilities to learn image characteristics on its own. The architecture of CNN is inspired by neurons of the brain as they can process and reprocess the huge amount of data by adjusting the weights and biases in the network. Spatial and temporal dependencies of the image are successfully captured by CNN with the help of relevant filters. The network is trained better to understand the image dataset and act accordingly. Different variations of CNN are available are LeNet, ZFNet, AlexNet, GoogleNet, and ResNet.

CNN extracts essential information from the image using multiple hidden layers. These layers are convolution, ReLu, pooling, and fully connected layers. The convolution layer extracts key features from the input image. Different filters are used in CNN to perform convolution operations. It will consider every image in the form of pixels. Each pixel in the image is coloured one and associated with some value. A convoluted feature matrix is computed from these pixel values of an image. Rectified linear unit (ReLu) comes into the picture once feature maps are extracted. This output of the convolution layers in the form of feature maps is passed to the next layer (ReLu) in the network. All negative values become zero after performing operations on each element. Therefore, the network was introduced with non-linearity and rectified feature map as an output. Hence, the original image is processed several times using ReLu and convolution layers to find the exact number of features from an input image. Further, dimensions of the feature maps are reduced using down-sampling operation and generate output as pooled featured map. Further, the flattening process is used to convert pooled feature maps to a long continuous linear vector. Finally, this flattened image is fed to the fully connected layer to perform the classification of images.

CNN is crucial in the identification of human emotions. There are several CNN-related apps available, but they don't always predict human emotions with great accuracy. CNN is used to determine an individual's emotions from their speech (Alnuaim, A. A et al. 2022). The challenge of recognizing human emotions through speech is difficult since choosing correct and useful features is not simple. The features were classified using 1D CNN, which achieved accuracy rates of 97.09%, 96.44%, and 83.33% for various datasets. Another study illustrated how hybrid CNN may be used to recognize emotions in speech (Puri, T et al. 2022). Three categories, including good, negative, and more specific emotions, are used to categorize customer emotions. Audio recordings from the Ryerson Audio-Visual Database of Emotional Speech and Song (RAVDESS) were used as a dataset for speech emotion detections. For classification purposes, emotions are categorized into various classes. For speech classification, two-dimensional CNN is utilized, and it produces better results than other approaches. CNN is capable of classifying different stages of emotions by capturing the facial expressions of an individual. It can be trained based on the huge collection of image datasets of facial expressions of the person in different situations.

Recurrent Neural Networks (RNNs)

RNN is a powerful, robust neural network algorithm that uses internal memory architecture. RNN is a bit old as compared to other algorithms and was developed in the 1980s. The need for processing relatively a huge amount of data which needs a huge computation power gives birth to LSTM in the 1990s depicts the need for RNNs as a base. Internal memory is the heart of RNN as they remember the exact input and are very accurate in predicting future events. It is usually preferred to analyse sequential data such as stock market, time series, weather, text, audio, and video data. Due to remembering past events deeply and sequentially, the RNN algorithm is more popular in predicting future events more accurately. It is derived from a feed-forward network and has the capabilities to remember past events. On the other hand, a simple feed-forward network was unable to remember past events and can't deal with sequential datasets, and worked only on the current inputs.

For understanding the working principle of RNN, we must know how the feed-forward network works. In this type of network, information is passed only in a single direction through input to hidden and hidden to output layers. Feed-forward networks are poor in predicting the future as they cannot remember the past information except how they are trained. On the other side, RNN works through a loop and feedback system. Decision-making is performed by considering the current input and also what the network has learned in its past like a human brain.

Usually, RNN has a short-term memory. However, LSTM has a long-term memory. We will try to understand with the help of an example. Suppose you have sequential data such as "2468" as an input to feed into the network. If you are feeding this information to the feed-forward network, it will read the numbers in the sequence as 2,4,6,8. By the time it will reach 8, it will forget about 2, 4, and 6 and be unable to predict the next number in the sequence. However, if this information is processed by RNN, it will remember the past information due to its internal memory. It remembers the output in the sequence before feeding the information across the next layers in the network. Hence, RNN has inputs based on the past and current. We should also note that RNN assigns the weights for current as well as previous inputs in the network.

RNN works as a sequence of neural networks which will assign the weights and train using the backpropagation process.

A recurrent neural network model is proposed to detect emotional intelligence based on different demographic variables (Prabha, R et al. 2022) . Recurrent models have an advantage over regression models when it comes to predicting EI using sociological factors because they can predict emotional intelligence with significant correlations in most of its dimensions. The proposed method provides a planning basis for addressing potential deficiencies in each group by estimating the level of EI in various groups based on demographics. Modern categorical emotion predictions are made in real-time using a Recurrent Neural Network (RNN) based emotion detection model that takes into account the conversation context and the individual party states. Real-time prediction capabilities, empirical evaluation, and two benchmark datasets are used to assess the performance of the proposed approach and model (Chamishka, S et al. 2022). The suggested method considerably outperformed current state-of-the-art models, reporting good accuracy rates for six fundamental emotions for the dataset.

Long Short-Term Memory (LSTM)

RNNs are extended further in terms of memory is called termed LSTM. Therefore, it is very good for remembering long past term information which has a long time gap in between. LSTM facilitates RNNs to memorize information for a long gap of time because it uses internal memory to keep the required information. LSTM can perform different operations in its memory like reading, writing, and deleting. It can learn over time and keeps the information that is needed for future prediction and forget the unnecessary information. LSTM works on the concept of three gates: input gate, output gate, and forget gate. These gates are important to figure out which information is needed or not. Forget gate will delete the information which is not needed and the output gate will impact the output at its current state. LSTM uses analog gates in terms of sigmoid, as they have a range from 0 to 1. Analog nature helps them to do the backpropagation process. The problem of vanishing gradient descent is rectified using the LSTM network as it keeps the gradient steep and low training time with boosted accuracy.

A study proposed a data selection, feature extraction, feature selection, and classification phased LSTM-based approach for emotion identification through EEG signals (Algarni, M wt al. 2022). This emotional model approach is useful to understand the unusual behaviour and diagnosis of psychiatric. Emotions are analysed through physiological signalling using a common pre-processed database. The dataset's wavelet characteristics, statistical features, and Hurst exponent were extracted. Feature selection task is performed using a Binary Gray Wolf Optimizer. The stacking bi-directional Long Short-Term Memory (Bi-LSTM) model was employed to identify human emotions during the categorization step. With an average accuracy for valence, arousal, and liking, the proposed methodology outperformed the methods employed in previous research work. It has demonstrated a strong performance for the emotion detection model using this approach.

Another study takes into account the categorization of three fundamental classes of emotions, namely positive, negative, and neutral, as well as the categorization of four negative classes of emotions using the genres of sadness, disgust, anger, and surprise (Sakalle, A et al. 2021). To identify emotions using EEG signals, this work introduces a long short-term memory deep learning (LSTM) network. This method's main objective is to evaluate the LSTM model's classification performance. Evaluation of human ehaviour across genders and age groups is the secondary objective. To compare the performance of different deep learning models for classification, we looked at multilayer perceptron (MLP), K-nearest Neighbors (KNN), Support Vector Machine (SVM), LIB-Support Vector Machine (LIB-SVM), and LSTM. The analysis reveals that, for four classes of emotions, the classification accuracy of the LSTM-based deep learning model is 83.12 percent, 86.94 percent, 91.67 percent, and 94.12 percent for cross-validations that are 50-50, 60-40, 70-30, and tenfold. According to 50-50, 60-40, 70-30, and 10-fold cross-validation, the classification accuracy for three classes of emotions is 81.33 percent, 85.41 percent, 89.44 percent, and 92.66 percent.

DEEP LEARNING METHODS FOR EMOTIONAL INTELLIGENCE

The topic of deep learning, a relatively new area of computer science, is the capacity of computers to learn without being explicitly programmed. Thanks to deep learning, a system may comprehend in terms of several class labels and learn from experience. In other words, machine learning is a system that enhances the efficiency and performance of a collection of domains via experience. Picture identification, character recognition, and weather forecasting are just a few of the numerous pattern recognition used for deep learning. Massive volumes of data can be analysed using machine learning (ML) to quickly spot relevant trends and patterns. By adding emotional intelligence to it, artificial intelligence can broaden its body of knowledge and provide new and more complex solutions.

This section presents an overlay of studies that will lead to illustrating the application of deep learning in emotional intelligence. Nowadays, Emotional intelligence (EI) introduced as a recent area of research to help and understand human perspective, which is beneficial to society. Rationally, it refers to the ability to recognize emotion's expression, recognition, adaption in thought process, and normalize emotions in individuals and with other people Mayer, J. et al. (2004). This will help the researchers or students by understanding and regulating emotion through emotional intelligence identification. The various existing methods are discussed here to explore the possibilities of standard DL algorithms for implementing various EI components. The methodologies described here state an increasing trend to apply DL on EI components, and Fuzzy based systems, Neural Networks, SVM, deep neural networks, evolutionary algorithms, and their combinations are recently used in emotional modelling which can be utilized to learn and develop models for emotional intelligence.

For developing a model for emotional intelligence, we should start by understanding the meaning of emotion and associated behavioural outcomes. Usually, it can be observed that emotions are directly reflected in the judgment of the inner state of the body and external state well through the expression of oneself. This supports us to retort rapidly to the atmosphere. In decision-making, there is a significant role of the perception of human intelligence which can be determined by the emotions of a person. Furthermore, the societal prospect of emotions is equally significant. Deep neural networks got recognition in every field and work efficiently with diverse and huge amounts of data even with real-time scenarios (Devan, P., & Khare, N. 2020). The authors presented the exploration of the emotion identification of audio and image visualization of expressions (Lu, X. 2021). An improved convolution neural network-Bi-directional Long Short-Term Memory (CNN-BiLSTM) technique is investigated. The simulation of the algorithm has been carried out to validate the performance of the model and the results of the simulation showed that the accuracy attained by the proposed CNN-BiLSTM algorithm is 98.75%.

The Deep Emotion Model

In this section, a deep emotion model is presented that explicates the emotion cycle through the proposed model as per the perspective of partner robots. The emotion model figures out the fact that robots can attain an understanding of humans. To empathize with the emotions of people, the robots should have their feelings. This may lead to the acceptance of robots in human life. The simulation results showed that the model demonstrated feasible conduct of the emotional behaviour.

The proposed computational model consists of three layers to present emotion: the first layer reacts bodily to stimuli extremely fast, the second layer accesses memories so that stimuli can be appraised via experiences, and the third layer predicts and acts in the future. These are inferred from the preceding implications.

Design and Implementation of the Emotion Model

This part presents the employment of the 3-layered deep emotion model as it is discussed above. The proposed design incorporates the RAM, LSTM, and DDPG Deep Neural Networks to implement the model, mainly at the first and third layers. The second layer deals with the management of the overall learning by applying a normal smoothing approach and maintains the emotional data repository to provide a support system to the other two layers. The following section describes the design and implementation of the 3-layer emotional model (Laz Hieida, C. et al. 2018).

The Appraisal Layer

The Appraisal layer responds to stimuli instantly through the body which is denoted as an exterior appraisal. This section expresses the body, i.e. interior appraisal which is irrespective of exterior expression. This layer explains the dependency of emotion on the body. Responses are programmed distinctly, they may lead to faults that may become the reason of the overfitting of stimuli.

The Emotional Memory Layer

To overcome the above-mentioned issue, the second layer the Emotional Memory layer is presented to provide storage features to the model to get the stimuli evaluated through know-how. Hence this layer is responsible to overwhelm the irrelevant responses and can respond to significant problems simultaneously. Therefore, the output of the appraisal layer, which is modulated by the emotional memory layer to be precise, can be considered as the perception of dimensionally reduced evaluated results of the external and internal worlds, i.e., internal representation. Hence, the results obtained by the appraisal layer can be referred to as interceptions.

The Decision-Making Layer

The third is Decision Making layer uses the output obtained by the appraisal layer and composes it with the input stimuli for underlying implication and estimation presented in Fig. 2. Then towards the prediction, decisions are obtained by applying input stimuli and underlying error in prediction. Finally, optimized decisions are obtained by the application of rewards on reinforcement learning in the third layer. In this emotion model, a controlling technique of the internal condition of the agent is exploited, which is referred to as "homeostasis". Here, the objective is not to keep the emotional condition constant by regulating homeostasis, whereas frequent changes in emotions are not preferred. The model signifies the regular changes in mean value as "mood". Further, the neural output sequences of the emotional phases are identified as emotional feelings. The emotion memory layer deposits experiences as periodic

Figure 3. Three-layer Deep emotion Model

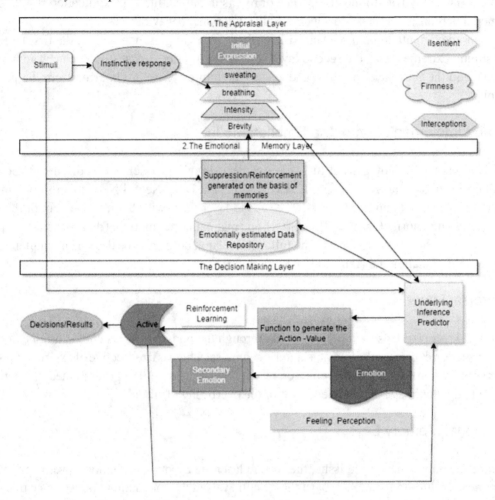

memories, then emotional assessment is carried out at this layer. It is necessary to mention here that the actual learning procedure is carried out at the second and third layers of the model.

Discussion

The first layer of the model determined a procedure to obtain valence values with arousal values using graphical stimuli exploiting the RAM. The first layer brought up some challenging results that are sub-stantiated the first layer is reasonable for obtaining man-kind instant response in contrast to the stimuli. Then decision-making is carried out by exploiting the second and third layers. The third layer is equipped with convolutional LSTM and DDPG to cope with continuous activities. It has resulted, in the agent being trained for a chosen smile and being capable to detect different emotions. At last, the complete model with all three layers is experimented with and analysed. It showed that the model including the second layer outperformed the model that was experimented with without a second layer. In the future, the model can be investigated for other critical tasks, such as implementing a robot in reality.

Skip-RNN Based Temporal Emotion Detection Model

Detection of emotion is getting progressive recognition due to its significance in interactions among people physically or virtually in real life. Various emotion models are developed for the identification of the emotional health of humans. The dimension-based emotion methods are getting important, using continuous values to estimate the kind of emotion and level of emotion (like arousal and valence) at regular intervals of time. The models the emotion by forming various subtle compositions of multiple emotional statuses. Moreover, the state of emotion can be referred to as a continuously growing and evenly process of changes regularly over time (Huang, J. et al. 2021).

To fulfil this instead of a single frame input a window consisting of continuous feature frames is introduced to provide an enhanced time series-based Feature frame model. The redundancy generated in frames can be controlled by applying frame skipping and time-based pooling. The model utilizes the skip-RNN to attain long-term time-based variations by skipping irrelevant features for streams of emotion identification.

Hence, while developing a condensed frame-level prediction for temporal emotion identification, it is critical to include long-term temporal context information. Two techniques that make use of long-term temporal contexts use parameter-level presentations and can learn long-term dependencies from short-term parameter presentations.

Method

This method involves the model which learns long-term temporal perspective data to increase the performance of the continuous emotion detection process. At the feature level, it pre-processes the features with a large window of consecutive frames to cover the temporal contexts. Additionally, a skip-RNN approach is utilized to target the more valuable information for modelling long sequences of continuous emotion detection.

Data Processing Step

At this step, the integration of four data processing approaches is used as a whole to treat temporal context at the feature level. The method uses a window containing concatenated feature frames from the past and the future in successive order of the emotional features to form input for the model. The inputs are represented as contexts created in the form of a stack of overlapping frames, whereas some contexts are created by frame skipping instead of overlapping. These methods lead to redundant emotional features in the window, which is taken care of by the application of temporal pooling to obtain the mean of the features despite using concatenation at this stage. The span of the window is considered a parameter for optimization.

Skip RNN Model

The skip RNN uses an input vector $y = (y_1, y_2 \ldots y_t)$ and obtain the sequence as an output vector) $z = (z_1, z_2 \ldots z_t)$ by application of parameter based state transition system I which consider states from t=1 to T:

Figure 4. Structure of skip-RNN at time stamp t

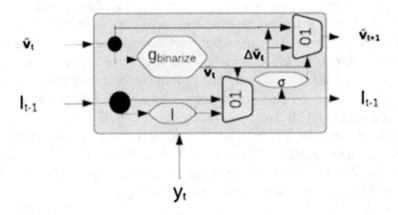

$$i_t = I\left(i_{n-1}, \ldots y_t\right)$$

The skip RNN updates the binary state through a gate, $v_t \hat{I} \{0,1\}$, when $v_t = 0$ the state of RNN is same as in previous time stamp and when $v_t = 1$ for updated state of the RNN. At any time stamp t the possibility of $v_{t+1} \hat{I} \{0,1\}$, is applicable for the update at t+1 is anticipated for RNN (Huang, J. et al. 2021). The characterisation of the final design is depicted in Fig 4 can be as follows:

$$v_t = g_{binarize}\left(\tilde{v}_t\right)$$

$$v_t = v_t.I\left(i_{t-1}, y_t\right) + \left(1 - v_t\right).I_{t-1}$$

$$\delta\tilde{v}_t = \sigma(M_p i_t + b_p)$$

$$\tilde{v}_{t+1} = v_t.\delta\tilde{v}_t + \left(1 - v_t\right).(\tilde{v}_t + \min(\delta\tilde{v}_t, 1 - \tilde{v}_t)$$

In the above equations, MP denotes a mass vector, bp is a directional bias, σ represent the sigmoid function, and $g_{binarize} \hat{I}[0,1]$ denotes a function to transform the input into binary value. Additionally, $g_{binarize}$ evaluates the step function, vt = round_off(vt), and its derivatives $\dfrac{dg_{binarize}}{dy} = 1$ during a reverse pass (Schuller, B. et al. 2003). Therefore, the model is capable of learning to minimize the objective loss function by applying backpropagation with no extra parameter involvement.

When a state update releases, the pre formation of the stat update gate will be done by incrementing the time stamp $v_t + 1$ by the value δv_t. Hence state update is reflected by setting $v_t = 1$ and whenever a skip of state update is there then v_t is clear; $v_t = 0$, that permits more efficient implementation of frames without performing any computations. Which in turn results in ignoring repeated computations due to the skip of frames, this makes the skip RNN to protect the important frames hidden across a long duration. The window segment-level audio features are figured ended a 4-s period, which in turn gave 88 features.

Results and Discussion

The (AVEC 2017) database is used to demonstrate the model's performance and the benefits of the presented method. The data set consists of natural person-person conversation which is a combined acoustic, graphical, and written text modalities. These are annotated time variant streams of combined data in the form of the emotional parameters, comprising arousal for the intense emotion and valence for the positive emotion.

The experimentation of the method is performed on AVEC 2017 database, which reveals the improved performance and advantages of using skip RNN. In this method, techniques for integrating long-term temporal context information for emotion sequence detection were presented (Huang, J. et al. 2021). It is observed that a longer window is needed to model the temporal emotional contexts. Further, improvement in the performance of skip LSTM can be done in the future and it is advisable to extend it to multimodal emotion fusion of temporal modelling.

The results revealed that the improved window length results in better performance, hence increased window length is essential to present the temporal emotional model. As per the result of experimentation, it is proved that the length of the valence window is more than the arousal, so, valence followed larger temporal contexts. Finally, it is observed that the visual features and the audio features are alike but visual features accord longer windows.

The experiments also showed that it is necessary to lighten the redundancy of feature frames of emotional contexts. The advantage of skip-LSTM is also exemplified to model the long-term temporal relevancies that skip the irrelevant information and concentrates on crucial emotional contexts. Hence, skip-LSTM models are more suitable to model continuous emotions consisting of complex states of emotions due to the critical contextual information.

Based on the results it can be concluded that the skip-LSTM leads to surprising results in continuous emotion identification. Further, with the application of skip-LSTM, the multi-modal temporal emotion fusion can be modelled.

Hybrid Prediction Models for the Identification of Temporal Emotional States

In this era, social media is providing an excellent means of interaction among users to convey their emotions focused on any real–life event or a topic, which resulted in a noteworthy contribution to effective public opinions (Çakıt, E., Karwowski, et. al 2020). Sentimental analysis is a method to bring up people's emotions and thoughts in the form of text that can be fed as input to a machine.

Since some social media groups can establish a combined phenomenon through their emotional states. Hence, an appropriate methodology is needed to carry out the analysis of Twitter messages, so they can impact social emotions. To understand the causal subtleties of social barometer facts, it is vital to predicting the upcoming reaction and emotional states of significant social groups. This study looked into the application of three supervised soft computing approaches for the prediction of emotional states expressed through the Twitter platform (Campos V et al., 2017):

(1)   FTS- Fuzzy Time Series-based prediction
(2)   ANN- FTS-based prediction, and
(3)   ANFIS -Adaptive Neuro-Fuzzy Inference systems.

Modelling

Forecasting demands a complete understanding of the system's inherent subtleties and also precise metrics of the real-time condition of the system. The basic subtleties of mood-related systems are unidentified, thus it is a must to estimate or interpret from evidence. Since, a tiny mistake in assessing the present emotion state value would grow exponentially over time, diminishing forecast accuracy, the inability to correctly measure the state of a nonlinear system is extremely important.

Results and Discussion

This study is conducted based on the LIWC pointers extracted from Twitter_ data, at regular time interval data points to carry out the analysis of emotion subtleties of the Manchester United Football Club (Campos V et al. 2017). This work used three soft computing models to investigate the subtleties of selected emotional states of people ('swear (anger)', 'negative emotions,' and 'positive emotions') as carried by Twitter data and to forecast future emotional states for a large social group. By relying solely on standard statistical approaches in social data analysis, one may be unable to completely comprehend and predict patterns in important transitions over some time and beyond a restricted time frame. To overcome present constraints in clarifying and identifying the early warning signals associated with big social datasets, soft computing techniques are an efficient solution.

Given the ambiguous nature of Twitter data, estimating the impact of socio-political acts based on emotional feelings has limited use. For big social groups' future emotional states and behaviour to be predicted, it is essential to comprehend the dynamics behind social barometer data. Using Twitter data, soft computing models were used to study the dynamics of three different human emotional states—"swear (anger)," "sad emotions," and "positive emotions"—and to forecast future emotional states for a big social group. One might not be able to fully understand the trends in social media data if they simply use approaches that have been used for a long time to evaluate data from social media. It's necessary to use soft computing methods to get over the existing limits in describing.

ANFIS model has the potential to outperform other soft computing approaches because of its adaptive learning ability. Soft computing methodologies have the potential to aid in social network and cultural domain analyses, address model imprecision, and uncertainty, and determine anomalous behaviour in the support of real-time social and emotional situational awareness for tactical decision-making and rapid socio-cultural assessment and training.

LSTM-Based Wireless Brainwave Driven System for Emotion Recognition

Emotions are an integral part of human life which make the person feel positive and negative in a situation, which may result in physical or psychological critical health issues. The proposed model uses a convenient brainwave-driven system to classify an emotion as positive, negative, or neutral emotion. Further negative emotion is divided into four subclasses: sad, hatred, annoyed and amazed. The model is designed to attain two main objectives; the first objective is the assessment of the classification metrics

Figure 5. Flow chart of hybrid ANFIS model for emotional intelligence

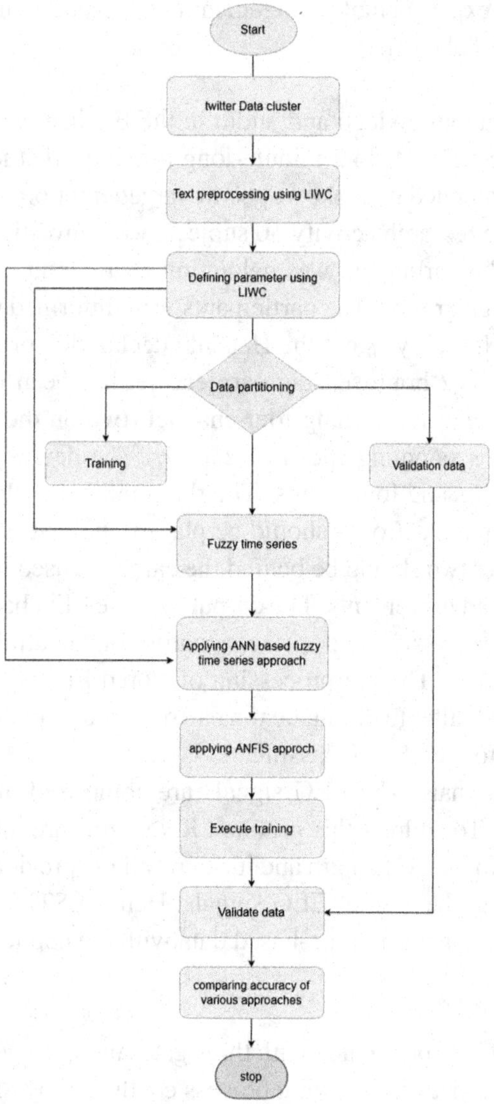

for the LSTM network used to conduct emotion recognition through ECG values. The second objective is the assessment of the behavioural patterns of people who belongs to distinct age, class, and gender. The model is tested with publically available ECG data sets DEEP and SEED, with self-reported feelings. The results showed the class of 18-25 years of age has come up with the largest number of emotion recognition. When it is observed concerning gender females are found to be high emotion active (Sakalle, A et al. 2021).

Method

The proposed model uses the experimental arrangement that includes stimuli, subject, device explanation, signal pre-processing, and classifier.

- Stimuli: movie clips containing video and audio in the English language are chosen that aid the subject to have real experience. 1- to 2-minute-long film clips that featured both independent and integrated information intended to evoke a specific target emotion.
- Subjects: to carry out the research activity 50 subjects were investigated out of the 25 were males and 25 were females. The participant was belonging to different cultures and educational backgrounds from different age groups. The participants were informed priory regarding cope and the process of carrying out the study as per the Helsinki declaration principle.
- Devices used: The MUSE 2 brain-sensing earpiece set has been used to record neuro-psychological signals. It is a brainwave reading four-channel (two on the forehead and two behind the ears) EEG headset with a sampling speed of 256 Hz. The device is equipped with seven EEG electrodes: three references and four inputs. The three reference electrodes are to be kept on the forehead and the four input electrodes should be placed, the first two at the left and right side of the forehead and the other two should be behind the ears. It is used to eliminate the noise from the data acquired through head movements. The output of these EEG bands is fed on the LSTM-based deep learning network for classifying positive, negative, and neutral emotions.
- Pre-processing EEG signals: The pre-processing of stored EEG signals is performed by passing through a regulating notch filter to eliminate the narrow bandwidth (45 to 64 Hz) signals. Then the rectified signals are fed to the LSTM classifier.
- Classification of EEG Signals: The EEG signals are comprised of long sequences, which cannot be learned by RNN. To address this problem RNN units are interchanged with LSTM units. LSTM will not respond to interval length and it can recall the previous values even after a gap, this feature is advantageous in the case of EEG signals. Hence LSTM network is a better choice for learning long-term dependencies in time-based data with the application of temporal correlations to obtain better results.

The LSTM network model is implemented with three gates input, forget and output gate. These gates are playing the main role in the decision-making process conducted by the LSTM network model. The forget gate initially helps in deciding which information should be stored and which should be rejected from the cell state, the finally sigmoid layer will carry out the decision.

Results and Discussion

This work reported the human emotion recognition system which processes brain wave signals using the LSTM network model. The LSTM model classifies the emotional states of subjects using brain wave evaluation. The system comprises four segments: elicitation segment, EEG data recording segment, feature reduction segment, and classification segment to obtain emotion class labels. Various experiments are carried out to validate the result obtained by the system and a comparative analysis with the existing methods is also done. The results proved that the proposed method performed better concerning the accuracy and the method is sound enough in the identification of various equivalent, distinguished emotions across the present state-of-the-art. Whereas the dataset is imbalanced, still the remembering capacity value is described in a way that the classifier is classifying the minority classes efficiently.

Analysis of Emotional Intelligence for Nurses

For students in a variety of topics or fields, including nursing students, the EI is associated with post-positive results. Higher academic achievement, better nursing leadership and practice performance, better patient safety, and better stress management are all related to higher EI. While there is a growing corpus of research on the emotional intelligence (EI) of nursing students, nothing has been done to track EI from the beginning to the end of the program (Just, M. A et al. 2017).

Design

Data is gathered four times over the study period, which spans from the start of the first year to the end of the first year, during which time students' emotional intelligence (EI) was tested using the Assessing Emotional Scale (AES).

The primary participants in the data collection were students who were enrolled in a PG in nursing (Foster, K., Fethney, J., et. al 2017). Dealing with complicated emotions is a part of the nursing profession. In addition to helping the patients process their trauma, they must cope with their trauma-related reactions. Emotional intelligence (EI) is essential for well-treated patients and workplace wellbeing because the work environment is generally high-pressure and stressful and demands a high level of EI.

Data Analysis

If there are any changes in the mean scores, the (LMM) Linear Mixed Model can be employed successfully to conduct the study. Since LMM enables the researchers to predict the correlations within specific data over time, it can be utilized for the repeated measure. It is possible to include additional covariates because LMM can handle datasets with numerous missing data points, it is chosen over ANOVA (Just, M. A et al. 2017).

The outcomes show that EI can progress while a student is enrolled in classes. It suggests that by enhancing nursing education, EI may be able to improve. But specific EI training can also be used to attain this outcome.

Speaker Emotions Detection using CNN for Human-Computer Interaction

Any human relationship depends on emotions, and the majority of real-time HCI systems rely on user input to make the system smarter. More complicated inputs are used by human-computer interaction systems, such as audio or spoken orders that include emotions. Numerous real-time applications rely on deriving the spoken words' emotions, yet due to a lack of balanced training data, emotion detection and categorization are challenging (Bang, J., Hur, T., Kim, et. al 2018). Lack of adequate knowledge of the necessary features is harming the procedures. As a result, the approaches cannot reliably identify emotions. In HCI, the field of emotion research is expanding quickly. The way a person behaves when their emotions are detected is determined by their feelings. It will enable the researchers to create a compelling human-computer interface for the system. A variety of users of human-computer interaction may benefit from spoken emotion recognition. For instance, a machine may react based on how the user is feeling. It is particularly crucial to investigate 1D CNN methods for tackling this issue when spoken orders are the main mode of communication (Alnuaim, A. A et al. 2022).

Dataset

The Basic Arabic Vocal Emotions Dataset, a collection of Arabic words recorded in.wav file in various emotional states, was used. The following ratings were given to seven different types of words: (0-like, 1-unlike, 2-this, 3-file, 4-good, 5- neutral, and 6-bad). Each phrase is said at one of three levels, each of which corresponds to a different feeling: 0 for a bad emotion (such as being fatigued), 1 for a neutral mood, and 2 for a pleasant emotion, which can be either positive or negative (happiness, joy, sadness, and anger).

The file also includes the following six descriptor sections:

(1) Speaker_id (int).
(2) Gender of the speaker (m or f).
(3) Speaker age(int).
(4) Word spoken (int from 0 to 6).
(5) Emotion spoken (int from 0 to 2).
(6) Record id(int).

The dataset contains 1935 recordings, recorded on 61 participants which included 45 men and 16 women (Alnuaim, A. A et al. 2022).

To develop a model for emotional recognition using a 1D convolution neural network and only five convolutional layers used in the model's architecture. To limit the number of parameters and eliminate the need for irrelevant data, they are connected via a max-pooling layer.

Results and Discussion

The model was built to pick up on the speaker's feelings. The model produced results for ER accuracy of 97.09% (BAVED), 96.44% (ANAD), and 83.33% (SAVEE), respectively (Alnuaim, A. A et al. 2022). It has been noted that adding additional speech units to the dataset might produce a classification model for speech emotion recognition that is substantially more successful. Utilizing programmable devices to detect human emotions from the speech is still a difficult problem since there are still mjor difficulties in understanding emotions because they vary by age, gender, and cultural variances.

SER research is becoming increasingly popular as a result of technological developments in emotional recognition because it helps us to create better user experiences and gives the system the ability to comprehend the varied emotional states of people in a much more thorough manner. Effective emotion detection is the cornerstone for assisting individuals in growing in emotional intelligence by assisting them in becoming more aware of their feelings.

Automated RNN model for Emotional Intelligence

The daily task of managing social or emotional situations heavily relies on emotional intelligence. EI is a term used to describe a collection of abilities, dispositions, and skills that affect how a person reacts to stress and environmental changes. One cannot constantly be conscious of their feelings or the various influences on their emotional state. Due to the aforementioned factors, artificial emotional intelligence, often known as emotion detection, is currently a growing study field. Artificial emotional intelligence (AI) can be applied to the decision-making process and becoming more prevalent in the healthcare industry to assist those who are experiencing anxiety or sadness. To extract the representations of the data, a potent learning technique is needed. For waveform extraction by emotional state assessment, a learning technique is also needed. Recurrent neural networks are capable of making high-precision predictions more effectively than linear models. To forecast a pattern that includes the EI and the following characteristics: age, gender, occupation, marital status, and education. The proposed RNN model makes it easier for people to recognize flaws in various EI states (Prabha, R et al. 2022).Training of the model is carried out by exploiting 1000 images over 600 faces, using Bio Vid Emo DB datasets to extract different subsets of faces and use each subset as a product.

Model

Face recognition is being explored using the deep learning methods:

1. Segmentation-based approach.
2. Region Proposal Networks (RPN)

Deep learning has outperformed other algorithmic approaches where models were developed using deep learning techniques and conventional computer vision techniques were used to retrieve features. Face segmentation has been demonstrated to be less effective than a regional proposal network. The face segmentation procedure involves determining whether or not each pixel in the image is a part of a face. Using a region proposal network, the model is specially trained to identify the precise region of the face. For emotion detection, an RNN model with one hidden layer and 15 connected bidirectional LSTMs was created. The dataset's shortest sequences, which start less than a minute after the input layer and have a predetermined size of 150 frame vectors, are used to extract the geometric features. 36 different vector sizes were used to reproduce the participant's face expression (Prabha, R et al. 2022).

Results and Discussion

The evaluation of the recurrent neural network with long short-term memory uses a hidden layer of 15 bidirectional LSTM with connected cells. In terms of two used features, the LSTM RNN performed better than the other machine learning techniques. This study reveals how well video features may be used to identify emotions, particularly outrage and disgust, which can be distinguished from one another. The suggested approach is useful for healthcare issues, particularly in psychiatric treatment facilities where it helps patients better comprehend their feelings and lessen their anxiety and sadness. These models can be utilized as an additional tool in the resolution of emotional problems.

CONCLUSION

To assist people for behavingappropriately in public, deep learning methods are crucial in understanding people's emotions. Emotional intelligence is crucial for people to communicate effectively in society. An individual's emotions might help them to perform wisely in daily activities. Other people can be informed about a person's health situation and able to comprehend the feelings underlying that person's concern with the help of emotional intelligence. The various deep learning techniques are investigated for determining emotional intelligence are presented from different emotional data environments. Detailed design with their implementation approaches are presented with results followed by discussions. Many emotional intelligence applications and their corresponding dataset descriptions and their impact on people's emotions are discussed. This chapter comprised with a required number of studies on deep learning potential to comprehend human emotions. In future the present techniques can be integrated to utilize their feature in combination and can also blend with optimization techniques to aid in the emotional intelligence field. Hence, the chapter presented emotional artificial intelligence by applications of deep learning techniques for the researchers to understand and apply the knowledge for carrying out their research in the field of emotional intelligence.

REFERENCES

Algarni, M., Saeed, F., Al-Hadhrami, T., Ghabban, F., & Al-Sarem, M. (2022). Deep Learning-Based Approach for Emotion Recognition Using Electroencephalography (EEG) Signals Using Bi-Directional Long Short-Term Memory (Bi-LSTM). *Sensors (Basel)*, *22*(8), 2976. doi:10.339022082976 PMID:35458962

Alnuaim, A. A., Zakariah, M., Alhadlaq, A., Shashidhar, C., Hatamleh, W. A., Tarazi, H., Shukla, P. K., & Ratna, R. (2022). Human-Computer Interaction with Detection of Speaker Emotions Using Convolution Neural Networks. *Computational Intelligence and Neuroscience*, *2022*, 2022. doi:10.1155/2022/7463091 PMID:35401731

Bang, J., Hur, T., Kim, D., Huynh-The, T., Lee, J., Han, Y., Banos, O., Kim, J.-I., & Lee, S. (2018). Adaptive data boosting technique for robust personalized speech emotion in emotionally-imbalanced small-sample environments. *Sensors (Basel)*, *18*(11), 3744. doi:10.339018113744 PMID:30400224

Çakıt, E., Karwowski, W., & Servi, L. (2020). Application of soft computing techniques for estimating emotional states expressed in Twitter® time series data. *Neural Computing & Applications*, *32*(8), 3535–3548. doi:10.100700521-019-04048-5

Campos, V., Jou, B., Giro-i-Nieto, X., Torres, J., & Chang, S. (2017). Skip RNN: learning to skip state updates in recurrent neural networks. ICLR.

Chamishka, S., Madhavi, I., Nawaratne, R., Alahakoon, D., De Silva, D., Chilamkurti, N., & Nanayakkara, V. (2022). A voice-based real-time emotion detection technique using recurrent neural network empowered feature modelling. *Multimedia Tools and Applications*, *81*(24), 1–22. doi:10.100711042-022-13363-4

Devan, P., & Khare, N. (2020). An efficient XGBoost–DNN-based classification model for network intrusion detection system. *Neural Computing & Applications*, *32*(16), 12499–12514. doi:10.100700521-020-04708-x

Dollmat, K. S., & Abdullah, N. A. (2021). Machine learning in emotional intelligence studies: A survey. *Behaviour & Information Technology*, 1–18.

Ekman, P., Friesen, W., & Hager, J. (2002). Facial Action Coding System: The Manual on CD ROM. A Human Face.

Foster, K., Fethney, J., McKenzie, H., Fisher, M., Harkness, E., & Kozlowski, D. (2017). Emotional intelligence increases over time: A longitudinal study of Australian pre-registration nursing students. *Nurse Education Today*, *55*, 65–70. doi:10.1016/j.nedt.2017.05.008 PMID:28528126

Huang, J., Liu, B., & Tao, J. (2021). Learning long-term temporal contexts using skip RNN for continuous emotion recognition. *Virtual Reality & Intelligent Hardware*, *3*(1), 55–64. doi:10.1016/j.vrih.2020.11.005

Just, M. A., Pan, L., Cherkassky, V. L., McMakin, D. L., Cha, C., Nock, M. K., & Brent, D. (2017). Machine learning of neural representations of suicide and emotion concepts identifies suicidal youth. *Nature Human Behaviour*, *1*(12), 911–919. doi:10.103841562-017-0234-y PMID:29367952

Khare, N., Devan, P., Chowdhary, C. L., Bhattacharya, S., Singh, G., Singh, S., & Yoon, B. (2020). SMO-DNN: Spider monkey optimization and deep neural network hybrid classifier model for intrusion detection. *Electronics (Basel)*, *9*(4), 692. doi:10.3390/electronics9040692

Laddha, S., Mnasri, S., Alghamdi, M., Kumar, V., Kaur, M., Alrashidi, M., Almuhaimeed, A., Alshehri, A., Alrowaily, M. A., & Alkhazi, I. (2022). COVID-19 Diagnosis and Classification Using Radiological Imaging and Deep Learning Techniques: A Comparative Study. *Diagnostics (Basel)*, *12*(8), 1880. doi:10.3390/diagnostics12081880 PMID:36010231

Laz Hieida, C., Horii, T., & Nagai, T. (2018). *Deep emotion: A computational model of emotion using deep neural networks.* arXiv preprint arXiv:1808.08447.

Lu, X. (2021). Deep learning based emotion recognition and visualization of figural representation. *Frontiers in Psychology*, 12. PMID:35069400

Mayer, J. D., Salovey, P., & Caruso, D. R. (2004). Emotional Intelligence: Theory, Findings, and Implications. *Psychological Inquiry*, *15*(3), 197–215. doi:10.120715327965pli1503_02

Prabha, R., Anandan, P., Sivarajeswari, S., Saravanakumar, C., & Babu, D. V. (2022, January). Design of an Automated Recurrent Neural Network for Emotional Intelligence Using Deep Neural Networks. In *2022 4th International Conference on Smart Systems and Inventive Technology (ICSSIT)* (pp. 1061-1067). IEEE. 10.1109/ICSSIT53264.2022.9716420

Prentice, C., Dominique Lopes, S., & Wang, X. (2020). Emotional intelligence or artificial intelligence– an employee perspective. *Journal of Hospitality Marketing & Management*, *29*(4), 377–403. doi:10.1080/19368623.2019.1647124

Puri, T., Soni, M., Dhiman, G., Ibrahim Khalaf, O., & Raza Khan, I. (2022). Detection of emotion of speech for RAVDESS audio using hybrid convolution neural network. *Journal of Healthcare Engineering*, *2022*, 2022. doi:10.1155/2022/8472947 PMID:35265307

Rautela, K., Kumar, D., & Kumar, V. (2022). Dual-modality synthetic mammogram construction for breast lesion detection using U-DARTS. *Biocybernetics and Biomedical Engineering*.

Sakalle, A., Tomar, P., Bhardwaj, H., Acharya, D., & Bhardwaj, A. (2021). A LSTM based deep learning network for recognizing emotions using wireless brainwave driven system. *Expert Systems with Applications, 173,* 114516. doi:10.1016/j.eswa.2020.114516

Schuller, B., Rigoll, G., & Lang, M. (2003, April). Hidden Markov model-based speech emotion recognition. In *2003 IEEE International Conference on Acoustics, Speech, and Signal Processing, 2003. Proceedings (ICASSP'03)* (Vol. 2). IEEE.

Sharma, J., Sharma, S., Kumar, V., Hussein, H. S., & Alshazly, H. (2022). Deepfakes Classification of Faces Using Convolutional Neural Networks. *Traitement du Signal, 39*(3).

Sharma, S., & Kumar, V. (2022). A Comprehensive Review on Multi-objective Optimization Techniques: Past, Present and Future. *Archives of Computational Methods in Engineering,* 1–29. doi:10.100711831-022-09778-9

Compilation of References

Abdelsalam, M. M., & Zahran, M. A. (2021). A Novel Approach of Diabetic Retinopathy Early Detection Based on Multifractal Geometry Analysis for OCTA Macular Images Using Support Vector Machine. *IEEE Access: Practical Innovations, Open Solutions, 9*, 22844–22858. doi:10.1109/ACCESS.2021.3054743

Abdolali, Shahroudnejad, Hareendranathan, Jaremko, Noga, & Punithakumar. (2020). *A systematic review on the role of artificial intelligence in sonographic diagnosis of thyroid cancer: Past, present and future.* CoRR abs/2006.05861.

Abdollahi, H., Mahoor, M., Zandie, R., Sewierski, J., & Qualls, S. (2022). Artificial emotional intelligence in socially assistive robots for older adults: A pilot study. *IEEE Transactions on Affective Computing, 1.* doi:10.1109/TAFFC.2022.3143803

Acharjya, D. P., & Chowdhary, C. L. (2018). Breast cancer detection using hybrid computational intelligence techniques. In *Handbook of Research on Emerging Perspectives on Healthcare Information Systems and Informatics* (pp. 251–280). IGI Global. doi:10.4018/978-1-5225-5460-8.ch011

Agrafioti, F., Hatzinakos, D., & Anderson, A. K. (2012). ECG Pattern Analysis for Emotion Detection. *IEEE Transactions on Affective Computing, 3*(1), 102–115. doi:10.1109/T-AFFC.2011.28

Ahmad, S. F., Alam, M. M., Rahmat, M., Mubarik, M. S., & Hyder, S. I. (2022). Academic and Administrative Role of Artificial Intelligence in Education. *Sustainability, 14*(3), 1101. doi:10.3390u14031101

Ahmed, J., Ward, N., Otto, J., & McMahill, A. (2022). How does emotional intelligence predict driving behaviors among non-commercial drivers? *Transportation Research Part F: Traffic Psychology and Behaviour, 85*, 38–46. doi:10.1016/j.trf.2021.12.013

Ahmed, Z. A., Aldhyani, T. H., Jadhav, M. E., Alzahrani, M. Y., Alzahrani, M. E., Althobaiti, M. M., Alassery, F., Alshaflut, A., Alzahrani, N. M., & Al-Madani, A. M. (2022). Facial Features Detection System To Identify Children With Autism Spectrum Disorder: Deep Learning Models. *Computational and Mathematical Methods in Medicine, 2022.* doi:10.1155/2022/3941049 PMID:35419082

Akinwalere, S. N., & Ivanov, V. (2022). Artificial Intelligence in Higher Education: Challenges and Opportunities. *Border Crossing, 12*(1), 1–15. doi:10.33182/bc.v12i1.2015

Al Faruqi, U. (2019). Future service in industry 5.0. *Jurnal Sistem Cerdas, 2*(1), 67–79. doi:10.37396/jsc.v2i1.21

Al Machot, F., Elmachot, A., Ali, M., Al Machot, E., & Kyamakya, K. (2019). A Deep-Learning Model for Subject-Independent Human Emotion Recognition Using Electrodermal Activity Sensors. *Sensors (Basel), 19*(7), 1659. doi:10.339019071659 PMID:30959956

Alam, M. M. (2009). The relationships between emotional intelligence and job satisfaction: Empirical findings from a higher education institution in Malaysia. *Journal of Health Care Professionals and Social Sciences, 5*(2), 124–139. doi:10.46745/ilma.jbs.2009.05.02.04

Alamsjah, F., & Asrol, M. (2021, December). Inter-island Logistics and the Role of an Agile Supply Chain to Achieve Supply Chain Performance: Initial Findings. In *2021 IEEE International Conference on Industrial Engineering and Engineering Management (IEEM)* (pp. 270-274). IEEE. 10.1109/IEEM50564.2021.9672866

Albashrawi, M., Yu, J., Binsawad, M., & Asiri, Y. (2022). Moving to Digital-Healthy Society: Empathy, Sympathy, and Wellbeing in Social Media. *Pacific Asia Journal of the Association for Information Systems*, *14*(2), 6.

Algarni, M., Saeed, F., Al-Hadhrami, T., Ghabban, F., & Al-Sarem, M. (2022). Deep Learning-Based Approach for Emotion Recognition Using Electroencephalography (EEG) Signals Using Bi-Directional Long Short-Term Memory (Bi-LSTM). *Sensors (Basel)*, *22*(8), 2976. doi:10.339022082976 PMID:35458962

Al-Hanawi, M. K., Khan, S. A., & Al-Borie, H. M. (2019). Healthcare human resource development in Saudi Arabia: Emerging challenges and opportunities - a critical review. *Public Health Reviews*, *40*(1), 1–16. doi:10.118640985-019-0112-4 PMID:30858991

Al-Kadi, M. I., Reaz, M. B. I., & Ali, M. A. M. (2013). Evolution of electroencephalogram signal analysis techniques during anesthesia. *Sensors (Basel)*, *13*(5), 6605–6635. doi:10.3390130506605 PMID:23686141

Alloghani, M., Thron, C., & Subair, S. (2022). Cognitive Computing, Emotional Intelligence, and Artificial Intelligence in Healthcare. In *Artificial Intelligence for Data Science in Theory and Practice* (pp. 109–118). Springer. doi:10.1007/978-3-030-92245-0_5

Alnuaim, A. A., Zakariah, M., Alhadlaq, A., Shashidhar, C., Hatamleh, W. A., Tarazi, H., Shukla, P. K., & Ratna, R. (2022). Human-Computer Interaction with Detection of Speaker Emotions Using Convolution Neural Networks. *Computational Intelligence and Neuroscience*, *2022*, 2022. doi:10.1155/2022/7463091 PMID:35401731

Alotaiby, T., Abd El-Samie, F. E., Alshebeili, S. A., & Ahmad, I. (2015). A review of channel selection algorithms for EEG signal processing. *EURASIP Journal on Advances in Signal Processing*, *2015*(1), 1–21. doi:10.118613634-015-0251-9

Al-Shweiki, J. (2021). *Re: Which Image resolution should I use for training for deep neural networks?* ResearchGate.

Alzayed, M. A., Miller, S. R., & McComb, C. (2022). Does Empathy Beget Creativity? Investigating the Role of Trait Empathy in Idea Generation and Selection. In *Design Computing and Cognition'20* (pp. 437–454). Springer. doi:10.1007/978-3-030-90625-2_26

Ameera, A., Saidatul, A., & Ibrahim, Z. (2019, June). Analysis of EEG spectrum bands using power spectral density for pleasure and displeasure state. *IOP Conference Series. Materials Science and Engineering*, *557*(1), 012030. doi:10.1088/1757-899X/557/1/012030

Anupam, A., Mohan, N. J., Sahoo, S., & Chakraborty, S. (2021). Preliminary Diagnosis of COVID-19 Based on Cough Sounds Using Machine Learning Algorithms. *2021 5th International Conference on Intelligent Computing and Control Systems (ICICCS)*, 1391–1397. 10.1109/ICICCS51141.2021.9432324

Aouani, H., & Ayed, Y. B. (2020). Speech emotion recognition with deep learning. *Procedia Computer Science*, *176*, 251–260. doi:10.1016/j.procs.2020.08.027

APTOS: Diabetic retinopathy detection kaggle. (2019). Https://Www.Kaggle.Com/c/Aptos2019-Blindness-Detection/Data

Araújo, T., Aresta, G., Mendonça, L., Penas, S., Maia, C., Carneiro, Â., Mendonça, A. M., & Campilho, A. (2020). Data augmentation for improving proliferative diabetic retinopathy detection in eye fundus images. *IEEE Access: Practical Innovations, Open Solutions*, *8*, 182462–182474. doi:10.1109/ACCESS.2020.3028960

Arnone, R., Cascio, M. I., & Parenti, I. (2019). The role of Emotional Intelligence in health care professionals' burnout. *European Journal of Public Health*, *29*(Supplement_4), ckz186–ckz553. doi:10.1093/eurpub/ckz186.553

Aslam, F., Aimin, W., Li, M., & Ur Rehman, K. (2020). Innovation in the era of IoT and industry 5.0: Absolute innovation management (AIM) framework. *Information (Basel)*, *11*(2), 1–24. doi:10.3390/info11020124

Aslam, S., & Ashraf, I. (2014). Data mining algorithms and their applications in education data mining. *International Journal (Toronto, Ont.)*, *2*(7).

Avola, D., Cinque, L., Fagioli, A., Filetti, S., Grani, G., & Rodolà, E. (2021). *Knowledge-Driven Learning via Experts Consult for Thyroid Nodule Classification*. ArXiv, abs/2005.14117.

Ayata, D., Yaslan, Y., & Kamasak, M. E. (2018). Emotion Based Music Recommendation System Using Wearable Physiological Sensors. *IEEE Transactions on Consumer Electronics*, *64*(2), 196–203. doi:10.1109/TCE.2018.2844736

Aziza, E. Z., el Amine, L. M., Mohamed, M., & Abdelhafid, B. (2019). Decision tree CART algorithm for diabetic retinopathy classification. *2019 6th International Conference on Image and Signal Processing and Their Applications (ISPA)*, 1–5.

Badrulhisham, N. A. S., & Mangshor, N. N. A. (2021, July). Emotion Recognition Using Convolutional Neural Network (CNN). *Journal of Physics: Conference Series*, *1962*(1), 012040. doi:10.1088/1742-6596/1962/1/012040

Bae, J., Kim, M., & Lim, J. S. (2020, October). Feature Extraction Model Based on Inception V3 to Distinguish Normal Heart Sound from Systolic Murmur. In *2020 International Conference on Information and Communication Technology Convergence (ICTC)* (pp. 460-463). IEEE. 10.1109/ICTC49870.2020.9289317

Baghcheghi, N., & Koohestani, H. R. (2022). The predictive role of a tendency toward mobile learning and emotional intelligence in Internet addiction in healthcare professional students. *Journal of Advances in Medical Education & Professionalism*, *10*(2), 113. PMID:35434145

Baker, D., & Salas, E. (1997). Team performance and assessment measurement: Theory, methods, and applications. Erlbaum.

Balakrishnan, S., Janet, J., & Rani, S. S. (2019). Symbiotic transformational technology on the rise: artificial intelligence in emotional intelligence. *CSI Communications Magazine, 43*, 14-17.

Bali, M. M., Kumalasani, M. P., & Yunilasari, D. (2022). Artificial Intelligence in Higher Education: Perspicacity Relation between Educators and Students. *Journal of Innovation in Educational and Cultural Research*, *3*(2), 146–152. doi:10.46843/jiecr.v3i2.88

Bang, J., Hur, T., Kim, D., Huynh-The, T., Lee, J., Han, Y., Banos, O., Kim, J.-I., & Lee, S. (2018). Adaptive data boosting technique for robust personalized speech emotion in emotionally-imbalanced small-sample environments. *Sensors (Basel)*, *18*(11), 3744. doi:10.339018113744 PMID:30400224

Baykal, E. (2022). The Relationship Between Spiritual Well-Being and Life Satisfaction During COVID-19. In Handbook of Research on Interdisciplinary Perspectives on the Threats and Impacts of Pandemics (pp. 425-443). IGI Global.

Bebarta, D. K., Das, T. K., Chowdhary, C. L., & Gao, X. Z. (2021). An intelligent hybrid system for forecasting stock and forex trading signals using optimized recurrent FLANN and case-based reasoning. *International Journal of Computational Intelligence Systems*, *14*(1), 1763–1772. doi:10.2991/ijcis.d.210601.001

Belk, R. (2022). Artificial Emotions and Love and Sex Doll Service Workers. *Journal of Service Research*. doi:10.1177/10946705211063692

Belyaev, S.A. (2021). Development of strategic development measures healthcare institutions. *Regional Bulletin, 1*(57), 5-7.

Bhardwaj, A., Gupta, A., Jain, P., Rani, A., & Yadav, J. (2015, February). Classification of human emotions from EEG signals using SVM and LDA Classifiers. In *2015 2nd International Conference on Signal Processing and Integrated Networks (SPIN)* (pp. 180-185). IEEE. 10.1109/SPIN.2015.7095376

Bhardwaj, C., Jain, S., & Sood, M. (2021). Transfer learning based robust automatic detection system for diabetic retinopathy grading. *Neural Computing & Applications*, *33*(20), 13999–14019. Advance online publication. doi:10.100700521-021-06042-2

Bhatkar, A. P., & Kharat, G. (2016). Diagnosis of Diabetic Retinopathy Using Principal Component Analysis (PCA). *International Conference on Smart Trends for Information Technology and Computer Communications*, 768–778. 10.1007/978-981-10-3433-6_92

Bhattacharya, S., Maddikunta, P. K., Pham, Q. V., Gadekallu, T. R., Chowdhary, C. L., Alazab, M., & ... . (2021). Deep learning and medical image processing for coronavirus (COVID-19) pandemic: A survey. *Sustainable Cities and Society*, *65*, 65. doi:10.1016/j.scs.2020.102589 PMID:33169099

Birks, Y., McKendree, J., & Watt, I. (2009). Emotional intelligence and perceived stress in healthcare students: A multi-institutional, multi-professional survey. *BMC Medical Education*, *9*(1), 1–8. doi:10.1186/1472-6920-9-61 PMID:19761603

Blair, K., Hansen, P., & Oehlberg, L. (2021, June). Participatory Art for Public Exploration of Algorithmic Decision-Making. In *Companion Publication of the 2021 ACM Designing Interactive Systems Conference* (pp. 23-26). 10.1145/3468002.3468235

Bolton, A., Goosen, L., & Kritzinger, E. (2021c). The Integration and Implementation of the Internet of Things Through Digital Transformation: Impact on Productivity and Innovation. In P. Tomar (Ed.), Integration and Implementation of the Internet of Things Through Cloud Computing (pp. 85-112). IGI Global.

Bolton, T., Goosen, L., & Kritzinger, E. (2020). Security Aspects of an Empirical Study into the Impact of Digital Transformation via Unified Communication and Collaboration Technologies on the Productivity and Innovation of a Global Automotive Enterprise. Communications in Computer and Information Science, 1166, 99-113.

Bolton, A. D., Goosen, L., & Kritzinger, E. (2021a). Unified Communication Technologies at a Global Automotive Organization. In M. Khosrow-Pour (Ed.), *Encyclopedia of Organizational Knowledge, Administration, and Technologies* (pp. 2592–2608). IGI Global. doi:10.4018/978-1-7998-3473-1.ch179

Bolton, A. D., Goosen, L., & Kritzinger, E. (2022a). Emerging Technologies for Innovation and Productivity Management in the Automotive Industry: Impact of Digital Transformation on Communication. In *Emerging Technologies for Innovation Management in the Software Industry (pp. 60-85)*. IGI Global. doi:10.4018/978-1-7998-9059-1.ch003

Bolton, A., Goosen, L., & Kritzinger, E. (2016). Enterprise Digitization Enablement Through Unified Communication and Collaboration. *Proceedings of the Annual Conference of the South African Institute of Computer Scientists and Information Technologists*. ACM. 10.1145/2987491.2987516

Bolton, A., Goosen, L., & Kritzinger, E. (2021b). An Empirical Study into the Impact on Innovation and Productivity Towards the Post-COVID-19 Era: Digital Transformation of an Automotive Enterprise. In L. C. Carvalho, L. Reis, & C. Silveira (Eds.), *Handbook of Research on Entrepreneurship, Innovation, Sustainability, and ICTs in the Post-COVID-19 Era* (pp. 133–159). IGI Global. doi:10.4018/978-1-7998-6776-0.ch007

Bolton, A., Goosen, L., & Kritzinger, E. (2022b). Challenges and Emerging Strategies for a Global Automotive Enterprise Towards a Post COVID-19 Era: The Impact of Digital Transformation. In *Challenges and Emerging Strategies for Global Networking Post-COVID-19 (pp. 76-109)*. IGI Global. doi:10.4018/978-1-7998-8856-7.ch005

Bong, S. Z., Murugappan, M., & Yaacob, S. (2012). Analysis of electrocardiogram (ECG) signals for human emotional stress classification. *Communications in Computer and Information Science, 330*, 198–205. doi:10.1007/978-3-642-35197-6_22

Borges, E., Fonseca, C., Baptista, P., Leite Queiros, C. M., & Baldonedo-Mosteiro, M. (2019). Compassion fatigue among nurses workingon an adultemergencyandurgent care unit. *Revista Latino-Americana de Enfermagem, 27*, e3175. doi:10.1590/1518-8345.2973.3175 PMID:31596410

Bota, P., Wang, C., Fred, A., & Silva, H. (2020). Emotion Assessment Using Feature Fusion and Decision Fusion Classification Based on Physiological Data: Are We There Yet? *Sensors (Basel), 20*(17), 4723. doi:10.339020174723 PMID:32825624

Boxall, P. F., Purcell, J., & Wright, P. (2007). The goals of HRM. In Oxford Handbook of Human Resource Management. Oxford University Press.

Bradley, M. M., & Lang, P. J. (1994). Measuring emotion: The self-assessment manikin and the semantic differential. *Journal of Behavior Therapy and Experimental Psychiatry, 25*(1), 49–59. doi:10.1016/0005-7916(94)90063-9 PMID:7962581

Branch, J. W., & Burgos, D. (2021). *Radical Solutions for Digital Transformation in Latin American Universities: Artificial Intelligence and Technology 4.0 in Higher Education.* Springer.

Breiman, L. (1996). Bagging predictors. *Machine Learning, 24*(2), 123–140. doi:10.1007/BF00058655

Breiman, L. (1996). Stacked regressions. *Machine Learning, 24*(1), 49–64. doi:10.1007/BF00117832

Britto, M., Fuller, S., Kaplan, H., Kotagal, U., Lannon, C., Margolis, P., Muething, S., Schoettker, P., & Seid, M. (2018). Using a network organisational architecture to support the development of Learning. *Healthcare Systems. BMJ Quality & Safety, 27*(11), 937–946. doi:10.1136/bmjqs-2017-007219 PMID:29438072

Bruce, M. L., & Pearson, J. L. (2022). Designing an intervention to prevent suicide: PROSPECT (prevention of suicide in primary care elderly: collaborative trial). *Dialogues in Clinical Neuroscience.* PMID:22033641

Buche, A., Chandak, D., & Zadgaonkar, A. (2013). *Opinion mining and analysis: a survey.* arXiv preprint arXiv:1307.3336.

Bulagang, A. F., Weng, N. G., Mountstephens, J., & Teo, J. (2020). A review of recent approaches for emotion classification using electrocardiography and electrodermography signals. *Informatics in Medicine Unlocked, 20*, 100363. doi:10.1016/j.imu.2020.100363

Burgund, E. D. (2021). Left Hemisphere Dominance for Negative Facial Expressions: The Influence of Task. *Frontiers in Human Neuroscience, 15*, 549. doi:10.3389/fnhum.2021.742018 PMID:34602999

Burns, M. (2018). *Digital Transformation In The Education Industry: 5 Trends.* Retrieved from https://www.digitalistmag.com/future-of-work/2018/05/10/5-digital-transformationtrends-in-education-industry-06164785

Businge, J., Openja, M., Kavaler, D., Bainomugisha, E., Khomh, F., & Filkov, V. (2019, February). Studying android app popularity by cross-linking github and google play store. In *2019 IEEE 26th International Conference on Software Analysis, Evolution and Reengineering (SANER)* (pp. 287-297). IEEE. 10.1109/SANER.2019.8667998

Buskila, Y., Bellot-Saez, A., & Morley, J. W. (2019). Generating brain waves, the power of astrocytes. *Frontiers in Neuroscience, 13*, 1125. doi:10.3389/fnins.2019.01125 PMID:31680846

Cai, S. (2022). Does social participation improve cognitive abilities of the elderly? *Journal of Population Economics, 35*(2), 591–619. doi:10.100700148-020-00817-y

Çakıt, E., Karwowski, W., & Servi, L. (2020). Application of soft computing techniques for estimating emotional states expressed in Twitter® time series data. *Neural Computing & Applications*, *32*(8), 3535–3548. doi:10.100700521-019-04048-5

Campos, V., Jou, B., Giro-i-Nieto, X., Torres, J., & Chang, S. (2017). Skip RNN: learning to skip state updates in recurrent neural networks. ICLR.

Cao, K., Xu, J., & Zhao, W.-Q. (2019). Artificial intelligence on diabetic retinopathy diagnosis: An automatic classification method based on grey level co-occurrence matrix and naive Bayesian model. *International Journal of Ophthalmology*, *12*(7), 1158–1162. doi:10.18240/ijo.2019.07.17 PMID:31341808

Cao, W., Czarnek, N., Shan, J., & Li, L. (2018). Microaneurysm detection using principal component analysis and machine learning methods. *IEEE Transactions on Nanobioscience*, *17*(3), 191–198. doi:10.1109/TNB.2018.2840084 PMID:29994317

Carrel, A. (2018). Legal intelligence through artificial intelligence requires emotional intelligence: A new competency model for the 21st century legal professional. *Ga. St. UL Rev*, *35*, 1153.

Cavus, N., Mohammed, Y. B., Gital, A. Y. U., Bulama, M., Tukur, A. M., Mohammed, D., Isah, M. L., & Hassan, A. (2022). Emotional Artificial Neural Networks and Gaussian Process-Regression-Based Hybrid Machine-Learning Model for Prediction of Security and Privacy Effects on M-Banking Attractiveness. *Sustainability*, *14*(10), 5826. doi:10.3390u14105826

Cekic, M., Bakiskan, C., & Madhow, U. (2022). *Neuro-Inspired Deep Neural Networks with Sparse, Strong Activations*. arXiv preprint arXiv:2202.13074.

Celani, G., Battacchi, M. W., & Arcidiacono, L. (1999). The understanding of the emotional meaning of facial expressions in people with autism. *Journal of Autism and Developmental Disorders*, *29*(1), 57–66. doi:10.1023/A:1025970600181 PMID:10097995

Chakrabarty, N. (2018). A deep learning method for the detection of diabetic retinopathy. *2018 5th IEEE Uttar Pradesh Section International Conference on Electrical, Electronics and Computer Engineering (UPCON)*, 1–5.

Chamishka, S., Madhavi, I., Nawaratne, R., Alahakoon, D., De Silva, D., Chilamkurti, N., & Nanayakkara, V. (2022). A voice-based real-time emotion detection technique using recurrent neural network empowered feature modelling. *Multimedia Tools and Applications*, *81*(24), 1–22. doi:10.100711042-022-13363-4

Chandrasekhar, U., & Chowdhary, C. L. (2013). Classification of ECG beats using features from two-stage two-band wavelet decomposition. *Journal of Theoretical and Applied Information Technology*, *49*(3), 922–928.

Channi, H. K., Shrivastava, P., & Chowdhary, C. L. (2022). Digital Transformation in Healthcare Industry: A Survey. In *Next Generation Healthcare Informatics* (pp. 279–293). Springer. doi:10.1007/978-981-19-2416-3_16

Chauhan, V. K., Dahiya, K., & Sharma, A. (2019). Problem formulations and solvers in linear SVM: A review. *Artificial Intelligence Review*, *52*(2), 803–855. doi:10.100710462-018-9614-6

Chen, X., Xie, H., Zou, D., & Hwang, G. J. (2020). Application and theory gaps during the rise of Artificial Intelligence in Education. *Computers and Education: Artificial Intelligence, 1*.

Chen, L., Chen, P., & Lin, Z. (2020). Artificial intelligence in education: A review. *Institute of Electrical and Electronics Engineers Access*, *8*, 75264–75278. doi:10.1109/ACCESS.2020.2988510

Chen, X., Zou, D., Xie, H., Cheng, G., & Liu, C. (2022). Two Decades of Artificial Intelligence in Education. *Journal of Educational Technology & Society*, *25*(1), 28–47.

Chen, Y., Chang, R., & Guo, J. (2021). Emotion Recognition of EEG Signals Based on the Ensemble Learning Method: AdaBoost. *Mathematical Problems in Engineering, 2021,* 2021. doi:10.1155/2021/8896062

Cherry, K. (2015). *Are people with high IQs more successful.* Retrieved from about education: http://psychology. about. com/od/intelligence/a/does-high-iq-equal-success. htm

Chi, J., Walia, E., Babyn, P., Wang, J., Groot, G., & Eramian, M. (2017). Thyroid Nodule Classification in Ultrasound Images by Fine-Tuning Deep Convolutional Neural Network. *Journal of Digital Imaging, 30*(4), 477–486. doi:10.100710278-017-9997-y PMID:28695342

Chowdhary, C. L. (2021). Simple Linear Iterative Clustering (SLIC) and Graph Theory-Based Image Segmentation. In Handbook of Research on Machine Learning Techniques for Pattern Recognition and Information Security (pp. 157-170). IGI Global.

Chowdhary, C. L., & Acharjya, D. P. (2018). Singular Value Decomposition–Principal Component Analysis-Based Object Recognition Approach. In Bio-Inspired Computing for Image and Video Processing (pp. 323-341). Chapman and Hall/CRC. doi:10.1201/9781315153797-12

Chowdhary, C. L., & Srivatsan, R. (2022). *Non-invasive Detection of Parkinson's Disease Using Deep Learning.* Academic Press.

Chowdhary, C. L., Darwish, A., & Hassanien, A. E. (2021). Cognitive Deep Learning: Future Direction in Intelligent Retrieval. In Research Anthology on Artificial Intelligence Applications in Security (pp. 2152-2163). IGI Global.

Chowdhary, C. L., Muatjitjeja, K., & Jat, D. S. (2015). *Proceedings of Emerging Trends in Networks and Computer Communications '15.* Academic Press.

Chowdhary, C. L. (2011). Linear feature extraction techniques for object recognition: Study of PCA and ICA. *Journal of the Serbian Society for Computational Mechanics, 5*(1), 19–26.

Chowdhary, C. L. (2022). Agile Supply Chain: Framework for Digitization. In *Innovative Supply Chain Management via Digitalization and Artificial Intelligence* (pp. 73–85). Springer. doi:10.1007/978-981-19-0240-6_5

Chowdhary, C. L., & Acharjya, D. P. (2016). A hybrid scheme for breast cancer detection using intuitionistic fuzzy rough set technique. *International Journal of Healthcare Information Systems and Informatics, 11*(2), 38–61. doi:10.4018/IJHISI.2016040103

Chowdhary, C. L., & Acharjya, D. P. (2017). Clustering algorithm in possibilistic exponential fuzzy C-mean segmenting medical images. In *Journal of Biomimetics, biomaterials and biomedical engineering* (Vol. 30, pp. 12–23). Trans Tech Publications Ltd. doi:10.4028/www.scientific.net/JBBBE.30.12

Chowdhary, C. L., & Acharjya, D. P. (2020). Segmentation and feature extraction in medical imaging: A systematic review. *Procedia Computer Science, 167,* 26–36. doi:10.1016/j.procs.2020.03.179

Chowdhary, C. L., Alazab, M., Chaudhary, A., Hakak, S., & Gadekallu, T. R. (2021). *Computer Vision and Recognition Systems Using Machine and Deep Learning Approaches: Fundamentals.* Technologies and Applications. Institution of Engineering and Technology.

Chowdhary, C. L., & Channi, H. K. (2022). Deep Learning Empowered Fight Against COVID-19: A Survey. In *Next Generation Healthcare Informatics* (pp. 251–264). Springer. doi:10.1007/978-981-19-2416-3_14

Chowdhary, C. L., Das, T. K., Gurani, V., & Ranjan, A. (2018). An improved tumour identification with gabor wavelet segmentation. *Research Journal of Pharmacy and Technology, 11*(8), 3451–3456. doi:10.5958/0974-360X.2018.00637.6

Chowdhary, C. L., Goyal, A., & Vasnani, B. K. (2019). Experimental assessment of beam search algorithm for improvement in image caption generation. *Journal of Applied Science and Engineering*, 22(4), 691–698.

Chowdhary, C. L., Khare, N., Patel, H., Koppu, S., Kaluri, R., & Rajput, D. S. (2022). Past, present and future of gene feature selection for breast cancer classification–a survey. *International Journal of Engineering Systems Modelling and Simulation*, 13(2), 140–153. doi:10.1504/IJESMS.2022.123355

Chowdhary, C. L., Mittal, M., Pattanaik, P. A., & Marszalek, Z. (2020). An efficient segmentation and classification system in medical images using intuitionist possibilistic fuzzy C-mean clustering and fuzzy SVM algorithm. *Sensors (Basel)*, 20(14), 3903. doi:10.339020143903 PMID:32668793

Chowdhary, C. L., Muatjitjeja, K., & Jat, D. S. (2015, May). Three-dimensional object recognition based intelligence system for identification. In *2015 International Conference on Emerging Trends in Networks and Computer Communications (ETNCC)* (pp. 162-166). IEEE. 10.1109/ETNCC.2015.7184827

Chowdhary, C. L., Patel, P. V., Kathrotia, K. J., Attique, M., Perumal, K., & Ijaz, M. F. (2020). Analytical study of hybrid techniques for image encryption and decryption. *Sensors (Basel)*, 20(18), 5162. doi:10.339020185162 PMID:32927714

Chowdhary, C. L., Sai, G. V. K., & Acharjya, D. P. (2016). Decreasing false assumption for improved breast cancer detection. *J. Sci. Arts*, 35(2), 157–176.

Chubarova, T.V. (2021). Effective healthcare as a condition for the reproduction of human potential: modern challenges for social policy. *Economic Security, 4*(3), 607–628.

Chumwatana, T. (2015). *Using sentiment analysis technique for analyzing Thai customer satisfaction from social media.* Academic Press.

Cohen, S. G., Ledford, G. Jr, & Spreitzer, G. (1996). A predictive model of self-managing work team effectiveness. *Human Relations*, 49(5), 643–676. doi:10.1177/001872679604900506

Courtiol, E., & Wilson, D. A. (2015). The olfactory thalamus: Unanswered questions about the role of the mediodorsal thalamic nucleus in olfaction. *Frontiers in Neural Circuits*, 9, 49. doi:10.3389/fncir.2015.00049 PMID:26441548

Cybenko, G. (1989). Approximation by superpositions of a sigmoidal function. *Mathematics of Control, Signals, and Systems*, 2(4), 303–314. doi:10.1007/BF02551274

Dar, M. N., Akram, M. U., Khawaja, S. G., & Pujari, A. N. (2020). CNN and LSTM-Based Emotion Charting Using Physiological Signals. *Sensors (Basel)*, 20(16), 4551. doi:10.339020164551 PMID:32823807

Das, T. K., Chowdhary, C. L., & Gao, X. Z. (2020). Chest X-ray investigation: a convolutional neural network approach. In Journal of Biomimetics, Biomaterials and Biomedical Engineering (Vol. 45, pp. 57-70). Trans Tech Publications Ltd.

Davy, A. (2003). *Components of a smart device and smart device interactions.* Telecommunications Software and Systems Group.

De Arriba Pérez, F., Santos-Gago, J. M., Caeiro-Rodríguez, M., & Fernández Iglesias, M. J. (2018). Evaluation of commercial-off-The-Shelf wrist wearables to estimate stress on students. *Journal of Visualized Experiments*, (136). Advance online publication. doi:10.3791/57590 PMID:29985338

Decenciere, E., Cazuguel, G., Zhang, X., Thibault, G., Klein, J.-C., Meyer, F., Marcotegui, B., Quellec, G., Lamard, M., Danno, R., Elie, D., Massin, P., Viktor, Z., Erginay, A., Laÿ, B., & Chabouis, A. (2013). TeleOphta: Machine learning and image processing methods for teleophthalmology. *IRBM*, 34(2), 196–203. doi:10.1016/j.irbm.2013.01.010

Decencière, E., Zhang, X., Cazuguel, G., Lay, B., Cochener, B., Trone, C., Gain, P., Ordonez, R., Massin, P., Erginay, A., Charton, B., & Klein, J.-C. (2014). Feedback on a publicly distributed image database: the messidor database. *Image Analysis & Stereology*, *33*(3), 231. doi:10.5566/ias.1155

Deshpande, A., Estrela, V. V., & Patavardhan, P. (2021). The DCT-CNN-ResNet50 architecture to classify brain tumors with super-resolution, convolutional neural network, and the ResNet50. *Neuroscience Informatics*, *1*(4), 100013. doi:10.1016/j.neuri.2021.100013

Dessai, A., & Virani, H. (2021). Emotion Detection Using Physiological Signals. *2021 International Conference on Electrical, Computer and Energy Technologies (ICECET)*, 1-4. 10.1109/ICECET52533.2021.9698729

Devan, P., & Khare, N. (2020). An efficient XGBoost–DNN-based classification model for network intrusion detection system. *Neural Computing & Applications*, *32*(16), 12499–12514. doi:10.100700521-020-04708-x

Devedžić, V. (2004). Web intelligence and artificial intelligence in education. *Journal of Educational Technology & Society*, *7*(4), 29–39.

do Nascimento, C. F., de Moraes Batista, A. F., Duarte, Y. A. O., & Chiavegatto Filho, A. D. P. (2022). Early identification of older individuals at risk of mobility decline with machine learning. *Archives of Gerontology and Geriatrics*, *100*, 104625. doi:10.1016/j.archger.2022.104625 PMID:35085986

Dollmat, K. S., & Abdullah, N. A. (2022). Machine learning in emotional intelligence studies: A survey. *Behaviour & Information Technology*, *41*(7), 1485–1502. doi:10.1080/0144929X.2021.1877356

Domínguez-Jiménez, J., Campo-Landines, K., Martínez-Santos, J., Delahoz, E., & Contreras-Ortiz, S. (2020). A machine learning model for emotion recognition from physiological signals. *Biomedical Signal Processing and Control*, *55*, 101646. doi:10.1016/j.bspc.2019.101646

Dubina, Y.Y. (2021). On approaches to assessing the cost effectiveness of the development of the healthcare sector. *State and Municipal Administration. Scientific Notes, 1*, 263-267.

Duh, E. J., Sun, J. K., & Stitt, A. W. (2017). Diabetic retinopathy: Current understanding, mechanisms, and treatment strategies. *JCI Insight*, *2*(14), e93751. doi:10.1172/jci.insight.93751 PMID:28724805

Durkin, J., Usher, K., & Jackson, D. (2019). Embodying compassion: A systematic review of the views of nurses and patients. *Journal of Clinical Nursing*, *28*(9-10), 1380–1392. doi:10.1111/jocn.14722 PMID:30485579

Durrani, H. (2016). Healthcare and healthcare systems: Inspiring progress and future prospects. *mHealth*, *2*(3), 1–9. PMID:28293581

Dwivedi, Y. K., Hughes, L., Ismagilova, E., Aarts, G., Coombs, C., Crick, T., Duan, Y., Dwivedi, R., Edwards, J., Eirug, A., Galanos, V., Ilavarasan, P. V., Janssen, M., Jones, P., Kar, A. K., Kizgin, H., Kronemann, B., Lal, B., Lucini, B., ... Williams, M. D. (2021). Artificial Intelligence (AI): Multidisciplinary perspectives on emerging challenges, opportunities, and agenda for research, practice and policy. *International Journal of Information Management*, *57*, 101994. doi:10.1016/j.ijinfomgt.2019.08.002

Dzedzickis, A., Kaklauskas, A., & Bucinskas, V. (2020). Human Emotion Recognition: Review of Sensors and Methods. *Sensors (Basel)*, *20*(3), 592. doi:10.339020030592 PMID:31973140

Efron, B., & Tibshirani, R. J. (1994). *An introduction to the bootstrap*. CRC Press.

Egger, M., Ley, M., & Hanke, S. (2019). Emotion Recognition from Physiological Signal Analysis: A Review. *Electronic Notes in Theoretical Computer Science*, *343*, 35–55. doi:10.1016/j.entcs.2019.04.009

Ekman, P., Friesen, W., & Hager, J. (2002). Facial Action Coding System: The Manual on CD ROM. A Human Face.

Electrodermal activity. (n.d.). In *Wikipedia*. Retrieved March 21, 2022, from https://en.wikipedia.org/wiki/Electrodermal_activity

Emotion classification. (n.d.). In *Wikipedia*. Retrieved March 21, 2022, from https://en.wikipedia.org/wiki/Emotion_classification

Emotion Recognition from Physiological Signal Analysis. (n.d.). Retrieved March 21, 2022, from https://www.researchgate.net/publication/333061423_Emotion_Recognition_from_Physiological_Signal_Analysis_A_Review

Empowering A. I. Leadership: AI C-Suite Toolkit. (n.d.). Retrieved March 21, 2022, from https://www3.weforum.org/docs/WEF_Empowering_AI_Leadership_2022.pdf

Erol, B. A., Majumdar, A., Benavidez, P., Rad, P., Choo, K. K. R., & Jamshidi, M. (2019). Toward artificial emotional intelligence for cooperative social human–machine interaction. *IEEE Transactions on Computational Social Systems*, 7(1), 234–246. doi:10.1109/TCSS.2019.2922593

Eszes, D. J., Szabó, D. J., Russell, G., Lengyel, C., Várkonyi, T., Paulik, E., Nagymajtényi, L., Facskó, A., Petrovski, G., & Petrovski, B. É. (2021). Diabetic Retinopathy Screening in Patients with Diabetes Using a Handheld Fundus Camera: The Experience from the South-Eastern Region in Hungary. *Journal of Diabetes Research*, 2021, 2021. doi:10.1155/2021/6646645 PMID:33628836

Eurostat: Healthcare personnel statistics - nursing and caring professionals. (2022). https://ec.europa.eu/eurostat/statistics-explained/index.php?title=Healthcare_personnel_statistics_-_nursing_and_caring_professionals

Fahimirad, M., & Kotamjani, S. S. (2018). A review on application of artificial intelligence in teaching and learning in educational contexts. *International Journal of Learning and Development*, 8(4), 106–118. doi:10.5296/ijld.v8i4.14057

Fan, Y., Lam, J. C., & Li, V. O. (2018, October). Multi-region ensemble convolutional neural network for facial expression recognition. In *International Conference on Artificial Neural Networks* (pp. 84-94). Springer. 10.1007/978-3-030-01418-6_9

Fariselli, L., Freedman, J., Ghini, M., & Valentini, F. (2008). *Stress, emotional intelligence, and performance in healthcare*. Academic Press.

Federal Service of State Statistic. (2022). https://rosstat.gov.ru/folder/13721

Fei, Z., Yang, E., Yu, L., Li, X., Zhou, H., & Zhou, W. (2022). A Novel deep neural network-based emotion analysis system for automatic detection of mild cognitive impairment in the elderly. *Neurocomputing*, 468, 306–316. doi:10.1016/j.neucom.2021.10.038

Feng, H., Golshan, H. M., & Mahoor, M. H. (2018). A wavelet-based approach to emotion classification using EDA signals. *Expert Systems with Applications*, 112, 77–86. doi:10.1016/j.eswa.2018.06.014

Ferdinando, H., Seppanen, T., & Alasaarela, E. (2016). Comparing features from ECG pattern and HRV analysis for emotion recognition system. *2016 IEEE Conference on Computational Intelligence in Bioinformatics and Computational Biology (CIBCB)*. 10.1109/CIBCB.2016.7758108

Ferdinando, H., Seppänen, T., & Alasaarela, E. (2017). Enhancing emotion recognition from ECG signals using supervised dimensionality reduction. *Proceedings of the 6th International Conference on Pattern Recognition Applications and Methods*. 10.5220/0006147801120118

Fernández Sánchez, J. (2014). TI-RADS classification of thyroid nodules based on a score modified regarding the ultrasound criteria for malignancy. *Revista Argentina de Radiología*, 78(3), 138–148.

Flogie, A., & Aberšek, B. (2022). Artificial intelligence in education. In O. Lutsenko & G. Lutsenko (Eds.), *Active Learning: Theory and Practice* (pp. 97–118). doi:10.5772/intechopen.96498

Foroutannia, A., Akbarzadeh-T, M. R., & Akbarzadeh, A. (2022). A deep learning strategy for EMG-based joint position prediction in hip exoskeleton assistive robots. *Biomedical Signal Processing and Control, 75*, 103557. doi:10.1016/j.bspc.2022.103557

Foster, K., Fethney, J., McKenzie, H., Fisher, M., Harkness, E., & Kozlowski, D. (2017). Emotional intelligence increases over time: A longitudinal study of Australian pre-registration nursing students. *Nurse Education Today, 55*, 65–70. doi:10.1016/j.nedt.2017.05.008 PMID:28528126

Fredrickson, B. L. (2004). The broaden–and–build theory of positive emotions. *Philosophical Transactions of the Royal Society of London. Series B, Biological Sciences, 359*(1449), 1367–1377. doi:10.1098/rstb.2004.1512 PMID:15347528

Frey, J., Mühl, C., Lotte, F., & Hachet, M. (2013). *Review of the use of electroencephalography as an evaluation method for human-computer interaction.* arXiv preprint arXiv:1311.2222.

Fuan, W., Hongkai, J., Haidong, S., Wenjing, D., & Shuaipeng, W. (2017). An adaptive deep convolutional neural network for rolling bearing fault diagnosis. *Measurement Science & Technology, 28*(9), 095005. doi:10.1088/1361-6501/aa6e22

Gadekallu, T. R., Srivastava, G., Liyanage, M., Iyapparaja, M., Chowdhary, C. L., Koppu, S., & Maddikunta, P. K. R. (2022). Hand gesture recognition based on a Harris hawks optimized convolution neural network. *Computers & Electrical Engineering, 100*, 107836. doi:10.1016/j.compeleceng.2022.107836

Gales, M., & Young, S. (2008). The application of hidden Markov models in speech recognition. *Foundations and Trends® in Signal Processing, 1*(3), 195-304.

Ganskaia, I., & Abaimov, S. (2022). *Before and After: Machine learning for perioperative patient care.* arXiv preprint arXiv:2201.08095.

Gillis, A. S. (2020). What is iot (internet of things) and how does it work? *IoT Agenda, TechTarget, 11.*

Gjoreski, M., Gjoreski, H., Luštrek, M., & Gams, M. (2017). Deep affect recognition from R-R intervals. *Proceedings of the 2017 ACM International Joint Conference on Pervasive and Ubiquitous Computing and Proceedings of the 2017 ACM International Symposium on Wearable Computers.* 10.1145/3123024.3125608

Gmurman, V. (2003). *Theory of probability and mathematical statistics.* Higher School.

Goar, V. K., Yadav, N. S., Chowdhary, C. L., & Mittal, M. (2021). An IoT and artificial intelligence-based patient care system focused on COVID-19 pandemic. *International Journal of Networking and Virtual Organisations, 25*(3-4), 232–251. doi:10.1504/IJNVO.2021.120169

Goda, A., Shimura, T., Murata, S., Kodama, T., Nakano, H., & Ohsugi, H. (2020). Psychological and Neurophysiological Effects of Robot Assisted Activity in Elderly People With Cognitive Decline. *Gerontology & Geriatric Medicine, 6.* doi:10.1177/2333721420969601 PMID:33241078

Goel, T., Murugan, R., Mirjalili, S., & Chakrabartty, D. K. (2021). OptCoNet: An optimized convolutional neural network for an automatic diagnosis of COVID-19. *Applied Intelligence, 51*(3), 1351–1366. doi:10.100710489-020-01904-z PMID:34764551

Goksel, N., & Bozkurt, A. (2019). Artificial intelligence in education: Current insights and future perspectives. In *Handbook of Research on Learning in the Age of Transhumanism* (pp. 224–236). IGI Global. doi:10.4018/978-1-5225-8431-5.ch014

Goleman, D. (2011). The brain and emotional intelligence: New insights. *Regional Business*, 94-95.

Goosen, L. (2015). Educational Technologies for an ICT4D MOOC in the 21st Century. In D. Nwaozuzu, & S. Mnisi (Ed.), *Proceedings of the South Africa International Conference on Educational Technologies* (pp. 37 - 48). Pretoria: African Academic Research Forum.

Goosen, L. (2018a). Sustainable and Inclusive Quality Education Through Research Informed Practice on Information and Communication Technologies in Education. In L. Webb (Ed.), *Proceedings of the 26th Conference of the Southern African Association for Research in Mathematics, Science and Technology Education (SAARMSTE)* (pp. 215 - 228). Gabarone: University of Botswana.

Goosen, L., & Mukasa-Lwanga, T. (2017). Educational Technologies in Distance Education: Beyond the Horizon with Qualitative Perspectives. In U. I. Ogbonnaya, & S. Simelane-Mnisi (Ed.), *Proceedings of the South Africa International Conference on Educational Technologies* (pp. 41 - 54). Pretoria: African Academic Research Forum.

Goosen, L. (2004). *Criteria and Guidelines for the Selection and Implementation of a First Programming Language in High Schools.* Potchefstroom Campus: North West University.

Goosen, L. (2018b). Trans-Disciplinary Approaches to Action Research for e-Schools, Community Engagement, and ICT4D. In T. A. Mapotse (Ed.), *Cross-Disciplinary Approaches to Action Research and Action Learning* (pp. 97–110). IGI Global. doi:10.4018/978-1-5225-2642-1.ch006

Goosen, L. (2018c). Ethical Data Management and Research Integrity in the Context of e-Schools and Community Engagement. In C. Sibinga (Ed.), *Ensuring Research Integrity and the Ethical Management of Data* (pp. 14–45). IGI Global. doi:10.4018/978-1-5225-2730-5.ch002

Goosen, L. (2018d). Ethical Information and Communication Technologies for Development Solutions: Research Integrity for Massive Open Online Courses. In C. Sibinga (Ed.), *Ensuring Research Integrity and the Ethical Management of Data* (pp. 155–173). IGI Global. doi:10.4018/978-1-5225-2730-5.ch009

Goosen, L. (2019). Research on Technology-Supported Teaching and Learning for Autism. In L. Makewa, B. Ngussa, & J. Kuboja (Eds.), *Technology-Supported Teaching and Research Methods for Educators* (pp. 88–110). IGI Global. doi:10.4018/978-1-5225-5915-3.ch005

Goosen, L., & Naidoo, L. (2014). Computer Lecturers Using Their Institutional LMS for ICT Education in the Cyber World. In C. Burger, & K. Naudé (Ed.), *Proceedings of the 43rd Conference of the Southern African Computer Lecturers' Association (SACLA)* (pp. 99-108). Port Elizabeth: Nelson Mandela Metropolitan University.

Goshvarpour, A., Abbasi, A., & Goshvarpour, A. (2017). An accurate emotion recognition system using ECG and GSR signals and matching pursuit method. *Biomedical Journal, 40*(6), 355–368. doi:10.1016/j.bj.2017.11.001 PMID:29433839

Gray, W. D. (Ed.). (2007). *Integrated models of cognitive systems* (Vol. 1). Oxford University Press. doi:10.1093/acprof:oso/9780195189193.001.0001

Greco, A., Valenza, G., Citi, L., & Scilingo, E. P. (2017). Arousal and valence recognition of affective sounds based on Electrodermal activity. *IEEE Sensors Journal, 17*(3), 716–725. doi:10.1109/JSEN.2016.2623677

Guan, C., Mou, J., & Jiang, Z. (2020). Artificial intelligence innovation in education: A twenty-year data-driven historical analysis. *International Journal of Innovation Studies, 4*(4), 134–147. doi:10.1016/j.ijis.2020.09.001

Gulapalli, A. S., & Mittal, V. K. (2022). Detection of Alzheimer's Disease Through Speech Features and Machine Learning Classifiers. In *Intelligent Sustainable Systems* (pp. 627–639). Springer. doi:10.1007/978-981-16-6309-3_59

Guo, H., Huang, Y., Lin, C., Chien, J., Haraikawa, K., & Shieh, J. (2016). Heart rate variability signal features for emotion recognition by using principal component analysis and support vectors machine. *2016 IEEE 16th International Conference on Bioinformatics and Bioengineering (BIBE)*. 10.1109/BIBE.2016.40

Gururaj, C., & Tunga, S. (2020). AI based feature extraction through content based image retrieval. *Journal of Computational and Theoretical Nanoscience*, *17*(9-10), 4050–4054. doi:10.1166/jctn.2020.9018

Hackman, J. R. (1990). Groups that work (and those that don't): Creating conditions for effective teamwork. Jossey-Bass.

Hackman, J. R. (1987). *Handbook of Organizational Behavior.* Prentice-Hall.

Haenlein, M., & Kaplan, A. (2019). A brief history of artificial intelligence: On the past, present, and future of artificial intelligence. *California Management Review*, *61*(4), 5–14. doi:10.1177/0008125619864925

Haldane, V., De Foo, C., Abdalla, S. M., Jung, A.-S., Tan, M., Wu, S., Chua, A., Verma, M., Shrestha, P., Singh, S., Perez, T., Tan, S. M., Bartos, M., Mabuchi, S., Bonk, M., McNab, C., Werner, G. K., Panjabi, R., Nordström, A., & Legido-Quigley, H. (2021). Health systems resilience in managing the COVID-19 pandemic: Lessons from 28 countries. *Nature Medicine*, *27*(6), 964–980. doi:10.103841591-021-01381-y PMID:34002090

Halili, S. H. (2019). Technological advancements in education 4.0. *The Online Journal of Distance Education and E-Learning, 7*(1), 63-69.

Hany, F., Ye, L., Seppänen, T., & Alasaarela, E. (2014). Emotion Recognition by Heart Rate Variability. *Australian Journal of Basic and Applied Sciences, 8*(14), 50-55.

Harper, R., & Southern, J. (2020). A Bayesian Deep Learning Framework for End-To-End Prediction of Emotion from Heartbeat. *IEEE Transactions on Affective Computing*, 1–1. doi:10.1109/TAFFC.2020.2981610

Hassan, M. M., Alam, M. G., Uddin, M. Z., Huda, S., Almogren, A., & Fortino, G. (2019). Human emotion recognition using deep belief network architecture. *Information Fusion*, *51*, 10–18. doi:10.1016/j.inffus.2018.10.009

Havaei, F., Ji, X. R., & Boamah, S. A. (2022). Workplace predictors of quality and safe patient care delivery among nurses using machine learning techniques. *Journal of Nursing Care Quality*, *37*(2), 103–109. doi:10.1097/NCQ.0000000000000600 PMID:34593739

Holmes, W., Bialik, M., & Fadel, C. (2019). *Artificial intelligence in education: Promises and Implications for Teaching and Learning.* Center for Curriculum Redesign.

Hope-Hailey, V., Gratton, L., McGovern, P., Stiles, P., & Truss, P. (1997). A Chameleon Function? HRM in the '90s. *Human Resource Management Journal*, *7*(3), 5–18. doi:10.1111/j.1748-8583.1997.tb00421.x

Hornung, O., & Smolnik, S. (2022). AI invading the workplace: Negative emotions towards the organizational use of personal virtual assistants. *Electronic Markets*, *32*(1), 123–138. doi:10.100712525-021-00493-0

Hsiu, H., Lin, S. K., Weng, W. L., Hung, C. M., Chang, C. K., Lee, C. C., & Chen, C. T. (2022). Discrimination of the Cognitive Function of Community Subjects Using the Arterial Pulse Spectrum and Machine-Learning Analysis. *Sensors (Basel)*, *22*(3), 806. doi:10.339022030806 PMID:35161551

Huang, J., Liu, B., & Tao, J. (2021). Learning long-term temporal contexts using skip RNN for continuous emotion recognition. *Virtual Reality & Intelligent Hardware*, *3*(1), 55–64. doi:10.1016/j.vrih.2020.11.005

Huang, X., Zou, D., Cheng, G., Chen, X., & Xie, H. (2021). Trends, research issues and applications of artificial intelligence in language education. *Journal of Educational Technology & Society*, *24*(3), 238–255.

Hu, H., Wang, S., Bezemer, C. P., & Hassan, A. E. (2019). Studying the consistency of star ratings and reviews of popular free hybrid Android and iOS apps. *Empirical Software Engineering*, 24(1), 7–32. doi:10.100710664-018-9617-6

Hur, W. M., Shin, Y., & Moon, T. W. (2022). Linking motivation, emotional labor, and service performance from a self-determination perspective. *Journal of Service Research*, 25(2), 227–241. doi:10.1177/1094670520975204

Hwang, G. J., Xie, H., Wah, B. W., & Gašević, D. (2020). Vision, challenges, roles and research issues of Artificial Intelligence in Education. *Computers and Education: Artificial Intelligence, 1*.

İnce, R., Adanır, S. S., & Sevmez, F. (2021). The inventor of electroencephalography (EEG): Hans Berger (1873–1941). *Child's Nervous System*, 37(9), 2723–2724. doi:10.100700381-020-04564-z PMID:32140776

Ivanov, V.N., & Suvorov, A.V. (2021). Modern problems of the development of Russian healthcare. Part 1. *Problems of Forecasting, 6*(189), 59-71.

Jagan Mohan, N., Murugan, R., Goel, T., & Roy, P. (2020b). Optic Disc Segmentation in Fundus Images using Operator Splitting Approach. *2020 Advanced Communication Technologies and Signal Processing (ACTS)*, 1–5. doi:10.1109/ACTS49415.2020.9350504

Jagan Mohan, N., Murugan, R., Goel, T., Mirjalili, S., & Roy, P. (2021). A novel four-step feature selection technique for diabetic retinopathy grading. *Physical and Engineering Sciences in Medicine*, 44(4), 1351–1366. doi:10.100713246-021-01073-4 PMID:34748191

Jagan Mohan, N., Murugan, R., Goel, T., & Roy, P. (2020a). An improved accuracy rate in microaneurysms detection in retinal fundus images using non-local mean filter. *International Conference on Machine Learning, Image Processing, Network Security and Data Sciences*, 183–193. 10.1007/978-981-15-6315-7_15

Jahanara, S., & Padmanabhan, S. (2021). *Detecting autism from the facial image*. Academic Press.

Jaiswal, A., Raju, A. K., & Deb, S. (2020, June). Facial emotion detection using deep learning. In *2020 International Conference for Emerging Technology (INCET)* (pp. 1-5). IEEE.

Janiesch, C., Zschech, P., & Heinrich, K. (2021). Machine learning and deep learning. *Electronic Markets*, 31(3), 685–695. doi:10.100712525-021-00475-2

Javaid, M., Haleem, A., Singh, R. P., Haq, M. I., Raina, A., & Suman, R. (2020). Industry 5.0: Potential applications in COVID-19. *Journal of Industrial Integration and Management*, 5(04), 507–530. doi:10.1142/S2424862220500220

Jawabri, K. H., & Sharma, S. (2021). Physiology, cerebral cortex functions. In *StatPearls* [internet]. StatPearls Publishing.

Jiang, H., Yang, K., Gao, M., Zhang, D., Ma, H., & Qian, W. (2019). An interpretable ensemble deep learning model for diabetic retinopathy disease classification. *2019 41st Annual International Conference of the IEEE Engineering in Medicine and Biology Society (EMBC)*, 2045–2048.

Jianhua, W., Nan, L., & Hui, G. (2009, October). Static Scheduling Model and Algorithms of Agile Supply Chain Under Definite Demands. In *2009 Second International Conference on Intelligent Computation Technology and Automation* (Vol. 3, pp. 984-987). IEEE. 10.1109/ICICTA.2009.703

Juncos-Rabadán, O., & Iglesias, F. J. (1994). Decline in the elderly's language: Evidence from cross-linguistic data. *Journal of Neurolinguistics*, 8(3), 183–190. doi:10.1016/0911-6044(94)90025-6

Just, M. A., Pan, L., Cherkassky, V. L., McMakin, D. L., Cha, C., Nock, M. K., & Brent, D. (2017). Machine learning of neural representations of suicide and emotion concepts identifies suicidal youth. *Nature Human Behaviour*, 1(12), 911–919. doi:10.103841562-017-0234-y PMID:29367952

Jyostna Devi, B., & Veeranjaneyulu, N. (2019). Facial emotion recognition using deep cnn based features. *International Journal of Innovative Technology and Exploring Engineering, 8*(7).

Kadadi, S., & Bharamanaikar, S.R. (2020). Role of Emotional Intelligence on in Healthcare Industry. *Drishtikon: A Management Journal, 11*(1), 1-37.

Kaggle, Inc. Diabetic retinopathy detection . (2016). Available at Https://Www.Kaggle.Com/c/Diabetic-Retinopathy-Detection

Kanjo, E., Younis, E. M., & Ang, C. S. (2019). Deep learning analysis of mobile physiological, environmental and location sensor data for emotion detection. *Information Fusion, 49*, 46–56. doi:10.1016/j.inffus.2018.09.001

Kanjo, E., Younis, E. M., & Sherkat, N. (2018). Towards unravelling the relationship between on-body, environmental and emotion data using sensor information fusion approach. *Information Fusion, 40*, 18–31. doi:10.1016/j.inffus.2017.05.005

Karan, A., & Wadhera, R. (2021). Healthcare System Stress Due to Covid-19: Evading an Evolving Crisis. *Journal of Hospital Medicine, 16*(2), 127–135. doi:10.12788/jhm.3583 PMID:33523798

Karani, F. (2014). Spatial heterogeneity of the US healthcare organization in the context of reform. *American Journal of Economics and Control Systems Management, 4*(2), 47-54.

Kassani, S. H., Kassani, P. H., Khazaeinezhad, R., Wesolowski, M. J., Schneider, K. A., & Deters, R. (2019). Diabetic Retinopathy Classification Using a Modified Xception Architecture. *2019 IEEE International Symposium on Signal Processing and Information Technology (ISSPIT)*, 1–6. 10.1109/ISSPIT47144.2019.9001846

Katsigiannis, S., & Ramzan, N. (2018). DREAMER: A Database for Emotion Recognition Through EEG and ECG Signals From Wireless Low-cost Off-the-Shelf Devices. *IEEE Journal of Biomedical and Health Informatics, 22*(1), 98–107. doi:10.1109/JBHI.2017.2688239 PMID:28368836

Katzenback, J. R., & Smith, D. K. (2003). The wisdom of teams. Harvard Business School Press.

Kauppi, T., Kalesnykiene, V., Kamarainen, J.-K., Lensu, L., Sorri, I., Uusitalo, H., Kälviäinen, H., & Pietilä, J. (2006). DIARETDB0: Evaluation database and methodology for diabetic retinopathy algorithms. Machine Vision and Pattern Recognition Research Group, Lappeenranta University of Technology, 73, 1–17.

Kaya, H., Senyuva, E., & Bodur, G. (2018). The relationship between critical thinking and emotional intelligence in nursing students: A longitudinal study. *Nurse Education Today, 68*, 26–32. doi:10.1016/j.nedt.2018.05.024 PMID:29883912

Keren, G., Kirschstein, T., Marchi, E., Ringeval, F., & Schuller, B. (2017). End-to-end learning for dimensional emotion recognition from physiological signals. *2017 IEEE International Conference on Multimedia and Expo (ICME)*. 10.1109/ICME.2017.8019533

Khachnaoui, H., Guetari, R., & Khlifa, N. (2018). A review on Deep Learning in thyroid ultrasound Computer-Assisted Diagnosis systems. *2018 IEEE International Conference on Image Processing, Applications and Systems (IPAS)*, 291-297. 10.1109/IPAS.2018.8708866

Khan, A. N., Ihalage, A. A., Ma, Y., Liu, B., Liu, Y., & Hao, Y. (2021). Deep learning framework for subject-independent emotion detection using wireless signals. *PLoS One, 16*(2), e0242946. doi:10.1371/journal.pone.0242946 PMID:33534826

Khan, M., Minbashian, A., & MacCann, C. (2021). College students in the western world are becoming less emotionally intelligent: A cross-temporal meta-analysis of trait emotional intelligence. *Journal of Personality, 89*(6), 1176–1190. doi:10.1111/jopy.12643 PMID:33872392

Khan, R., & Debnath, R. (2020). Human distraction detection from video stream using artificial emotional intelligence. *International Journal of Image, Graphics and Signal Processing, 10*(2), 19–29. doi:10.5815/ijigsp.2020.02.03

Khare, N., Devan, P., Chowdhary, C. L., Bhattacharya, S., Singh, G., Singh, S., & Yoon, B. (2020). SMO-DNN: Spider monkey optimization and deep neural network hybrid classifier model for intrusion detection. *Electronics (Basel), 9*(4), 692. doi:10.3390/electronics9040692

Khosravi, M., & Hassani, F. (2022). From emotional intelligence to suicidality: A mediation analysis in patients with borderline personality disorder. *BMC Psychiatry, 22*(1), 1–11. doi:10.118612888-022-03891-6 PMID:35361178

Kim, J. Y., Liu, N., Tan, H. X., & Chu, C. H. (2017). Unobtrusive monitoring to detect depression for elderly with chronic illnesses. *IEEE Sensors Journal, 17*(17), 5694–5704. doi:10.1109/JSEN.2017.2729594

Kim, J., & Sohn, M. (2022). Graph Representation Learning-Based Early Depression Detection Framework in Smart Home Environments. *Sensors (Basel), 22*(4), 1545. doi:10.339022041545 PMID:35214446

Kitchen, K., & Drexel, B. (2021). *Quantum computing: A national security primer.* Academic Press.

Klussman, K., Curtin, N., Langer, J., & Nichols, A. L. (2022). The importance of awareness, acceptance, and alignment with the self: A framework for understanding self-connection. *Europe's Journal of Psychology, 18*(1), 120–131. doi:10.5964/ejop.3707 PMID:35330854

Koelstra, S., Muhl, C., Soleymani, M., Jong-Seok Lee, Yazdani, A., Ebrahimi, T., Pun, T., Nijholt, A., & Patras, I. (2012). DEAP: A Database for Emotion Analysis;Using Physiological Signals. *IEEE Transactions on Affective Computing, 3*(1), 18–31. doi:10.1109/T-AFFC.2011.15

Kolski, C., Boy, G. A., Melançon, G., Ochs, M., & Vanderdonckt, J. (2020). Cross-fertilisation between human-computer interaction and artificial intelligence. In *A guided tour of artificial intelligence research* (pp. 365–388). Springer. doi:10.1007/978-3-030-06170-8_11

Konadath, S., Chatni, S., Lakshmi, M. S., & Saini, J. K. (2017). Prevalence of communication disorders in a group of islands in India. *Clinical Epidemiology and Global Health, 5*(2), 79–86. doi:10.1016/j.cegh.2016.08.003

Koudelková, Z., Strmiska, M., & Jašek, R. (2018). Analysis of brain waves according to their frequency. *Int. J. Of Biol. And Biomed. Eng., 12*, 202–207.

Krakovsky, M. (2018). Artificial (emotional) intelligence. *Communications of the ACM, 61*(4), 18–19. doi:10.1145/3185521

Kramer, H. (1999). *Mathematical methods of statistics.* University Press.

Kritzinger, E., Loock, M., & Goosen, L. (2019). Cyber Safety Awareness – Through the Lens of 21st Century Learning Skills and Game-Based Learning. *Lecture Notes in Computer Science, 11937*, 477–485. doi:10.1007/978-3-030-35343-8_51

Kumar, S., & Singh, S. K. (2021). *Brain Computer Interaction (BCI): A Way to Interact with Brain Waves.* Academic Press.

Kumari, N., & Singh, S. N. (2016, January). Sentiment analysis on E-commerce application by using opinion mining. In 2016 6th International Conference-Cloud System and Big Data Engineering (Confluence) (pp. 320-325). IEEE. doi:10.1109/CONFLUENCE.2016.7508136

Kumar, V., Zarrad, A., Gupta, R., & Cheikhrouhou, O. (2022). COV-DLS: Prediction of COVID-19 from X-Rays Using Enhanced Deep Transfer Learning Techniques. *Journal of Healthcare Engineering, 2022.* doi:10.1155/2022/6216273 PMID:35422979

Kwet, M., & Prinsloo, P. (2020). The 'smart' classroom: A new frontier in the age of the smart university. *Teaching in Higher Education, 25*(4), 510–526. doi:10.1080/13562517.2020.1734922

Lacouz, I., & Midler, G. (2021). Antique US Government and State Health. *American Journal of Law & Medicine*, *47*(1), 104–122.

Laddha, S., Mnasri, S., Alghamdi, M., Kumar, V., Kaur, M., Alrashidi, M., Almuhaimeed, A., Alshehri, A., Alrowaily, M. A., & Alkhazi, I. (2022). COVID-19 Diagnosis and Classification Using Radiological Imaging and Deep Learning Techniques: A Comparative Study. *Diagnostics (Basel)*, *12*(8), 1880. doi:10.3390/diagnostics12081880 PMID:36010231

Lameras, P., & Arnab, S. (2021). Power to the Teachers: An Exploratory Review on Artificial Intelligence in Education. *Information (Basel)*, *13*(1), 14. doi:10.3390/info13010014

Lane, R. D., Nadel, L., & Kaszniak, A. W. (2002). Cognitive Neuroscience. *Cognitive Neuroscience of Emotion*, 407.

Lawler, E. E. III, & Mohrman, S. A. (2003). HR as a Strategic Partner: What Does It Take to Make it Happen? *Human Resource Planning*, *26*(5), 15.

Laz Hieida, C., Horii, T., & Nagai, T. (2018). *Deep emotion: A computational model of emotion using deep neural networks*. arXiv preprint arXiv:1808.08447.

Lazareva, N.V. (2021). Resource potential of the healthcare system. *Problems of improving the organization of production and management of industrial enterprises: Interuniversity collection of scientific papers, 1*, 32-37.

LeCun, Y., Bengio, Y., & Hinton, G. (2015). Deep learning. *Nature, 28*(521), 7553.

LeCun, Y., Bengio, Y., & Hinton, G. (2015). Deep learning. *Nature, 521*(7553), 436-444.

Lee, M. S., Lee, Y. K., Pae, D. S., Lim, M. T., Kim, D. W., & Kang, T. K. (2019). Fast Emotion Recognition Based on Single Pulse PPG Signal with Convolutional Neural Network. *Applied Sciences (Basel, Switzerland)*, *9*(16), 3355. doi:10.3390/app9163355

Lee, M., Lee, Y. K., Lim, M.-T., & Kang, T.-K. (2020). Emotion Recognition Using Convolutional Neural Network with Selected Statistical Photoplethysmogram Features. *Applied Sciences (Basel, Switzerland)*, *10*(10), 3501. doi:10.3390/app10103501

Libbrecht, P., & Goosen, L. (2015). Using ICTs to Facilitate Multilingual Mathematics Teaching and Learning. In *Mathematics Education and Language Diversity* (pp. 217–235). Springer.

Li, C., Xu, C., & Feng, Z. (2016). Analysis of physiological for emotion recognition with the IRS model. *Neurocomputing*, *178*, 103–111. doi:10.1016/j.neucom.2015.07.112

Lim, N. (2016). Cultural differences in emotion: Differences in emotional arousal level between the East and the West. *Integrative Medicine Research*, *5*(2), 105–109. doi:10.1016/j.imr.2016.03.004 PMID:28462104

Lin, Y. P., & Jung, T. P. (2017). Improving EEG-based emotion classification using conditional transfer learning. *Frontiers in Human Neuroscience*, *11*, 334. doi:10.3389/fnhum.2017.00334 PMID:28701938

Li, R., Ren, C., Zhang, X., & Hu, B. (2022). A novel ensemble learning method using multiple objective particle swarm optimization for subject-independent EEG-based emotion recognition. *Computers in Biology and Medicine*, *140*, 105080. doi:10.1016/j.compbiomed.2021.105080 PMID:34902609

Li, T. M., Chao, H. C., & Zhang, J. (2019). Emotion classification based on brain wave: A survey. *Human-centric Computing and Information Sciences*, *9*(1), 1–17. doi:10.118613673-019-0201-x

Liu, M., Fan, D., Zhang, X., & Gong, X. (2016). Human emotion recognition based on galvanic skin response signal feature selection and SVM. *2016 International Conference on Smart City and Systems Engineering (ICSCSE)*. 10.1109/ICSCSE.2016.0051

Li, X., Zhang, P., Song, D., Yu, G., Hou, Y., & Hu, B. (2015). *EEG based emotion identification using unsupervised deep feature learning.* Academic Press.

Loria, A. A. (2022, January 20). *The Role of Artificial Intelligence in Modern Education.* Retrieved from https://www.depedbataan.com/resources/4/the_role_of_artificial_intelligence_in_modern_education.pdf

Lucey, P., Cohn, J. F., Kanade, T., Saragih, J., Ambadar, Z., & Matthews, I. (2010, June). The extended cohn-kanade dataset (ck+): A complete dataset for action unit and emotion-specified expression. In *2010 IEEE Computer Society Conference on Computer Vision and Pattern Recognition-Workshops* (pp. 94-101). IEEE.

Lu, X. (2021). Deep learning based emotion recognition and visualization of figural representation. *Frontiers in Psychology*, 12. PMID:35069400

Machine learning. (n.d.). In *Wikipedia*. Retrieved March 21, 2022, from https://en.wikipedia.org/wiki/Machine_learning

Ma, J., Zeng, Z., & Fang, K. (2022). Emotionally savvy employees fail to enact emotional intelligence when ostracized. *Personality and Individual Differences*, *185*, 111250. doi:10.1016/j.paid.2021.111250

Makridakis, S. (2017). The forthcoming Artificial Intelligence (AI) revolution: Its impact on society and firms. *Futures*, *90*, 46–60. doi:10.1016/j.futures.2017.03.006

Malik, G., Tayal, D. K., & Vij, S. (2019). An analysis of the role of artificial intelligence in education and teaching. In *Recent Findings in Intelligent Computing Techniques* (pp. 407–417). Springer. doi:10.1007/978-981-10-8639-7_42

Martens, D., & Johann, T. (2017, May). On the emotion of users in app reviews. In *2017 IEEE/ACM 2nd International Workshop on Emotion Awareness in Software Engineering (SEmotion)* (pp. 8-14). IEEE. 10.1109/SEmotion.2017.6

Martins Van Jaarsveld, G. (2020). The effects of COVID-19 among the elderly population: A case for closing the digital divide. *Frontiers in Psychiatry*, *11*, 1211. doi:10.3389/fpsyt.2020.577427 PMID:33304283

Matsubara, M., Augereau, O., Sanches, C. L., & Kise, K. (2016). Emotional arousal estimation while reading comics based on physiological signal analysis. *Proceedings of the 1st International Workshop on comics ANalysis, Processing and Understanding.* 10.1145/3011549.3011556

Mattingly, V., & Kraiger, K. (2019). Can emotional intelligence be trained? A meta-analytical investigation. *Human Resource Management Review*, *29*(2), 140–155. doi:10.1016/j.hrmr.2018.03.002

Mayer, J. D., & Salovey, P. (1997). *Emotional development and emotional intelligence.* Basics Books.

Mayer, J. D., Caruso, D. R., & Salovey, P. (2016). The ability model of emotional intelligence: Principles and updates. *Emotion Review*, *8*(4), 290–300. doi:10.1177/1754073916639667

Mayer, J. D., Salovey, P., & Caruso, D. R. (2004). Emotional Intelligence: Theory, Findings, and Implications. *Psychological Inquiry*, *15*(3), 197–215. doi:10.120715327965pli1503_02

McArthur, D., Lewis, M., & Bishary, M. (2005). The roles of artificial intelligence in education: Current progress and future prospects. *Journal of Educational Technology*, *1*(4), 42–80.

Menard, M., Richard, P., Hamdi, H., Dauce, B., & Yamaguchi, T. (2015). Emotion Recognition based on Heart Rate and Skin Conductance. *2nd International Conference on Physiological Computing Systems*, 26-32.

Mikolajczak, L., Bodarwe, K., Laloyaux, O., Hansenne, M., & Nelis, D. (2010). Association between frontal EEG asymmetries and emotional intelligence among adults. *Personality and Individual Differences*, *48*(2), 177–181. doi:10.1016/j.paid.2009.10.001

Milcent, C. (2016). Evolution of the Health System. Inefficiency, Violence, and Digital Healthcare. *China Perspectives (Online)*, *4*(4), 39–50. doi:10.4000/chinaperspectives.7112

Minhad, K.N., Ali, S.H., & Reaz, M.B. (2017). A design framework for human emotion recognition using electrocardiogram and skin conductance response signals. *Journal of Engineering Science and Technology, 12*, 3102-3119.

Miranda-Correa, J. A., Abadi, M. K., Sebe, N., & Patras, I. (2021). AMIGOS: A Dataset for Affect, Personality and Mood Research on Individuals and Groups. *IEEE Transactions on Affective Computing, 12*(2), 479–493. doi:10.1109/TAFFC.2018.2884461

Mohan, N. J., Murugan, R., & Goel, T. (2022). Machine Learning Algorithms for Hypertensive Retinopathy Detection through Retinal Fundus Images. *Computer Vision and Recognition Systems: Research Innovations and Trends*, 39.

Mohan, N. J., Murugan, R., & Goel, T. (2020). Investigations of Diabetic Retinopathy Algorithms in Retinal Fundus Images. *International Journal of Image Processing and Pattern Recognition, 6*(1), 14–26.

Mohan, N. J., Murugan, R., Goel, T., & Roy, P. (2021a). Exudate Detection with Improved U-Net Using Fundus Images. *2021 International Conference on Computational Performance Evaluation (ComPE)*, 560–564. 10.1109/ComPE53109.2021.9752239

Mohan, N. J., Murugan, R., Goel, T., & Roy, P. (2021b). Exudate Localization in Retinal Fundus Images Using Modified Speeded Up Robust Features Algorithm. *2020 IEEE-EMBS Conference on Biomedical Engineering and Sciences (IECBES)*, 367–371. 10.1109/IECBES48179.2021.9398771

Mohan, N. J., Murugan, R., Goel, T., & Roy, P. (2022). Fast and Robust Exudate Detection in Retinal Fundus Images Using Extreme Learning Machine Autoencoders and Modified KAZE Features. *Journal of Digital Imaging, 35*(3), 496–513. Advance online publication. doi:10.100710278-022-00587-x PMID:35141807

Mohrman, S. A., Cohen, S. G., & Mohrman, A. M. (1995). *Designing team-based organizations: new forms for knowledge work*. Jossey-Bass.

Momtaz, P. P. (2021). CEO emotions and firm valuation in initial coin offerings: An artificial emotional intelligence approach. *Strategic Management Journal, 42*(3), 558–578. doi:10.1002mj.3235

Monett, D., & Stolte, H. (2016, September). Predicting star ratings based on annotated reviews of mobile apps. In *2016 Federated Conference on Computer Science and Information Systems (FedCSIS)* (pp. 421-428). IEEE. 10.15439/2016F141

Morales Rodríguez, F. M., Lozano, J. M. G., Linares Mingorance, P., & Pérez-Mármol, J. M. (2020). Influence of smartphone use on emotional, cognitive and educational dimensions in university students. *Sustainability, 12*(16), 6646. doi:10.3390u12166646

Morana, S., Gnewuch, U., Jung, D., & Granig, C. (2020). The Effect of Anthropomorphism on Investment Decision-Making with Robo-Advisor Chatbots. ECIS.

Morris, R. S., Tignanelli, C. J., deRoon-Cassini, T., Laud, P., & Sparapani, R. (2022). Improved prediction of older adult discharge after trauma using a novel machine learning paradigm. *The Journal of Surgical Research, 270*, 39–48. doi:10.1016/j.jss.2021.08.021 PMID:34628162

Mousavi, M., Parvin, S., Farid, F., Bahrainian, A., & Asghanejad Farid, A. (2016). Evaluation of emotional intelligence training efficiency aimed at improving the quality of life, reducing symptoms of anxiety and depression among the elderly in Tehran nursing home. *Journal of Fundamentals of Mental Health, 18*(Special Issue), 520–526.

Mukeshimana, M., Ban, X., Karani, N., & Liu, R. (2017). Multimodal emotion recognition for human-computer interaction: A survey. *System, 9*, 10.

Muthusamy, H., Polat, K., & Yaacob, S. (2015). Improved emotion recognition using gaussian mixture model and extreme learning machine in speech and glottal signals. *Mathematical Problems in Engineering, 2015*, 2015. doi:10.1155/2015/394083

Nahavandi, S. (2019). Industry 5.0—A human-centric solution. *Sustainability, 11*(16), 4371. doi:10.3390u11164371

Najafpour, J., Keshmiri, F., Rahimi, S., Bigdeli, Z., Niloofar, P., & Homauni, A. (2020). Effect of emotional intelligence on the quality of nursing care from the perspectives of patients in educational hospitals. *Journal of Patient Safety & Quality Improvement, 8*(1), 37–43.

Najar, T. (2022, January). Lean-Agile supply chain innovation performance; the mediating role of dynamic capability, innovation capacity, and relational embeddednes. In *Supply Chain Forum: An International Journal* (pp. 1-22). Taylor & Francis.

Naji, M., Firoozabadi, M., & Azadfallah, P. (2013). Classification of music-induced emotions based on information fusion of forehead Biosignals and electrocardiogram. *Cognitive Computation, 6*(2), 241–252. doi:10.100712559-013-9239-7

Nakisa, B., Rastgoo, M. N., Rakotonirainy, A., Maire, F., & Chandran, V. (2018). Long Short Term Memory Hyperparameter Optimization for a Neural Network Based Emotion Recognition Framework. *IEEE Access: Practical Innovations, Open Solutions, 6*, 49325–49338. doi:10.1109/ACCESS.2018.2868361

Nanchen, G., Abutalebi, J., Assal, F., Manchon, M., Démonet, J. F., & Annoni, J. M. (2017). Second language performances in elderly bilinguals and individuals with dementia: The role of L2 immersion. *Journal of Neurolinguistics, 43*, 49–58. doi:10.1016/j.jneuroling.2016.09.004

Năstasă, L. E., & Fărcaş, A. D. (2015). The effect of emotional intelligence on burnout in healthcare professionals. *Procedia: Social and Behavioral Sciences, 187*, 78–82. doi:10.1016/j.sbspro.2015.03.015

National Collaborating Centre for Mental Health. (2009). Borderline personality disorder: Treatment and management. British Psychological Society.

Nayak, Holla, Akshayakumar, & Gururaj. (2021). Machine Learning Methodology toward identification of Mature Citrus fruits. In Computer Vision and Recognition Systems using Machine and Deep Learning Approaches IET Computing series vol. 42. The Institution of Engineering and Technology. doi:10.1049/PBPC042E_ch16

Ndhlovu, N. J., & Goosen, L. (2021). Re-Envisioning and Restructuring E-Learning Through Engagement With Underprivileged Communities: The Impact of Effectively Using ICTs in Classrooms. In C. Bosch, D. J. Laubscher, & L. Kyei-Blankson (Eds.), *Re-Envisioning and Restructuring Blended Learning for Underprivileged Communities* (pp. 66–87). IGI Global. doi:10.4018/978-1-7998-6940-5.ch004

Newell, A., Shaw, J. C., & Simon, H. A. (1956). *Problem solving in humans and computers.* Rand Corp.

Nguyen, D. T., Kang, J. K., Pham, T. D., Batchuluun, G., & Park, K. R. (2020, March 25). Ultrasound Image-Based Diagnosis of Malignant Thyroid Nodule Using Artificial Intelligence. *Sensors (Basel), 20*(7), 1822. doi:10.339020071822 PMID:32218230

Nikhila, Nathan, Ataide, Illanes, Friebe, & Abbineni. (2019). Lightweight Residual Network for The Classification of Thyroid Nodules. *IEEE EMBS.*

Njemanze, I. (2016). *What Does Being a Strategic HR Business Partner Look Like in Practice?* Retrieved from Cornell University, ILR School site: http://digitalcommons.ilr.cornell.edu/student/101

OECD: Health at a Glance 2021: OECD Indicators. (2021). OECD Publishing. doi:10.1787/ae3016b9-

Ogawa, S., Lee, T. M., Nayak, A. S., & Glynn, P. (1990). Oxygenation-sensitive contrast in magnetic resonance image of rodent brain at high magnetic fields. *Magnetic Resonance in Medicine, 14*(1), 68–78. doi:10.1002/mrm.1910140108 PMID:2161986

Oliveira-Dias, D., Maqueira, J. M., & Moyano-Fuentes, J. (2022). The link between information and digital technologies of industry 4.0 and agile supply chain: Mapping current research and establishing new research avenues. *Computers & Industrial Engineering, 167,* 108000. doi:10.1016/j.cie.2022.108000

On national goals and strategic objectives of the development of the Russian Federation for the period up to 2024 . (2022). Decree of the President of the Russian Federation dated 07.05.2018 No. 204. http://www.consultant.ru/document/cons_doc_LAW_335693/

Oran, O. (2016, June 7). *Wall Street hopes artificial intelligence software helps it hire loyal bankers.* Retrieved September 25, 2017, from https://www.reuters.com/article/us-banks-hiring-ai/wall-streethopes-artificial-intelligencesoftware-helps-it-hire-loyalbankers-idUSKCN0YT163

Orlov, A. (2004). *Econometrica.* Exam.

Ostertagova, E., & Ostertag, O. (2013). Methodology and Application of One-way ANOVA. *American Journal of Mechanical Engineering, 1*(7), 256–261.

Owoc, M. L., Sawicka, A., & Weichbroth, P. (2019, August). Artificial intelligence technologies in education: benefits, challenges and strategies of implementation. *International Federation for Information Processing (IFIP) International Workshop on Artificial Intelligence for Knowledge Management* (pp. 37-58). Cham: Springer.

Ozdemir, M. A., Elagoz, B., Alaybeyoglu, A., Sadighzadeh, R., & Akan, A. (2019, October). *Real time emotion recognition from facial expressions using CNN architecture. In 2019 medical technologies congress (tiptekno).* IEEE.

Özdemir, V., & Hekim, N. (2018). Birth of industry 5.0: Making sense of big data with artificial intelligence, "the internet of things" and next-generation technology policy. *OMICS: A Journal of Integrative Biology, 22*(1), 65–76. doi:10.1089/omi.2017.0194 PMID:29293405

Padmanabha, A. G. A., Appaji, M. A., Prasad, M., Lu, H., & Joshi, S. (2017). Classification of diabetic retinopathy using textural features in retinal color fundus image. *2017 12th International Conference on Intelligent Systems and Knowledge Engineering (ISKE),* 1–5.

Panigrahi, R., Borah, S., Bhoi, A. K., Ijaz, M. F., Pramanik, M., Jhaveri, R. H., & Chowdhary, C. L. (2021). Performance assessment of supervised classifiers for designing intrusion detection systems: A comprehensive review and recommendations for future research. *Mathematics, 9*(6), 690. doi:10.3390/math9060690

Parimala, M., Priya, R. S., Reddy, M. P., Chowdhary, C. L., Poluru, R. K., & Khan, S. (2021). Spatiotemporal-based sentiment analysis on tweets for risk assessment of event using deep learning approach. *Software, Practice & Experience, 3*(51), 550–570. doi:10.1002pe.2851

Pearce, E., & Sivaprasad, S. (2020). A review of advancements and evidence gaps in diabetic retinopathy screening models. *Clinical Ophthalmology (Auckland, N.Z.), 14,* 3285–3296. doi:10.2147/OPTH.S267521 PMID:33116380

Pedraza, L., Vargas, C., Narvaez, F., Duran, O., Munoz, E., & Romero, E. (2015). An open access thyroid ultrasound-image database. *Proceedings of the 10th International Symposium on Medical Information Processing and Analysis.*

Pedro, F., Subosa, M., Rivas, A., & Valverde, P. (2019). *Artificial intelligence in education: Challenges and opportunities for sustainable development.* United Nations Educational, Scientific and Cultural Organization.

Perez-Rosero, M. S., Rezaei, B., Akcakaya, M., & Ostadabbas, S. (2017). Decoding emotional experiences through physiological signal processing. *2017 IEEE International Conference on Acoustics, Speech and Signal Processing (ICASSP)*. 10.1109/ICASSP.2017.7952282

Phan, T. D. T., Kim, S. H., Yang, H. J., & Lee, G. S. (2021). EEG-Based Emotion Recognition by Convolutional Neural Network with Multi-Scale Kernels. *Sensors (Basel)*, *21*(15), 5092. doi:10.339021155092 PMID:34372327

Philip, B., Trevor, H., Christopher, M., & Shivakumar, V. (2003). An exploration of sentiment summarization. In *Proceedings of AAAI* (pp. 12-15). AAAI.

Picard, R. W. (2008). *Toward machines with emotional intelligence*. Academic Press.

Picard, R. W. (2003). Affective computing: Challenges. *International Journal of Human-Computer Studies*, *59*(1-2), 55–64. doi:10.1016/S1071-5819(03)00052-1

Pinkovetskaia, I., Nuretdinova, Y., Nuretdinov, I., & Lipatova, N. (2021). Mathematical modeling on the base of functions density of normal distribution. *Revista de La Universidad del Zulia*, *12*(33), 34–49. doi:10.46925//rdluz.33.04

Pivec, M. (Ed.). (2006). *Affective and emotional aspects of human-computer interaction: game-based and innovative learning approaches* (Vol. 1). IOS Press.

Podhorecka, M., Pyszora, A., Woźniewicz, A., Husejko, J., & Kędziora-Kornatowska, K. (2022). Empathy as a Factor Conditioning Attitudes towards the Elderly among Physiotherapists—Results from Poland. *International Journal of Environmental Research and Public Health*, *19*(7), 3994. doi:10.3390/ijerph19073994 PMID:35409677

Pollreisz, D., & TaheriNejad, N. (2017). A simple algorithm for emotion recognition, using physiological signals of a smart watch. *2017 39th Annual International Conference of the IEEE Engineering in Medicine and Biology Society (EMBC)*. doi:10.1109/EMBC.2017.8037328

Posentseva, Y. S., Mustenko, N. S., & Khomutinnikov, A. D. (2020). Analysis of Health System Efficiency: Main Trends of Development and Prospects of Modernization. *Proceedings of the Southwest State University. Series: Economics, Sociology and Management*, *10*(3), 123-139.

Prabha, R., Anandan, P., Sivarajeswari, S., Saravanakumar, C., & Babu, D. V. (2022, January). Design of an Automated Recurrent Neural Network for Emotional Intelligence Using Deep Neural Networks. In *2022 4th International Conference on Smart Systems and Inventive Technology (ICSSIT)* (pp. 1061-1067). IEEE. 10.1109/ICSSIT53264.2022.9716420

Prentice, C., Dominique Lopes, S., & Wang, X. (2020). Emotional intelligence or artificial intelligence–an employee perspective. *Journal of Hospitality Marketing & Management*, *29*(4), 377–403. doi:10.1080/19368623.2019.1647124

Preston, S. H. (2007). The changing relation between mortality and level of economic development. *International Journal of Epidemiology*, *36*(3), 484–490. doi:10.1093/ije/dym075 PMID:17550952

Puri, T., Soni, M., Dhiman, G., Ibrahim Khalaf, O., & Raza Khan, I. (2022). Detection of emotion of speech for RAVDESS audio using hybrid convolution neural network. *Journal of Healthcare Engineering*, *2022*, 2022. doi:10.1155/2022/8472947 PMID:35265307

Puspitasari, R., Budimansyah, D., Sapriya, S., & Rahmat, R. (2022, January). The Influence of Emotional Intelligence, Moral Intelligence and Intellectual Intelligence on Characters Caring for the Environmental School Students in the Perspective of Civic Education. In *Annual Civic Education Conference (ACEC 2021)* (pp. 343-348). Atlantis Press. 10.2991/assehr.k.220108.062

Qin, H., & Wang, G. (2022, January). Benefits, Challenges and Solutions of Artificial Intelligence Applied in Education. In *11th International Conference on Educational and Information Technology (ICEIT)* (pp. 62-66). IEEE. 10.1109/ICEIT54416.2022.9690739

Quellec, G., Charrière, K., Boudi, Y., Cochener, B., & Lamard, M. (2017). Deep image mining for diabetic retinopathy screening. *Medical Image Analysis*, *39*, 178–193. doi:10.1016/j.media.2017.04.012 PMID:28511066

Qummar, S., Khan, F. G., Shah, S., Khan, A., Shamshirband, S., Rehman, Z. U., Khan, I. A., & Jadoon, W. (2019). A deep learning ensemble approach for diabetic retinopathy detection. *IEEE Access: Practical Innovations, Open Solutions*, *7*, 150530–150539. doi:10.1109/ACCESS.2019.2947484

Rachmawati, I., Multisari, W., Triyono, T., Simon, I. M., & da Costa, A. (2021). Prevalence of Academic Resilience of Social Science Students in Facing the Industry 5.0 Era. *International Journal of Evaluation and Research in Education*, *10*(2), 676–683. doi:10.11591/ijere.v10i2.21175

Ragot, M., Martin, N., Em, S., Pallamin, N., & Diverrez, J. (2017). Emotion recognition using physiological signals: Laboratory vs. wearable sensors. *Advances in Human Factors in Wearable Technologies and Game Design*, 15-22. doi:10.1007/978-3-319-60639-2_2

Rahul, Uppunda, Sumukh, Vinayaka, & Gururaj. (2022). Self-Driving Car using Behavioral Cloning. In *Fundamentals and Methods of Machine and Deep Learning: Algorithms, Tools and Applications*. Wiley Publications. doi:10.1002/9781119821908.ch16

Rajaraman, V. (2014). John McCarthy—Father of artificial intelligence. *Resonance*, *19*(3), 198–207. doi:10.100712045-014-0027-9

Rakova, T. V. (2021). On the state of the Russian healthcare system before the coronavirus pandemic. *Azimuth of scientific research. Economics and Management*, *10*(2), 267–269.

Rakshit, R., Reddy, V. R., & Deshpande, P. (2016). Emotion detection and recognition using HRV features derived from photoplethysmogram signals. *Proceedings of the 2nd workshop on Emotion Representations and Modelling for Companion Systems*. 10.1145/3009960.3009962

Ranganathan, H., Chakraborty, S., & Panchanathan, S. (2016). Multimodal emotion recognition using deep learning architectures. *2016 IEEE Winter Conference on Applications of Computer Vision (WACV)*. 10.1109/WACV.2016.7477679

Rasker, P., van Vliet, T., van Den Broek, H., & Essens, P. (2001). *Team effectiveness factors: A literature review. TNO Technical report No.: TM-01-B007*.

Rautela, K., Kumar, D., & Kumar, V. (2022). A Systematic Review on Breast Cancer Detection Using Deep Learning Techniques. *Archives of Computational Methods in Engineering*, 1–31. doi:10.100711831-022-09744-5

Rautela, K., Kumar, D., & Kumar, V. (2022). Dual-modality synthetic mammogram construction for breast lesion detection using U-DARTS. *Biocybernetics and Biomedical Engineering*.

Ravi, A. (2018). *Pre-trained convolutional neural network features for facial expression recognition*. arXiv preprint arXiv:1812.06387.

Razmak, J., Pitzel, J. W., Belanger, C., & Farhan, W. (2022). Brushing up on time-honored sales skills to excel in tomorrow's environment. *Journal of Business & Industrial Marketing*, ahead-of-print.

Reddy, G. T., Bhattacharya, S., Ramakrishnan, S. S., Chowdhary, C. L., Hakak, S., Kaluri, R., & Reddy, M. P. K. (2020, February). An ensemble based machine learning model for diabetic retinopathy classification. In *2020 international conference on emerging trends in information technology and engineering (ic-ETITE)* (pp. 1-6). IEEE.

Reddy, G. T., Bhattacharya, S., Ramakrishnan, S. S., Chowdhary, C. L., Hakak, S., & Kaluri, R. (2020, February). An ensemble based machine learning model for diabetic retinopathy classification. *International conference on emerging trends in information technology and engineering (ic-ETITE)* (pp. 1-6). IEEE. 10.1109/ic-ETITE47903.2020.235

Reprintseva, E. (2020). Assessment of indicators of the development of the hospital healthcare network in Russia. *Regional Bulletin, 7*(46), 83-85.

Rodrigues, E. O., Conci, A., & Liatsis, P. (2020). ELEMENT: Multi-Modal Retinal Vessel Segmentation Based on a Coupled Region Growing and Machine Learning Approach. *IEEE Journal of Biomedical and Health Informatics, 24*(12), 3507–3519. doi:10.1109/JBHI.2020.2999257 PMID:32750920

Roll, I., & Wylie, R. (2016). Evolution and revolution in artificial intelligence in education. *International Journal of Artificial Intelligence in Education, 26*(2), 582–599. doi:10.100740593-016-0110-3

Romeo, L., Cavallo, A., Pepa, L., Bianchi-Berthouze, N., & Pontil, M. (2022). Multiple instance learning for emotion recognition using physiological signals. *IEEE Transactions on Affective Computing, 13*(1), 389–407. doi:10.1109/TAFFC.2019.2954118

Roopa, N. (2019). Emotion Recognition from Facial Expression using Deep Learning. *International Journal of Engineering and Advanced Technology.*

Roxo, M. R., Franceschini, P. R., Zubaran, C., Kleber, F. D., & Sander, J. W. (2011). The limbic system conception and its historical evolution. *TheScientificWorldJournal, 11*, 2427–2440. doi:10.1100/2011/157150 PMID:22194673

Rubeis, G. (2022). iHealth: The ethics of artificial intelligence and big data in mental healthcare. *Internet Interventions: the Application of Information Technology in Mental and Behavioural Health, 28*, 100518. doi:10.1016/j.invent.2022.100518 PMID:35257003

Sadiku, M. N., Musa, S. M., & Chukwu, U. C. (2022). Artificial Intelligence in Education. *International Journal of Scientific Advances, 2*(1), 5–11.

Sadri, S., Shahzad, A., & Zhang, K. (2021, February). Blockchain traceability in healthcare: Blood donation supply chain. In *2021 23rd International Conference on Advanced Communication Technology (ICACT)* (pp. 119-126). IEEE.

Saganowski, S., Dutkowiak, A., Dziadek, A., Dziezyc, M., Komoszynska, J., Michalska, W., Polak, A., Ujma, M., & Kazienko, P. (2020). Emotion Recognition Using Wearables: A Systematic Literature Review - Work-in-progress. *2020 IEEE International Conference on Pervasive Computing and Communications Workshops (PerCom Workshops).* 10.1109/PerComWorkshops48775.2020.9156096

Sakalle, A., Tomar, P., Bhardwaj, H., Acharya, D., & Bhardwaj, A. (2021). A LSTM based deep learning network for recognizing emotions using wireless brainwave driven system. *Expert Systems with Applications, 173*, 114516. doi:10.1016/j.eswa.2020.114516

Salam, S., Jianqiu, Z., Pathan, Z. H., & Lei, W. (2017, December). Strategic barriers in the effective integration of ICT in the public schools of Pakistan. In *Proceedings of the International Conference on Computer Science and Artificial Intelligence* (pp. 169-172). New York: ACM. 10.1145/3168390.3168422

SalaryExplorer. (2022). http://www.salaryexplorer.com/

Saluja, R. (2021). *Steps taken by developed nations to protect the wildlife.* KIIT School of Law.

Samantaray, S., Deotale, R., & Chowdhary, C. L. (2021). Lane detection using sliding window for intelligent ground vehicle challenge. In *Innovative Data Communication Technologies and Application* (pp. 871–881). Springer. doi:10.1007/978-981-15-9651-3_70

Samosir, F. J., Hulu, V. T., Julpa, A., & Sinurat, Y. T. (2022). Mental Health Exploration And Screening In Adults And Elderly Age Groups. *International Journal of Health and Pharmaceutical*, *2*(1), 29–35.

Samsonovich, A. V. (2012, July). An approach to building emotional intelligence in artifacts. *Workshops at the Twenty-Sixth AAAI Conference on Artificial Intelligence.*

Santamaria-Granados, L., Munoz-Organero, M., Ramirez-Gonzalez, G., Abdulhay, E., & Arunkumar, N. (2019). Using deep Convolutional neural network for emotion detection on a physiological signals dataset (AMIGOS). *IEEE Access: Practical Innovations, Open Solutions*, *7*, 57–67. doi:10.1109/ACCESS.2018.2883213

Saragadam, N., Koushmitha, S., Arun, Y. N. K., & Chowdhary, C. L. (2022). Data Protection Using Multiple Servers for Medical Supply Chain System. In *Innovative Supply Chain Management via Digitalization and Artificial Intelligence* (pp. 195–207). Springer. doi:10.1007/978-981-19-0240-6_11

Sarkar, P., & Etemad, A. (2021). Self-supervised ECG Representation Learning for Emotion Recognition. *IEEE Transactions on Affective Computing*, 1–1. doi:10.1109/TAFFC.2020.3014842

Sarno, R., Munawar, M. N., Nugraha, B. T., Sarno, R., Munawar, M., & Nugraha, B. (2016). Real-time electroencephalography-based emotion recognition system. *Int. Rev. Comput. Softw. IRECOS*, *11*(5), 456–465. doi:10.15866/irecos. v11i5.9334

Sarro, F., Harman, M., Jia, Y., & Zhang, Y. (2018, August). Customer rating reactions can be predicted purely using app features. In *2018 IEEE 26th International Requirements Engineering Conference (RE)* (pp. 76-87). IEEE. 10.1109/RE.2018.00018

Schlaegel, C., Engle, R. L., & Lang, G. (2022). The unique and common effects of emotional intelligence dimensions on job satisfaction and facets of job performance: An exploratory study in three countries. *International Journal of Human Resource Management*, *33*(8), 1562–1605. doi:10.1080/09585192.2020.1811368

Schmidt, P., Reiss, A., Dürichen, R., & Laerhoven, K. V. (2019). Wearable-Based Affect Recognition—A Review. *Sensors (Basel)*, *19*(19), 4079. doi:10.339019194079 PMID:31547220

Schuller, B., Rigoll, G., & Lang, M. (2003, April). Hidden Markov model-based speech emotion recognition. In *2003 IEEE International Conference on Acoustics, Speech, and Signal Processing, 2003. Proceedings (ICASSP '03)* (Vol. 2). IEEE.

Schuller, D., & Schuller, B. W. (2018). The age of artificial emotional intelligence. *Computer*, *51*(9), 38–46. doi:10.1109/MC.2018.3620963

Selvaraj, J., Murugappan, M., Wan, K., & Yaacob, S. (2013). Classification of emotional states from electrocardiogram signals: A non-linear approach based on hurst. *Biomedical Engineering Online*, *12*(1), 44. doi:10.1186/1475-925X-12-44 PMID:23680041

Senior, K. R. (2010). *The eye: the physiology of human perception.* The Rosen Publishing Group, Inc.

Senthilkumar, M., & Chowdhary, C. L. (2019). An AI-Based Chatbot Using Deep Learning. In *Intelligent Systems* (pp. 231–242). Apple Academic Press. doi:10.1201/9780429265020-12

Sha'abani, M. N. A. H., Fuad, N., Jamal, N., & Ismail, M. F. (2020). kNN and SVM classification for EEG: A review. *InECC, E2019*, 555–565. doi:10.1007/978-981-15-2317-5_47

Shaees, S., Naeem, H., Arslan, M., Naeem, M. R., Ali, S. H., & Aldabbas, H. (2020, September). Facial emotion recognition using transfer learning. In *2020 International Conference on Computing and Information Technology (ICCIT-1441)* (pp. 1-5). IEEE.

Shanthi, T., & Sabeenian, R. S. (2019). Modified Alexnet architecture for classification of diabetic retinopathy images. *Computers & Electrical Engineering*, *76*, 56–64. doi:10.1016/j.compeleceng.2019.03.004

Sharma, J., Sharma, S., Kumar, V., Hussein, H. S., & Alshazly, H. (2022). Deepfakes Classification of Faces Using Convolutional Neural Networks. *Traitement du Signal, 39*(3).

Sharma, S., & Kumar, V. (2022). A Comprehensive Review on Multi-objective Optimization Techniques: Past, Present and Future. *Archives of Computational Methods in Engineering*, 1–29. doi:10.100711831-022-09778-9

Sharma, S., Oberoi, J. S., Gupta, R. D., Saini, S., Gupta, A. K., & Sharma, N. (2022). Effect of agility in different dimensions of manufacturing systems: A review. *Materials Today: Proceedings*, *63*, 264–267. doi:10.1016/j.matpr.2022.03.054

Sharp, G., Bourke, L., & Rickard, M. J. (2020). Review of emotional intelligence in health care: An introduction to emotional intelligence for surgeons. *ANZ Journal of Surgery*, *90*(4), 433–440. doi:10.1111/ans.15671 PMID:31965690

Shen, C. W., & Ho, J. T. (2020). Technology-enhanced learning in higher education: A bibliometric analysis with latent semantic approach. *Computers in Human Behavior*, *104*, 104. doi:10.1016/j.chb.2019.106177

Shi, H., Yang, L., Zhao, L., Su, Z., Mao, X., Zhang, L., & Liu, C. (2017). Differences of heart rate variability between happiness and sadness emotion states: A pilot study. *Journal of Medical and Biological Shimmer Solicits Clinical Research Community Input on Expanded*. Retrieved March 21, 2022, from https://shimmersensing.com/news/shimmer-solicits-clinical-research-community-input-on-expanded-open-wearables-initiative-owear/

Shishkin, S. V., Sheiman, I. M., Abdin, A. A., Boyarsky, S. G., & Sazhina, S. V. (2017). *Russian healthcare in the new economic conditions: challenges and prospects. Report of the Higher School of Economics on the problems of the development of the healthcare system*. Publishing House of the Higher School of Economics.

Shkolnikov, V., Andreev, E., Tursun-zade, R., & Leon, D. (2019). Patterns in the relationship between life expectancy and gross domestic product in Russia in 2005–15: A cross-sectional analysis. *Lancet: Public Health, 4*.

Shukla, J., Barreda-Angeles, M., Oliver, J., Nandi, G. C., & Puig, D. (2021). Feature extraction and selection for emotion recognition from Electrodermal activity. *IEEE Transactions on Affective Computing*, *12*(4), 857–869. doi:10.1109/TAFFC.2019.2901673

Shu, L., Xie, J., Yang, M., Li, Z., Li, Z., Liao, D., Xu, X., & Yang, X. (2018). A Review of Emotion Recognition Using Physiological Signals. *Sensors (Basel)*, *18*(7), 2074. doi:10.339018072074 PMID:29958457

Shu, L., Yu, Y., Chen, W., Hua, H., Li, Q., Jin, J., & Xu, X. (2020). Wearable emotion recognition using heart rate data from a smart bracelet. *Sensors (Basel)*, *20*(3), 718. doi:10.339020030718 PMID:32012920

Singer, T., & Klimecki, O. M. (2014). Empathy and compassion. *Current Biology*, *24*(18), R875–R878. doi:10.1016/j.cub.2014.06.054 PMID:25247366

Singh, S., Sharma, C., Sharma, S., & Verma, N. K. (2021, September). Re-Learning Emotional Intelligence through Artificial Intelligence. In *2021 9th International Conference on Reliability, Infocom Technologies and Optimization (Trends and Future Directions) (ICRITO)* (pp. 1-5). IEEE. 10.1109/ICRITO51393.2021.9596091

Singh, B., Bhattacharya, S., Chowdhary, C. L., & Jat, D. S. (2017). A review on internet of things and its applications in healthcare. *Journal of Chemical and Pharmaceutical Sciences*, *10*(1), 447–452.

Singh, C., Kumar, A., Nagar, A., Tripathi, S., & Yenigalla, P. (2019, December). Emoception: An inception inspired efficient speech emotion recognition network. In *2019 IEEE Automatic Speech Recognition and Understanding Workshop (ASRU)* (pp. 787-791). IEEE. 10.1109/ASRU46091.2019.9004020

Singh, D., Kaur, M., Jabarulla, M. Y., Kumar, V., & Lee, H. N. (2022). Evolving fusion-based visibility restoration model for hazy remote sensing images using dynamic differential evolution. *IEEE Transactions on Geoscience and Remote Sensing, 60*, 1–14. doi:10.1109/TGRS.2022.3155765

Siuly, S., Li, Y., & Zhang, Y. (2016). EEG signal analysis and classification. *IEEE Transactions on Neural Systems and Rehabilitation Engineering, 11*, 141–144.

Smith, L. M., Heaven, P. C. L., & Ciarrochi, J. (2008). Trait emotional intelligence, conflict communication patterns, and relationship satisfaction. *Personality and Individual Differences, 44*(6), 1314–1325. doi:10.1016/j.paid.2007.11.024

Smith, R., Killgore, W. D., Alkozei, A., & Lane, R. D. (2018). A neuro-cognitive process model of emotional intelligence. *Biological Psychology, 139*, 131–151. doi:10.1016/j.biopsycho.2018.10.012 PMID:30392827

Sokanto, G. L., & Bruise, S. (2021). Regional policy for health care reform in the United States. Administration approaches from Obama to Trump. *American Review of Public Administration, 51*(2), 62–77.

Soleymani, M., Lichtenauer, J., Pun, T., & Pantic, M. (2012). A Multimodal Database for Affect Recognition and Implicit Tagging. *IEEE Transactions on Affective Computing, 3*(1), 42–55. doi:10.1109/T-AFFC.2011.25

Somayaji, S. R. K., Alazab, M., Manoj, M. K., Bucchiarone, A., Chowdhary, C. L., & Gadekallu, T. R. (2020, December). A framework for prediction and storage of battery life in iot devices using dnn and blockchain. In *2020 IEEE Globecom Workshops (GC Wkshps)* (pp. 1-6). IEEE.

Song, W., Li, S., Liu, J., Qin, H., Zhang, B., Zhang, S., & Hao, A. (2018). Multitask cascade convolution neural networks for automatic thyroid nodule detection and recognition. *IEEE Journal of Biomedical and Health Informatics, 23*(3), 1215–1224. doi:10.1109/JBHI.2018.2852718 PMID:29994412

Soomro, T. A., Gao, J., Khan, M. A. U., Khan, T. M., & Paul, M. (2016). Role of image contrast enhancement technique for ophthalmologist as diagnostic tool for diabetic retinopathy. *2016 International Conference on Digital Image Computing: Techniques and Applications (DICTA)*, 1–8. 10.1109/DICTA.2016.7797078

Spatz, D. (2000). Team-building in construction. *Practice Periodical on Structural Design and Construction, 5*(3), 93–105. doi:10.1061/(ASCE)1084-0680(2000)5:3(93)

Sreelakshmi, P., & Sumithra, M. D. (2019). Facial Expression Recognition robust to partial Occlusion using MobileNet. *International Journal of Engineering Research & Technology (Ahmedabad), 8*(06).

Sreevidya, P., Veni, S., & Ramana Murthy, O. V. (2022). Elder emotion classification through multimodal fusion of intermediate layers and cross-modal transfer learning. *Signal, Image and Video Processing, 16*(5), 1–8. doi:10.100711760-021-02079-x PMID:35069919

Srivastava, S., Misra, R., Pathak, D., & Sharma, P. (2021). Boosting Job Satisfaction Through Emotional Intelligence: A Study on Health Care Professionals. *Journal of Health Management, 23*(3), 414–424. doi:10.1177/09720634211035213

Srujana, K. S., Kashyap, S. N., Shrividhiya, G., Gururaj, C., & Induja, K. S. (2022). Supply Chain Based Demand Analysis of Different Deep Learning Methodologies for Effective Covid-19 Detection. In *Innovative Supply Chain Management via Digitalization and Artificial Intelligence* (pp. 135–170). Springer. doi:10.1007/978-981-19-0240-6_9

Stavrianos, P., Pavlopoulos, A., & Maglogiannis, I. (2022). Enabling Speech Emotional Intelligence as a Service in Homecare Platforms. In *Pervasive Healthcare* (pp. 119–144). Springer. doi:10.1007/978-3-030-77746-3_9

Steinmetz, J. D., Bourne, R. R. A., Briant, P. S., Flaxman, S. R., Taylor, H. R. B., Jonas, J. B., Abdoli, A. A., Abrha, W. A., Abualhasan, A., Abu-Gharbieh, E. G., Adal, T. G., Afshin, A., Ahmadieh, H., Alemayehu, W., Alemzadeh, S. A. S., Alfaar, A. S., Alipour, V., Androudi, S., Arabloo, J., ... Vos, T. (2021). Causes of blindness and vision impairment in 2020 and trends over 30 years, and prevalence of avoidable blindness in relation to VISION 2020: the Right to Sight: an analysis for the Global Burden of Disease Study. *The Lancet. Global Health*, *9*(2), e144–e160. doi:10.1016/S2214-109X(20)30489-7 PMID:33275949

Stuss, D. T., & Benson, D. F. (2019). The frontal lobes and control of cognition and memory. In *The frontal lobes revisited* (pp. 141–158). Psychology Press. doi:10.4324/9781315788975-8

Su, J., & Yang, W. (2022). Artificial intelligence in early childhood education: A scoping review. *Computers and Education: Artificial Intelligence, 3*.

Subramanian, R., Wache, J., Abadi, M. K., Vieriu, R. L., Winkler, S., & Sebe, N. (2018). ASCERTAIN: Emotion and Personality Recognition Using Commercial Sensors. *IEEE Transactions on Affective Computing*, *9*(2), 147–160. doi:10.1109/TAFFC.2016.2625250

Suhaimi, N. S., Mountstephens, J., & Teo, J. (2020). EEG-based emotion recognition: A state-of-the-art review of current trends and opportunities. *Computational Intelligence and Neuroscience*, *2020*. doi:10.1155/2020/8875426 PMID:33014031

Suleman, M., Malik, A., & Hussain, S. S. (2019). Google play store app ranking prediction using machine learning algorithm. *Urdu News Headline, Text Classification by Using Different Machine Learning Algorithms, 57*.

Suresh, K. P., & Urolagin, S. (2020, January). Android App Success Prediction based on Reviews. In *2020 International Conference on Computation, Automation and Knowledge Management (ICCAKM)* (pp. 358-362). IEEE. 10.1109/IC-CAKM46823.2020.9051529

Surve, A. A. (2020). *Impact Of Artifical Intelligence In Human Resource Management* [Doctoral Dissertation]. University of Mumbai.

Syarif, I., Zaluska, E., Prugel-Bennett, A., & Wills, G. (2012, July). Application of bagging, boosting and stacking to intrusion detection. In *International Workshop on Machine Learning and Data Mining in Pattern Recognition* (pp. 593-602). Springer. 10.1007/978-3-642-31537-4_46

Tamilarasi, F. C., & Shanmugam, J. (2020, June). Convolutional neural network-based autism classification. In *2020 5th International Conference on Communication and Electronics Systems (ICCES)* (pp. 1208-1212). IEEE. 10.1109/ICCES48766.2020.9137905

Tangkraingkij, P. (2016). Significant frequency range of brain wave signals for authentication. *Software Engineering, Artificial Intelligence, Networking and Parallel Distributed Computing*, *2015*, 103–113.

Tang, Y. Y., Tang, R., Posner, M. I., & Gross, J. J. (2022). Effortless training of attention and self-control: Mechanisms and applications. *Trends in Cognitive Sciences*, *26*(7), 567–577. doi:10.1016/j.tics.2022.04.006 PMID:35537920

Tannenbaum, S., Beard, R., & Salas, E. (1992). Teambuilding and its influence on team effectiveness: An examination of conceptual and empirical developments. In *Issues, theory, and research in industrial/organizational psychology* (pp. 117–153). Elsevier Science. doi:10.1016/S0166-4115(08)62601-1

Tavakoli, M., Mehdizadeh, A., Aghayan, A., Shahri, R. P., Ellis, T., & Dehmeshki, J. (2021). Automated Microaneurysms Detection in Retinal Images Using Radon Transform and Supervised Learning: Application to Mass Screening of Diabetic Retinopathy. *IEEE Access: Practical Innovations, Open Solutions*, *9*, 67302–67314. doi:10.1109/ACCESS.2021.3074458

Taylor, S., Jaques, N., Chen, W., Fedor, S., Sano, A., & Picard, R. (2015). Automatic identification of artifacts in electrodermal activity data. *2015 37th Annual International Conference of the IEEE Engineering in Medicine and Biology Society (EMBC)*. 10.1109/EMBC.2015.7318762

Teglasi, H., Caputo, M. H., & Scott, A. L. (2022). Explicit and implicit theory of mind and social competence: A social information processing framework. *New Ideas in Psychology, 64*, 100915. doi:10.1016/j.newideapsych.2021.100915

Tessler, F. N., Middleton, W. D., & Grant, E. G. (2018, April). Thyroid Imaging Reporting and Data System (TI-RADS): A User's Guide. *Radiology, 287*(1), 29–36. doi:10.1148/radiol.2017171240 PMID:29558300

Tessler, F. N., Middleton, W. D., Grant, E. G., Hoang, J. K., Berland, L. L., Teefey, S. A., Cronan, J. J., Beland, M. D., Desser, T. S., Frates, M. C., Hammers, L. W., Hamper, U. M., Langer, J. E., Reading, C. C., Scoutt, L. M., & Stavros, A. T. (2017). ACR thyroid imaging, reporting and data system (TI-RADS): White paper of the ACR TI-RADS committee. *Journal of the American College of Radiology, 14*(5), 587–595. doi:10.1016/j.jacr.2017.01.046 PMID:28372962

The Conversation. (n.d.). *In-depth analysis, research, news and ideas from.* Retrieved March 21, 2022, from https://theconversation.com/The

The Healthcare Development Strategy of the Russian Federation for the period up to 2025 . (2022). http://www.kremlin.ru/acts/news/60708

The professionals point. (n.d.). https://theprofessionalspoint.blogspot.com/2019/02/knn

Theckedath, D., & Sedamkar, R. R. (2020). Detecting affect states using VGG16, ResNet50 and SE-ResNet50 networks. *SN Computer Science, 1*(2), 1–7. doi:10.100742979-020-0114-9

Thiviya, T., Nitheesram, R., Srinath, G., Ekanayake, E. M. U. W. J. B., & Mehendran, Y. (2019). *Mobile Apps' Feature Extraction Based On User Reviews Using Machine Learning.* Academic Press.

Topic, A., & Russo, M. (2021). Emotion recognition based on EEG feature maps through deep learning network. *Engineering Science and Technology, an International Journal, 24*(6), 1442-1454.

Travnikova, D.A., & Shubina, E.Y. (2020). Analysis and evaluation of the dynamics of indicators of the development of the Russian healthcare system. *Issues of Sustainable Development of Society, 10,* 142-149.

Tsao, H.-Y., Chan, P.-Y., & Su, E. C.-Y. (2018). Predicting diabetic retinopathy and identifying interpretable biomedical features using machine learning algorithms. *BMC Bioinformatics, 19*(9), 111–121. doi:10.118612859-018-2277-0 PMID:30367589

Uden, L., & Guan, S. (2022). Neuroscience and Artificial Intelligence. In Handbook of Research on New Investigations in Artificial Life, AI, and Machine Learning (pp. 212-241). IGI Global. doi:10.4018/978-1-7998-8686-0.ch009

Ur Rehman, M., Abbas, Z., Khan, S. H., & Ghani, S. H. (2018). Diabetic retinopathy fundus image classification using discrete wavelet transform. *2018 2nd International Conference on Engineering Innovation (ICEI)*, 75–80.

Usman, I., & Almejalli, K. A. (2020). Intelligent Automated Detection of Microaneurysms in Fundus Images Using Feature-Set Tuning. *IEEE Access: Practical Innovations, Open Solutions, 8*, 65187–65196. doi:10.1109/ACCESS.2020.2985543

Vadhiraj, V. V., Simpkin, A., O'Connell, J., Singh Ospina, N., Maraka, S., & O'Keeffe, D. T. (2021). Ultrasound image classification of thyroid nodules using machine learning techniques. *Medicina, 57*(6), 527. doi:10.3390/medicina57060527 PMID:34074037

Vaishnavi, K., Kamath, U. N., Rao, B. A., & Reddy, N. S. (2022). Predicting Mental Health Illness using Machine Learning Algorithms. *Journal of Physics: Conference Series, 2161*(1), 012021. doi:10.1088/1742-6596/2161/1/012021

Van Pay, B. (2018). *How AI is reinventing HR*. Academic Press.

Venkata Phanikrishna, B., Pławiak, P., & Jaya Prakash, A. (2021). *A Brief Review on EEG Signal Pre-processing Techniques for Real-Time Brain-Computer Interface Applications*. Academic Press.

Vlasova, O.V. (2021). Trends in the development of the region's of the healthcare system in the current socio-economic conditions. *Science and Practice of Regions, 3*(24), 47-51.

Vojković, L., Kuzmanić Skelin, A., Mohovic, D., & Zec, D. (2021). The Development of a Bayesian Network Framework with Model Validation for Maritime Accident Risk Factor Assessment. *Applied Sciences (Basel, Switzerland), 11*(22), 10866. doi:10.3390/app112210866

Wadley, G., Kostakos, V., Koval, P., Smith, W., Webber, S., Cox, A., . . . Slovák, P. (2022, April). The Future of Emotion in Human-Computer Interaction. In *CHI Conference on Human Factors in Computing Systems Extended Abstracts* (pp. 1-6). 10.1145/3491101.3503729

Walker, S. A., Double, K. S., Kunst, H., Zhang, M., & MacCann, C. (2022). Emotional intelligence and attachment in adulthood: A meta-analysis. *Personality and Individual Differences, 184*, 111174. doi:10.1016/j.paid.2021.111174

Wang, C., Chen, D., Hao, L., Liu, X., Zeng, Y., Chen, J., & Zhang, G. (2019). Pulmonary image classification based on inception-v3 transfer learning model. *IEEE Access: Practical Innovations, Open Solutions, 7*, 146533–146541. doi:10.1109/ACCESS.2019.2946000

Wang, J., Luo, J., Liu, B., Feng, R., Lu, L., & Zou, H. (2020). Automated diabetic retinopathy grading and lesion detection based on the modified R-FCN object-detection algorithm. *IET Computer Vision, 14*(1), 1–8. doi:10.1049/iet-cvi.2018.5508

Wang, W., & Fu, W. (2007, August). Hybrid Petri Net Based Modelling and Simulation of Agile Supply Chain Dynamic Systems. In *2007 IEEE International Conference on Automation and Logistics* (pp. 2560-2565). IEEE. 10.1109/ICAL.2007.4339011

Wang, X., Xu, B., & Guo, Y. (2022). Fuzzy Logic System-Based Robust Adaptive Control of AUV with Target Tracking. *International Journal of Fuzzy Systems*, 1–9. doi:10.100740815-022-01356-2

Wei, W., Jia, Q., Feng, Y., & Chen, G. (2018). Emotion recognition based on weighted fusion strategy of multichannel physiological signals. *Computational Intelligence and Neuroscience, 2018*, 1–9. doi:10.1155/2018/5296523 PMID:30073024

Weng, H. C., Chen, H. C., Chen, H. J., Lu, K., & Hung, S. Y. (2008). Doctors' emotional intelligence and the patient-doctor relationship. *Medical Education, 42*(7), 703–711. doi:10.1111/j.1365-2923.2008.03039.x PMID:18588649

Weng, Y., & Lin, F. (2022). Multimodal Emotion Recognition Algorithm for Artificial Intelligence Information System. *Wireless Communications and Mobile Computing, 2022*, 2022. doi:10.1155/2022/9236238

Wentzel, E. (2010). *The theory of probability*. KnoRus.

White, D., & Katsuno, H. (2022). Artificial emotional intelligence beyond East and West. *Internet Policy Review, 11*(1).

Wilson, V., & Djamasbi, S. (2015). Human-computer interaction in health and wellness: Research and publication opportunities. *AIS Transactions on Human-Computer Interaction, 7*(3), 97–108. doi:10.17705/1thci.00067

Wislow, E. (2017). *Top ways to use artificial intelligence in HR*. Academic Press.

Wolpert, D. H. (1992). Stacked generalization. *Neural Networks, 5*(2), 241–259. doi:10.1016/S0893-6080(05)80023-1 PMID:18276425

World health statistics 2020: Monitoring health for the SDGs, sustainable development goals. (2020). World Health Organization.

Wyczesany, M., & Ligeza, T. S. (2015). Towards a constructionist approach to emotions: Verification of the three-dimensional model of affect with EEG-independent component analysis. *Experimental Brain Research, 233*(3), 723–733. doi:10.100700221-014-4149-9 PMID:25424865

Xu, K., Feng, D., & Mi, H. (2017). Deep convolutional neural network-based early automated detection of diabetic retinopathy using fundus image. *Molecules (Basel, Switzerland), 22*(12), 2054. doi:10.3390/molecules22122054 PMID:29168750

Yang, Z., & Li, D. (2019, July). Application of logistic regression with filter in data classification. In *2019 Chinese Control Conference (CCC)* (pp. 3755-3759). IEEE. 10.23919/ChiCC.2019.8865281

Yıldız, G., & Dizdaroğlu, B. (2020, October). Traffic Sign Recognition via Transfer Learning using Convolutional Neural Network Models. In *2020 28th Signal Processing and Communications Applications Conference (SIU)* (pp. 1-4). IEEE. 10.1109/SIU49456.2020.9302399

Yonck, R. (2020). *Heart of the machine: Our future in a world of artificial emotional intelligence.* Arcade.

Yoo, G., Seo, S., Hong, S., & Kim, H. (2016). Emotion extraction based on multi bio-signal using back-propagation neural network. *Multimedia Tools and Applications, 77*(4), 4925–4937. doi:10.100711042-016-4213-5

Yuniartika, W., Anwar, S., Kamil, A. R., & Herlinah, L. (2022). The effectiveness of yoga therapy to reduce the level of depression among elderly in the community. *Jurnal Ners dan Kebidanan Indonesia, 9*(4).

Yu, Q., Jiang, T., Zhou, A., Zhang, L., Zhang, C., & Xu, P. (2017). Computer-aided diagnosis of malignant or benign thyroid nodes based on ultrasound images. *European Archives of Oto-Rhino-Laryngology, 274*(7), 2891–2897. doi:10.100700405-017-4562-3 PMID:28389809

Yu, S., Xiao, D., & Kanagasingam, Y. (2018). Machine learning based automatic neovascularization detection on optic disc Region. *IEEE Journal of Biomedical and Health Informatics, 22*(3), 886–894. doi:10.1109/JBHI.2017.2710201 PMID:29727291

Zawacki-Richter, O., Marín, V. I., Bond, M., & Gouverneur, F. (2019). Systematic review of research on artificial intelligence applications in higher education–where are the educators? *International Journal of Educational Technology in Higher Education, 16*(39), 1–27. doi:10.118641239-019-0171-0

Zhang, D., Bu, W., & Wu, X. (2017). Diabetic retinopathy classification using deeply supervised ResNet. *2017 IEEE SmartWorld, Ubiquitous Intelligence & Computing, Advanced & Trusted Computed, Scalable Computing & Communications, Cloud & Big Data Computing, Internet of People and Smart City Innovation (SmartWorld/SCALCOM/UIC/ATC/CBDCom/IOP/SCI),* 1–6.

Zhang, J., Wen, X., & Whang, M. (2022). Empathy evaluation by the physical elements of the advertising. *Multimedia Tools and Applications, 81*(2), 2241–2257. doi:10.100711042-021-11637-x

Zhang, K., Ren, W., Luo, W., Lai, W. S., Stenger, B., Yang, M. H., & Li, H. (2022). Deep image deblurring: A survey. *International Journal of Computer Vision, 130*(9), 2103–2130. doi:10.100711263-022-01633-5

Zhang, N., Gupta, A., Chen, Z., & Ong, Y. S. (2021). Evolutionary machine learning with minions: A case study in feature selection. *IEEE Transactions on Evolutionary Computation.*

Zhang, X., Xu, C., Xue, W., Hu, J., He, Y., & Gao, M. (2018). Emotion Recognition Based on Multichannel Physiological Signals with Comprehensive Nonlinear Processing. *Sensors (Basel), 18*(11), 3886. doi:10.339018113886 PMID:30423894

Zhang, Z. (2016). Introduction to machine learning: K-nearest neighbors. *Annals of Translational Medicine, 4*(11), 218. doi:10.21037/atm.2016.03.37 PMID:27386492

Zhao, L., Yang, L., Shi, H., Xia, Y., Li, F., & Liu, C. (2017). Evaluation of consistency of HRV indices change among different emotions. *2017 Chinese Automation Congress (CAC).* 10.1109/CAC.2017.8243625

Zhao, M., & Jiang, Y. (2020). Great expectations and challenges of artificial intelligence in the screening of diabetic retinopathy. *Eye (London, England), 34*(3), 418–419. doi:10.103841433-019-0629-2 PMID:31827269

Zheng, W. L., Zhu, J. Y., & Lu, B. L. (2017). Identifying stable patterns over time for emotion recognition from EEG. *IEEE Transactions on Affective Computing, 10*(3), 417–429.

Zhou, J., Yang, X., Zhang, L., Shao, S., & Bian, G. (2020). Multisignal VGG19 network with transposed convolution for rotating machinery fault diagnosis based on deep transfer learning. *Shock and Vibration, 2020.* doi:10.1155/2020/8863388

Zhou, Y., Wang, B., He, X., Cui, S., & Shao, L. (2020). DR-GAN: Conditional generative adversarial network for fine-grained lesion synthesis on diabetic retinopathy images. *IEEE Journal of Biomedical and Health Informatics.* PMID:33332280

Zyukin, D.A. (2020). On the results of the resource optimization process in the healthcare system. *Politics, Economics and Innovation, 6*(35), 1-7.

About the Contributors

Chiranji Lal Chowdhary is an Associate Professor in the School of Information Technology & Engineering at VIT University, where he has been since 2010. He received a B.E. (CSE) from MBM Engineering College at Jodhpur in 2001, and M. Tech. (CSE) from the M.S. Ramaiah Institute of Technology at Bangalore in 2008. He received his PhD in Information Technology and Engineering from the VIT University Vellore in 2017. From 2006 to 2010 he worked at M.S. Ramaiah Institute of Technology in Bangalore, eventually as a Lecturer. His research interests span both computer vision and image processing. Much of his work has been on images, mainly through the application of image processing, computer vision, pattern recognition, machine learning, biometric systems, deep learning, soft computing, and computational intelligence. He has given a few invited talks on medical image processing. Professor Chowdhary is editor/co-editor of 8 books and is the author of over forty articles on computer science. He filed two patents deriving from his research. He was selected in the Stanford University List of Top 2% Scientists Worldwide for 2021. Google Scholar Link: https://scholar.google.com/citations?user=PpJt13oAAAAJ&hl=en.

* * *

Yash Agrawal is a blockchain developer at Intellibuzz. He holds a bachelor's degree in computer engineering from the University of Mumbai, India. His research interests include various machine learning algorithms, computer vision, natural language processing and cryptography.

Mohsen Aghabozorgi Nafchi obtained a Master of Information Technology from Shiraz University (Iran) in 2013. Since then, he has been teaching at Higher education Institutions, Iran. He is doing researching in different subjects especially Human Computer Interaction (HCI), Psychology, User Experience, and Educational Technologies. Also, Social Media, Smart Healthcare, Blockchain, Internet of Things, Data Mining, Big Data, Learning Analytics, Opinion Mining, machine learning and deep learning are other most his interested areas for continuing to carry out fundamental research. He has taught people with visual impairment and collaborates with them at university. In this experience, he has become familiar with the challenges and obstacles that people with visual impairment faced during study and work in society. He always attempts to improve the quality of life of people with disability and looks for finding new ways to use the capacity of them in society. Research on new technologies and their applications to provide services for people in the society, especially people with disability and the elderly is one of areas of his interests. So, He is designing new mobile applications related to people with disabilities, aging and health care. Among his previous projects, the effect of playing chess on children with learning disabilities, the factors affecting the acceptance of health applications, the acceptance of e-government, and the acceptance of e-learning among people can be mentioned. Also, in order to increase the spread of climate change, the challenges of climate refugees, the economic impact of climate change, the role of international law and new technologies to reduce the damages related to climate change among refugees are other his research areas. At last, His main aim is to use new technologies for improving the quality of life of humanity not to destroy environment and mankind.

Vanmathi C. received her Ph.D. degree in Information Technology and Engineering from VIT University, M.Tech (IT) from Sathyabama University and B.E. Computer Science from Madras University. She is working as an Associate Professor in the School of Information Technology at VIT University, Vellore Campus, India. She is having 17 years of research experience. Her area of research includes Deep Learning, Blockchain Technology, Computer Vision, Soft Computing, Cyber Physical Systems and Internet of Things. She is a member of Computer society of India and Soft Computing Research Society.

Amita Dessai is currently pursuing her Ph.D. at Goa College of Engineering, Goa. She has received her B.E. degree in Electronics & Telecommunication Engineering & Master's degree in ECI, Goa University, Goa, India. She is currently working as Associate Professor and has work experience of more than 15 years. Her current research interests include biomedical signal processing and machine learning. She is a life member of IETE and ISTE.

Tripti Goel obtained her Bachelor of Engineering (Hons) from Maharishi Dayanand University in 2004. She obtained her MTech in 2008 from Chottu Ram State College of Engineering, Haryana and Ph.D in 2017 from BPS Mahilla Vishwavidyalaya, Haryana. She joined Bhagwan Mahaveer Institute of Engineering and Technology, Haryana as Lecturer in August 2005. After completing her M.Tech. She joined Guru Premsukh Memorial College of Engg. As lecturer in 2009 and became a Senior Lecturer in 2012. She joined at NIT, Delhi as an Assistant Professor in July 2015. After that she Joined National Brain Research Center, Gurugram as Research Scientist in February 2018. She joined NIT, Silchar as an Assistant Professor in June 2018. Her research interest which includes Medical Image Processing, Machine Learning, Deep Learning, Pattern Recognition, Neuroimaging.

Leila Goosen is a full professor in the Department of Science and Technology Education of the University of South Africa. Prof. Goosen was an Associate Professor in the School of Computing, and the module leader and head designer of the fully online signature module for the College for Science, Engineering and Technology, rolled out to over 92,000 registered students since the first semester of 2013. She also supervises ten Masters and Doctoral students, and has successfully completed supervision of 43 students at postgraduate level. Previously, she was a Deputy Director at the South African national Department of Education. In this capacity, she was required to develop ICT strategies for implementation. She also promoted, coordinated, managed, monitored and evaluated ICT policies and strategies, and drove the research agenda in this area. Before that, she had been a lecturer of Information Technology (IT) in the Department for Science, Mathematics and Technology Education in the Faculty of Education of the University of Pretoria. Her research interests have included cooperative work in IT, effective teaching and learning of programming and teacher professional development.

C. Gururaj received his B.E. degree in Electronics and Communication and M.Tech degree in Electronics, both from Visvesvaraya Technological University, Belagavi his PhD from Jain University, Bengaluru. He is currently working in the department of Electronics and Telecommunication Engineering, BMS College of Engineering, Bengaluru. He has more than 50 publications to his credit with high citations that are indexed in portals such as Scopus, Web of Science, Google scholar, Vidwan, etc. He has received multiple awards and grants throughout his 18 years career. His areas of interest are Image Processing, VLSI Design, Machine Learning, Deep Learning, Artificial Intelligence and Engineering Education.

Kamalakannan J. is an Associate Professor at School of Information Technology and Engineering, VIT University, Vellore, India. He has completed his Bachelors in Electronics and Communication Engineering and Masters in Computer Science and Engineering from Madras University, he has completed his Ph.D at School of Computing Science and Engineering, VIT University, India. His area of research includes Medical Imaging, Image processing, Data Analytics, Big data, Machine Learning, Deep learning, IoT, etc.

Jevin Jain is a computer science graduate with an MBA in marketing and data analytics post graduation. He is currently working as a Product Manager at India's leading P2P investment company.

Sujigarasharma K. completed his Bachelor of Science in Computer Science at Vellore Institute of Technology Vellore, India. His area of Interest includes Deep Learning, Machine Learning, Data Mining, Data Analytics and IoT.

Avani K. V. H. at the time of writing this paper is pursuing her graduate degree in Electronics and Telecommunication Engineering from BMS College of Engineering, Bengaluru, India. She would graduate in 2022. Her areas of interest are Image Processing, Machine Learning and Deep Learning.

Swetank Kaushik is a student of B.Tech. (IT) at Vellore Institute of Technology, Vellore.

Neelu Khare is presently working as Associate Professor Senior in the School of Information Technology and Engineering at VIT, Vellore, India 2012. Overall she has 15 years of Academic and Research experience. She completed her Ph.D. degree from Maulana Azad National Institute of Technology Bhopal, India in the year 2011. She has published 53 research papers in International Journals and conferences, 5 Book Chapters, and published 2 patents in Patent India. She has guided 4 Ph.D. students. Her areas of interest are Data Science, Machine Learning, Deep Learning, Soft computing techniques, Network Intrusion Detection, IoT, and Bio-informatics.

Sagar M. received the Master of Technology degree from Jawaharlal Technological University Hyderabad in 2016. He is currently working towards Ph.D Degree in Deep Learning at Vellore Institute of Technology (VIT University), Vellore. His main research interest includes cyber-physical systems, deep learning, and cyber security.

Sowmya M. received B.E. Degree in Computer Science and Engineering from Visvesvaraya Technological University, Belagavi India in June 2010. She acquired Master's degree in Software Engineering from Visvesvaraya Technological University, Belagavi, India in Jan 2016. She is pursuing Ph D in Computer Science and Engineering from Visvesvaraya Technological University, Belagavi, India since 2020. At present she is working as Assistant Professor at GSSS Institute of Technology for women, Mysuru. Her research interest includes Internet of Things. Computer Networks and wireless Communication.

Deeksha Manjunath at the time of writing this paper is pursuing her undergraduate degree in Electronics and Telecommunication Engineering from BMS College of Engineering, Bengaluru, India. She would graduate in 2022. Her areas of interest are Signal and Image Processing.

Subramaniam Meenakshi Sundaram is currently working as Professor and Head in the Department of Computer Science and Engineering at GSSS Institute of Engineering and Technology for Women, Mysuru. He obtained Bachelor Degree in Computer Science & Engineering from Bharathidasan University, Tiruchirappalli in 1989, M. Tech from National Institute of Technology, Tiruchirappalli in 2006 and Ph.D. in Information and Communication Engineering from Anna University Chennai in 2014. He has published 53 papers in refereed International Journals, presented 3 papers in International Conferences and has delivered more than 40 seminars. He is a reviewer of Springer – SN Computer Science, Soft Computing Journal, International Journal of Ah Hoc Network Systems, Journal of Engineering Science and Technology, Taylor's University, Malaysia and International Journal of Computational Science & Engineering, Inderscience Publishers, UK. He has organized more than 40 seminars / Workshops / FDPs. He has attended more than 45 Workshops / Seminars. His area of interest includes Computer Networks, Wireless Communication, Software Engineering, Optical Networks and Data Mining. He is a Life Member of Indian Society for Technical Education (ISTE) and a member of Computer Society of India (CSI). He has 30+ Years of teaching experience and 13 years of research experience. One research scholar has completed Ph D and seven others are pursuing Ph.D. in VTU Belagavi, India under his guidance.

Akshat Mishra is a student of B.Tech. (IT) at Vellore Institute of Technology, Vellore.

Tejaswini R. Murgod received BE degree in Computer Science and Engineering from Visveshwarya Technological University, Belagavi India during June 2008. She acquired Master's degree in Software Engineering from Visveshwarya Technological University, Belagavi, India in Jan 2015. She received Ph D in Computer Science and Engineering from Visveshwarya Technological University, Belagavi, India in February 2022. At present she is working as Assistant Professor at GSSS Institute of Technology for women, Mysuru. Her research interest includes underwater communication, Optical networks and wireless networks. She has published 15 research papers in refereed journals and has been awarded excellent researcher award in December 2021.

Jagan Mohan Nagula is currently pursuing his Ph.D. at the National Institute of Technology Silchar in Bio-Medical Image Processing. He received his Master's degree in Embedded Systems from JNTU Hyderabad. He received his Bachelor's degree in Electronics and Communication Engineering from JNTU Hyderabad. Before enrolling in his Ph.D., he worked as an Assistant Professor in the Department of Electronics and Communication Engineering at Chaitanya Bharathi Institute of Technology (CBIT) Gandipet, Hyderabad. He published four journal publications, six conferences, and two book chapters. His area of interest includes bio-medical image processing, medical imaging, machine learning, deep learning, computer vision, pattern recognition, retinal image analysis.

Prabhavathy P. is working as an Associate Professor in School of Information Technology and Engineering, VIT University, Vellore. Her research area includes computational intelligence, data mining, data science, machine learning and deep learning. She has published around 20 journal papers in her research filed. She is life member of CSI and IEEE. She is also part of various school activity committees. She has published number of papers in international conferences. She had completed funded project from ISRO, SAC, Ahmadabad, Gujarat on "Development of Automated Web based Online Feature Tracking system using Shape Adaptive Curvelet with PCA and Haralick Texture Feature".

Visvanathan P. completed his M.E. in Computer Science and Engineering from Anna University, India in year 2007 and B.E from University of Madras, Tamilnadu, India in 1999. At present he is pursuing his Ph.D from School of Information Technology and Engineering, VIT, Vellore, India. His research area includes machine learning, deep learning, transfer learning, and optimization techniques.

Iuliia Pinkovetskaia, Professor of Economics, is working at the Institute of Economics and Business in Ulyanovsk State University for 16 years. She is an active researcher. Her research interests are related to educational policy, public administration, economic analysis, statistical and mathematical methods, management of enterprises and organizations, entrepreneurship, organization of higher and secondary education, investment policy, innovation development, improvement of research methodology, industry specifics of business, digitalization, and ICT. Since 2004, she has published more than 300 research papers and participated in many international and Russian conferences. She is the author of 64 research papers in journals indexed in Web of Science database and 24 research papers in journals indexed in Scopus database. She has published 12 research monographs and 10 higher education books. She published four patents deriving from her research. She is a member of the editorial boards in several journals.

Kanchana R. completed her M.E. in Electronics and communication Engineering from Anna University, India and B.Tech from University of Madras, Tamilnadu, India. Her research area includes knowledge discovery databases, genetic algorithms, machine learning, deep learning, transfer learning, and optimization techniques.

Murugan R. received his B.E. degree in Electronics and Communication Engineering, and M.E. degree in Embedded System Technologies from Anna University, Chennai, Tamilnadu, in 2005, and 2010 respectively. He received his Ph.D. degree from Information and Communication Engineering, Centre for Research, Anna University, Chennai, Tamilnadu, India. He is working as an Assistant Professor, in the Department of Electronics and Communication Engineering, National Institute of Technology Silchar since 15th June 2018. He published more than 26 journal publications, 22 conference proceedings, 2 books, 9 book chapters and 4 patents in his credit. His area of interest which includes Bio-medical signal and image processing, medical imaging, Retinal image analysis, computer vision, pattern recognition, machine learning, and deep learning.

Parvathi R. is a Professor of School of Computing Science and Engineering at VIT University, Chennai since 2011. She received the Doctoral degree in the field of spatial data mining in the same year. Her teaching experience in the area of computer science includes more than two decades and her research interests include data mining, big data and computational biology.

Rathi R. received her Ph.D. degree from VIT, Vellore. She completed her M.E. in Computer Science and Engineering from Anna University, India in year 2006 and B.Tech from University of Madras, Tamilnadu, India in 2003. At present she is working as an Assistant Professor [senior] in the School of Information Technology and Engineering, VIT, Vellore, India. She has authored many papers and published research articles. Her research area includes Rough set, Knowledge discovery databases, Genetic algorithms, Machine Learning, Deep Learning, Transfer Learning and optimization Techniques.

Niranjan Rajpurohit is an Assistant Professor (HR&OB), Jaipuria Institute of Management, Jaipur.

Mangayarkarasi Ramaiah received her Ph.D. Degree in Information Technology and Engineering from VIT University, M.E. Computer Science from Anna University. She is working as an Associate Professor in the School of Information Technology and Engineering at VIT University, Vellore Campus, India. She is having 19 years of research experience. Her research interest includes Computer Vision, Image Processing, Machine Learning, Deep Learning and Internet of Things.

Hemalatha S. is currently working as an Associate Professor in the School of Information Technology (SITE) in VIT University, Vellore. She received her Ph.D. degree in Computer Science and Engineering from VIT University, Vellore in August 2017. She completed ME in Computer Science and Engineering from VIT University, Vellore, in 2004 and received BE degree in Computer Science and Engineering from University of Madras, Chennai in 2000. Her current research interests includes image processing, video processing, image segmentation and classification, texture enhancement and analysis and data mining. She has authored many papers in reputed international journals and conferences. She is a life member of Computer Society of India (CSI).

Santhakumari Sadhasivam is a Research Scholar at School of Information Technology and Engineering, VIT University, Vellore, India. She has completed her Bachelors in Computer Science and Engineering from University of Madras and Masters in Computer Science and Engineering from Dr. M. G. R. Educational Research Institute, Chennai. Her area of research includes data analytics, big data, machine learning, deep learning, etc.

Zahra Alidousti Shahraki got her master degree in computer architecture at university of Isfahan, Iran (2011-2014).Since then (Oct 2014), she has been teaching at Technical and Vocational University, Iran, and also she is research director of Researcher's Women community in Shahrekord, Iran (Oct 2019-now). Her interest is the study of the topics of Quantum intelligence, Human Computer Interaction (HCI), Psychology, User Experience, Educational Technologies, Cognitive Science, Computer Architecture, Image Processing, Machine Learning and Deep learning. Her recent activities are related to challenges of learning for children, people with disability and elderly people, working with her colleague at university. She is doing research about new artificial intelligence technologies and effects of them in societies. In her research, she always wants to know more about how we can develop new technologies and what effects are to be expected on humanity. She got a Diploma degree in Mathematics Fields at NODET high school (2004 – 2006). (NODET: National Organization for Development of Exceptional Talents). Her high school was an organization that recruits students for middle and high-schools through a two-step set of exams at each level. The organization is aimed to provide a unique educational environment for the exceptionally talented students and the teachers. Zahra and her colleagues carry out research projects and works related to their province and they take steps to solve the problems and needs of the province. One of the important projects that are being carried out now is to study the health challenges of the people especially aging women and the youth and provide solutions to eliminate unemployment among the youth of the province.

Brijendra Singh is presently working as Assistant Professor Senior in the School of Information Technology and Engineering at VIT, Vellore, India 2010. Overall he has 12 years of academic and research experience. He completed his Ph.D. degree from Vellore Institute of Technology, Vellore, India. He has published 14 research papers in national and international journals, and two book chapters. His areas of interest are machine learning, deep learning, and soft computing techniques.

Pattabiraman Venkatasubbu, Professor, School of Computer Science and Engineering, Vellore Institute of Technology (VIT) – Chennai Campus, has 20 years of professional experience, out of which he spent as much as 18 years in teaching and research and the remaining 2 years in industry. He has published more than 50 papers in various national and international peer-reviewed journals in the last five years. He has also presented several papers in international conferences. His research expertise covers a wide range of subject areas, including Knowledge Discovery and Data Mining, Big Data Analytics, Machine Learning, Deep Learning, Database technologies, etc.

Hassanali Gulamali Virani is currently working as Professor and Head of the Electronics and Telecommunication Department of Goa College of Engineering, Goa, India. He has completed his Bachelor's Degree in Electronics & Telecommunication Engineering from Goa College of Engineering, Goa University in the year 1991. He has completed an M. Tech. in Industrial Electronics in September 2004 at the National Institute of Technology, Karnataka. He has Ph.D. degree from Indian Institute of Technology, Bombay. He has more than 25 years of teaching experience. His areas of research include Signal processing and Machine learning, Devices, Nanoelectronics, Control systems and Wireless Sensor Networks. He has paper publications in IEEE Transactions on Electron Devices and several other reputed journals and conferences. He is a fellow member of IETE, life member of IETE and ISTE.

Index

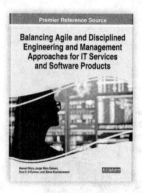

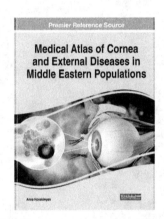

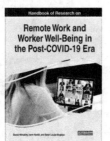

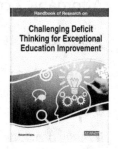